THE BELFAST URBAN MOTORWAY

Engineering, ambition and social conflict

Wesley Johnston

Published 2014 by Colourpoint Books
an imprint of Colourpoint Creative Ltd
Colourpoint House, Jubilee Business Park
21 Jubilee Road, Newtownards, BT23 4YH
Tel: 028 9182 6339
Fax: 028 9182 1900
E-mail: info@colourpoint.co.uk
Web: www.colourpoint.co.uk

First Edition, First Impression

A catalogue record for this book is available from the British Library.

Designed by April Sky Design, Newtownards
Tel: 028 9182 7195
Web: www.aprilsky.co.uk

Printed by GPS Colour Graphics Limited, Belfast

ISBN 978-1-78073-047-9

Front cover: Divis Street junction on Westlink close to completion in late 1982.
Rear cover: Photomontage of the Belfast Urban Motorway at Ormeau Road, 1967.

Dr Wesley Johnston grew up in Omagh, County Tyrone. His PhD was in Software Engineering but he has always had a fascination with local history. His studies of old maps led him to explore the history of the local road network, eventually setting up a web site on the topic in 2006. Since then he has continued to both research the history of roads in Northern Ireland and act as a commentator on the current road network and its future development. He maintains an archive of historical material relating to all aspects of the local road network. He currently lives in Belfast with his wife and daughter, both of whom are very patient when Wesley makes detours to photograph obscure pieces of transport infrastructure.

CONTENTS

An appeal: *There must be an abundance of remarkable material on the Northern Ireland road network in private ownership. I would love the opportunity to make contact with anyone who has photographs or archive material on (a) any aspect of the development of our road network or (b) Craigavon New City. I can be e-mailed at roads@wesleyjohnston.com or contacted on Twitter @niroads. I also maintain a web site full of information about the current road network, its history and plans for future road schemes at www.wesleyjohnston.com/roads.*

To my Father

who nurtured my fascination with transport

AUTHOR'S PREFACE

The Belfast Urban Motorway was the most audacious road scheme never to see the light of day.

Yet, few in the city today have even heard of it. When I first dusted off the covers of the almost forgotten 1967 plans in Belfast Central Library and saw the scale of the proposals for a fully elevated three-lane motorway encircling the city centre, it took my breath away. So began a seven-year research project to trace the story of this remarkable plan from its genesis before the Second World War, through its remarkable rise, and fall, before its eventual transformation into the Westlink and M3 that we know today.

Yet this book is about much more than civil engineering – although I do devote a generous amount of space to this aspect of the story. Fundamentally, it is a story about the contradictory needs of the people of Belfast and what they were and were not prepared to accept – and pay for – to keep their city moving.

To fully understand it we need to set aside the issues that are foremost in the city today, and go back in time to eras with different mindsets and different world views.

The story encompasses all the significant issues in Belfast's recent history – the Second World War, socialism versus capitalism, housing, public transport, the rise of the private car, pollution, the class war, redevelopment, centralised planning, the 'Troubles', gentrification, traffic congestion, architecture, environmentalism and global warming.

The story of the Belfast Urban Motorway is also the story of how the fabric of the city's transport system came into being. As such, it is vital reading for anyone seeking to understand Belfast's urban development, the transport system that exists today, and who seeks to influence the city's direction in the years to come.

There are many elements of the 1967 plan that we would fundamentally disagree with today. But rather than going down the easy path of derision and scorn, perhaps it should instead cause us to stop and think. Perhaps, in a few decades' time, our children and grandchildren, with different world views, and priorities that we cannot foresee, will look back and judge the decisions we are making today just as harshly.

Many people have helped me with my research on this book, and I offer them my sincere thanks. In particular I wish to acknowledge, in no particular order, the assistance of Roy Spiers, Lionel Walsh and Colin McBurney at DRD Roads Service; Grahame Fraser; Denis O'Hagan; T Jackson McCormick; Aubrey Dale; Tim Morton; Billy McCoubrey; Frankie Quinn; Declan Hill and Mark Hackett at the Forum for Alternative Belfast; John Eltham; Gary Potter; Paul Savage; Norman Johnston and my editor Rachel Irwin at Colourpoint.

Wesley Johnston
January 2014

CHAPTER 1
SETTING THE SCENE

The Growth of Belfast

The town of Belfast originally grew up along the banks of the River Farset, close to where it flows into the River Lagan. The location in Irish, *Béal Feirste* ('mouth of the Farset'), gave its name to the city and indeed the river still flows beneath High Street today, sealed in a culvert since 1770.[1] While it proved straightforward to bridge the humble River Farset, carrying travelers efficiently over the adjacent River Lagan has proved to be a persistent problem for the city, from its foundation to the present day. Before the 1680s the only way across to the east bank at Ballymacarrett was either by boat or by utilising a ford, the site of which almost certainly lay a few dozen metres upstream of today's Queen's Bridge.[2]

At this time, the Lagan at Belfast was considerably wider than it is today, and the first bridge to the constructed, the appropriately named Long Bridge (completed in 1682) had a total span of 260 metres (840 feet), comprising 21 narrow arches.[3] This is in contrast to the modern Queen's Bridge, on the same site, which has a much shorter span of 115 metres (375 feet).

The Long Bridge, Belfast, as painted by Andrew Nicholl (1804–86). It was demolished in 1840. *(Andrew Nicholl, BELUM.U1696, © National Museums Northern Ireland, Collection Ulster Museum)*

Before the nineteenth century, the urban area remained almost exclusively on the west bank of the Lagan, with only limited development across the river in Ballymacarrett. By the mid nineteenth century, however, the city was rapidly industrialising. The growth of shipbuilding had led to the establishment of the Harland and Wolff shipyard on the eastern shore at Queen's Island, along with many other industries, such as the Sirocco engineering works at the north end of Short Strand (in 1881).

At the same time, the city's population burgeoned, growing from perhaps 19,000 people in 1802 to 71,000 in 1841, and reaching 349,000 by 1901.[4] This expansion led to increasing pressure on the city's transportation system. One of the main focal points of this pressure was the River Lagan itself, partly because the bulk of the population lived on the west bank of the Lagan while a significant level of employment was to be found on the east. Some of this traffic crossed the Lagan by ferries, as existed, for example, between Donegall Quay and Queen's Quay.[5] However, the rest used the bridge, and the ever increasing pressure on crossing points led to a sequence of bridge construction or improvement projects between the early nineteenth and late twentieth centuries.

In 1831, a second crossing was provided to relieve the Long Bridge. This five-arch toll bridge was erected about 700 metres (2,300 feet) upstream. It earned the name Halfpenny Bridge, although the toll was abolished after just 16 years.[3] In 1840, the Long Bridge was demolished and replaced, in 1844, by the Queen's Bridge, an elegant structure consisting of five sweeping stone arches. The structure was designed by Sir Charles Lanyon and John Frazer, and cost

Queen's Bridge, Belfast, showing its original 1844 stone arches and its later cantilevered iron extensions. *(Ardfern: Reproduced under the Creative Commons Attribution-Share Alike 3.0 Unported license)*

£27,000. However, even this structure quickly proved inadequate, and it was widened to 20 metres (65 feet) in 1885 by adding a cantilevered iron structure to each side of the bridge.[3] This work was carried out by JC Bretland. In 1863, a third bridge was opened at the edge of the city to carry the Ormeau Road over the Lagan. The bridge, known simply as Ormeau Bridge, consists of four stone arches.

When two arches of the Halfpenny Bridge collapsed without warning in 1886, it was replaced by the city's first iron bridge, named the Albert Bridge, which opened in 1890. The bridge was designed by JC Bretland and cost £36,500 to construct. It consists of three wrought iron arches mounted on stone piers. Yet another bridge, the King's Bridge, was constructed even further upstream at Stranmillis in 1911.[6]

Albert Bridge, Belfast, which opened in 1890. *(Author's collection)*

Transportation

The growth of the city led to an increasing need for transportation both within the city and linking to other urban centres. A rail link to Lisburn opened in 1839, with Ballymena, Carrickfergus and Holywood following in 1848, and Bangor in 1865. The construction of the Central Railway linked the east and west banks of the Lagan via a new railway bridge, the Lagan Viaduct, from 1884. The railway network continued to grow across Ireland.

An extensive system of trams was developed in Belfast from 1872. By 1895 the system was carrying 11 million passengers per year on the 39 km (24 mile) network,[1] and had facilitated the expansion of Belfast's new suburbs. Bus services began to take over from the trams from the 1920s, and trolleybuses from the Second World War.

A Belfast trolleybus on Royal Avenue in May 1968. *(Norman Johnston)*

With the partition of Ireland in 1921, Belfast became the capital city of the new state of Northern Ireland. Although part of the United Kingdom, Northern Ireland had its own devolved Parliament with considerable powers. The Parliament was based at Stormont, on the edge of east Belfast and was dominated by unionists who isolated the province as much as possible from the rest of the island and aligned it closely with Great Britain.

At this time, freight was carried predominantly on the railways, which fulfilled the dual role of ferrying both passengers and cargo. The railway network by the 1920s was extensive, reaching all the principal towns in the province, and was operated by three private companies. The Belfast and County Down Railway ran routes to Bangor, Newtownards, Donaghadee, Ballynahinch, Newcastle, Downpatrick and Ardglass, and had its Belfast terminus at Queen's Quay, on the east bank of the Lagan. The Northern Counties Committee (part of the LMS from 1923) operated trains to Carrickfergus, Larne, Ballymena, Cookstown, Coleraine, Londonderry and Strabane, and had its Belfast terminus at York Road, north of the city centre. The Great Northern Railway (GNR(I)) operated trains to Lisburn, Portadown, Dublin, Omagh, Fermanagh and Londonderry. Their terminus was at Great Victoria Street, to the west of the city centre. The GNR also owned the Central Railway which connected the three termini to the docks and to each other, albeit via a torturous route suitable only for goods wagons.

The Internal Combustion Engine

With the invention of the internal combustion engine, motorised vehicles began to appear on Ireland's roads from the turn of the twentieth century. By the late 1920s, wealthier members of society usually owned a motor car, private operators were setting up bus routes and lorries were appearing to carry freight on roads.

Believing it to be the most efficient way of operating road vehicles, Stormont took the decision in the mid 1930s to nationalise all bus and lorry operations. This meant that, with few exceptions, the government had a monopoly on bus and freight transport on the road

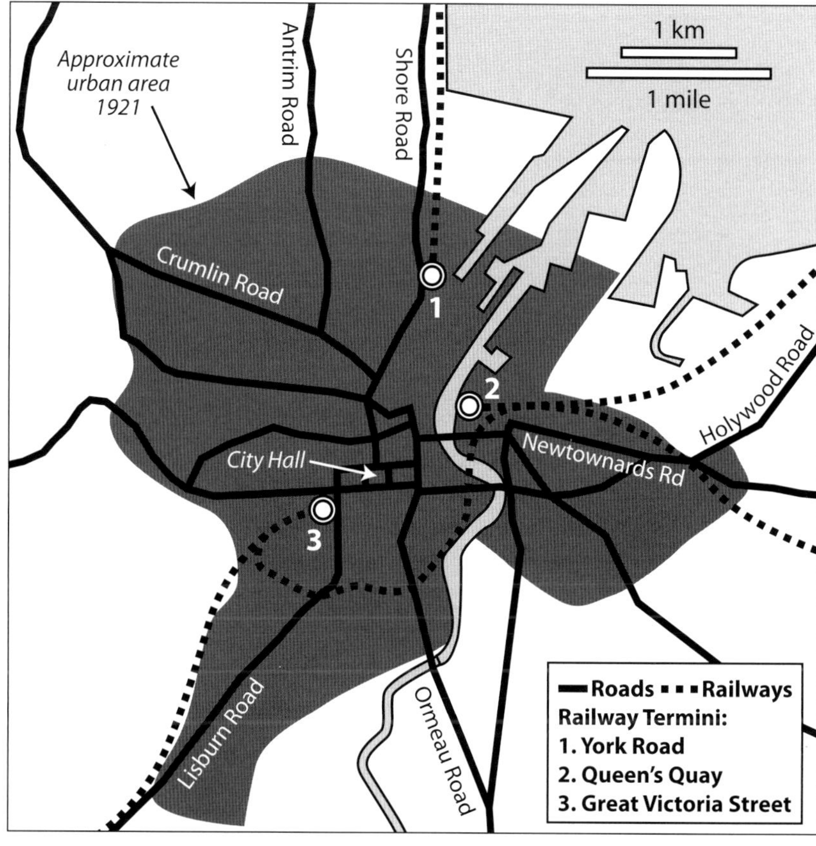

Main roads, railways and railway termini in Belfast in 1921.

network. These services were operated under the auspices of the Northern Ireland Road Transport Board from 1935.[8] The buses and lorries tended to be operated on routes and in areas not served by the railways, which remained the dominant option for freight movements between ports and main towns, and were still privately owned.

In Belfast in the 1920s and 1930s, the progressive adoption of motorised transport led to an increasing number of private cars and goods vehicles competing for road space with trams, buses, horse-drawn vehicles, cyclists and pedestrians. Many of the roads in the city had not been widened since they had been laid out, and traffic congestion began to become a serious problem at certain times of the day. Although most arterial routes into the city were bottlenecks, two of the most serious were the Queen's Bridge and Holywood Arches, the latter then being part of the main road from Belfast to Holywood and Bangor.

In the early 1920s Lord Pirrie (chairman of the Harland and Wolff shipyard and a member of the Northern Ireland Senate) is said to have become so concerned about the amount of traffic using the Queen's Bridge that he personally approached the Harbour authorities with a proposal to construct a moveable 'transport' bridge over the harbour. This proposal was, apparently, turned down.[9]

In Stormont in 1938, Independent Labour MP Jack Beattie was heard to lament:

> *...in view of the congestion of traffic which takes place at Ballymacarrett. I do not think you require to spend much money on expert advice. Common sense should lead you to understand clearly that the Queen's Bridge will never accommodate the growing amount of traffic that is taking place on it.*[7]

A more humorous assessment of the new conflicts being created by increasing numbers of cars on Northern Ireland's roads can be found in a comment by Unionist MP James Gamble in Stormont, during a debate on a new piece of traffic management legislation in 1934:

> *I speak also of pedal-cyclists and cattle that are being driven to and from the fairs. The person in charge of the cattle appears to think that he has the right to the whole of the road, and that motorists should stop and wait the convenience of the person who wants to*

A preserved Leyland Tiger PS1, built circa 1946-48, a bus typical of the NIRTB era. *(Norman Johnston)*

> *get the cattle past ... As regards pedestrian traffic, I find very often when motoring, especially about lighting-up time, that, even where there are very good footpaths, people walk in the middle of the road. Whether that is due to the good condition of the road or not I do not know, but I think that where there are footpaths the pedestrians should walk on them.*[10]

The government of the time agreed that the "cross river traffic problem" was becoming an increasingly important issue, as was the more general issue of transporting an ever-growing quantity of goods and people through the nineteenth century streets of the expanding city. It was already apparent that the trend towards a rising number of cars and lorries in the city was going to continue. If Belfast's streets were not to become gridlocked, something had to be done.

CHAPTER 2
PROPOSALS, PLANS AND WAR

The interest that the Ministry of Home Affairs of the Northern Ireland government was taking in the growing traffic problem is evidenced by two reports that they commissioned to examine solutions for the problem.

A Bypass at Sydenham

In 1936, Scottish engineer R Dundas Duncan was commissioned by the Ministry of Home Affairs to submit a report on the feasibility of constructing a new road to relieve the pressure on the Holywood Arches and Holywood Road.[1] Although other roads in the city, such as the Antrim and Lisburn Roads, were also heavily trafficked, there was more scope for a solution to the Holywood Arches problem due to the large amount of open, reclaimed land that existed to the north, beside the Bangor railway line.

There seems to have been talk of a new road through this land since at least 1930. However, problems during negotiations with the Harbour Commissioners, presumably related to land acquisition, appear to have scuppered these early attempts.[2] Duncan submitted his proposals in December 1936 and recommended the construction of a new road to connect Ballymacarrett and Tillysburn, to be known as the 'Sydenham By-pass Road'. The road would provide two traffic lanes in each direction.

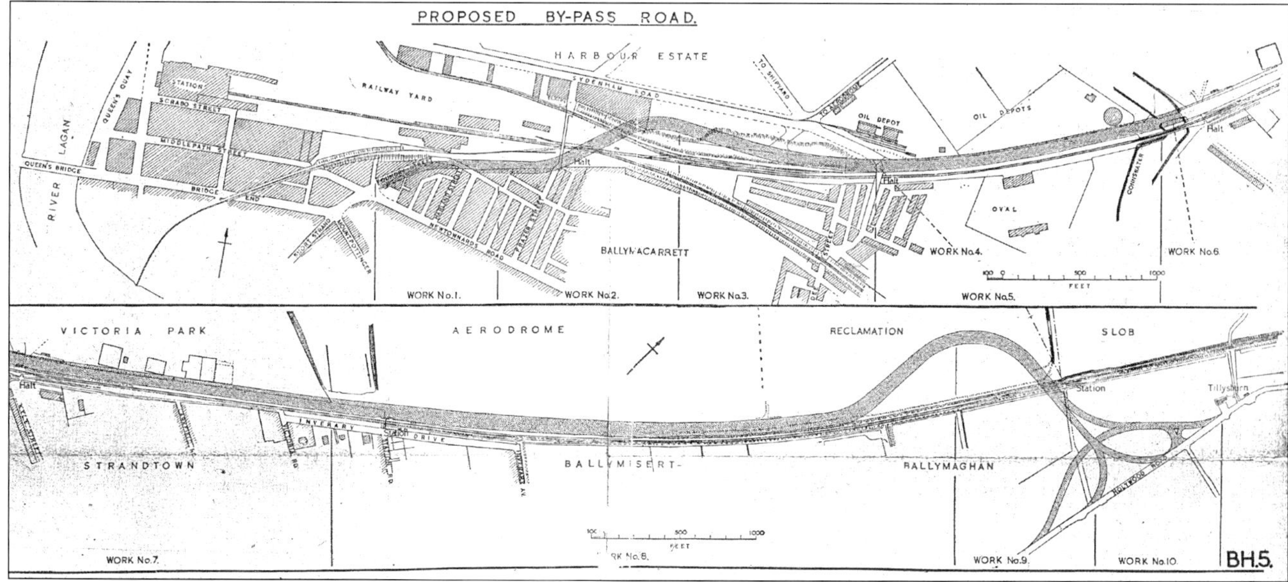

Plans for the proposed Sydenham Bypass, 1936. Note the elaborate freeflow one-way system proposed for Tillysburn at the eastern end. *(Belfast Newsletter)*

Although a short stretch of road on this route (running from Dee Street to Victoria Park) already existed, the bulk of the proposal would require the construction of an entirely new road on soft, reclaimed land. Since the proposed road would run parallel to the north side of the existing railway line, it would have to cross the line at both the Tillysburn and Ballymacarrett ends. It would also involve widening the existing bridge over the Connswater River and lengthening the bridge that carried Dee Street over the railway.

The Ministry of Home Affairs accepted Mr Duncan's report and employed him to design and build the road. The design process involved a further period of surveying work (there is a record of £600 being paid for survey reports for the Sydenham road in 1937).[3] Due to the uncertainty surrounding exactly how the new road should tie in with the exiting road network at the Queen's Bridge, when work did begin on the ground in 1938 it was limited to the central section from around Victoria Park to as far east as Tillysburn. Around 40 men were employed to widen the existing road at the Park by accumulating fill.[4]

As if to demonstrate how some things never change, politicians were soon demanding to know why the work was taking so long. Speaking in Stormont in March 1938, the Parliamentary Secretary for the Department of Home Affairs, JC Davison, made a statement describing the particular challenges of the project:

Any scheme of the magnitude of this road involves much difficult and detailed preparation before work can be commenced on an appreciable scale. The road will include a viaduct over the railways, an under-bridge at Dee Street, a widening of the bridge over the Connswater, a bridge under the railway at Tillysburn, another before the junction with the Holywood Road, an extensive embankment between the railway at Tillysburn and the Holywood Road, and a considerable amount of piling and difficult drainage.[4]

He then went on to describe some of the problems they had encountered. The original plan for a bridge over the railway at Tillysburn had to be abandoned after concerns were raised that it would conflict with aircraft at the newly established Sydenham Airport (today's Belfast City Airport). Plans for a bridge to connect the new road to the Newtownards Road at the city end were halted whenever doubt was expressed over whether this would be the best place to join it, as described in the next section.

Bridges and Tunnels

It was recognised early on that the Sydenham By-pass Road would not achieve its full potential if it was not coupled with an improved crossing of the River Lagan to relieve the Queen's Bridge. In other words, it was acknowledged that the road would simply feed the existing traffic jams more efficiently if the capacity of the Queen's Bridge was not also increased. This was generally taken to mean that a new crossing was also needed sufficiently close to the existing bridge that it would be a realistic alternative. For example, in 1937, Independent Labour MP Jack Beattie said in the Northern Ireland Parliament:

There is only one solution of the present difficulty and that is to build a bridge at Queen's Square or a little further down the quayside ... By the construction of a bridge over the river there to Middlepath Street the new road would proceed in a straight direction. That road would then suit the traffic coming from Antrim Road, Shore Road, and Lisburn Road. It would form a central position and relieve in a practical way the congestion on the two roads that we are trying to relieve.[5]

However, the question of how to provide this new crossing was not as straightforward as it may first appear, for three reasons. Firstly, the only place a new bridge could realistically be constructed was downstream of the existing bridge. However, this land was already engaged in intensive commercial activity and acquiring it would prove quite disruptive to the shipping merchants. Secondly, even if a site could be found for the bridge, such a structure would severely limit shipping in the Lagan by preventing all but the smallest ships sailing past it to unload at Queen's Quay or Donegall Quay. Finally, the Donegall Quay railway line ran along the west bank of the Lagan here. It passed under the end of Queen's Bridge in a tunnel, but at all other points was at ground level, effectively blocking bridge construction. A consensus appears to have developed that the only viable solutions were either a tunnel under the river, or some kind of moveable bridge that could accommodate shipping on the Lagan and freight on the railway line.

Nevertheless, there seems to have been a degree of reluctance on the part of the shipping industry to accept even a moveable bridge. Mr Beattie goes on to assert:

We cannot allow the Belfast Harbour Commissioners to stop the progress of Belfast because the road would interfere with a few individual ships when accommodation as good can be obtained for them elsewhere without causing anyone any inconvenience. I am supported in my opinion by many practically-minded people who say that if we allow the interference of the Harbour Board to prevent our having either a transport bridge or an underground tunnel we might as well cease to think of making the by-pass road a success.[5]

In 1938, the Ministry commissioned London consultancy firm Meik and Halcrow to examine the problem of the Queen's Bridge and how the traffic from the new Sydenham By-pass Road could be accommodated when it reached the Lagan. Announcing the appointment in Stormont, JC Davison said:

With regard to the most suitable route for the continuation of the [Sydenham By-pass] road from Sydenham towards the city, some difference of opinion exists, and among other suggestions the possibility of carrying the road by means of a tunnel underneath the river has been frequently mentioned. In these circumstances it has been thought advisable to engage the services of a very eminent expert – Mr Halcrow, of the well-known firm of Meik & Halcrow, London – who has been asked to investigate the question as to the best route for the continuation of the road from Sydenham towards the city, not merely from an engineering standpoint, but, in particular, from the point of view of finding out the best solution for the relief of traffic congestion.[4]

Meik and Halcrow submitted their report later in 1938. Their first proposal was to construct a second bridge to relieve the Queen's Bridge.[6] To keep it from interfering with shipping,

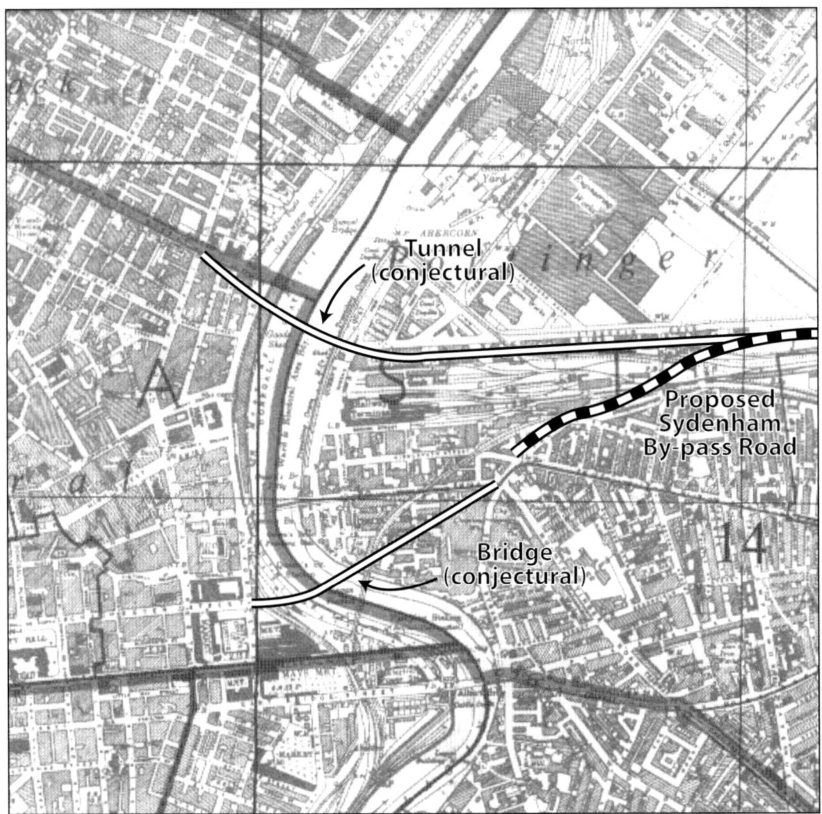

Conjectural map of Meik and Halcrow's proposals for Belfast. *(Base map Ordnance Survey, 1940)*

this proposed bridge would be sited upstream of the existing bridge, forming a connection between Chichester Street and the junction of Bridge End with the lower Newtownards Road. They also proposed that this should be followed at a later date by a new road tunnel linking the proposed Sydenham By-pass Road directly to the west bank of the Lagan at Great George's Street. A tunnel would ensure that the road did not conflict with shipping movements in the river, although it did mean that the entrance/exit points would have had to be much further from the river than a conventional low-level bridge, to allow for the road to descend to the required depth.

Foreign Influences

Meanwhile, the experience of foreign countries had started to influence planners in Northern Ireland. Other parts of the world were significantly more advanced in providing roads designed exclusively for motor vehicles.[7] The development of such roads was pioneered by the USA and Italy in the 1920s and 1930s, but by far the greatest influence on Northern Ireland's planners at the time was Germany's system of autobahnen (called 'motorways' in the UK) constructed under the Nazi government from 1933 to 1939. These were dual-carriageways, each 7.5 metres (25 feet) wide with no junctions on the level (ie other roads crossed over or under it via bridges), no pedestrians or animals, and which allowed sustained high speeds of 100 km/h (60 mph). By the beginning of the war, Germany had built 3200 km (2000 miles) of autobahnen.

In September 1937 a group of 224 delegates from the UK, having accepted an invitation by the Nazi government, visited and inspected the German motorway system.[8] Included in the party were two men from Northern Ireland: R Dundas Duncan, the engineer in charge of the Sydenham By-pass Road, and John Bates, the Inspector of Roads for the Ministry of Home Affairs.[9]

Duncan returned from Germany "full of enthusiasm"[9] and convinced that these types of road were key to solving the traffic problem on the main arteries into Belfast. The County Surveyors' Society in Great Britain came to a similar view after the visit and issued a report in May 1938 proposing a system of 1600 km (1000 miles) of 'motorways' connecting the main population centres of England, Scotland and Wales.

However, both the Westminster government and the Northern Ireland government were initially unconvinced of the need for roads requiring such high standards of design. Senior government figures seem not to have grasped the potential impact of such roads for the economy. They continued to talk as if the new roads would merely cater for existing traffic rather than having a more fundamental impact on the economy by allowing distant regions to more effectively engage in commerce.

Others argued that the investment would be a waste of money if only long-distance traffic used the motorways, on the basis that not many people travelled long distances, once again missing the potential of such roads to open up the nation. This is evidenced by an address by Frederick C Cook, the Chief Engineer in the Ministry of Transport in Great Britain, to the British Association in 1938, when he said:

> *In a densely roaded country such as ours, conditions would not permit the construction of a system of motorways which would be more than a small fraction of our 180,000 miles of public highways. Investigation on certain important routes has shown that through traffic ... varies from 17 to 25 per cent of the whole. It may therefore be expected that at least three-fourths of the traffic on those routes which motorways are designed to supplement would continue to use the existing roads including public service vehicles ... and all local traffic whether private or commercial.*[7]

A German autobahn constructed by the Nazi government in the late 1930s. Note the dual-carriageways, an innovation at the time. *(US Library of Congress)*

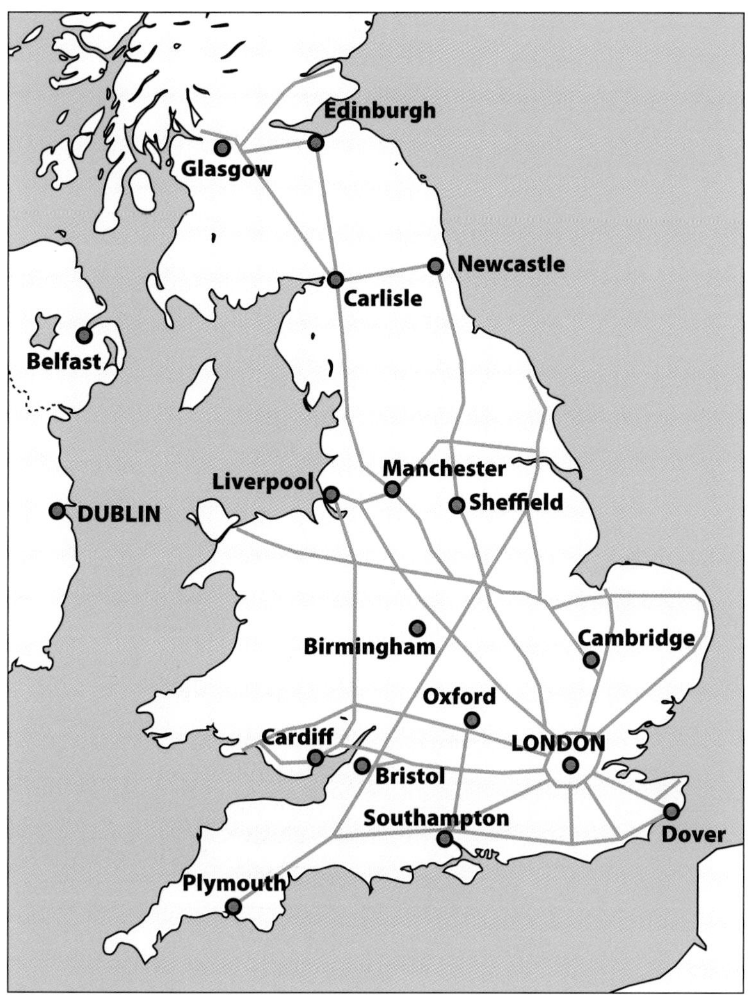

A motorway network for Great Britain as proposed by the Institution of Highway Engineers in 1936.

The Second World War

Meanwhile in Belfast, although there seems to have been general acceptance in government that a new bridge over the River Lagan was necessary, the outbreak of the Second World War in September 1939 meant that all work on the Sydenham By-pass Road was halted. With the exception of essential repairs, no work was carried out on the road network during the war and no further action was taken concerning Meik and Halcrow's proposed bridge and tunnel.

The breathing space provided by the war proved to be an extremely fruitful period for discussion and debate on how the increasing use of motor vehicles on roads in both Northern Ireland and the United Kingdom as a whole could be accommodated, although wartime austerity severely limited what could actually be implemented.

CHAPTER 3
POST-WAR PLANS

Belfast, in common with many other UK cities, suffered considerable damage during the Blitz. Towards the end of the war, increasing attention was given to the inevitable issue of post-war reconstruction. A series of reports were commissioned and published and, although their implementation was impossible due to the war and the dire economic state of the country afterwards, they were clearly driven by a genuine sense of need and a desire to create a better world. As they looked at Belfast's Blitz-damaged streets, sub-standard nineteenth century housing and a congested and antiquated road system, planners increasingly saw an opportunity to create a better city, one that would leave behind the imperial era and embrace technology and industry. At its heart would be a modern road system suitable for the post-war world.

Increasing Ambition

During the second half of the 1940s, the UK government's attitude to 'motorways' began to thaw. In June 1945 Major HE Aldington, Chief Engineer of the Ministry of War Transport in Great Britain, presented a paper on the subject of post-war road development.[1] He argued that it was impossible to upgrade existing roads to a sufficient standard to be a fast and safe means of long distance travel. He instead advocated a separate network of roads for the exclusive use of vehicles and established a set of guidelines for their construction. Under his proposals,

Key features of a motorway.

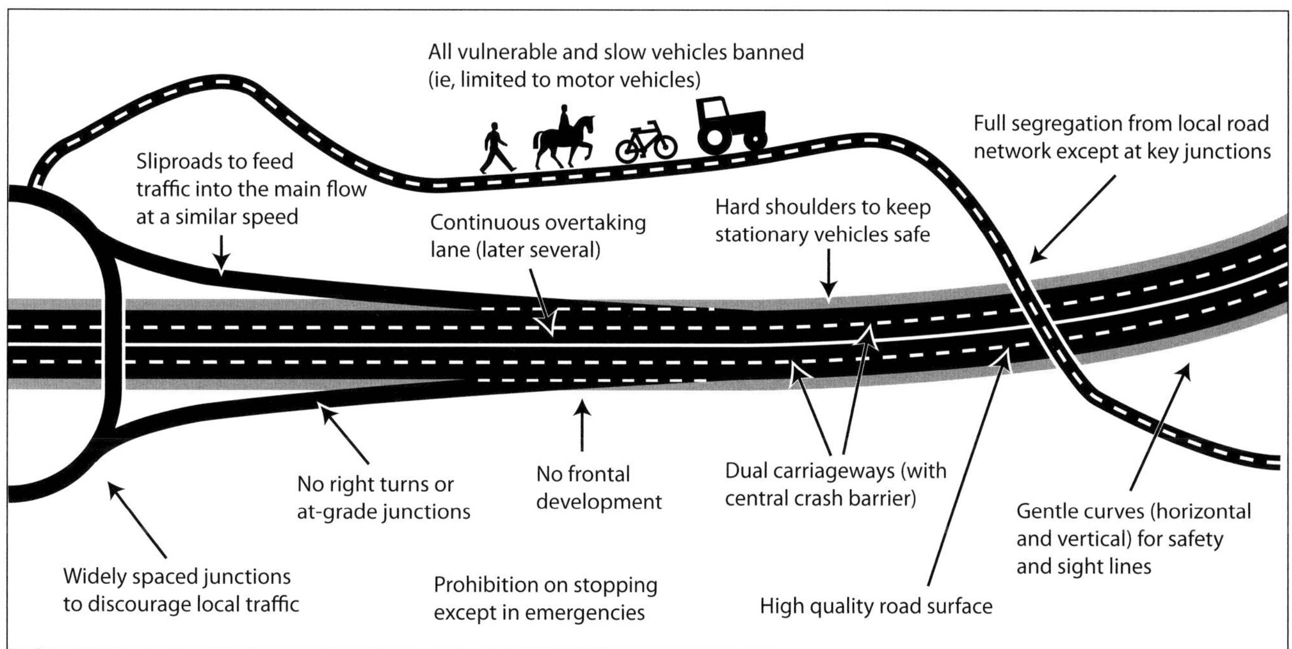

such roads would (amongst other things) (a) consist of two parallel carriageways to segregate traffic travelling in opposite directions; (b) have no intersections on the level; (c) would allow joining traffic to accelerate to the same speed as traffic already on the road before merging; (d) have consistent, gentle curves to permit high speeds; (e) be equipped with a simplified system of signage; and (f) have a 'hard' shoulder to allow vehicles to be easily moved off the road if they broke down.

By 1949 the Westminster government had become convinced that a system of motorways was needed and passed the *Special Roads Act (1949)* to allow their construction. *The Roads Act (Northern Ireland) (1948)* had been passed in December 1948 and gave the Northern Ireland Parliament similar powers, and this was later supplemented by the *Special Roads Act (Northern Ireland) (1963)*. Post-war economic turmoil, however, prevented any actual construction. Planners must have looked with envy to the United States which, having been spared the urban destruction and near-bankruptcy of war, engaged in a massive programme of both urban and rural motorway construction to support an increasingly prosperous car-based economy, especially after the national system of 'Interstates' was introduced in 1956.

The Pennsylvania Turnpike, an early US 'motorway', seen in 1942. Today it is part of Interstate 76. *(Arthur Rothstein, US Library of Congress)*

Nevertheless, despite the lack of any actual construction in Northern Ireland, the plans became progressively more ambitious. In August 1942 the Minister of Home Affairs had appointed English planner WR Davidge to prepare planning proposals for Northern Ireland, but principally for the Belfast area. An interim report ('Planning Proposals for the Belfast Area') had been completed in September 1944 and made a number of proposals.[2] The main one was to construct a network of three ring roads in Belfast: an inner one encircling the city centre, an intermediate one about one to two miles from the centre, and an outer one beyond the edge of the urban area. The ring roads were to be constructed at ground level with conventional junctions where they met existing roads. The ring road plan was approved in principle by Belfast Corporation on 26 February 1948, but no work took place at that time.[3]

In addition, the report proposed the construction of three new radial routes into the city to relieve pressure on the Antrim Road, Lisburn Road and Holywood (Bangor) Road. Unlike the ring roads, these three roads were envisaged as motorways. These became known as the North Approach, South Approach and East Approach respectively. Some believe that the inclusion of these proposals was a direct result of R Dundas Duncan (the engineer who had been appointed to construct the Sydenham Bypass in 1938) being involved by the commission.[2,4] A second report in 1946 proposed to extend the South Approach to Portadown, and urged that it "be undertaken at the earliest possible date".[2]

The development of motorways outside Belfast is a remarkable story in itself, but is beyond the scope of this book, which will hereafter focus on the urban motorways around the central area of the city.

Captain Perceval-Maxwell, who was the Parliamentary Secretary of the Ministry of Commerce, announced that the government had accepted the recommendations of the Planning Commission on 13 November 1946:

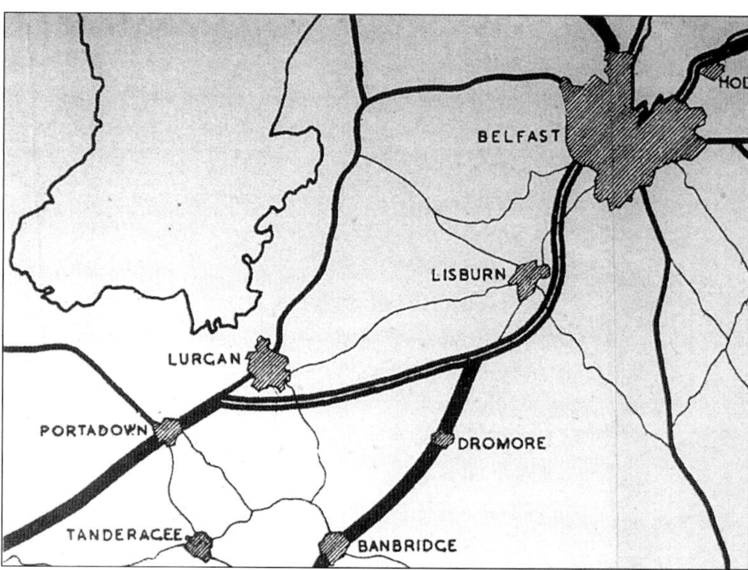

1946 Planning Commission proposals for Belfast. Note that the South Approach road passed to the south of Lurgan in this proposal.

> *The Government accepts the Planning Commission's recommendations that approach roads to Belfast should be constructed. The construction of one from the east, that is the Sydenham by-pass, was begun at public expense in 1938 and will be completed. Two others will, in consultation with the local authorities concerned, be undertaken. One from the south will by-pass Lisburn and the suburban area which has grown up between Lisburn and Belfast; the other from the north will by-pass Glengormley and relieve the present Antrim Road within the city. In view of the cost of constructing roads of this kind and their value to the traffic of the Province, the Government is prepared to construct them at public expense.*[5]

He added that: "I am able to announce that the Government will accept full responsibility for the construction and maintenance of arterial or trunk roads and intends that the Ministry of Commerce shall become the highway authority for such roads."[5] However, he recognised that this could not be achieved in the near future and noted that it would be an immensely complex task to plan, and expensive to implement.

Legislation dating from 1937 *(The Roads Act (Northern Ireland))* was invoked to make these proposals possible and was then supplemented by *The Roads Act (Northern Ireland) (1948)*, which established a system of centrally-managed trunk roads. Some work was carried out on the Sydenham Bypass in the second half of 1946, and again between March and December 1947 when men were employed by direct labour to lay concrete slabs. Work was again stopped in January 1948 due to financial constraints.[6]

The Cross-River Traffic Problem

During the 1940s, further attention was also being given to the cross-river traffic problem. A 1944 report by the Planning Commission proposed a bridge approximately on the line

1944 Planning Commission proposals for a street-level ring road encircling Belfast city centre which was largely, but not entirely, to be built by widening existing streets. The dots denote tree-lined boulevards. A bridge is shown crossing the Lagan downstream from the Queen's Bridge. Note the link road through Ormeau Park.

of Meik and Halcrow's tunnel (ie, not far from where the M3 bridge is today) but raised high enough so as not to interfere with road and rail traffic on the quays.[6] It would still have been too low to accommodate shipping, however. Since Donegall Quay was still an important dock at this time, the so-called Green Committee published a report in 1946 recommending that the bridge be moved upstream to connect High Street to Middlepath Street.[6] This bridge would be less likely to conflict with shipping and would still be at a high enough level to avoid interfering with the Donegall Quay railway or traffic on the quays.

However Major HE Aldington, the same engineer who had produced the report on post-war road development for the UK in 1945, later challenged the assumption that a new bridge was necessary. Aldington had been commissioned to prepare a report on the cross-river traffic problem in light of the Green Committee's proposals, and he presented his report in 1950[6] with a second one in 1951.[7] Aldington argued that it was not the Queen's Bridge itself that lacked capacity, but the road system around it, and that by improving the flow of traffic and pedestrians on its approaches, the single bridge should have sufficient capacity for some years to come. His proposals included the provision of roundabouts at either end of the bridge, two pedestrian underpasses under the Lagan, downstream of the bridge, and a one-way system in the city centre with an associated at-grade ring road around it.[8]

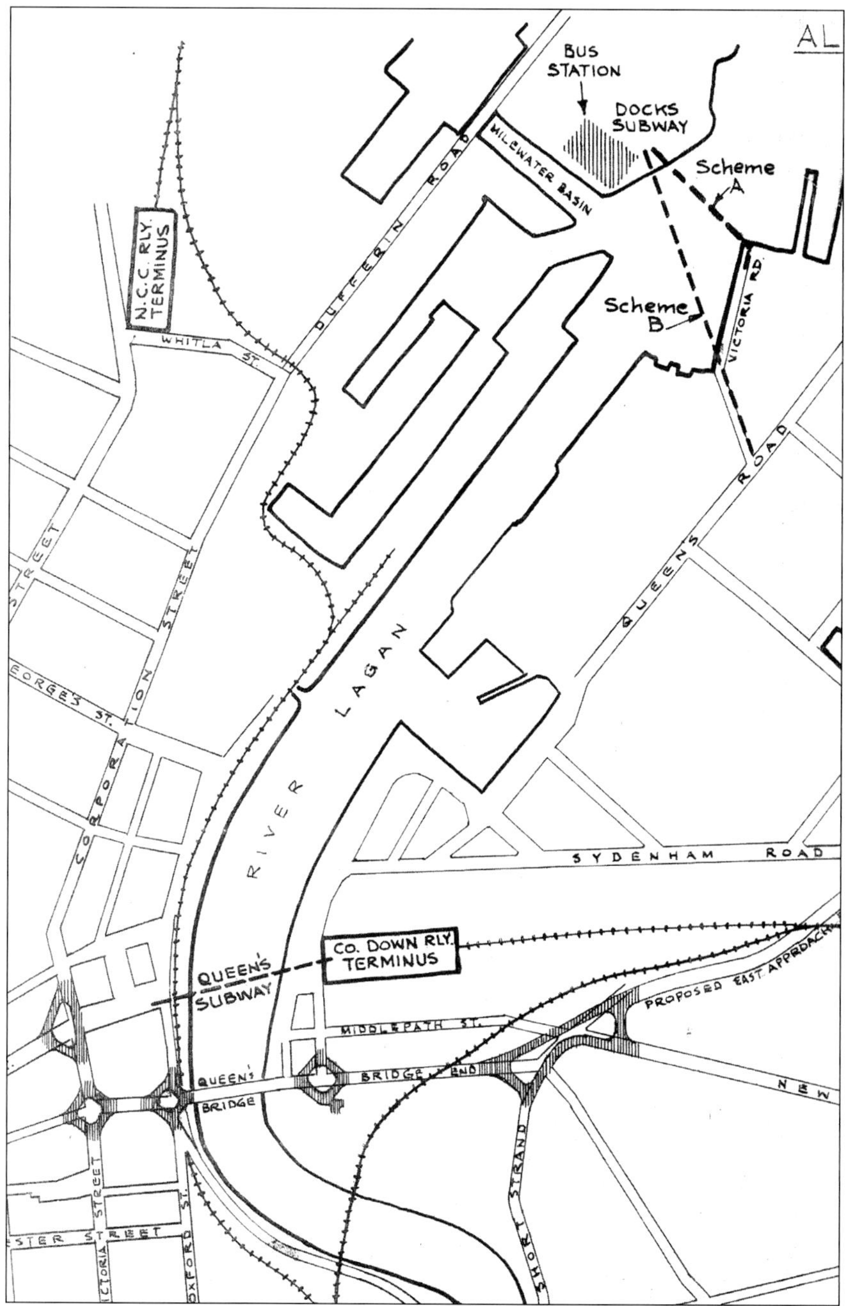

Aldington's 1950 proposals for improved junctions on either side of Queen's Bridge, and new subways. *(Deputy Keeper of the Records, Public Record Office of Northern Ireland LA/7/8/K/1)*

The Stormont government was not, however, convinced by Major Aldington's report, as evidenced by a comment made in Stormont three years later, when Lord Glentoran noted that:

> *[Major Aldington] advised that if certain improvement works were carried out at the approaches to the bridges, other arrangements were put into effect, and pedestrian subways were constructed, an additional bridge would not be necessary. The Belfast Corporation are not satisfied that these proposals would satisfactorily solve the problem, and have ordered the preparation of detailed alternative schemes.*[9]

Whether they genuinely disagreed with Aldington's analysis, or merely had their hearts set on a new bridge, is not clear. In the end, Mr Aldington's proposals for a one-way system were implemented, but the remaining measures were rejected.[8] The bridge remained busy. In 1950, almost 24,000 vehicles were crossing the Queen's Bridge daily,[7] which contrasts with the figure of around 18,000 in the year 2000.[10]

With little or no money available, talking was the only option. Discussions seemingly went round in circles with the authorities failing to reach a definite decision on what should be done, and spending hours of time debating proposal after proposal. In 1954, for example, Lord Glentoran commented that the latest idea was for "the construction of a second bridge to be sited close by, and possibly of a further bridge sited between McConnell's Weir and the Ormeau Bridge".[11] One MP even proposed in the same debate "to cover over the river entirely from the Queen's Bridge upwards, and provide better access to various parts of the city" – a proposal which, thankfully, was not taken seriously.

Over time, traffic engineers gained more experience of the dynamics of modern traffic flow. Eventually those in leadership came to understand that in seeking to make journey times faster (or at least, to prevent them getting slower) the provision of new, high-capacity roads would not achieve the desired aim if they merely terminated at the usual bottlenecks. In other words, in urban areas, the capacity of junctions is more important than the capacity of the links between them, a fact that Aldington had understood. Ulster Unionist MP Henry Holmes put this realisation into words, in 1954, when he asked:

> *What is the good of speeding up traffic on the Bangor and Newtownards roads if that traffic is going to run into a bottleneck at either the Queen's Bridge or the Albert Bridge roads? What is the good of speeding up traffic on the Newcastle-Ballynahinch road if that traffic is going to be congested at the Ormeau Bridge? What is the good of speeding up traffic on the Portadown-Lisburn road if it is going to run into a bottleneck at Shaftesbury Square? The same applies to the Antrim Road and to the Shore Road.*[11]

This is just one illustration of how, by the mid 1950s, it had been recognised that the cross-river traffic problem was a more complex issue than merely increasing capacity at the Queen's Bridge. Rather, it had become integrated into the wider debate of a city-wide traffic management strategy. From this point on, discussions on new river crossings were always associated with other major road projects in Belfast – initially the Sydenham By-pass, and later the ring road proposals.

Developments in Transport

During the Second World War fuel was in such scarce supply that "if you weren't an essential worker you didn't get a petrol ration".[12] This meant that those people who did own cars in 1939 often mothballed them and awaited the end of the war. Almost everybody had to use either public transport or horse-drawn vehicles. This led to an era of huge patronage on the railways and trolleybuses, resulting in an almost complacent approach to their operation. According to transport historian Norman Johnston, "if the bus was there, it filled up". At the time, "if you wanted to go somewhere you could go by train, or partly by train and partly by bus. You could do anything you wanted by public transport. The trains were losing money, but the trains were still there."[12]

The trains were indeed losing money. Wages were rising, making the railways less profitable, and the rolling stock had not been substantially upgraded since the 1920s. Since as far back as the 1930s, there had been a trend of more and more goods traffic transferring to lorries, leading to a further loss of income for the railway companies. Norman Topley worked on the railways during the period and recalled that the changes to freight traffic were inevitable for economic reasons:

> *A good illustration was those towns on the Clogher Valley – Augher, Clogher, Fivemiletown – every pound weight of coal that was burned in those towns was transferred by shovels from broad gauge wagons to narrow gauge wagons at Tynan railway station. And when you picture that compared with taking it direct by road there's no comparison ... Of course all the railwaymen frowned upon the lorries because they could see it was their living going, if you look at it from that point of view. But you had to be sensible about the thing.*[13]

Passenger transport followed a similar trend. Prior to the outbreak of the Second World War, private motorcars had been growing in popularity. Their appeal was obvious: door-to-door transportation, no waiting on platforms or at bus stops, travel at any time of day and the freedom to travel anywhere. However, the war prevented people from purchasing or using cars in great numbers. Norman Johnston explains that "a latent demand for cars had built up during the late 1940s."[12] This demand could not really be met until the Conservatives came to power in Westminster in 1951 and brought in sweeping economic changes.

> *It took until 1956 for the demand from the 1940s, the backlog, to be used up. Even though cars were of a poor quality in the 1950s people bought them. There was no foreign competition. From the mid 1950s prosperity was increasing, wages were rising and people had more money in their pockets. There was a new market emerging in the 1950s: people who aspired to own a car. It wouldn't necessarily be a new car – maybe three or four years old – and so because you got a good price for a used car, the middle classes changed their cars every few years.*[12]

A preserved Ford Prefect, manufactured 1956–62, a vehicle typical of the cars being used on Belfast's streets at the time. *(Norman Johnston)*

Joyce Topley, who worked on the railways with his brother Norman, was able to describe the situation before the war in these terms: "You'd see the commuter trains coming in to York Road station and Great Victoria Street station and Queen's Quay station. It just unloaded, train after train of commuters."[13] But after the war people's views had been transformed. People were no longer content to take the bus or train if they could afford a car, and so people began to purchase cars in ever increasing numbers. While our modern, ecologically-informed world view primarily considers public transport in terms of its sustainability and environmental credentials, and the private car in terms of pollution and congestion, the public of the 1950s associated the private car very much with freedom, success and social achievement.

By the mid 1950s the Stormont government had reached the conclusion that road transport was the future. Norman Johnston describes their attitude in these terms: "Their view was that life was modernising and more and more people would own cars. In contrast the railways were steam, viewed as dirty and regarded as a costly luxury. The Northern Ireland government basically wanted to close most of them".[12] Norman Topley has a slightly more cynical view: "Their attitude would be 'if we keep the railways open we have to finance them, but if the man buys his own car we haven't to pay for it'. That's the thinking."[13]

But the government had realised that the railways were in trouble long before the 1950s. In 1948 they set up the Ulster Transport Authority (UTA) to manage goods and public transport in Northern Ireland. It absorbed the debt-ridden NIRTB, which has hitherto been responsible for most bus and road freight transportation, and nationalised the railway lines of the Belfast and County Down Railway (BCDR) and the Northern Counties Committee (NCC). The northern section of the Great Northern Railway (GNR(I)) was nationalised in 1951, after it became inevitable that it was going to go bankrupt, and became part of the UTA in 1958. The UTA was given the hopeless task of becoming profitable within five years, and the only way to achieve this was to close down the least lucrative lines. Virtually all the BCDR lines (with the exception of the Belfast to Bangor line) were closed in 1950 with large chunks of the NCC

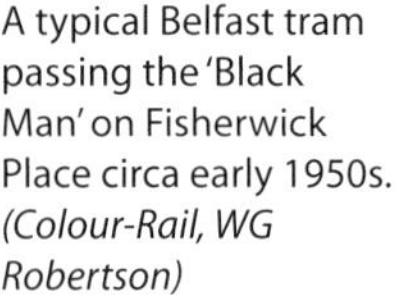

A typical Belfast tram passing the 'Black Man' on Fisherwick Place circa early 1950s. *(Colour-Rail, WG Robertson)*

network following swiftly.[14] Huge swathes of the (GNR(I)) were closed between 1955 and 1957, where huge political opposition from the affected areas encountered an equally resolved government that pressed ahead regardless.

During this same period, the use of public transport in Belfast reached its peak. Until the 1950s, trams were the most common vehicle, after which they were replaced by trolleybuses, which were themselves largely replaced by buses from the late 1960s. But regardless of the particular mode of public transport, the total number of journeys per year rose steadily from around 50 million at the start of the First World War, to around 150 million by 1941 and reached a peak of over 280 million in the mid 1950s[15] before starting its long decline.

Traffic on Belfast's streets was rising rapidly, not only because of the rise in car ownership, but because the transfer of freight from railway to road had put hundreds more lorries onto the congested streets of Belfast. It is therefore not surprising that in the 1960s planners more or less assumed that the future of transportation lay with providing new roads. This thinking was to inform the vast majority of what was planned during the 1950s and 1960s.

Work Commences on the Approach Roads

Following the 1946 decision to proceed with the Approach roads, detailed design work got underway and this continued for a number of years. It was not until late 1952 that the government indicated that some money might soon be available for commencing construction work.[2] Some advance contracts (construction of bridges) were carried out on the North and South Approach roads between 1956 and 1959, but no work was carried out on the roads themselves until 1959, when construction began on the South Approach road.

Hightown Road bridge, Glengormley, seen in 1958 when it sat in a pit in anticipation of the future construction of the North Approach road. *(T Jackson McCormick)*

On 6 June 1956 the Minister of Commerce, Lord Glentoran, announced that the government had decided to further expand the plans for the Approach Roads. The reason given was that "traffic on our roads has grown, and is continuing to grow, at a greater rate within a widening area from Belfast than could have been foreseen some years ago".[16] In other words, the plans announced in 1946 were no longer sufficient to meet the anticipated demand from road users. Instead of halting at Glengormley, the North Approach (M2) would now go to Ballymena, while the South Approach (M1) would go all the way to Dungannon. The East Approach would not stop at Tillysburn, but would now continue to Bangor, while an entirely new road, referred to as the South East Approach, was tentatively proposed to relieve the Saintfield Road from Carryduff into the city. It is important to stress that these proposals did not suggest that all of the roads would be 'motorways' in the modern sense, but they were certainly envisaged to be dual-carriageways.

This announcement is significant because is indicates that a shift was underway in the Northern Ireland government's understanding of the role of the Approach Roads. They had initially been proposed as relief roads for the arterial roads of the city, but were now also being viewed as a means to efficiently connect more distant towns and industry to Belfast. The fact that providing a network of fast roads into the heart of the city would likely result in thousands more vehicles entering the central area of the city was not overlooked by the government. A year later, Lord Glentoran commented in Stormont that:

> *It may be expected that the approach roads, when completed, will be likely to attract traffic to them, and that such traffic will disperse into the city road network. I am aware that the Belfast Corporation has under consideration the provision of new routes in the city from the termini of these roads or the reconstruction of the existing streets. It has, in particular, actively in hand the question of improving the cross-river communications.*[17]

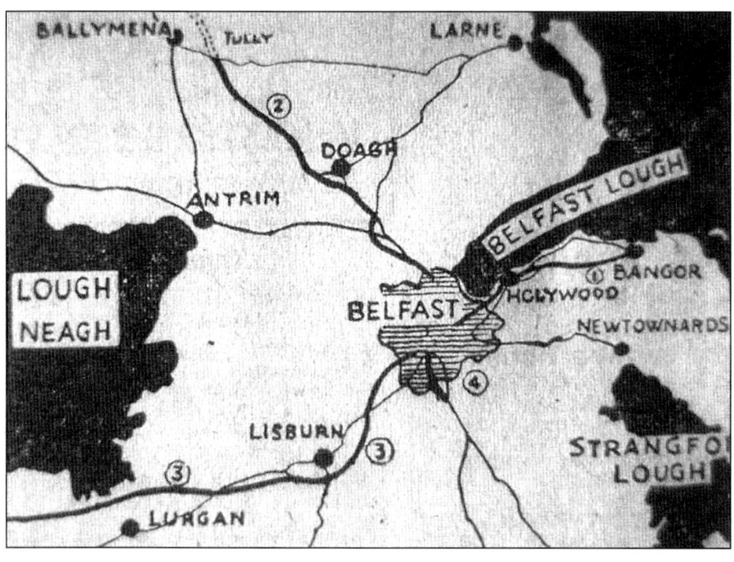

Motorway proposals for the Belfast area as announced in June 1956. Note that the North Approach runs via Doagh, rather than Antrim, and the South Approach now passes to the north of Lurgan. *(Northern Ireland Executive/Belfast Telegraph)*

Up to this point, the plans for the city centre had consisted of little more than ground level ring roads, but it was now realised that a more radical approach was needed if all this traffic was going to be absorbed effectively by the city centre. It is also interesting to note that the idea that there might be a limit to how much traffic the city centre could physically absorb had not yet been raised, let alone addressed.

Finances had finally enabled work on the East Approach (the Sydenham Bypass) to recommence in earnest by 1954[18] and the road was officially opened on 23 November 1959, almost 20 years after work had begun. Since the issue of how best to tie the new road in to the proposed new river crossing had never been resolved, despite hours of talking, the engineers threw up their hands and took the only course of action open to them, which was to simply connect the Bypass to the existing lower Newtownards Road via a T-junction. This was an unsatisfactory arrangement that caused massive tailbacks on opening day[19] and undoubtedly prevented the road from achieving its full potential in its early years.[20]

The Sydenham Bypass did not have motorway restrictions when it opened, even though this was the ultimate intention. However, it did claim the accolade of being the first modern dual-carriageway to open on the island of Ireland. Although the concept of a 'motorway' was widely understood by 1959 (the UK's first motorway, the Preston Bypass, had opened in December 1958)[1] the relaxed attitude that many people had to the new road was typified by football supporters attending the nearby Oval, who sometimes parked their cars on the central reservation!

The pre-existing East Road, seen here in 1957 at the point it crossed the Connswater River near Victoria Park. East Road was subsumed by the Sydenham Bypass. *(Via DRD Roads Service)*

Work underway on the Sydenham Bypass in 1958, most notably on the reconstruction of the existing Connswater bridge that hitherto carried East Road. The original arrangement at Dee Street is visible on the left. *(Via DRD Roads Service)*

The new Dee Street bridge seen looking south west in 1958 shortly after its completion. Although Dee Street already crossed over the railway line here, the bridge was rebuilt to accommodate the Sydenham Bypass, which opened the following year. *(T Jackson McCormick)*

The Sydenham Bypass as seen in 1970, 11 years after its completion. Dee Street bridge is in the foreground. Note the priority T-junction where traffic signals exist today. Note also the low traffic levels! *(Via DRD Roads Service)*

Aerial view of the Tillysburn roundabout at the eastern end of the Sydenham Bypass in December 1964. The roundabout was replaced with a signalised junction in 1988, although the outline of the original roundabout is still plainly visible today. *(Via DRD Roads Service)*

Chaotic scenes marred the opening day of the Sydenham Bypass, 23 November 1959, as hundreds of vehicles attempted to merge with the existing traffic at the bottom of the Newtownards Road. The 'no through road' sign was presumably there for the benefit of those unfamiliar with the concept of a dual-carriageway. *(Belfast Telegraph)*

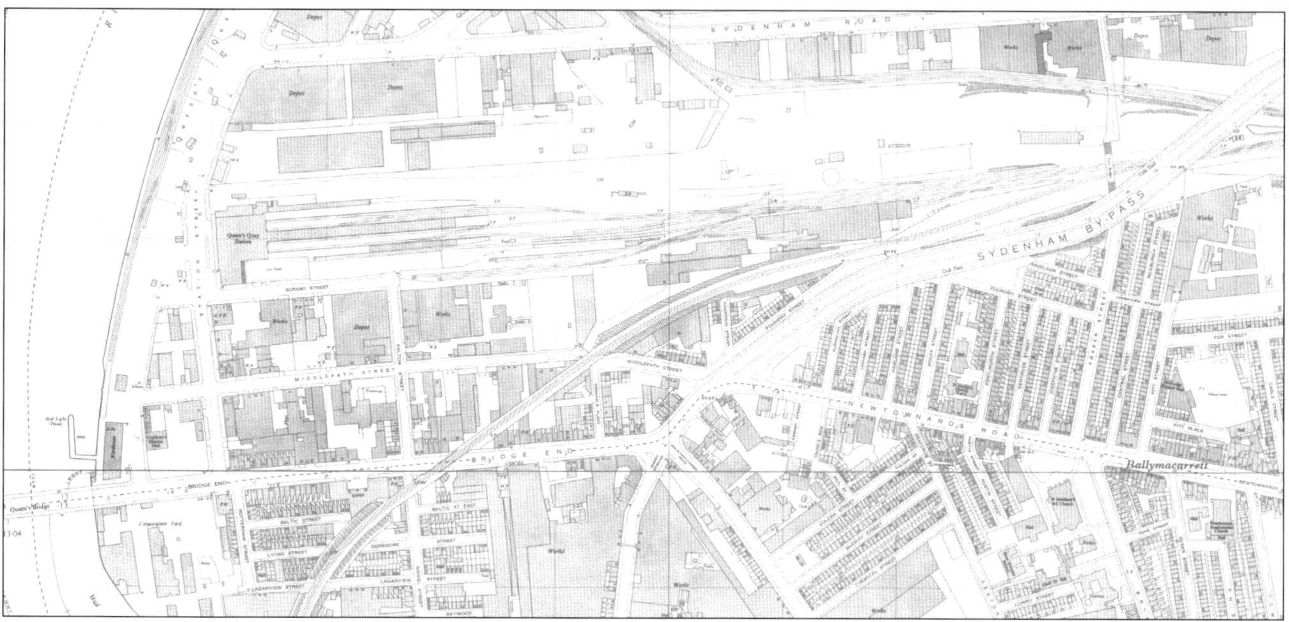

The original terminus of the Sydenham Bypass on the Newtownards Road as shown on a 1963 map. *(LPS/Ordnance Survey of Northern Ireland)*

Inner City Regeneration

During the Blitz of 1941, almost 57,000 houses had been destroyed in Belfast[15] and thousands of those that had survived were of a very poor standard and were classed as 'slums'. Although the government had constructed emergency prefabricated housing and rebuilt some of the damaged sites, there had been no serious efforts to deal with the more widespread issue of housing deprivation before the mid 1950s. What was needed was a scheme to systematically rebuild entire neighbourhoods.

On 6 November 1956, the Northern Ireland government passed the verbosely named *Housing (Miscellaneous Provisions) and Rent Restriction Law (Amendment) Act (Northern Ireland) (1956)*. This Act gave the government the right to define certain properties as 'unfit'

Westbourne Street, on the Newtownards Road, showing houses destroyed during the Blitz of 1941. *(Belfast Telegraph)*

and mark them for redevelopment. Almost 100,000 houses (about a quarter of all houses in Northern Ireland) were allocated under this Act and as a result vast areas of the working class inner city were earmarked for reconstruction. The majority of these were to the west of the city centre (the Crumlin Road, Shankill Road and Divis Street areas) and to the south (Sandy Row, Donegall Road and The Markets), with more limited allocations in the east (such as Short Strand) and the north (for example around North Queen Street). The degree to which the existing residents of these communities supported the regeneration plans is debatable. While most welcomed the construction of better homes, some were rightly nervous about how exactly this would be carried out.

Work soon got underway building modern social housing on green field sites outside the city centre, for example at Rathcoole, Belvoir and Seymour Hill. However, very little work was carried out in the inner city regeneration areas during the early years of the process,[15] leading to the problem of 'planning blight', where private sector developers did not want to invest in the redevelopment areas leading to a further deterioration in the fabric of existing buildings and contributing to the malcontent of the communities living there.

Map of designated redevelopment areas in Belfast after 1956. *(Base map Ordnance Survey, 1940)*

The 1950s was an era of modernity, a reaction against the decadence of pre-war Europe, where function was the main aim of development, and planners at least viewed vast district-wide reconstruction projects as inherently good and progressive. After years of destruction and war, the new generation of planners were ready to discard the past with its fussy, stuffy architecture, and envisaged a prosperous future with construction dominated by concrete and steel; the materials of the new era.

The redevelopment plans thus provided town planners with a unique opportunity to modernise the urban fabric of the inner city on a massive scale. In addition, there was potential for great economic benefits to Northern Ireland (or, at least, to the ruling classes) by making large areas of the city centre available for investment. The area allocated for redevelopment was so big that the degree of opportunity available at this point was not to be paralleled at any time in the decades that have since elapsed.

By 1960, two major themes were converging. The recognised need for new high capacity roads in the city centre, coupled with the availability of hundreds of acres of land in the city centre, created a situation which carried with it a certain degree of inevitability.

CHAPTER 4
THE URBAN MOTORWAY

By the end of the 1950s Belfast was facing other difficulties in addition to the problems of congestion and sub-standard housing. The city's mobile population was deserting the inner city and moving to the suburbs, which were sprawling out from the edge of the older city at an alarming rate.[1] Many of those who had the means to commute chose to move to nearby towns such as Bangor and Newtownards, which mushroomed from this period onwards.

Belfast Corporation, the city's governing body, was a powerful organisation with wide ranging powers including the management of roads and most services in the city. Facing the problem of a falling population within their boundary and the urgent need to provide better housing, the Corporation began to pressurise the Stormont government to allow an expansion of the city limits in 1960.

The Stormont government recognised the dangers posed by a city that could expand unchecked into the surrounding countryside. These dangers not only included the risk of starving the rest of Northern Ireland of industrial development, by creating a single dominant city, but perhaps also of leaving Belfast Corporation too powerful for the government's comfort.[1] As a result, Stormont was not prepared to simply acquiesce to the Corporation's pressure and sought other ways to manage suburban growth.

On 26 April 1960, the Minister of Health and Local Government, John Andrews, announced that the government had decided to prepare a plan for the Belfast region. Although this approach was extremely popular in Great Britain at the time, this was the first occasion that such a plan was prepared for Northern Ireland. Mr Andrews said in Stormont:

> *Recognising the many problems ... in the city of Belfast and the surrounding area, the Government recently decided that the time was opportune to have this important area surveyed and a comprehensive plan drawn up for its future development.*[2]

He then announced the appointment of well-known planner Sir Robert Matthew:

> *It affords me the very greatest pleasure to be able to announce that Professor Matthew has agreed to act. Some years ago Professor Matthew carried out a regional survey and plan of the Clyde Valley, and is now engaged on large slum clearance operations for the Glasgow Corporation. Professor Matthew hopes to begin his survey very shortly.*[2]

Professor Matthew reported initially on housing, but his regional plan, which included detailed transport proposals, was not to be published until October 1962.[3]

The Urban Motorway is conceived

During the 1950s, City Planning Officer Victor Walshe had developed the proposals for the city centre ring road.[3] Walshe initially envisaged a ring constructed on the level with roundabouts at each radial encountered. However, it was soon realised that such a design would not work since the traffic loads at the roundabouts would exceed their capacity and cause significant congestion at these locations.

Belfast Corporation was concerned about the effect that the approach roads would have on city; the vast number of vehicles that would speed into the inner city would need to be distributed efficiently. The Corporation felt that the much-discussed inner ring road was the solution.

It must be noted that, while the rural motorway programme proceeded at a great pace, very little initially happened in Belfast. The expertise rested in the Ministry of Development's Roads Branch and gradually, under the advice and guidance of Ministry staff, Belfast Corporation accepted the need to further progress the plans for a ring road.[4]

Once again, the planners turned to Europe for inspiration. The construction of the first phase of the 'Grote Ring' urban motorway in Brussels in 1957 apparently spurred them to consider elevation as a possible alternative to a ground level road.[5] After consulting with the Ministry of Commerce, Walshe's plan was revised to become an 'urban motorway', known at the time as the 'Grade Separated Scheme'.[6] Under this approach the road would be an elevated dual-carriageway with two lanes in each direction, forming a triangle enclosing the city centre. The city planners based its design on Lord Glentoran's proposals of 1956, envisaging that it would have connections to each of the four proposed approach roads (motorways). The plan was that each of the four approach roads would terminate at a grade separated roundabout on the urban motorway.[6] These were not the only junctions; the road was to have "as many connections as possible to the city streets".[7] The speed limit would have been 30 mph.[5]

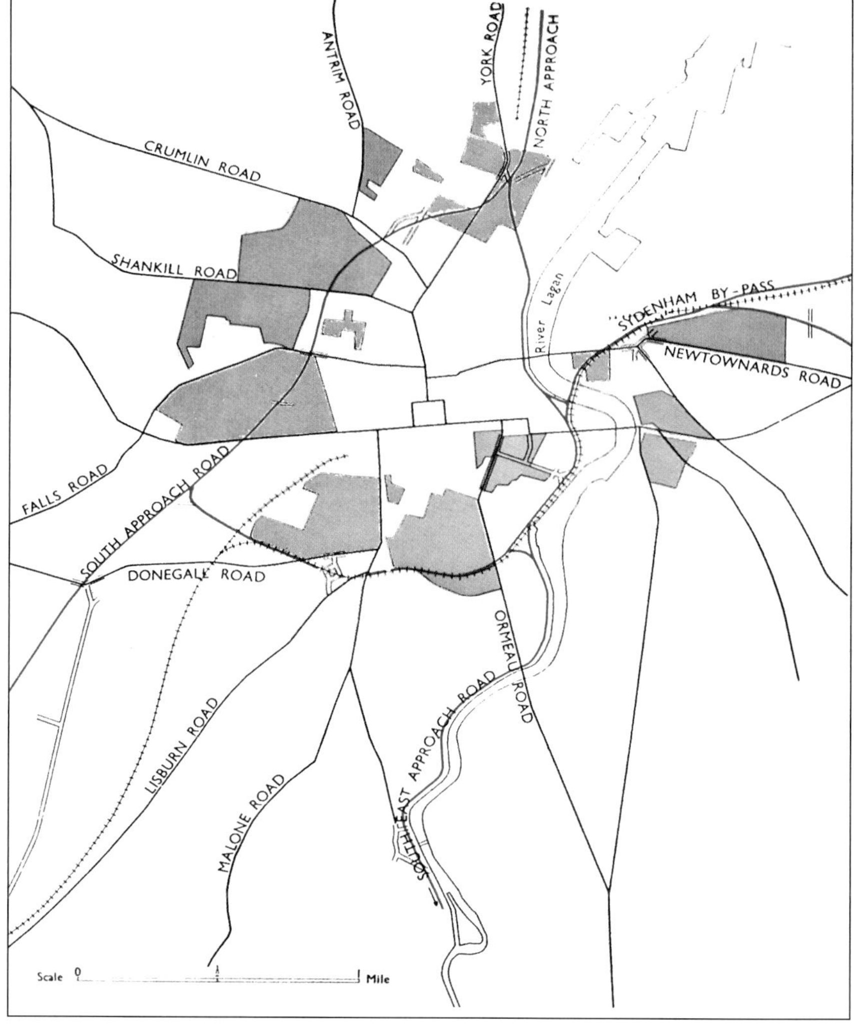

The late 1950s 'grade separated scheme' for a dual two-lane urban motorway encircling the city centre connecting to four approach roads. *(Matthew Plan)*

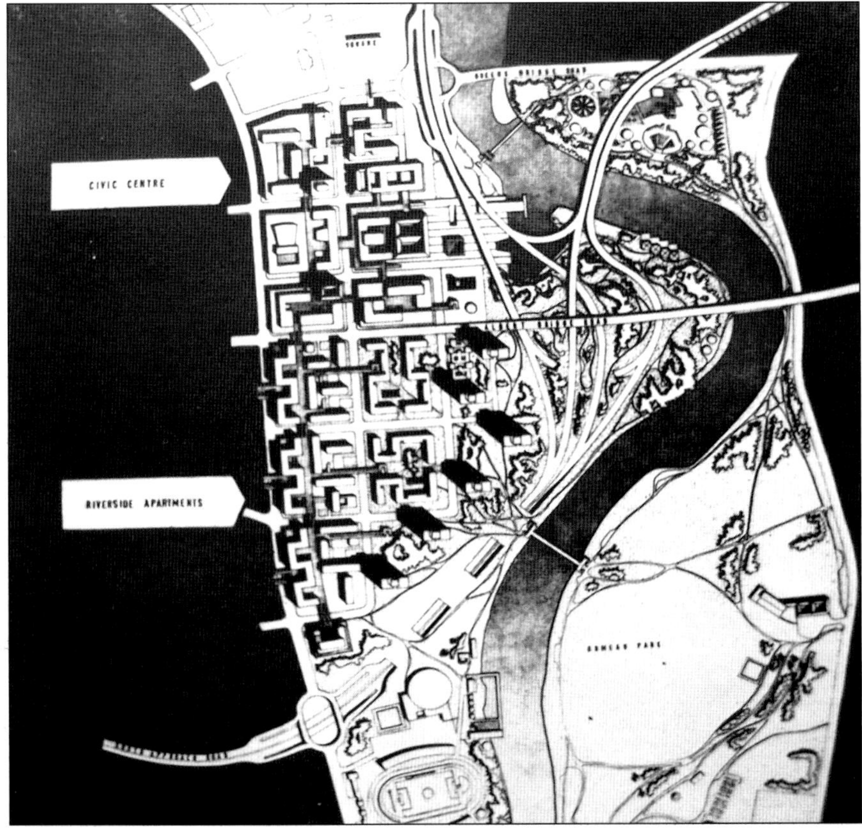

A 1962 artist's impression of the Urban Motorway and its connection to the East Approach road around the Markets area. Note that the layout of sliproads here is probably conjectural and not based on actual designs. *(Matthew Plan)*

Starting at the terminus of the South Approach (the M1) beside the Royal Victoria Hospital, the route was generally north easterly, sticking as far as possible to the redevelopment areas designated in 1956, before reaching the terminus of the North Approach (the M2) around York Street. It then turned sharply south east and ran along the west bank of the Lagan through Donegall Quay towards the Albert Bridge, where it was met by a proposed extension of the Sydenham Bypass. From then on it followed the route of the Central Railway line around the south edge of the city centre, meeting the South East Approach close to the gas works, and finally coming full circle. The fact that the Corporation routed the motorway along the line of the Central Railway reveals the extent to which planners at the time saw no future in rail transport.

These proposals were put to the Improvement Committee of Belfast Corporation and approved on 8 June 1961.[3] The plans were then sent to the Ministry of Commerce for approval.

The Matthew Plan

Meanwhile, Professor Matthew submitted his report 'Belfast Regional Survey and Plan' in October 1962.[8] The plan attracted criticism for being too limited in its geographical scope, and for pre-empting other economic plans,[1] but was nevertheless a milestone in planning in Northern Ireland. It brought a degree of high-level vision that had not been seen since the war years.

Matthew examined a number of issues, including the need for new housing, a growing population and the problem of the unrestrained growth of Belfast. His radical solution was to fence the city with what he called a 'stop line', beyond which the city would not be allowed to expand. Such was the success of this proposal that, with a few exceptions such as Poleglass and Cairnshill, this stop line remains more or less intact to the present day.

The people living in sub-standard housing in the city would instead be re-housed in seven existing towns, that would be greatly expanded, and one entirely new city, to be positioned in the countryside between Portadown and Lurgan. The city would later be named 'Craigavon'. These towns would also absorb the predicted growth in the total population of the region. The eight growth poles were as follows:[8]

TOWN	1961 POPULATION	PLANNED 1981 POPULATION
Antrim	3000	12000 (+300%)
Ballymena	15000	35000 (+133%)
Bangor	24000	31000 (+30%)
Carrickfergus	10000	18000 (+80%)
Craigavon Area	37000	100000 (+170%)
Downpatrick	4000	7000 (+75%)
Larne	16000	22000 (+38%)
Newtownards	13000	23000 (+77%)

Even without these large population movements, Matthew's words capture the degree to which traffic congestion in the city had already reached epic proportions:

> *All the main roads leading into Belfast are either overloaded or working to full capacity ... In each of the past two decades traffic has more than doubled and it is probable that it will continue to increase. The concentration of approximately 85% of traffic on 11% of the road mileage, and its further concentration in time, makes the relief of these main roads a matter of urgency.*[8]

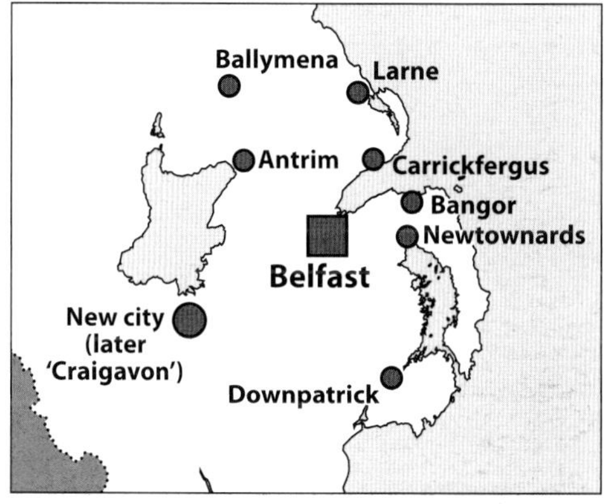

Belfast and the eight growth poles designated by the 1962 'Matthew Plan'.

Tim Morton recalls the traffic clearly:

> *Belfast was a seriously congested city at peak times – much more congested than it is [in 2006] ... My bus home from Inst to the Malone Road could take forever to stop-start its way out of the city centre if I was late away from school. The whole central area just seemed to be continually gridlocked.*[9]

The table below shows the degree of congestion in the city in 1960:[8]

ROAD	% OF CAPACITY
Antrim Road at Templepatrick	106%
Shore Road at Greencastle	176%
Bangor Road at Holywood	195%
Saintfield Road to Carryduff	185%
Lisburn Road at Dunmurry	231%

To make matters worse, the problem was increasing at a staggering rate. Between 1956 and 1966, the number of private cars in Belfast rose by approximately 240%, a rate of increase not seen even in the modern day.[8]

Matthew knew that his plans to move thousands of people out of Belfast would put even more pressure on the transport system of the Belfast area, since the Approach Roads would not only connect Belfast to other towns, but would become essential commuter routes. In keeping with the thinking of the day, Matthew's solution was a largely roads-based one, even though many of these towns had existing railway lines that ran into the heart of the city. Not only did he confirm the need for the four Approach Roads, but he suggested further dual-carriageways to Newtownards, Carrickfergus, Banbridge and Toome, as well as a dual-carriageway bypass round the east of the city.

Most importantly, he strongly endorsed Belfast Corporation's plan for an urban motorway in the city centre, since all the commuter and port traffic would be gravitating into the central area of the city.

> *The urban motorway system inside Belfast is essential to link the main roads feeding traffic into the central area of the city and the port facilities. It is essential that it should be completed at the earliest possible moment, yet some of the fundamentals necessary for its construction, the clearance and redevelopment programme and the future of the railways, have yet to be established.*[8]

That Matthew should come up with proposals so overwhelmingly based on roads is puzzling, given that just months earlier he is on record as advocating a much more balanced approach to transport, particularly towards the role of public transport and the effect of roads on the built heritage of cities.[10] Perhaps the opinions of the Northern Ireland government itself influenced Matthew during the process of his work.

With hindsight, scholars have acknowledged that the 'Matthew Plan' was "a high point in the history of regional planning" but note that "it was based on a range of assumptions that subsequently proved to be false" and "was cavalier in the way it dealt with people forced to move to the new regional centres and it relied too much on public funding".[1] One of these assumptions was the growth rate of Northern Ireland's population, a figure that proved to be greatly exaggerated, with the result that the new city of Craigavon (which had numerous other problems) was unable to achieve a critical mass and was never completed.

Nevertheless, the result of the 'Matthew Plan' at the time was to place the embryonic motorway system at the heart of the development of the Belfast region, to promote little enthusiasm for public transport, and to accept that Belfast would become a city of commuters. Much of the subsequent evolution of the region has been shaped by this fundamental policy decision. It also reinforced the trend of continuous growth in the use of private cars and helped make the plans for the urban motorway self-perpetuating. The table below shows how the use of public transport declined from the 1960s until the Millennium.

Means of travel into Belfast by commuters

MODE	1960	1971	1981	1991	2001
Bus	48%	37%	22%	14%	14%
Train	12%	6%	5%	3%	No data
Private Vehicles	40%	57%	71%	82%	84%

However, it would be disingenuous to wholly blame Belfast's transformation into a car-based commuter city on the 'Matthew Plan'. The move to the private car was already underway and it is likely that, even if no motorways had been built at all, private cars would still have come to dominate the city. It must be remembered that the planners at the time were simply coping with the consequences of this trend, and that in the 1960s the explosion in the use of private cars did not have the negative connotations that it does today.

Work on the motorways

By this point work was well underway on the approach roads. Work on the first stretch of the South Approach (the M1 motorway) had begun in 1959 with the main contract being awarded to Sir Alfred McAlpine and Son Ltd. The stretch from Belfast to Saintfield Road, Lisburn opened without fanfare on 10 July 1962. Tim Morton remembers the day well:

> *A kindly uncle drove me up and down to Lisburn. There was very little traffic and much of it was driving on the hard shoulder! The concept of the hard shoulder had not been properly understood and many thought it was simply a brightly coloured slow lane (it had a pink surfacing)!"*[9]

The M1 motorway during construction at Donegall Road (below the bottom of the picture) circa 1962. *(Photograph courtesy of DRD Roads Service)*

The completed M1 motorway seen here shortly before opening in July 1962. The wetland to the left is the Bog Meadows, today beneath the Boucher Road industrial estate. *(Photograph courtesy of DRD Roads Service)*

The 'temporary' terminus of the M1 motorway at Donegall Road, seen here shortly before opening in July 1962. *(Photograph courtesy of DRD Roads Service)*

At Belfast, this stretch of the M1 ended rather awkwardly at a temporary terminus on the Donegall Road, close to its junction with Broadway. There had been proposals to terminate the M1 closer to the city centre, on either Roden Street or Grosvenor Road. However, there was considerable local and political opposition to this, so the temporary terminus near Broadway was essentially a 'fall back' solution implemented ahead of a resolution to the debate.[11] It was therefore planned that the M1 would be extended from its temporary terminus on Donegall Road to meet the inner ring road (the urban motorway) at some undefined point in the future.

This part of the M1 was the first motorway in Ireland and work was carried out on the remaining sections of the M1 over the following six years, with the final stretch opening in January 1968. Work on the North Approach between the Shore Road at Greencastle and Sandyknowes near Glengormley would begin in September 1963. No work was carried out on the South East Approach and no further work was carried out on the East Approach.

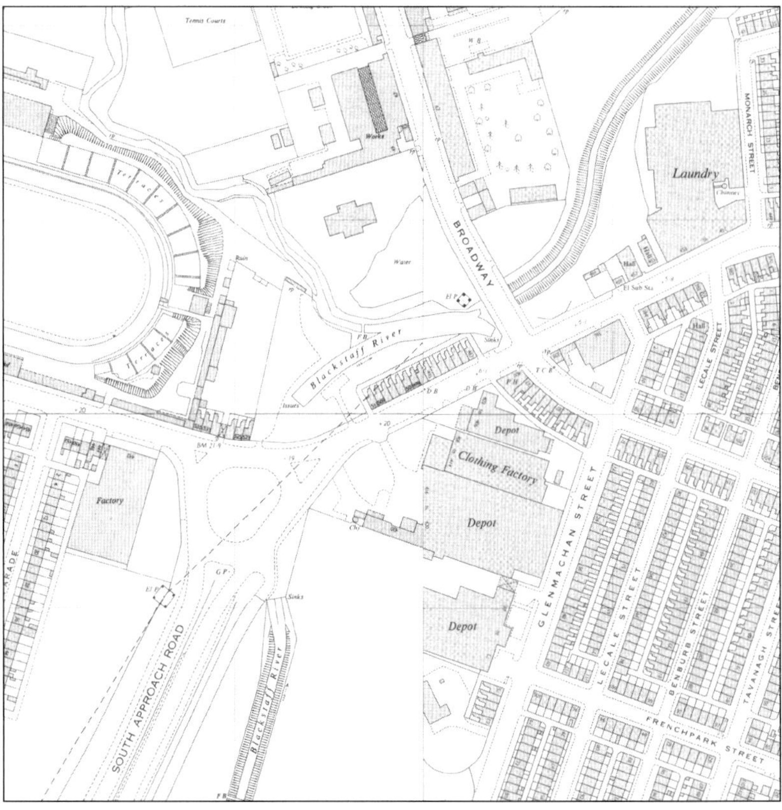

Map of the original terminus of the M1 motorway at Donegall Road (1965/1971). Note that it has been labelled 'South Approach Road', despite having being named 'M1' since its opening in 1962. *(LPS/ Ordnance Survey of Northern Ireland)*

1963 saw a new Prime Minister in Northern Ireland, Terence O'Neill, who appointed William Craig as Minister of Home Affairs (which took over responsibility for roads from the Ministry of Commerce at the same time). Craig initially kept his own counsel, absorbing the 1963 Benson Report[12] on the railways (discussed later in this chapter), the Matthew Plan[8] on the Belfast region of 1962 and, of course, the need to be seen making sound investments for the future. He finally made his intentions public in Stormont on 13 February 1964[13] when he announced the closure of large sections of the rail system, to be compensated by substantially increased investment in roads. These included plans to extend the motorway network as far as Coleraine, Londonderry and Newry.

In Belfast, there were plans to build yet more motorways: to Carrickfergus (M5), Larne (M6), and Dundonald (M7), the latter to be built along the route of the closed County Down railway line through suburban east Belfast. Another motorway (M8) would be built across the Lagan Valley from near Lisburn to the M4 south of Carryduff. Finally, it was planned to relieve pressure on the M1 by building a relief motorway (M11) which would run parallel to the M1 out of Belfast before diverging to pass round the north side of Lisburn and then continue to Newry.

Craig assessed his own announcement thus:

> *This is a formidable programme for an economy as small as ours; but the Government feel that unless a major effort of this kind is made we will not be able, as we wish to do, to show in Northern Ireland the lead in making adequate provision for using to the maximum the advantages of flexibility and efficiency which modern road vehicles offer to a developing industrial economy.*[13]

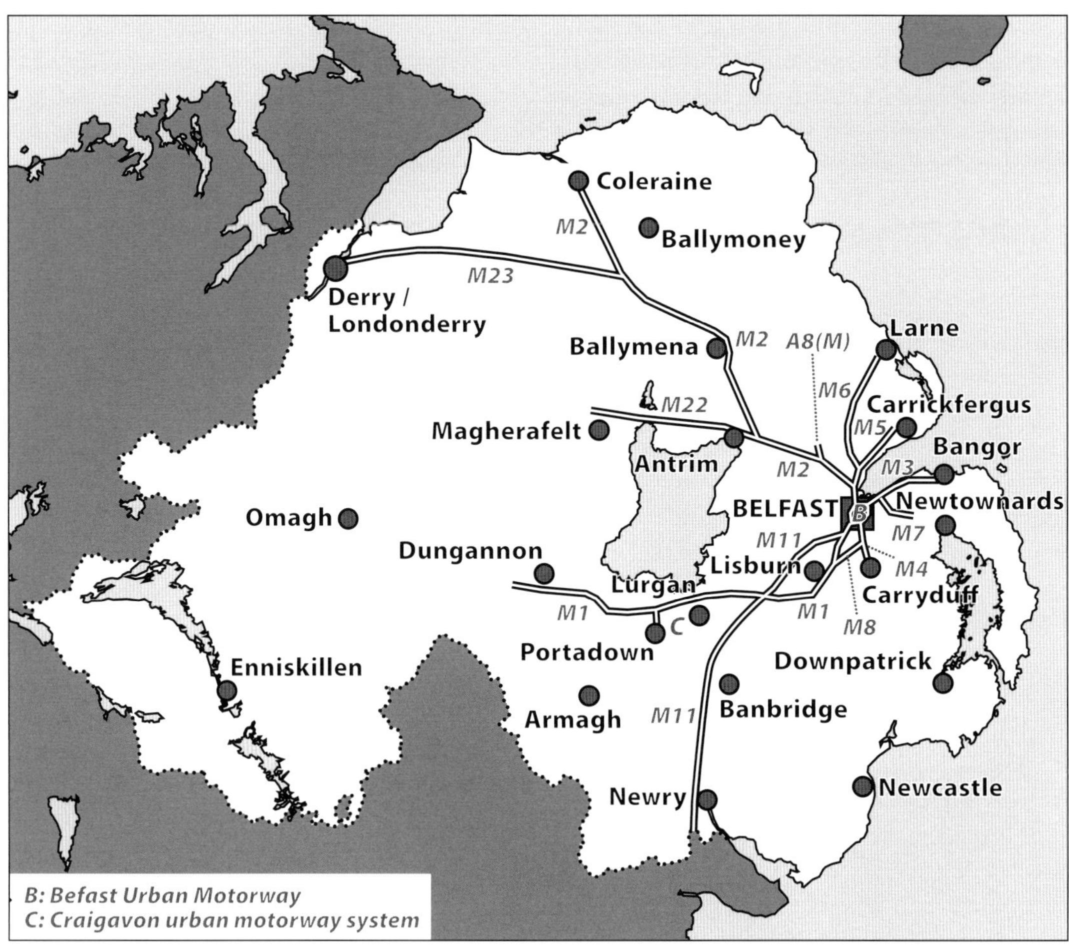

Proposed system of motorways for Northern Ireland as announced by William Craig in February 1964. These proposals marked the zenith of ambitions for the rural motorway network.

These plans were on such an unprecedented scale that even Ministers in London were taken aback by their ambition, but it must be noted that the proposals were still nothing more than statements of ambition, and would be properly scrutinised by engineers and economists over the coming years.

A New Bridge

Meanwhile, changes were already taking place on the railways. As has already been noted, those parts of the Great Northern Railway which lay in Northern Ireland were absorbed into the Ulster Transport Authority (UTA) in 1958. This included the Belfast Central Railway which connected the railways on the west of the city (terminating at Great Victoria Street), the east of the city (terminating at Queen's Quay) and those to the north of the city (terminating at York Road). The line crossed to the south of the city centre before traversing the Lagan via the rickety Lagan Viaduct, and then across Bridge End and Middlepath Street on a pair of rather low bridges. A length of line, suitable only for goods vehicles, also went north along Donegall Quay, under the western end of Queen's Bridge in a tunnel, serving the port and terminating near York Road.

The Central Railway and the Donegall Quay railway both caused problems for the urban planners because they prevented the development of the road system. As has already been discussed, the Donegall Quay railway was in the way of new river crossings, and the Middlepath Street bridge was so low that no new roads could feasibly be built to connect to the recently-opened Sydenham Bypass. These problems disappeared with the decision to close the Donegall Quay railway in 1959. The Central Railway closed in 1965, following the 1963 Benson Report, which proposed closing virtually all of the railways except for the three commuter lines into Belfast.[12]

These decisions have been characterised by road planners as unrelated events undertaken by the railway operators that just happened to make certain road proposals possible. The 1967 report into the Urban Motorway would later say neutrally that "by 1959 the UTA … had decided that the Donegall Quay railway … could be abandoned". JT Noble, writing in 1972, simply says, "the abandonment … freed the western bank of the River Lagan and opened the way to a convenient bridge site".[7]

This version of history, however, likely understates what actually happened behind the scenes. It seems likely that the road planners put considerable pressure on the UTA to abandon the railways in question, and that it was not a decision that the UTA made independently. Norman Johnston explains:

> *By 1958 the UTA had the ability to link all the termini in Belfast and replace them with a new central station. They didn't because [the government] weren't prepared to invest in infrastructure … A tremendous amount of freight arrived in Belfast and went to the docks by rail without touching the roads. If you were to dig deep enough you might find the planners approached the UTA and said 'do you really need the Donegall Quay railway'? You have all sorts of anecdotal evidence of efforts to get rid of the railways.*[14]

Nevertheless, it is true that the closure of the Donegall Quay railway removed the main obstacle that had prevented the construction of a new low-level bridge over the Lagan for the past 30 years. A new bridge was soon constructed adjacent to the Queen's Bridge, just 60 metres (210 feet) downstream. The structure consists of three steel arches mounted on reinforced concrete piers and at 24 metres (80 feet) across, it was even wider than the Queen's Bridge.

Considerable thought was put into how the new bridge could best be accommodated into the local road network and in particular the recently completed Sydenham Bypass. In the end the land around Middlepath Street was acquired to construct an ambitious one-way system 1.1 km (0.7 mile) in circumference, east of the river, between 1963 and 1966. The system, which required the removal of the now-redundant Middlepath Street railway bridge, allowed four lanes of traffic to circulate clockwise. The Sydenham Bypass was tied in to the eastern end of the system, with the two Lagan bridges at the western end. Two flyovers were constructed: Bridge End Flyover took traffic from the Sydenham Bypass directly onto the one-way system bypassing the Newtownards Road junction, while Station Street Flyover allowed traffic from Queen's Quay, then a key industrial area, to jump across to the westbound section without having to travel around the entire system.

Although the works resulted in big improvements to traffic flow across the river and particularly to the Sydenham Bypass, it also had the effect of converting the streetscape of

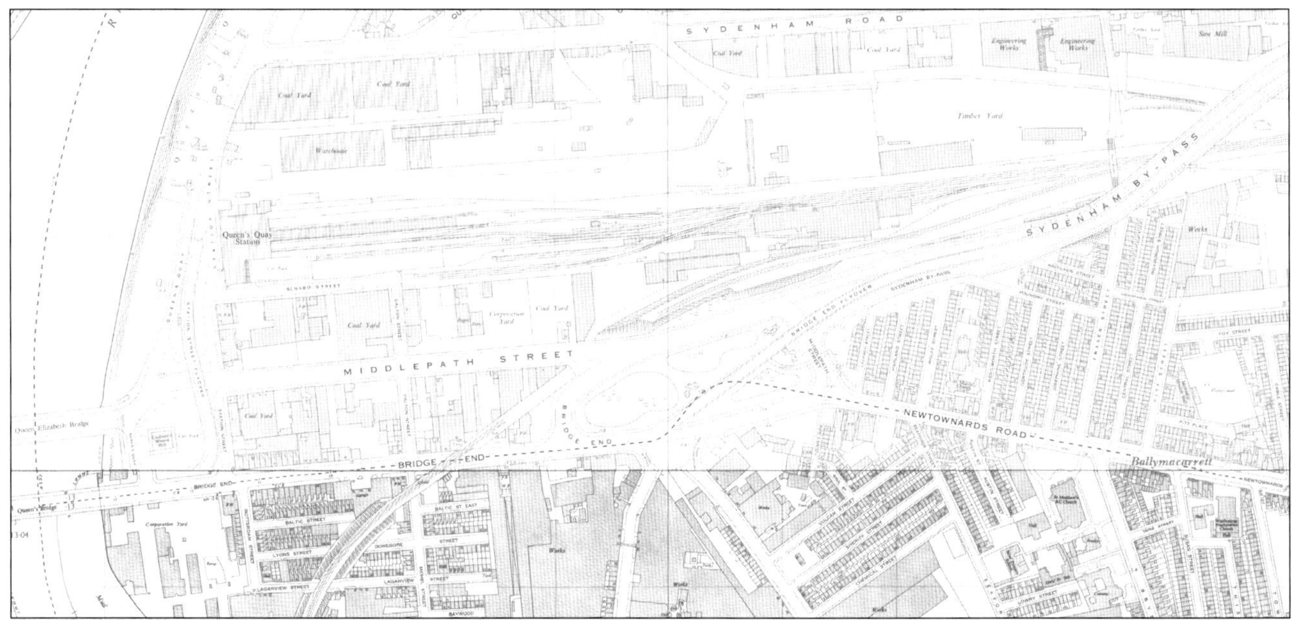

Map of the modified terminus of the Sydenham Bypass, the Queen Elizabeth Bridge, and the Middlepath Street/ Bridge End one-way system in 1970. *(LPS/ Ordnance Survey of Northern Ireland)*

Ballymacarrett into an expansive urban wasteland that persists to the present day, acting as a significant psychological barrier between the Newtownards Road/Short Strand area and the city centre. This phenomenon of severance would be recognised as one of the most significant problems associated with urban road schemes.[15] In 2011, the area was officially termed the 'Shatterzone'.[16]

The junction of Bridge End and Short Strand (to the left) in 2005. While highly functional, the road system here is a significant scar on the streetscape of the city. *(Author's collection)*

The Queen Elizabeth Bridge, which opened in 1966 to relieve the adjacent Queen's Bridge. *(Author's collection)*

The new bridge finally opened to traffic on 3 April 1966. There was considerable debate in Belfast Corporation concerning the name of the new bridge[17] with unionists wanting to name it in honour of former Ulster Unionist leader Sir Edward Carson. However, this was bitterly opposed by nationalists and by way of compromise the bridge was named the 'Queen Elizabeth Bridge', after the incumbent monarch who officially opened the eponymous bridge on 4 July 1966. As if to highlight the nature of the debate, the Queen's car was struck by a concrete block as it travelled along Great Victoria Street.[17]

The second bridge and one-way system eased the cross-river traffic problem to an extent, but in the face of rapidly rising traffic levels it was widely recognised, even before the bridge was completed, that a much more significant solution was urgently needed.[18] The decision by the UTA (acting on the recommendations of the Benson Report) to cease most rail freight transport in 1965 simply exacerbated the problem by putting hundreds more lorries onto the roads around the docks and the approach roads leading to the city centre (although it is likely that market forces would have led to this change regardless of UTA policy).

The Urban Motorway is approved

On 8 June 1961 the 'Grade Separated Scheme' was approved by Belfast Corporation and the proposal was sent to the Ministry of Commerce for its approval.[5] The Ministry referred the proposals to the Motorways Committee who (not surprisingly) accepted the scheme, but noted that the plans were "too modest in scale and that full grade separation should be planned at the intersection of the elevated roads with the cityward extensions to the approach roads".[5] In other words, they felt that the plan to terminate the M1, M2, etc at roundabouts should be altered to include fully free-flowing junctions instead.

This sentiment was echoed by City Surveyor JEF Anderson, who said in a letter dated 8 June 1961:

> *I am convinced that bold, even revolutionary, methods must be used to keep abreast of traffic growth and that completion dates for road schemes must be based on as rigid a time schedule as possible, and must not be allowed to be affected by side issues.*[5]

This statement demonstrates the strength of conviction, resolve and single-mindedness with which the planners were now approaching the question of the urban motorway which was clearly perceived to be the paramount and overriding planning issue in the city. It also highlights the degree of alarm that the planners must have felt when they observed the rate of traffic growth in the early 1960s.

In 1963 four engineers travelled to the United States to study the developing urban motorway systems there: Fred Chambers and Jackson McCormick from the Ministry of Home Affairs, City Surveyor JEF Anderson and Chief Planning Officer Jim Aitken.[19] During the course of about three weeks they visited New York, Baltimore, Philadelphia, Chicago, Oklahoma, Dallas, Los Angeles and San Francisco, although Anderson and Aitken returned to Northern Ireland part way through.[19]

Jackson McCormick recalls how the visit reinforced their view that the scheme should be grade separated: "we'd been thinking of changing anyway but what we saw reinforced our views … it really reinforced our view – that the elevated motorway was the proper answer for Belfast."[19]

The visit to America should have sounded alarm bells for the Belfast planners, as two of the key problems that would later plague the motorway scheme were already apparent there. Since the American motorway system had been started several decades earlier than the British system, there had been enough time for these issues to emerge.

Firstly, there was the issue of congestion. Already, in 1963, the motorways in Los Angeles were getting congested. McCormick comments that "there was congestion certainly on the Los Angeles [motorways]. They were flowing pretty full even at that time. And San Francisco was quite busy too."[19] Even allowing for the fact that these cities were many times larger than

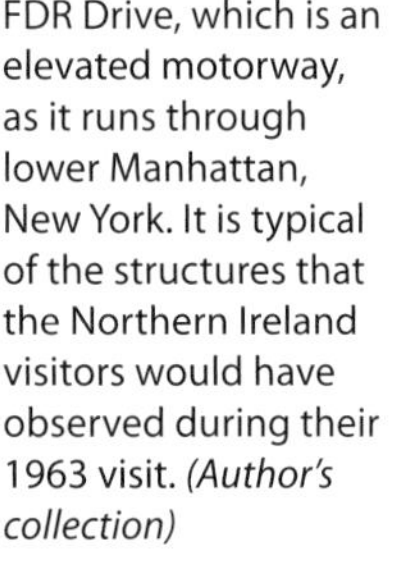

FDR Drive, which is an elevated motorway, as it runs through lower Manhattan, New York. It is typical of the structures that the Northern Ireland visitors would have observed during their 1963 visit. *(Author's collection)*

Part of an elevated road junction that towers above local streets as it connects FDR Drive to the Brooklyn Bridge, Manhattan. Although somewhat dilapidated today, it would have been almost new and very impressive to the Northern Ireland engineers during their 1963 visit. *(Author's collection)*

Belfast, the American experience showed that motorways attracted ever more traffic each year. The Belfast planners responded to this observation by scaling up their plans from dual two-lane to dual three-lane with hard shoulders (for various reasons, related to traffic dynamics, the capacity of a three-lane road is almost double that of a two-lane road).

Secondly, there was the issue of opposition from local residents to having large elevated motorways constructed through their neighbourhoods. Caught in the vision of a brave new world of fast and efficient personal transport, many planners genuinely seem not to have grasped the level of opposition that would meet any proposal to construct a large, noisy, elevated concrete structure through a residential area. The opposition was further polarised by the fact that, while it was the middle classes that would most benefit from the schemes, it was often the working classes that had to pay the bulk of the environmental price. To outside observers, many of the motorways that blasted their way through urban areas in the USA "seemed to have been accomplished without too much pain",[9] but in many ways this was because the communities through which they passed lacked a coherent voice and means with which to object, rather than because they were indifferent.

Planners such as Matthew have since been criticised for their 'cavalier' attitude towards the communities that would have to be removed to make way for the new road schemes.[1] The planners assumed that those who lived in the regeneration areas would be glad to leave their sub-standard housing, while ignoring the possibility that they may nevertheless wish to remain living in the same community, with the same neighbours and in the same part of the city. Tim Morton sums this attitude up:

> *There had perhaps been a somewhat cavalier attitude to the demolition of poor areas. In addition, there were substantial areas of housing in Belfast classified as slums and the contemporary view was that such housing was dispensable – and in fact, that the residents would be glad to be housed elsewhere with inside toilets.*[9]

The controversial Embarcadero Freeway, San Francisco, as seen in 1982. The structure was demolished in 1989. *(GeraldPHawkins: Licensed under the Creative Commons Attribution-Share Alike 3.0 Unported license)*

At the time of the trip to the USA there was evidence that local communities were starting to find their voice. Jackson McCormick recalls that "San Francisco's [motorway plan] was in trouble at that time, especially along the Embarcadero Freeway."[19] The Embarcadero Freeway was a plan for a highly controversial, elevated motorway along the northern waterfront of San Francisco. The first phase had opened in 1959. However, such was the degree of public opposition to this highly functional, but rather ugly, structure that the remaining phases of the scheme were eventually abandoned. The extant section was eventually demolished in 1989, ostensibly due to 'earthquake damage', and the waterfront restored to something of its former appearance. Highway planners were being told that, while roads were needed, they were not to be permitted to provide them at any price.

Despite making significant changes to the design after the visit to America, the planners in Belfast did not appear to have adequately grasped the degree to which local communities would be likely to oppose their grand plans. Although it would be unfair to criticise the decision to press ahead with an urban motorway, given the compelling and urgent need for it at the time, it would also be fair to say that project documents published during the rest of 1960s did not look at the proposals from the point of view of displaced residents in any meaningful way.

This is despite the fact that, in 1963, an influential report by Professor Sir Colin Buchanan, was published in Great Britain.[20] The 'Traffic in Towns' report recognised for the first time that transport was not the overriding consideration in town planning. The report famously says:

> *The American policy of providing motorways for commuters can succeed, even in American conditions, only if there is a disregard for all considerations other than the free flow of traffic which seems sometimes to be almost ruthless. Our British cities are not only packed with buildings, they are also packed with history and to drive motorways through them on the American scale would inevitably destroy much that ought to be preserved.*[20]

The report suggested (in quite a revolutionary way) limiting vehicle use in built-up urban areas through the selective application of pedestrianisation, one-way systems and parking restrictions, whilst nevertheless recommending the provision of fast, modern roads wherever possible.

The upgraded design was approved by Belfast Corporation in September 1964.[3] In a letter dated 7 September of that year, City Surveyor JEF Anderson explains the rationale for the road as the planners saw it at the time:

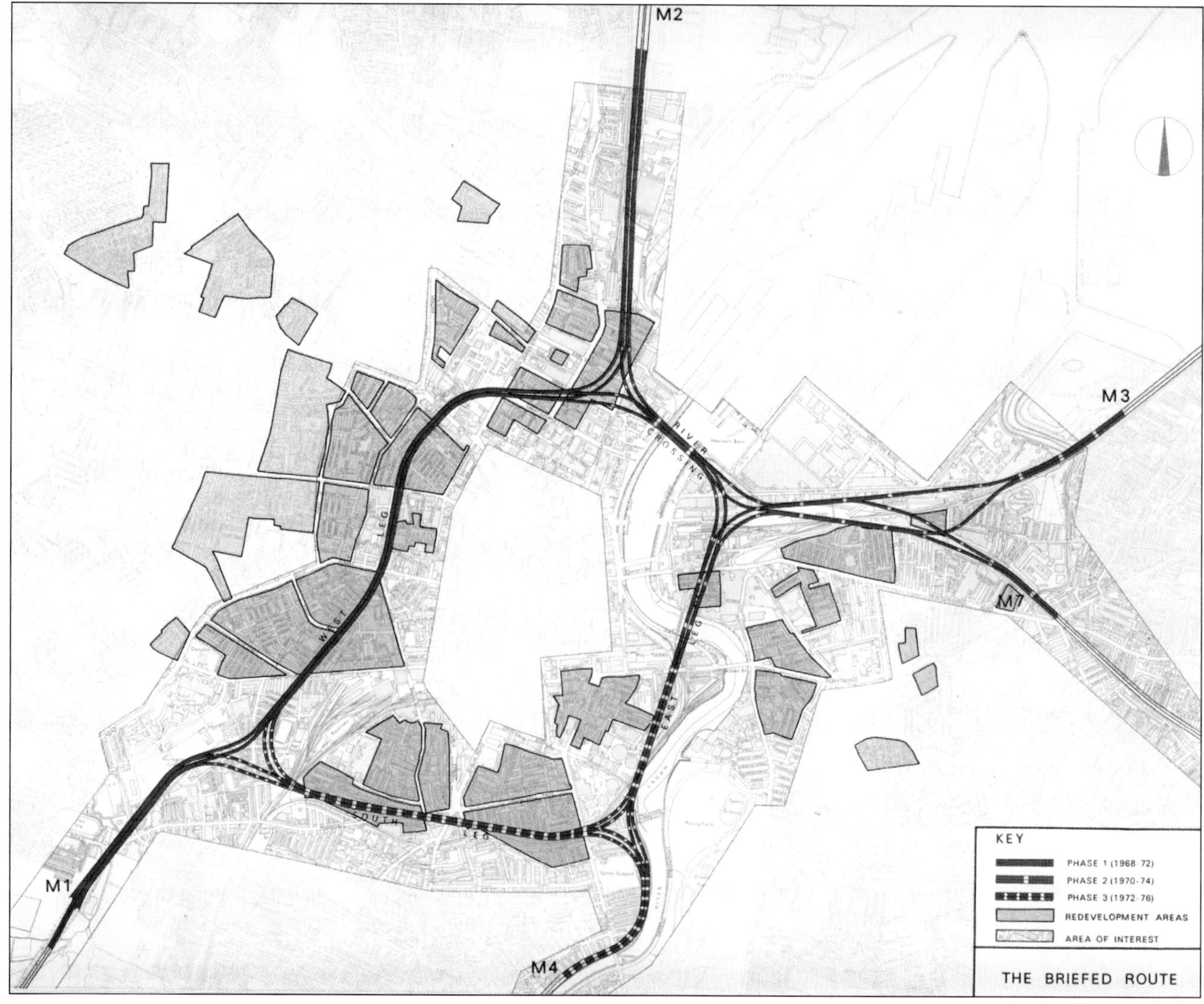

Belfast Corporations's plan for the Belfast Urban Motorway as of September 1964. The yellow shows redevelopment areas. *(Courtesy of DRD Roads Service)*

The purpose of the ring road is not merely to carry traffic between the approach roads, but to allow traffic from them to get into the central area of Belfast at as many points as possible, so that instead of having to pass through the city centre, traffic could go round the ring to the most convenient place and then enter the central area ... Having accepted the ring road solution, and it must be emphasised that this was an inescapable decision in the circumstances, the next question to be answered is where the ring should be situated..."[5]

In April 1965 R Travers Morgan and Partners were appointed to oversee the design and construction of the motorway. The company established an office in Belfast and, while the partners and some senior staff were from outside the province, most were recruited locally.[4] Two months later, the same company was appointed to oversee the project to tie the M1, M2, M3, M4 and the recently-announced M7 to the urban motorway. The team included not only employees of the company, but also several engineers from Belfast Corporation and the Northern Ireland government.[3] The final report, entitled 'Belfast Urban Motorway', was presented to the Corporation on 6 February 1967 and published in book form.[6]

CHAPTER 5
THE DREAM

The Proposal

The scheme outlined in the 'Report on the Belfast Urban Motorway' in February 1967 represents the zenith of ambition for motorways within the city of Belfast.[1] The proposed motorway was bold. Nothing on this scale had ever been considered in the city's history. It would tower at least six metres (20 feet) above street level. It was also ambitious in its timescale, and would require demolition on an immense scale. Had it

Photomontage of the Belfast Urban Motorway encircling the city centre, as envisaged in the 1967 report. *(Courtesy of DRD Roads Service)*

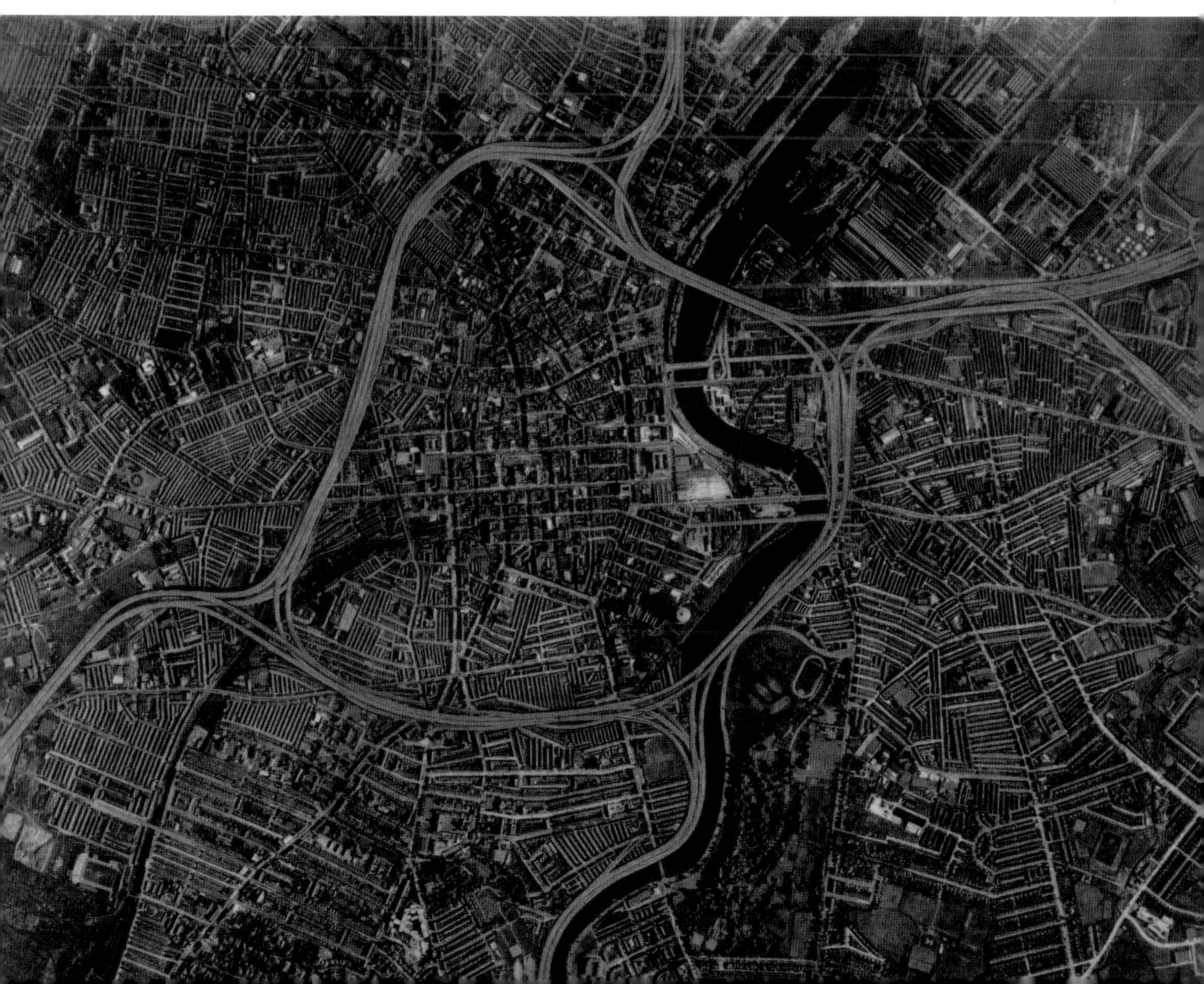

been implemented in full, the plans would have transformed the city both physically and in terms of the pattern of movement of people and goods.

The very restrictive terms of reference that R Travers Morgan were given for the study allowed them to do little more than appraise the scheme developed by Belfast Corporation. It was inevitable, therefore, that the general design and route of the motorway they proposed largely mirrored the design approved by the Corporation in 1964, albeit with a few key differences.

The scheme would have seen a fully elevated motorway constructed in a ring around the city centre. The road was generally three lanes wide, except within interchanges, where only two through lanes were required, and the main bridge over the River Lagan which was to be four lanes wide. There were to be freeflow junctions with the five existing and proposed approach roads – M1, M2, M3, M4 and M7 – as well as a number of interchanges to give access to the city streets. The structure was to be generally elevated to a height of 20–30 feet (6–9 metres) above ground level. However, to accommodate the freeflow junctions, some of

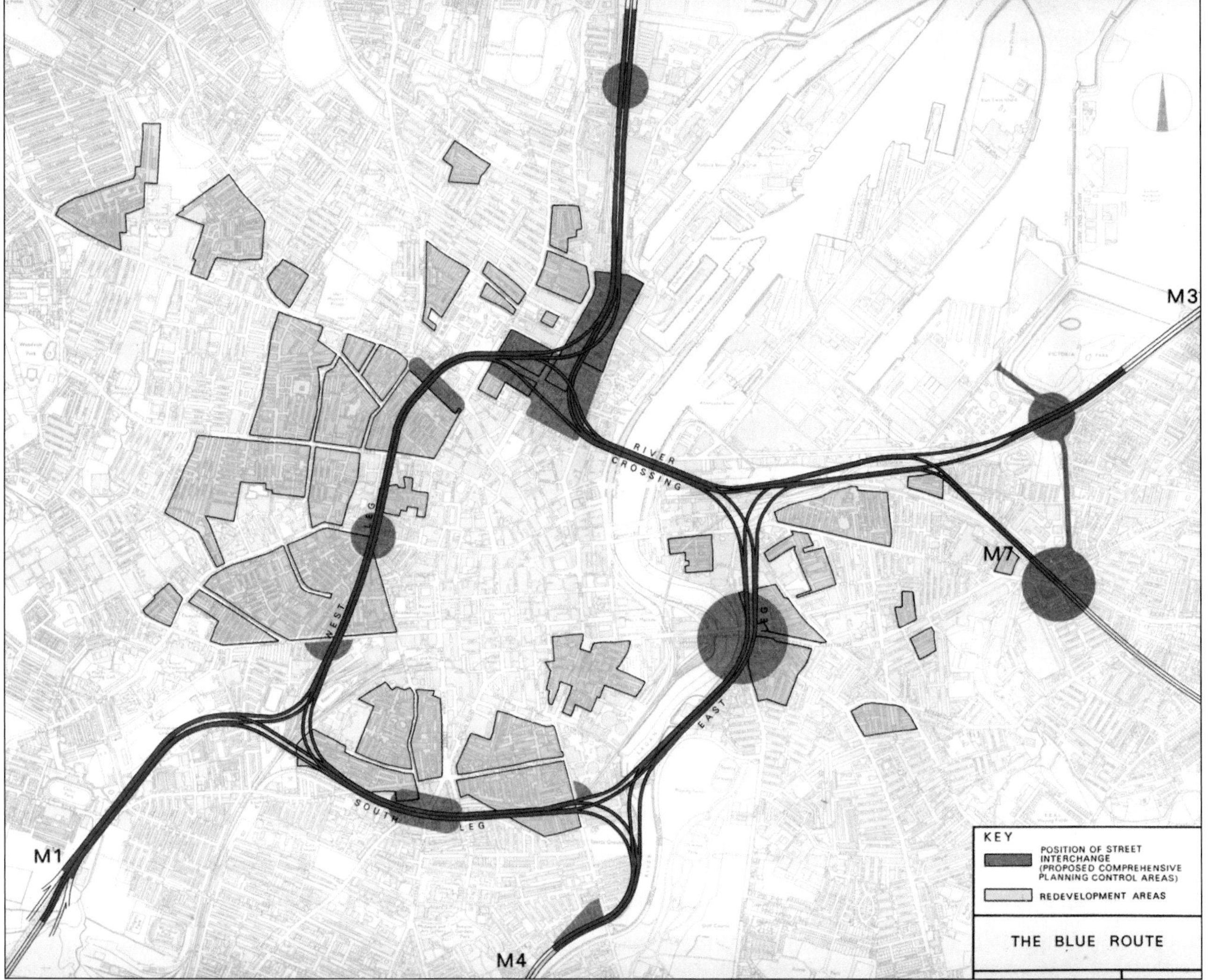

The design of the Belfast Urban Motorway as recommended by the 1967 report. The most significant differences from the 1964 design are the alignment of the eastern flank, the site of the M1 interchange, and the position of the Lagan bridge. *(Courtesy of DRD Roads Service)*

the flyovers were over 50 feet (15 metres) high, with part of the M1 interchange reaching a height of almost 70 feet (21 metres) above ground level.

The proposed Belfast Urban Motorway is shown opposite along with the approach motorways. This route was referred to as the 'blue route' to differentiate it from the 'red route', which was the design approved by the Corporation in 1964. The main differences between the 1964 'red' route and the 1967 'blue' route were:

- The M1 interchange was moved eastwards into the sidings of Great Victoria Street railway station rather than through residential properties south of Grosvenor Road.
- The river crossing at the harbour was moved upstream by about 300 metres so as to interfere less with shipping and improve traffic conditions on the ring.
- The interchange with the M3 and M7 was rearranged to reduce land take and increase the distance between junctions.
- The south eastern stretch was relocated from the west bank to the east bank of the River Lagan to lessen the impact on industrial property on Albertbridge Road and to provide better traffic flow.
- The southern stretch was shifted about 100 metres to the south, to the Lower Crescent area, as it was decided that passing directly through Bradbury Place would be unacceptably disruptive.

The Process

In appraising the route of the Urban Motorway, R Travers Morgan carried out a number of surveys. They undertook detailed studies of the topography of the city, the geology of the area of construction, land use patterns, locations of buildings of historic or other value, the positions of watercourses and the locations of electricity, gas and water utilities. These studies informed the engineering aspects of the proposals, and were used to more accurately estimate the costs of the various alternatives and rule out options that clearly could not or should not be constructed.

They also carried out travel surveys throughout greater Belfast to obtain data on the actual journeys people wanted to make. This involved interviews in 13,600 homes and with the drivers of 3,000 commercial vehicles. They claim to have interviewed 70% of motorists entering the greater Belfast area over the course of a typical day. Finally, they obtained details of all the public transport routes currently being operated, and their patronage.

These studies showed that less than 5% of vehicles on Belfast's roads were just passing through the city. 40% had either their origin or destination in the city, while 55% were journeys entirely within the city. In addition, it was found that 27% of people driving within the greater Belfast area were trying to get to the city centre itself.

It is worth noting that at no point was it considered appropriate to survey the general public about their thoughts on the proposed motorway itself. Neither was it considered necessary to seek the opinions of those whose homes or businesses lay on the route of the motorway. Instead, the public were informed of the completed proposals via the media and a series of leaflets in which the Urban Motorway was presented as a *fait accompli,* and which merely offered information on how the vesting of their properties would proceed.[2]

This is not to imply that the planners completely ignored these interest groups. The planners spent considerable time examining the effect of severance on communities and the necessity of preserving buildings of high historical, economic or social importance, examples of which included the Royal Victoria Hospital, Clifton House, the Gasworks and numerous churches. The route was adjusted in several locations in order to reduce impact on property; most notably the decision to move the route away from the residential areas of Grosvenor Road into the sidings of Great Victoria Street railway station, and the relocation of the eastern leg to the east bank of the Lagan to reduce impact on industry. In so doing, the planners managed to reduce the estimated number of houses to be demolished by over 20%, from 4860 to 3830.

However, it is apparent that the road was always the number one priority, and where a conflict arose between the needs of the road and the significance of a building, the road generally won. Unless a building had specific historical merit, it was seen purely as a financial choice. For example, the planners stated:

> *...many buildings of social importance ... have been assessed to have special quality only if they are of architectural or historical merit. Without such merit, the value of such buildings is directly measurable in cost, since the buildings can be replaced – often in better surroundings. This can sometimes apply even to churches where the congregation has moved due to the redevelopment around it, or where the size of the church is disproportionate to its needs.*[1]

In addition, the planners seem to have generally regarded working class homes as expendable (consistently, though not inaccurately at the time, referring to them as "poor quality") with an implicit assumption that relocating these residents should be seen as a bonus, as it provided an opportunity to provide better homes, but without considering that a community would be destroyed in the process. By contrast, the loss of more expensive middle class homes was

Belfast's Westlink, a classic example of a depressed road structure which attempts to reduce its impact by dropping below street level. *(Author's collection)*

Belfast's M3 motorway, a classic example of an elevated road structure which attempts to reduce severance by passing above the existing streets. *(Author's collection)*

phrased with implied regret, for example, "[the motorway] does however pass through an area of good quality housing near Cameron Street and Lower Crescent".

It had already been determined that constructing the Urban Motorway at ground level would lead to an unacceptable level of severance on surrounding communities and land use. This left the choice of an elevated structure, a depressed structure, or a mixture of the two. The planners admitted that from a social perspective, the depressed structure had advantages, because "the visual impact of an elevated structure can be considerable" and because the noise pollution from traffic is much reduced by a depressed road.

However, they also noted that physical severance is much greater for a depressed road since it is possible to pass beneath an elevated structure at any point, but movement is only possible over a depressed roadway by building bridges. We now know that elevated structures create enormous psychological severance, regardless of whether it is physically possible to pass beneath them, but this effect seems to have been underestimated in the plans for Belfast. The photomontage overleaf shows how planners anticipated the M4 would look as it met the Urban Motorway beside Ormeau Road. The most striking feature of this image is that it was placed in the report as a positive image, entirely without irony, and without comment on how those in the houses shown might perceive the structure.

The planners pointed out, correctly, that constructing a depressed road requires the wholesale removal of all existing utilities, whereas an elevated structure can rest on a series of isolated foundations. A depressed structure also has major problems related to drainage, particularly when constructed through areas with a high water table, such as those which exist near Shaftesbury Square, and adjacent to the River Lagan where the road would be below sea level.

Photomontage of M4 Interchange FIGURE 16

Photomontage of the proposed M4 interchange with the Belfast Urban Motorway. The Ormeau Road can be seen running along the left of the picture. Note that part of the junction is sited in the River Lagan itself. *(Courtesy of DRD Roads Service)*

In the end, therefore, the decision came down to economics. Given that the construction costs of retaining walls and excavation were estimated to far exceed the cost of an elevated structure, the planners decided that the motorway should be entirely elevated.

The route itself was based on that given to R Travers Morgan at project inception, and was informed by a number of considerations. One of the most important was the need to utilise, as far as possible, areas already earmarked for redevelopment. This was a particular factor for the western leg from the M1 to the M2, and to a lesser extent the eastern leg and M3/M7 interchange.

It was also important that the river crossing should not disrupt the operation of the Port of Belfast. With hindsight we know that in the decades that followed the Port would be relocated downstream, but this information was not known at the time, and so the planners expended enormous amounts of energy attempting to solve the problem. They compared the relative merits of:

- A high-level bridge, with a central span of 450 feet (137 metres) and a height of 90 feet (27 metres, or about 6 storeys) situated beside Abercorn Basin.
- A low-level bridge with a height of 35 feet (11 metres) situated a little further upstream, on the line of Great Patrick Street.
- A pair of submerged tunnels constructed within the bed of the Lagan.

The planners decided that for economic reasons, and to reduce the visual impact, the low level bridge was the correct choice.

(Above) Artist's impression of how a high-level bridge over the River Lagan would have looked. This structure would have allowed shipping to pass beneath. *(Courtesy of DRD Roads Service)*

(Below) Artist's impression of a low-level bridge over the River Lagan, which bears more than a passing resemblance to the M3 Lagan Bridge that was eventually built 30 years later. *(Courtesy of DRD Roads Service)*

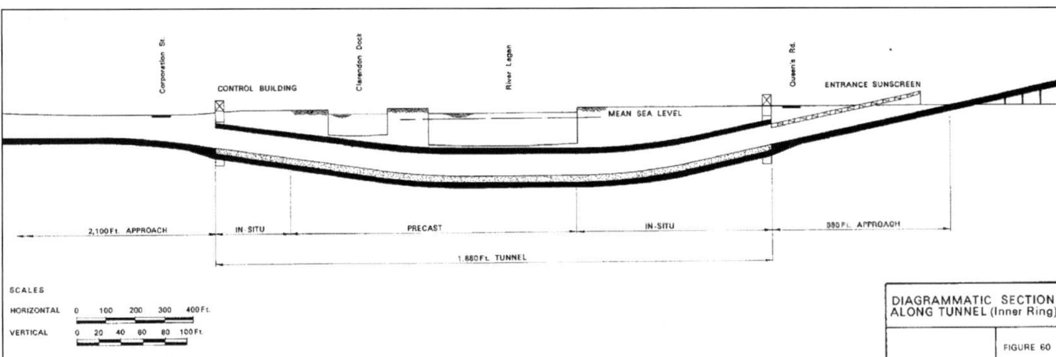

Longitudinal plan for the tunnel option, which was considered but rejected as a means of taking the Urban Motorway across the River Lagan. *(Courtesy of DRD Roads Service)*

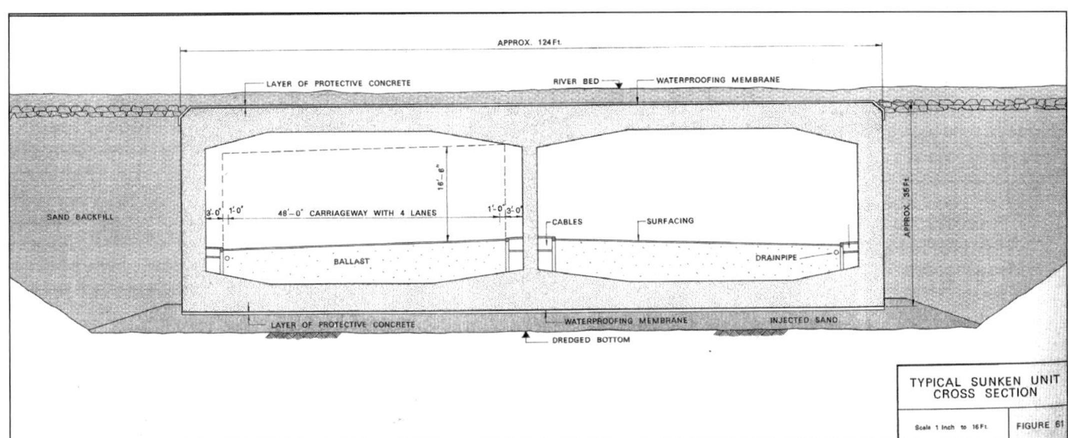

Cross-section of the tunnel option, which would have seen Urban Motorway housed in two parallel box structures. *(Courtesy of DRD Roads Service)*

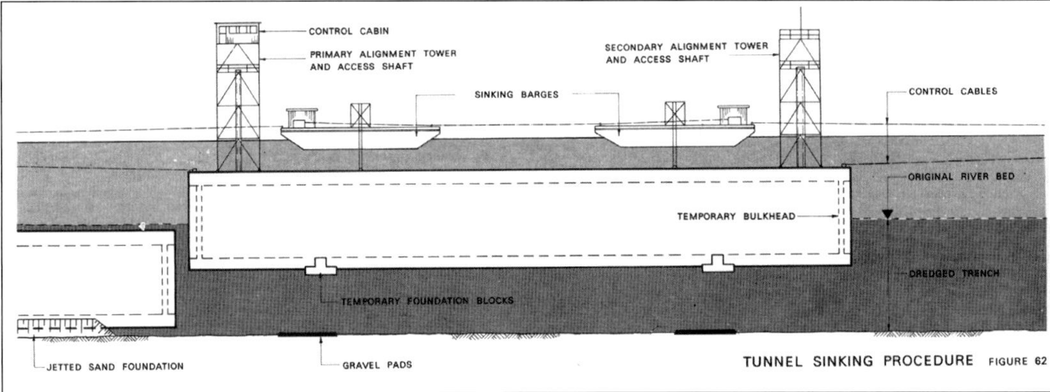

Illustration of how the tunnel could have been constructed from prefabricated sections lowered by barges. *(Courtesy of DRD Roads Service)*

To the south of the city, the briefed route had passed directly through Bradbury Place. However, the planners felt that this was unnecessarily disruptive and instead recommended a route along the line of the Central Railway. This is despite the fact that the Benson Report of 1963 had recommended that the Central Railway be retained. In August 1963 the Town Planning Committee of Belfast Corporation had responded to this recommendation by saying that they were "convinced in all the circumstances that the route of the grade separated road should be adhered and accordingly that the proposal in the Benson Report to retain the railway link should not be implemented."[3] It is striking that the reason given for not retaining the railway link is entirely due to the desire to use the land for a road, and not because of any perceived problem with the railway itself. As has already been said, however, we should not be too critical when applying the benefits of hindsight to the 1960s, an era when cars were the future and railways an anachronism. The planners did not address the issue in any serious way in the 1967 report, except to briefly comment that if the issue arose, "[the Central Railway] could be wholly or partly elevated between the two carriageways of the Ring Road". This was hardly a realistic option, given that the existing railway was actually well below ground level at this location.

In the final part of their report, the planners summarise the costs of the scheme, both in terms of money and in terms of demolition. Approximately two thirds of the financial cost of the scheme was estimated to be from construction, while one third was related to land acquisition and compensation to homeowners, commercial businesses, the Ulster Transport Authority, Belfast Harbour Commissioners, shipping companies and industry. In terms of demolition, the scheme would require the loss of 2,430 homes in redevelopment areas, and an additional 1,400 homes outside redevelopment areas, giving a total loss of 3,830 homes.

The total cost of the scheme was estimated to be £77.4 million in 1966 prices, which equates to approximately £1.1 billion in modern prices (2010).[4]

The Route

The diagram overleaf shows a reconstruction of how the Urban Motorway would have looked had it been built as originally intended. The road width has been exaggerated by a factor of two to make the lanes more visible, but is otherwise to scale. The lane markings at junctions are conjectural, but the number of lanes is accurate. A small number of changes have been made to the sliproads compared to what is shown in the 1967 document in light of modifications suggested in the 1969 Transportation Plan. In the following text, we will follow the route of the Urban Motorway clockwise, beginning at the M1.

The M1 at Belfast was opened as a dual two-lane motorway in 1962, five years before the Urban Motorway report was published. The M1 had a temporary terminus in the form of a roundabout on Donegall Road, close to its junction with Broadway. The report envisaged that the M1 would be widened to dual four-lanes in order to cater for the anticipated traffic increases that would occur during the 1970s and 1980s (traffic on the M1 more than doubled between 1962 and 1968[5]). Two of these lanes would split off on the way out of Belfast to form the M11 motorway around the north of Lisburn, with the remaining two lanes continuing as the existing M1 to Lisburn and beyond. The report also envisaged that the temporary junction at Broadway would be closed and replaced by a new junction, the 'Bog Meadows' junction, situated just under half a mile south west of Broadway along the M1.

The reconstructed M1 would rise up onto the elevated urban structure around the line of Tate's Avenue and be carried over Donegall Road and Broadway without any links to the local road network. Following the line of the Blackstaff River (the line today occupied by Westlink) the elevated M1 would continue as far as Roden Street, where there would be a freeflow junction with the Urban Motorway.

All four of the junctions where the Urban Motorway meets the radial motorways M1, M2, M3 and M4 were planned to be a variant of the 'Full Y' or 'Directional T' design. This is a

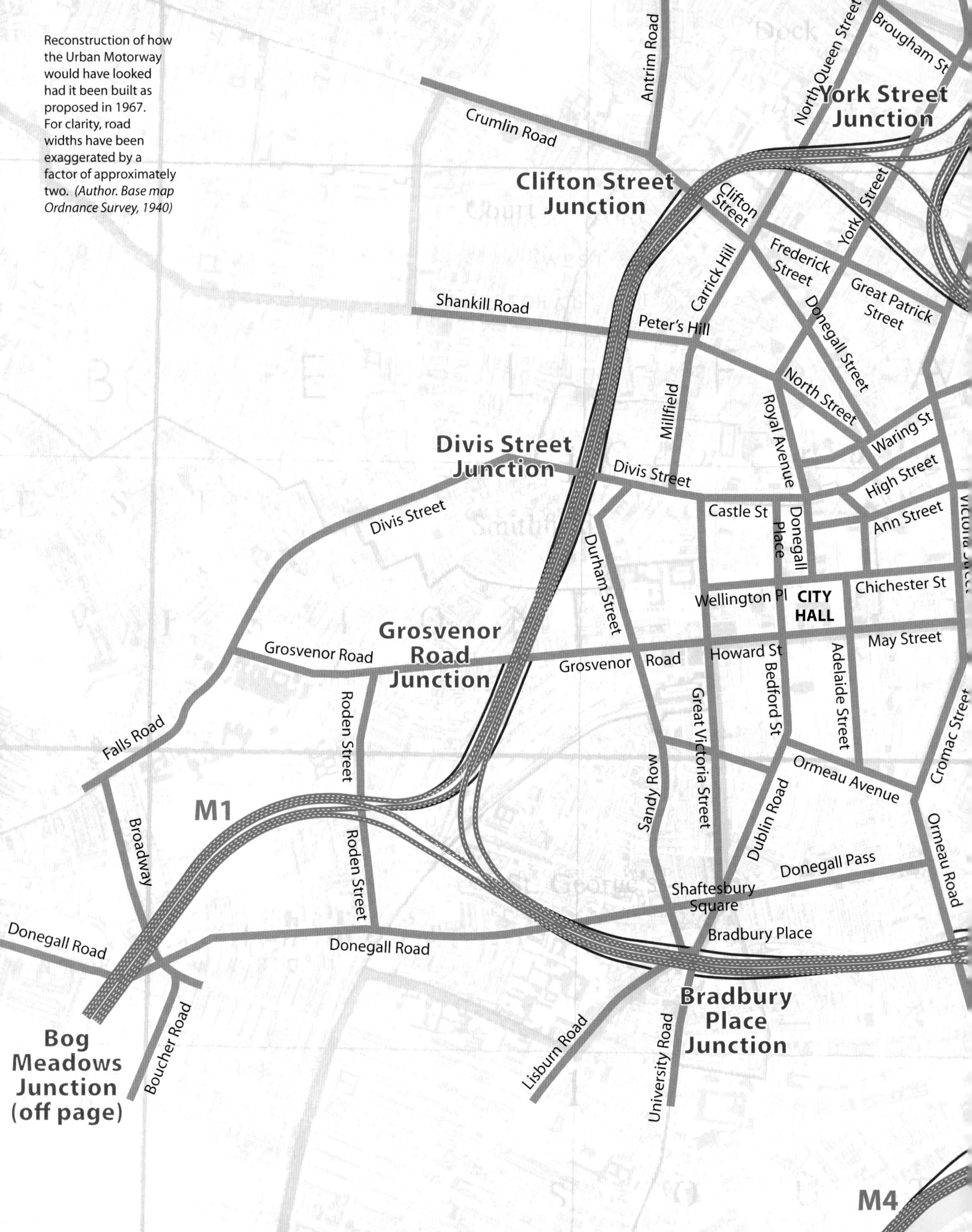

Reconstruction of how the Urban Motorway would have looked had it been built as proposed in 1967. For clarity, road widths have been exaggerated by a factor of approximately two. *(Author. Base map Ordnance Survey, 1940)*

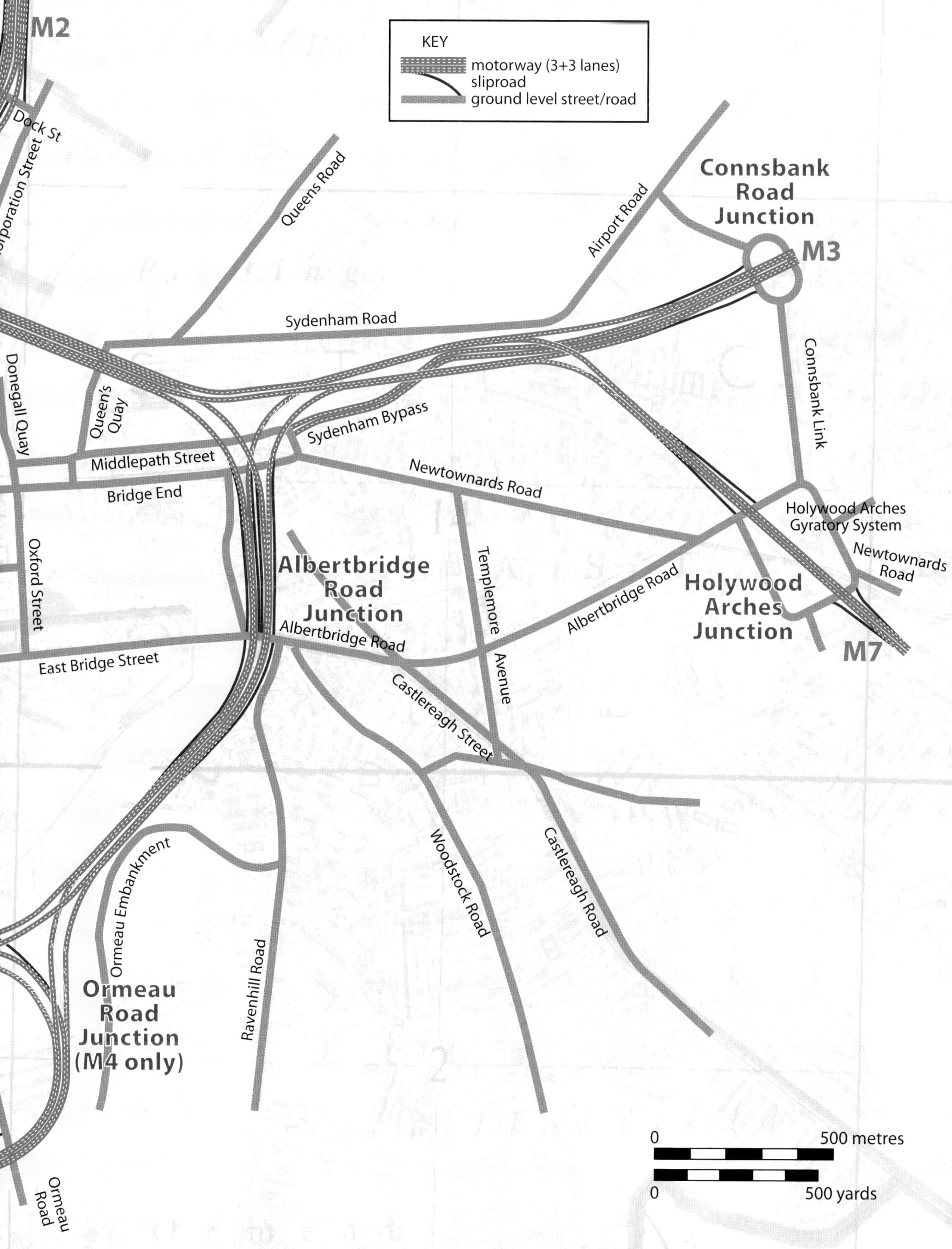
M2
KEY
motorway (3+3 lanes)
sliproad
ground level street/road
Dock St
Corporation Street
Queens Road
Connsbank Road Junction
Airport Road
M3
Sydenham Road
Donegall Quay
Queen's Quay
Connsbank Link
Sydenham Bypass
Middlepath Street
Newtownards Road
Bridge End
Holywood Arches Gyratory System
Newtownards Road
Oxford Street
Albertbridge Road Junction
Templemore Avenue
Albertbridge Road
Holywood Arches Junction
Albertbridge Road
M7
East Bridge Street
Castlereagh Street
Ormeau Embankment
Woodstock Road
Castlereagh Road
Ravenhill Road
Ormeau Road Junction (M4 only)
0
500 metres
0
500 yards
Ormeau Road

Full Y or Directional T Interchange

∗ = diverge or merge on right hand side

design that does not exist anywhere in the UK today, but can be found in the USA. The main reason it is not recommended in the UK is that it creates situations where sliproads diverge from the right hand side of the carriageway, and merge on the right, situations that are now regarded as dangerous in the UK because drivers are taught that they should only be in the right hand lane if overtaking. However, the design for Belfast was created when there was little real-life experience of urban motorways and such issues were not so obvious to planners.

Two lanes of the M1 link with the western leg of the Urban Motorway, while the remaining two link with the southern leg. It is here that we encounter our first junction – access to Grosvenor Road for traffic coming to and from the M1. For practical reasons, there was no access from the southern leg, and no access to and from the north. Continuing north, the elevated Urban Motorway (dual three-lanes in width) follows a route through the redevelopment areas west of the city centre, crossing over Grosvenor Road, Albert Street, Divis Street, Peter's Hill and Old Lodge Road in quick succession. This part of the route is almost exactly the same as that occupied by the modern Westlink. A full-access junction is provided down to street level at Divis Street, while access is provided to and from the south at Clifton Street.

The reason for the lack of access to and from the north at Clifton Street is due to the proximity of the freeflow M2 interchange, which we encounter where the Urban Motorway runs downhill and swings round to the east. The M2 interchange is a similar design to the M1 interchange, but occupying even more land. Indeed, virtually all the land between York Street

Photomontage of how the Urban Motorway would have looked passing over Clifton Street, here looking towards Carlisle Circus. *(Courtesy of DRD Roads Service)*

Model of the proposed M2/Urban Motorway interchange at York Street. The M2 is towards the top of the image. *(T Jackson McCormick – Motorway Archive Trust)*

and Corporation Street, including the residential area known as 'Sailortown', would be cleared for almost half a mile. Six sliproads would provide comprehensive access to and from the local road network from all three directions here.

At the time of the report's publication, the M2 motorway in Belfast existed only from Greencastle to Glengormley. Work on the dual-five lane 'foreshore' section, which would connect the M2 directly to the Urban Motorway, had begun in late 1966 but the scale of work meant it would not be completed until well into the 1970s. Nevertheless, it was anticipated that the M2 would rise up onto an elevated structure around Whitla Street and then merge with the Urban Motorway. This junction would soar over 60 feet (18 metres) into the air above York Street.

Two lanes from the M2 and two lanes from the Urban Motorway met in the air above Corporation Street before leaping across the Lagan on a low-level dual four-lane bridge on an alignment about 50 metres north of where the modern M3 Lagan Bridge is situated. Indeed, at first glance the photomontage of the proposed bridge could easily be mistaken for the bridge that was actually built 30 years later, such are their outward similarities.

On the east bank of the Lagan the Urban Motorway encounters its third freeflow interchange, this time with the M3. The M2 and M3 interchanges are so close together that there are no junctions between the two. The Sydenham Bypass had opened in 1959, and its terminus at Middlepath Street would remain in its existing form. However, the rest of the Bypass would be upgraded to motorway standard with a pair of elevated parallel carriageways built on each side of the terminus to connect it directly to the Urban Motorway. From there towards Holywood the M3 would be dual three-lane.

The M7 motorway to Dundonald would then diverge from the M3 roughly where the M3 crossed Dee Street. This would affect housing outside redevelopment areas, but the planners did not feel this was an issue as the housing was "mostly poor quality". The M7 would quickly join the route of the former County Down Railway line and return to ground level around Beersbridge Road. Due to the constricted land available for the M7, it was to be built as a dual two-lane motorway with only partial hard shoulders. Holywood Arches was to be transformed by the presence of an elevated motorway junction with the M7 soaring overhead and a new one-way system constructed through the surrounding streets. On the M3, a new junction at Connsbank Road would feed into the Harbour Estate and also connect to the Holywood Arches (and of all the proposals for this area of the city, the Connsbank Road junction is the only one that remains a live plan at the time of writing). The westbound carriageway of the M3 between Connsbank Road and the Urban Motorway was to be at a constant height of almost 60 feet (18 metres) to clear the existing Sydenham Bypass.

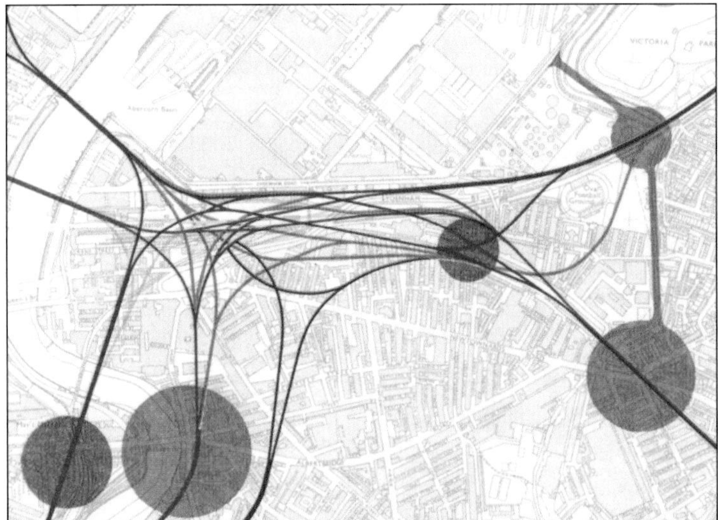

Map showing the various options considered for the troublesome M3/M7/Urban Motorway interchange. *(Courtesy of DRD Roads Service)*

The layout of the M3/M7 junction and their connection to the Urban Motorway proved the most problematic for the planners, who needed to provide enough 'weaving' room (space for drivers to change lanes) to safely and correctly negotiate the two junctions. Indeed, six different options were considered but in the end the chosen route combined the greatest possible weaving distances with the least disruption to existing development. The decision to place the Lagan bridge quite far upstream also provided much-needed distance between the M2 and M3 junctions.

Returning to the Urban Motorway at the M3 junction, the route then takes a sharp turn to the south along the east bank of the River Lagan. The route was originally to have crossed onto the west bank here, but it was moved to the east bank partly to reduce the impact on the 'high value' industrial properties on Albertbridge Road and Laganbank Road, but mainly because simulations showed that it led to much better traffic conditions on the ring road. Instead the road was routed through lower value industrial property and 'low quality' houses in redevelopment areas around Short Strand and the bottom of the Ravenhill Road. The route continued to follow the line of the Lagan as far as Ravenhill Reach, beside Ormeau Park, where it then re-crossed the river. The motorway was, of course, elevated on all these stretches. There was to be a full access junction at Albertbridge Road, but due to the proximity of the M3 junction there had to be two onslips and two offslips in the northerly direction, two of which were on right hand side of the motorway.

As it crossed the Lagan, the Urban Motorway met the fourth radial motorway, the M4, at a final freeflow junction. This junction was to be sited partly in an existing area of non-redevelopment housing on the lower Ormeau Road adjacent to the Gasworks, and partly in the River Lagan itself. The M4 was planned as a dual three-lane motorway hugging the west bank of the Lagan through the lower Ormeau area, passing over Ormeau Road, and then by being constructed literally above Stranmillis Embankment on an elevated structure. Access would be provided to and from the M4 here by a pair of sliproads, but there would be no access for vehicles on the Urban Motorway itself. Of all the proposals in the design for the

Urban Motorway, the M4 was by far the most visually intrusive, due to its riverside setting.

The final leg of the Urban Motorway ran as an elevated structure west from the Ormeau Road, generally following the line of the Central Railway line. It crossed over Bradbury Place at its junction with the University and Lisburn Roads and then crossed over Donegall Road roughly where City Hospital railway station now lies. Substantial areas of housing would have been lost on this stretch, some of which (on Donegall Road, Sandy Row and Ormeau Road) were redevelopment areas, and some of which were not. Notably in the latter category were the buildings of the Lower Crescent and the building that is today the Crescent Arts Centre.

A full access junction would be provided at Bradbury Place. In order to provide adequate access to the local road network, this would have required the permanent clearance of the south end of Sandy Row and the Upper and Lower Crescents. The Urban Motorway then completes the full circle by meeting its junction with the M1 motorway.

Traffic Flow Aspects

The planners designed the Urban Motorway for freeflow traffic conditions, even at peak times, but they did not anticipate great speed. The design speed was 50 mph, but it was acknowledged that at peak times speeds would be reduced to 30–40 mph, still an impressive average speed for the rush hour. It was assumed that each lane of the motorway would have a capacity of 1,500 'passenger car units' (PCUs) per hour. Theoretically this meant that a three-lane section of the Urban Motorway would have the capacity of almost 4,500 PCUs per hour. Since the Urban Motorway had two carriageways (clockwise and anticlockwise) the theoretical hourly capacity of a three-lane section of the motorway was around 9,000 PCUs. Whether or not the Urban Motorway could have attained this capacity in practice cannot be known without an accurate computerised traffic model, but the factor most likely to reduce the capacity was the high degree of weaving and merging inherent in the design.

A **passenger car unit (PCU)** is defined as the impact that one passenger car has on traffic factors such as speed or road space. If a car has a value of 1.0, then larger vehicles have higher values and smaller vehicles lower values. For example, a bus might have a value of 2.5 and a motorcycle a value of 0.4. Thus 100 buses would be 250 PCUs, while 100 motorcycles would be only 40 PCUs, reflecting their lower impact on the road.

Weaving occurs when traffic attempting to change lanes in one direction comes into direct conflict with traffic attempting to change lanes in the opposite manner. The design of the Urban Motorway, with four freeflow motorway interchanges and five street interchanges in the space of just four miles (7 km), combined with lanes that diverged and converged with the Urban Motorway, was a recipe for weaving problems. With the exception of drivers entering the motorway at one junction and leaving at the next junction along, many drivers would have to change lanes when entering the motorway and again when leaving. These movements would be in conflict with drivers who were completing the opposite manoeuvre at each junction, reducing traffic speeds and therefore lowering the capacity of the road.

In addition, most of the sliproads carrying traffic onto the motorway from the local road network merged with the motorway rather than continuing as a new lane (a 'lane gain'),

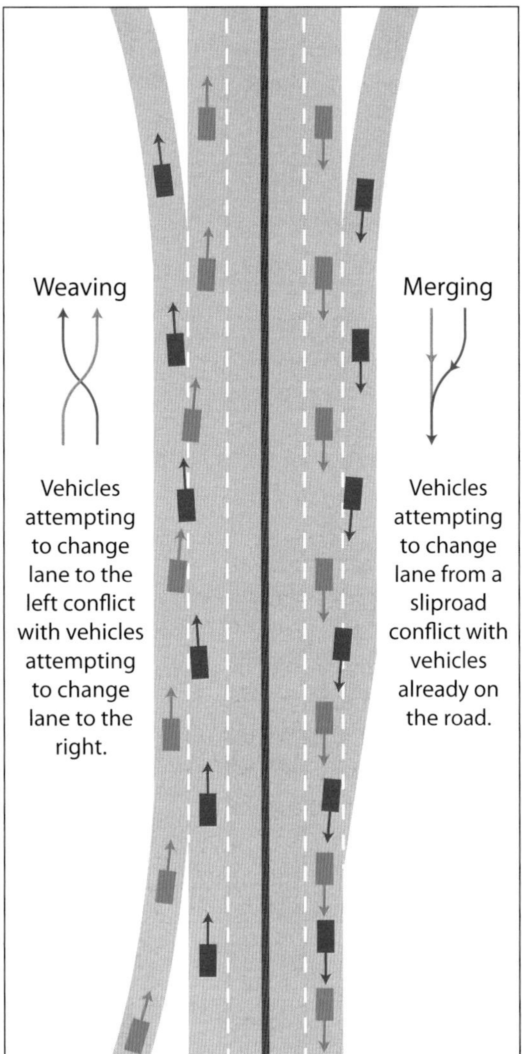

Weaving and merging, two problems that increasingly plague motorways as traffic levels increase.

creating further problems as drivers would attempt to merge into the traffic already on the ring. On the Urban Motorway a 'lane gain' approach was used at all four of the motorway interchanges to combat this effect.

Merging and weaving are two of the biggest sources of congestion on motorways, and in heavy traffic can eventually result in stop-start traffic conditions. Examples of these issues can be seen today on Belfast's road network. Merging problems routinely led to stationery traffic on the M2 motorway in the morning peak approaching Sandyknowes (at least until the 2009 upgrade) while similar problems continue to beset the junctions on the canyon section of the Westlink. There are weaving problems on the M3 Lagan Bridge in Belfast because vehicles wishing to exit the M3 are attempting to change lanes in the same space as traffic wishing to join. This leads to reduced speeds on the M3, which would likely result in stationery traffic were it not for the fact that the onslips are controlled by traffic signals, rather than having a continuous flow, which periodically releases the pressure on the weaving section.

Based on the experience of the modern Lagan Bridge, it could be said that 300 metres is the minimum distance over which weaving movements between two adjacent lanes can safely take place (although this is more than the minimum permitted by the current design manual). The design of the Urban Motorway indicates weaving distances of at least 500 metres, which would permit safe weaving even at peak times, albeit at reduced speeds. Some stretches (most notably the section between Bradbury Place and the M1 interchanges, where traffic would have to cross two lanes in quick succession) would likely have caused problems, but these issues may, in practice, have been ironed out during more detailed design phases.

Calculations suggested that the Urban Motorway would have led to significant improvements to traffic on the existing city streets. Those most improved would have been the Falls Road, Antrim Road, Shore Road, the Queen's Bridge/Queen Elizabeth Bridge one-way system, Newtownards Road, Ormeau Road, Donegall Street and, to a lesser extent, the majority of streets in the city centre. A few streets would have had a small increase in traffic, caused by traffic seeking to access the Urban Motorway at specific junctions. These included Crumlin Road, Clifton Street, York Street, Albertbridge Road and University Street. These increases were calculated to be much smaller than the decreases experienced on the other streets.

In terms of the traffic utilising the Urban Motorway, the 1967 report includes some preliminary traffic estimates that illustrate how the road would have performed had traffic levels stayed at their 1966 levels. These figures suggest that the road would have been running comfortably with traffic levels at only 20% of capacity on the southern section. On the busy Lagan Bridge, traffic levels would have been around 50% of the capacity of this stretch.

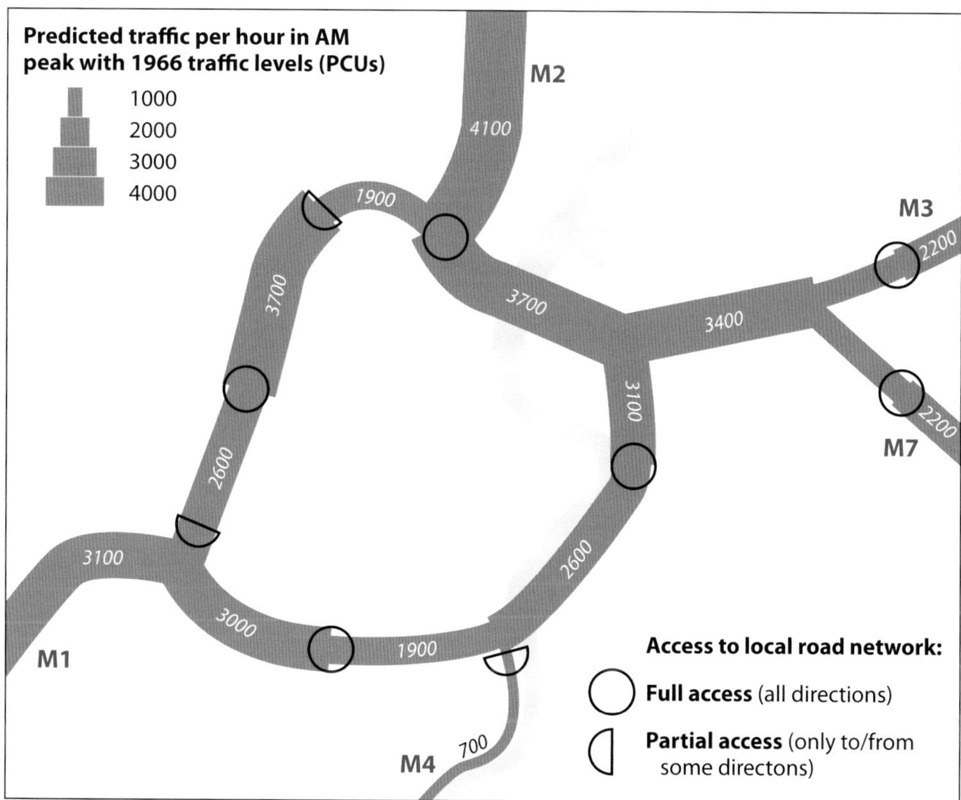

Predicted traffic loads on the Belfast Urban Motorway as predicted in 1967 assuming 1966 traffic levels.

Of course, traffic figures in 1966 were rapidly rising, and the report acknowledges this obvious fact. At the time the report was published, it was accepted that traffic levels would double over the following ten years. The fact that such a massive increase did not actually materialise is irrelevant since these were the figures that the designers were working to and assumed to be true for their purposes.

In 1967 it was assumed that the Urban Motorway would be completed by 1976 – ten years beyond the 1966 traffic figures being used. When a doubling of traffic levels is applied to the Urban Motorway, it was clear that by the time it was completed, sections of the road would already be running at capacity: "The Motorway will, in general terms, be in full use from the day it opens".[1] In other words, the road had essentially no future proofing. To their credit, the designers did not shy away from the implications of this crucial fact:

> *It follows that in the peak hour neither the currently envisaged system nor the existing street network is capable of handling substantial increases in traffic beyond 1976 and maintaining satisfactory operating conditions.*[1]

Therefore:

> *...in the period after the Motorway is opened there will be a need to implement traffic management measures ... [such as] the monitoring of traffic using the Motorway, control of access points by signals linked with a general area traffic control system and the like.*[1]

The inescapable conclusion was also spelled out:

> *It seems inevitable that unless vast resources are to be allotted to further highway construction and unless the nature of the City centre is to be changed fundamentally, public transport will have a more important role. A decision will therefore need to be made as to the level of future investment in highway development. This policy decision will need to consider the question of whether the free demand of the private motorist is to be met and if not, the amount of restraint of private vehicle use, particularly with respect to home-to-work journeys, which can be accepted … It seems inevitable that free demand by private motorists is an ideal that will not be achievable in Belfast at the stage of vehicle ownership in the 1980s.*[1]

These comments represent the first official acceptance that, while the Urban Motorway would have enormous benefits, it was not a magic bullet that would solve the city's traffic problems.

Engineering

The 1967 Report did not devote more than two pages to the engineering aspects of the Urban Motorway. However, the design was refined further during the following few years and a very detailed description of the design was published in the *Journal of the Institution of Highway Engineers* in 1972.[6] The discussion below is a summary highlighting the key points.

The engineers tasked with designing the structures began with four principles:

- The structure must have a high degree of standardisation to reduce costs and produce a uniform appearance.
- That the superstructure should have a minimal depth in order to ensure that the road surface was as low as possible, hence minimising the length of sliproads.
- The design should permit all forms of land use beneath the motorway, including construction of buildings.
- As far as possible, the design should allow maintenance to be carried out from road level, as the land beneath would be released for development.

The design of the motorway was refined following the 1967 Report, and used a set of standards based on a design speed of 50 mph. The two carriageways were to be constructed as separate elevated structures positioned at least 17 feet (5 metres) above ground level and no closer than 5 feet (1.5 metres) apart. The minimum curve radius was 800 feet (240 metres), the maximum gradient was 4% (6% on sliproads) and the maximum superelevation (the tilting of the carriageway on curves) was 1 in 14.5. The fineries of route selection were carried out with computer assistance.

Each carriageway consisted of two, three or four lanes 11 feet 6 inches (3.5 metres) wide, with a 10 foot (3.0 metre) near-side hard shoulder and a 6 foot (1.8 metre) off-side hard shoulder. Combined with the space required for the safety barriers and kerbs on each side, the total width of a four-lane carriageway was therefore 73 feet (22.3 metres), reducing to 50 feet (15.2 metres) for a two-lane carriageway. Single lane sliproads were to be 35 feet (10.7 metres) wide. Between the two adjacent carriageways was to be high mast lighting 80 feet (24 metres) above the carriageway level, but mounted on the ground, at 280 foot (85 metre) intervals along the motorway.

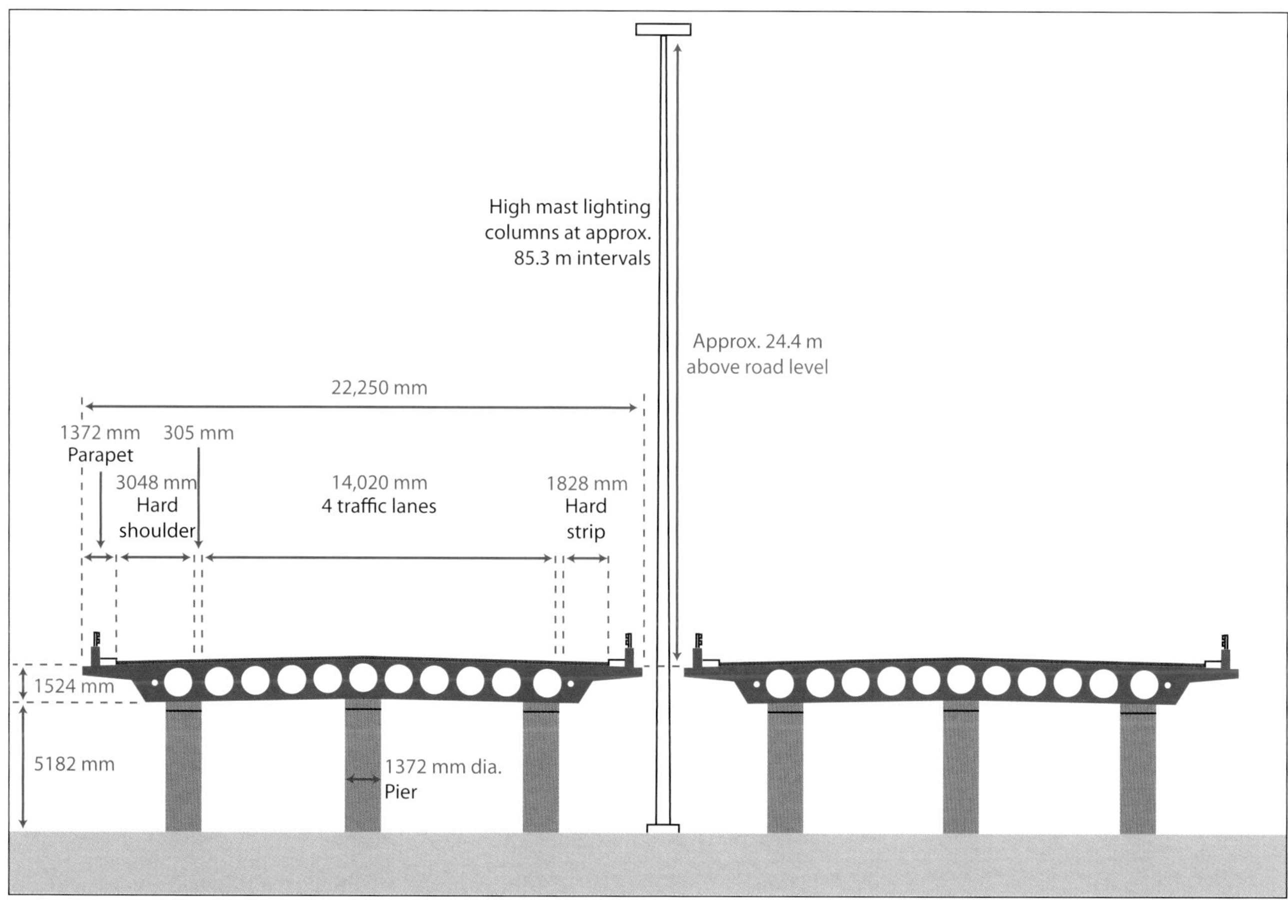

Cross-section of the twin elevated structures proposed to carry the Belfast Urban Motorway. Phase 1 was actually designed in imperial, but with the intention that Phases 2 and 3 would be designed in metric. *(Based on Noble, 1972 [6])*

During 1967, 100 boreholes were sunk along the western part of the route, and this found that solid sandstone bedrock was situated at a depth of 40–80 feet (12–24 metres), with overlying layers of glacial boulder clay, silt, sand and gravel. All piers and columns were therefore to be supported on 3 or 4 foot (0.9 or 1.2 metre) bored piles. For the majority of the route, the superstructure was to be supported on columns 4.5 feet (1.4 metres) in diameter. The western part of the scheme (from the M1 to the M2) required 1,075 columns arranged in fours, threes, twos or (for sliproads) singly, depending on the width of the motorway. There were also to be 45 piers of cellular construction where space was needed within.

With the exception of the Lagan Bridge and some of the motorway interchanges, the superstructure was to be of continuous flat slab reinforced concrete construction using a voided section in span, 5 feet (1.5 metres) in thickness. The western part of the scheme required 454 such spans, ranging from 35–125 feet (10.7–38.1 metres) in length, with the majority in the range 65–80 feet (19.8–24.4 metres). In the western part of the scheme, the northbound carriageway over York Street was to be carried on a four-span, prestressed, post-tensioned concrete structure of variable depth. Later parts of the motorway would presumably have featured similar designs. The superstructure was to be connected to the substructure by means of bearings, with the superstructure joined into sections ranging in length from 290–1,800 feet (90–550 metres), with expansion and rotation joints between.

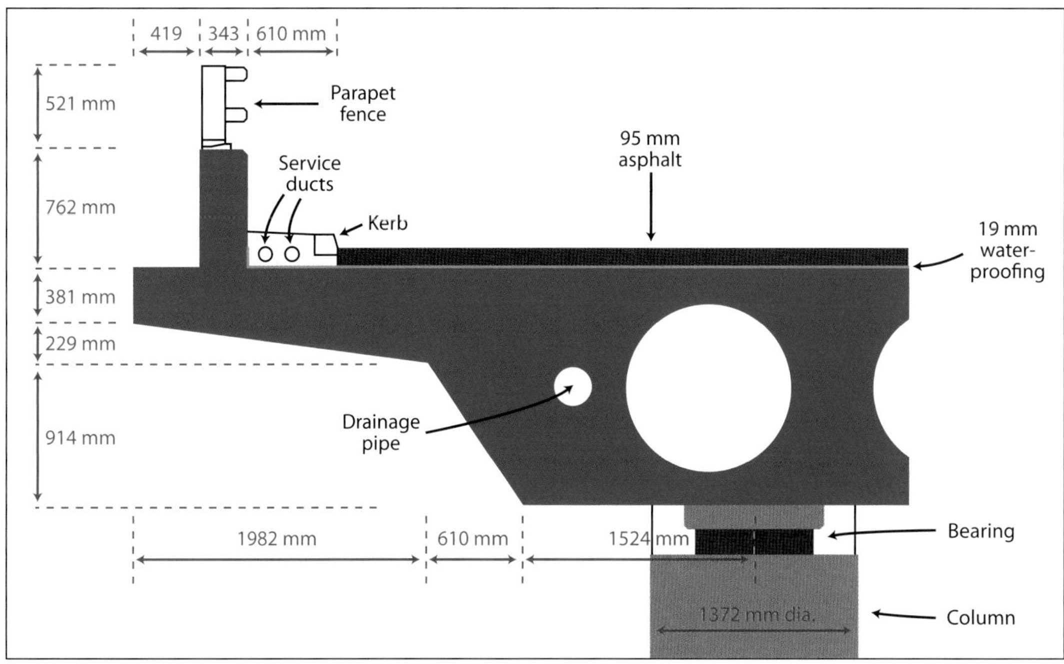

Closeup of the edge and parapet structure proposed for the Belfast Urban Motorway. *(Based on Noble, 1972[6])*

Approaching ground level the sliproads were initially to be of the voided slab construction, but then changed to reinforced concrete cellular construction, with bays 20, 40 or 60 feet (6, 12 or 18 metres) in length. Access to these cells was to be preserved to allow their use for storage or, in two cases, for electricity substations. Below an elevation of 8 feet (2.4 metres) the sliproads were to be constructed on fill between retaining walls.

At all points, for aesthetic reasons, the motorway was to have a tapered cantilever edge extending 8.5 feet (2.6 metres) from the main slab. This tapered edge was to include service ducts and a concrete plinth, 2.5 feet (0.8 metres) tall, surmounted by a two-rail metal crash barrier, 1.7 feet (0.5 metres) high. All street furniture was to be mounted on a nip protruding 1.4 feet (0.4 metres) beyond the parapet. The road surface was to have consisted of a waterproof prefabricated sheet, followed by a 2¼ inch (57 mm) hot rolled asphalt base course and a 1½ inch (38 mm) wearing course.

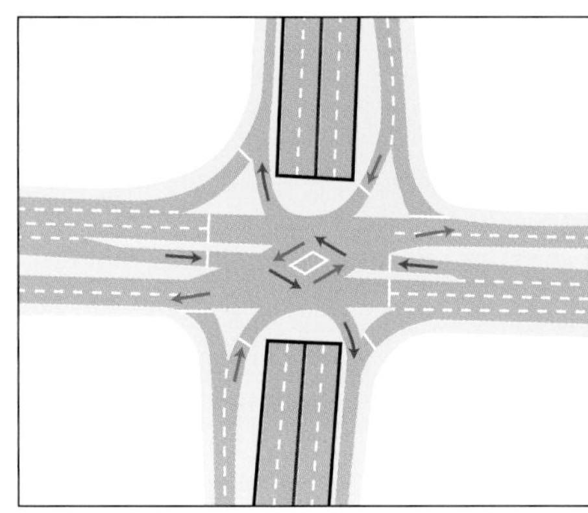

A single-point urban interchange ingeniously allows opposing right-turn movements to take place simultaneously, with the result that only three separate traffic light phases are required, thus increasing junction capacity.

As work progressed on the scheme after 1967, the design of the road changed from the reconstruction shown earlier in this chapter with various layouts of lanes, sliproads and bridges at the different junctions. These included designs for the street level interchanges. Notably, the 1972 paper shows a possible arrangement for Divis Street junction featuring a 'Single Point Urban Interchange' (SPUI) design. This is the design that was in fact adopted for Divis Street when the Westlink was constructed in the early 1980s, and at the time of writing, the junction remains the only example of the SPUI design in the entire United Kingdom.

Reconstruction Aspects

Clearly, the Urban Motorway would cause enormous destruction to the existing streetscape as it aggressively carved its way through the subtleties of the existing urban area. While the question of whether such a level of destruction was acceptable was not really dealt with, the fact that some form of alleviation would be required was at least recognised by the designers, who noted that "it is not enough merely to construct an elevated route through a city without associated development of the strip of land on which the road is built".[6] Redevelopment of this land was viewed as part-and-parcel of the scheme and planned with it.

Consultancy firm 'Building Design Partnership' had been commissioned by Belfast Corporation in October 1965 to advise on the development of the city centre.[7] In August 1968, in association with R Travers Morgan, they produced a report that outlined their advice on the issue of reconstruction around the site of the motorway.[8] The document covered not only the 300 acres required for the road itself, but adjacent redevelopment areas comprising a further 800 acres. As expected, the report merely discussed how buildings could be re-constructed around the Urban Motorway, not the impact of the Urban Motorway on the existing built environment.

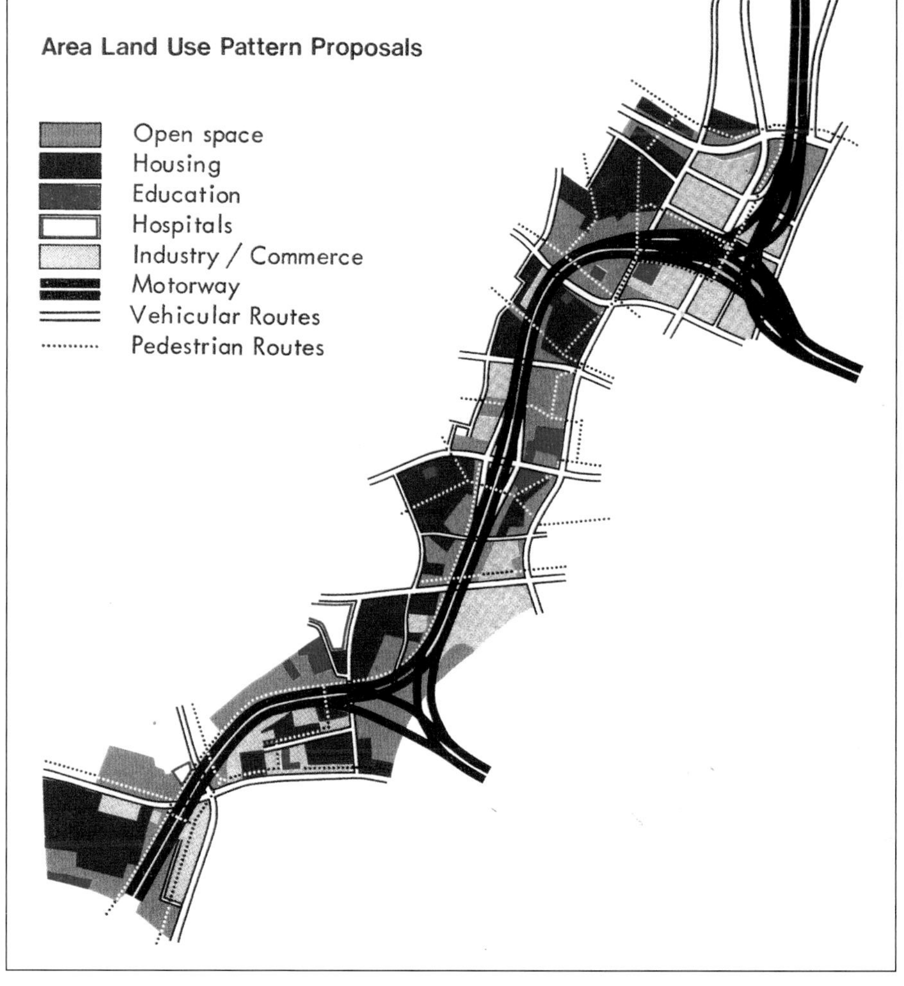

Proposed land uses along Phase 1 of the Urban Motorway. *(From the Urban Motorway West Leg Action Plan)*

The land directly beneath the motorway was not to be left derelict, but was to be used for car parking, commerce, warehousing, industrial, retail, storage or recreation. Adjacent land could be used for all these purposes, but also for parkland. Land more than 100 feet (30 metres) away could also be used for residential development. As far as possible, development beneath the motorway was to be directly linked to the land around it in order to reduce the severance effect of the structure. For example, adjacent to a new office complex, the land would be used for associated car parking. However, a linear car park running the length of the motorway would not be permitted, as it was thought that this would draw focus to the line of the motorway and create a psychological barrier.

The motorway would also create new severance within

Various artist's impressions of how the area beneath the Urban Motorway could be utilised. (Clockwise from top left) Public car park; warehouse; youth club; recreation area with children's play area. *(Belfast Urban Area Plan)*

existing communities. The report emphasised the importance of retaining links across the barrier through the plentiful provision of road and pedestrian access points, sightlines and parkland. Some areas, such as the Roden Street area, were highlighted as being at particular risk from severance while others, such as Donegall Road, were cited as examples of communities where existing severance (by the railway line) could actually be reduced through the redevelopment.

New housing constructed closest to the motorway was to be designed such that living areas and bedrooms, where noise was less tolerable, faced away from the motorway (although how this could actually work in practice is not explained). The report recognised that "road traffic is … the predominant source of annoyance from noise and no other single noise is of comparable importance".[8] It therefore recommended that baffles be attached to the railings of the motorway at key points, and that new homes close by should be built with noise insulation and double glazing as standard. In industrial areas, it recommended that commercial buildings be constructed to a considerable height adjacent to the motorway in order to double as a sound barrier.

Finally, the planners addressed the problem of how the buildings that are either not required for demolition, or are partially demolished, would look. These "will expose an undesirable foreground view of truncated buildings, severed roads and outworn properties [in a] confused state of untidiness and ugliness".[8] The recommendation was that the appearance of such buildings should be either improved by remedial work, or else demolished and the site redeveloped.

Artist's impression of (left) a pedestrian footway and (right) a pedestrian shopping centre beneath the Urban Motorway. *(Belfast Urban Area Plan)*

These proposals were developed in more detail in subsequent years, and by 1972 a much more detailed plan, involving a lot more trees, had been developed to help the motorway integrate into its urban setting.[9]

The efforts of the planners to reconstruct the land around the motorway are laudable and well-intentioned, but with the benefit of 40 years of hindsight it seems clear that they would have only partly succeeded. We now know that a towering concrete structure on the scale proposed attracts litter, graffiti, and anti-social behaviour. Major road junctions with no frontal development in otherwise built-up areas are barriers to pedestrians. As a result, pedestrians feel unsafe and tend to avoid these areas, which then reinforces the trend towards increasing urban abandonment. There is every likelihood that, at least in residential areas, the shadowy void beneath the motorway would have become a wasteland that would have eventually been fenced off by the authorities. In addition, experience has shown that artists' impressions of mothers pushing prams beneath overhead motorways rarely translate into reality.

Implementation

The 1967 report proposes an aggressive programme of works that would have seen the entire ring completed by 1976. This involved dividing the project into three phases. Since the only existing motorways were the M1 and M2, the western leg connecting these two would have been constructed first, followed by the northern (river crossing) leg and finally the eastern and southern legs. The second phase was later divided into two sub-phases, with the first consisting of the bridge and connection to the Sydenham Bypass only, and the second adding the links to the M7 and the stretch of the Urban Motorway linking to Albertbridge Road.

The three phases for construction of the Urban Motorway. Phase 2 was later divided into two further parts.

Construction/compensation costs and timings for each phase of the Urban Motorway				
PHASE	**CONSTR £**	**COMPENSATION £**	**TOTAL £ 1966 (2010 equivalent)** [4]	**WHEN**
1	19.4	8.2	27.6 (390)	Jan 69–Dec 72
2	20.0	10.2	30.2 (439)	Jan 71–Dec 74
3	14.1	5.5	19.6 (277)	Jan 73–Dec 76
ALL	53.5	23.9	77.4 (1090)	

Of the total cost of £77.4m, 92.5% was to be funded by central government grant, and 7.5% to be funded by Belfast Corporation.[10] The total cost in 2010 prices was a cool £1.09 bn.[4]

This is an extremely optimistic timetable, even by 1960s standards, as acknowledged in the report: "The project is feasible in all respects. But to complete it by 1976 requires the active cooperation of everyone concerned and the setting up and maintaining of a fast tempo of endeavour."[1] It was estimated that at any one time between 1,500 and 2,000 people would be working on the scheme itself, not to mention the labourers that would be required to re-house those displaced by the road.

During the course of the project a total of 4,220 new homes would need to be provided to re-house those displaced. As these would need to be provided between 1967 and January 1973, this amounts to around 700 new homes per year. Given that the existing housing programme in 1967 was producing 740 new homes per year to meet the existing waiting list of 7,000 applicants,[1] it is clear that at least a doubling of housing output would be required if the timetable was to be met. This, in the words of the planners, would make the housing situation "critical". These figures also ignore the fact that vesting of properties might not go smoothly, and that families would require reasonable notice (at least several months) to arrange a move.

What if?

This chapter outlines the planners' 'dream' of an urban motorway encircling Belfast city centre by 1976. Had the road been built, it would undoubtedly have transformed both the appearance of the city and the experience of the motorist. At off-peak times the road would, even today, have provided a fast route into the city centre from the suburbs, as well as providing an effective distributor for traffic crossing the central area merely to travel from one area to another. The road was technically feasible and, had the land already been free from existing development, it possibly could have been constructed within the timetable stated.

The planners anticipated that traffic levels would have doubled by the completion of the motorway in 1976, at which point the western and northern legs would have been running at capacity at peak times. For several reasons that are explored in later chapters, this did not occur. In fact, actual traffic figures suggest that the motorway would not have reached capacity at peak hours until around 1990. Of course, this ignores the fact that the motorway would have induced further traffic growth than actually occurred, so capacity may indeed have been reached during the mid 1980s.

We also know that traffic in Belfast increased by a further 50% between 1990 and 2006,[11] which would have caused the situation to deteriorate. The closely-spaced junctions and high degree of weaving inherent in the design makes the road very susceptible to congestion. Some limited additional capacity could probably have been provided at low cost during the 1990s by converting the hard shoulder into an additional lane. Nevertheless, it seems quite likely that the Belfast Urban Motorway would have become gridlocked at peak times, effectively ceasing to function, by the Millennium.

The road would also have had a significant detrimental impact on the streetscape of the city. The elevated structure would have dominated the surrounding area visually, audibly and through airborne pollution. The landscape around the modern elevated M3 motorway north of the city centre provides an illustration of how the area beneath could have looked. The large street junctions required would have decimated what are now thriving commercial areas such as Bradbury Place. In addition, the enormous scale of the freeflow motorway interchanges may have been acceptable beside the Harbour Estate, but the proposals to place these structures adjacent to rows of houses on the Ormeau Road or Donegall Road would have had a serious impact on the amenity of these areas. Finally, 1960s construction technology was such that bridge structures of that era tend to have a lifespan of around 50 years. Thus, in a worst-case scenario, the entire Urban Motorway may have required reconstruction around the period 2020–2030; at enormous expense and disruption given that the land beneath would have been developed in the interim.

Belfast's Corporation Street, as it is traversed by the M3 motorway, provides an illustration of how areas beneath the Urban Motorway could have looked in practice. *(Author's collection)*

Despite their best intentions, it seems unlikely that serious severance could have been avoided. Pedestrians would have felt intimidated walking in the shadows beneath the motorway, while the psychological effect of the barrier may well have proved even more effective than the physical one.

Despite strenuous denials at the time, there can also be little doubt that the Urban Motorway was an example of what is today called gentrification, the uprooting of working class communities to serve the interests of the middle classes. The planning documents betray an assumption that the working class communities are dispensable, and can be relocated without harm, and show little understanding of the significance of 'place' to community. Today it is accepted that any attempt to relocate a community merely succeeds in destroying it. The road would have primarily benefitted the car-owning middle classes, but the brunt of the cost would have been borne by the working class communities through which it was driven.

Finally, it seems most unlikely that the Urban Motorway could ever have been built by 1976. With several thousand commercial, industrial and residential properties to acquire, several thousand more new homes to be built, all the residents to be re-housed, new factories constructed, contracts let, materials sourced, components manufactured and labour recruited, the timetable seems hopelessly optimistic with hindsight.

Had the Urban Motorway been built, Belfast would be a very different place and no doubt debate would still be raging today about the wisdom and consequences of its construction.

CHAPTER 6
FALTERING

Reception of the Plan

The response from local politicians to the idea of an urban motorway was mixed, with opposition generally limited to those directly affected by the scheme. For example, in a letter dated January 1965 (ie two years before the final design was released) the Unionist Association in St Anne's Ward (comprising the south-west of the city centre and Falls Road) sent a strongly worded letter that seems reasonable when taken at face value: "It is appalling to consider the cold blooded inhumanity that regards human beings as no better than cattle to be moved round at official edict." and "There is no possible building ground inside the City Boundary where these extra 5000 [replacement] houses could be constructed ... presumably these 5000 families just vanish."[1] However, reading further suggests that the objections may not have been entirely philanthropic:

> *In St Anne's Ward 610 homes will be demolished, destroying the heart of the Ward's main polling station. These houses are all good residential property, none of them scheduled for slum clearance. There is already very bitter resentment and people are starting to leave the district. The more responsible, sensible people who are the backbone of any community, are going. Property and business values have dropped to slum clearance levels. A previously solid unionist community now shows an infiltration of other voters that might be anything from 10–20% ... How many other unionist seats will be lost is anyone's guess ... This scheme is political suicide on a really grand scale.*[1]

That such reasoning could be so explicitly stated demonstrates how solid the unionist government still believed itself to be on this, the eve of the civil rights movement and the 'Troubles'. The implication that the most important repercussion of the routing of the Urban Motorway through 610 homes would be the loss of a unionist seat to a nationalist politician indicates that the ordinary people of Belfast had little more of a voice through their local representatives than they had on their own.

Nevertheless, newspapers predominantly read by unionists enthusiastically welcomed the plan. The *Belfast Telegraph* proudly proclaimed on its front page that the plan would "shape the Belfast of 1976",[2] before noting that the scheme would employ over 2,000 people and that the effect on housing was much reduced from the earlier ring road proposals. An accompanying editorial poured scorn on the idea that the plan would "drain the life from the centre of the city" by noting that taking through traffic out would make the city centre "freer to serve its proper function". The effect on housing was recognised, but dismissed since "a large proportion ... would have been due for slum clearance".[3] Several pages were devoted to a detailed description of the plan.

In stark contrast the *Irish News*, read mostly by nationalists, reported the scheme more factually, while using an editorial to lambast the "paradox" of spending so much on a ring road at a time of housing shortage, rising unemployment and wage freezes: "human beings are less important than giant ring roads and fantastic fly-over [sic], that free-running traffic in the centre of the city merits greater consideration than parents and children".[4] After predicting that the huge cost would mean that the "disturbing" scheme would never happen, they concluded: "we still come back wondering about those without homes and those who will lose them". The divergent views of the two newspapers may have had as much to do with the social class and location of their readership, as it was to do with party politics.

For their part, Belfast Corporation received the plan[5] enthusiastically, and adopted it late in 1967.[6] Work began immediately on preparing Phase 1 (the M1 to M2 link) for the public inquiry and contract stages.

Such was the scale of the scheme that the Corporation initially had difficulties because so many members had declared an interest in property affected by the scheme. The situation rapidly degenerated to farce when:

> *...a substantial number of members left the meeting and others expressed themselves as very dissatisfied that the remaining members should be left to determine an issue of such tremendous importance to the City in the absence of those deemed to have a pecuniary interest.*"[7]

In the end, the situation was only resolved when the Ministry of Development gave special permission for members with a declared interest to nevertheless take part in the decision making process.[8]

Refining Traffic Forecasts

Consultancy firm R Travers Morgan, who produced the report into the Belfast Urban Motorway, had been appointed by Belfast Corporation in April 1965. In June 1965 the Ministry of Development had asked them to expand their remit to include a more general traffic and transportation study of the entire Greater Belfast area.[9] Some initial work from their traffic studies had informed the Urban Motorway report,[10] but the figures were preliminary and gave only a general idea of the expected traffic loads on the Urban Motorway since they did not model the roads in the rest of the city in detail.

As the traffic study progressed during 1967 and into 1968, more detailed traffic forecasts could be made. This resulted in periodic correspondence between R Travers Morgan and the Corporation indicating some cheap short-term solutions to particular bottlenecks. However, the work also began to reveal that the traffic flow models for the Urban Motorway, as published in 1967 were not accurate. In particular, they showed that the predicted usage of the southern and eastern legs of the Motorway had been over-estimated. While traffic levels on the western leg (Phase 1) were predicted to be high, and levels on the cross-harbour link (Phase 2) extremely high, traffic levels on the southern leg (Phase 3) were much lower, around a quarter of the flows expected on the cross-harbour link. Even at peak times, this part of the road was predicted to be operating at just over 50% capacity by 1986.[10]

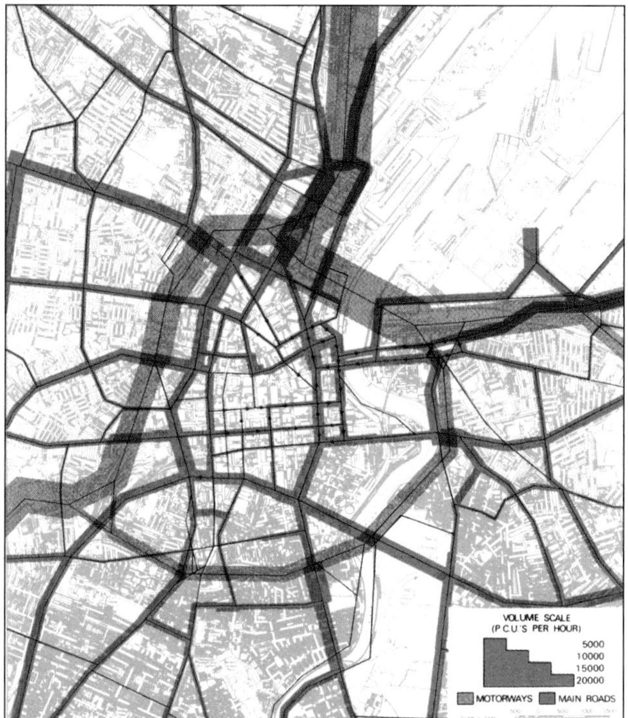

A map of amended traffic flow predictions in 1969, suggesting that the southern leg of the Urban Motorway would have been significantly under-utilised compared to the remainder. This map uses predicted 1986 traffic flows. *(Belfast Transportation Plan, Courtesy of DRD Roads Service)*

A map showing the uneven predicted utilisation of the Urban Motorway highlights the fact that the links between the M1 and M2, and the cross-harbour bridge were the two most important parts of the project. More significantly, it must surely have been difficult to avoid the thought that provision of the southern and eastern legs of the motorway may not even have been necessary *at all*. But perhaps, in the end, it was the simple fact that the Urban Motorway had always been planned to be a 'ring' that prevented this possibility from being seriously considered in 1968.

Nevertheless, the traffic figures did influence the planners to a certain degree. On 18 April 1968, the consultants wrote to the Corporation expressing the view that Phase 3 should be brought down to ground level, rather than being of the same elevated construction as the remainder of the ring.[10] This did not mean having traffic lights and roundabouts – it was still to be a motorway with flyovers at junctions – but that between junctions it should be built on the level. The motivation for such a move was to reduce the unit cost of this less-busy stretch, rather than for environmental or social reasons, and the Corporation appear to have readily accepted this recommendation.[11]

A month later, on 22 May 1968, R Travers Morgan submitted their report, *Travel in Belfast,* which summarised the findings of the traffic study that was being used to inform the general plan for Greater Belfast.[12]

Money Problems

By the late 1960s, the confident optimism displayed by the Northern Ireland government earlier in the decade began to falter. The predictions of a rapidly rising population and sustained economic growth began to turn sour in the face of an increasingly challenging financial climate in the UK, and a reduced population growth rate that began to dilute the case for new cities and the plans for major urban growth in the towns around Belfast. This is not to suggest that Northern Ireland was in decline – there was still population growth and economic success – but it was not on the scale that had been anticipated.

In addition, the grand plans for an extensive motorway network were coming into conflict with the cold realities of feasibility. Notions of constructing miles of motorway in just a few years were frustrated by high construction costs, a finite supply of construction material, the physical limits of the labour supply and the protracted time required to bring each road project to the point where construction could begin.

In late 1966, the Minister of Development (William K Fitzsimmons) had admitted:

> *...conditions have changed tremendously since the programme was first announced. Costs have risen and unexpected problems have been found in the building of motorways.*

Most important of all, the financial situation has not improved in keeping with the cost of building motorways.[13]

He also stated one way in which he proposed to tackle this problem:

I have decided that a special attempt must be made to bring down the cost of rural motorways to a level more in keeping with the traffic volumes they will carry.[13]

Essentially this meant that roads initially planned as motorways would instead be built as all-purpose dual-carriageways. This resulted in the hugely controversial decision to downgrade the final section of the M1, the Dungannon Bypass, to dual-carriageway standard (it was eventually opened as a single-carriageway in 1980 after further delays, and did not become dual-carriageway until 2010).

Despite Mr Fitzsimmons' comments about escalating costs, this does not seem to actually be the case. Indeed, it may be more the case that the government was initially over-optimistic about the expense. Writing later, in 1971, the chief motorway engineer at the Ministry of Development insisted, "the cost per mile of motorway has not risen significantly in the last 10 years".[14]

The pace of motorway construction slowed, particularly on the M2, which was less advanced than the M1.[9] When it became obvious that it was not going to be possible to construct all the planned motorways for several decades, decisions were made to carry out more limited road improvement schemes as interim measures. For example, despite the ambition to construct the M3 from the Belfast Urban Motorway to Bangor, the decision was made in late 1968 to construct the Holywood Throughpass on the existing A2 road to relieve the chronic congestion in the town. The Minister freely admitted that "a new road to motorway standards will cost at least £6 million [£79m in 2010 prices] and perhaps as much as £8 million [£106m] and the plain truth is that we cannot afford to build a road of this kind for a long time."[15,16] Plans were also put in place to upgrade the A1, parts of which were dualled in a piecemeal fashion during the 1970s and completed in the early 2000s.

The Stormont government was beginning to realise that a desperate *need* for road schemes did not automatically translate into having *enough money* to actually build them. Perhaps the government had become too ambitious in their plans, forgetting that Northern Ireland was still a small state on the periphery of the continent. These facts were very much in the minds of the

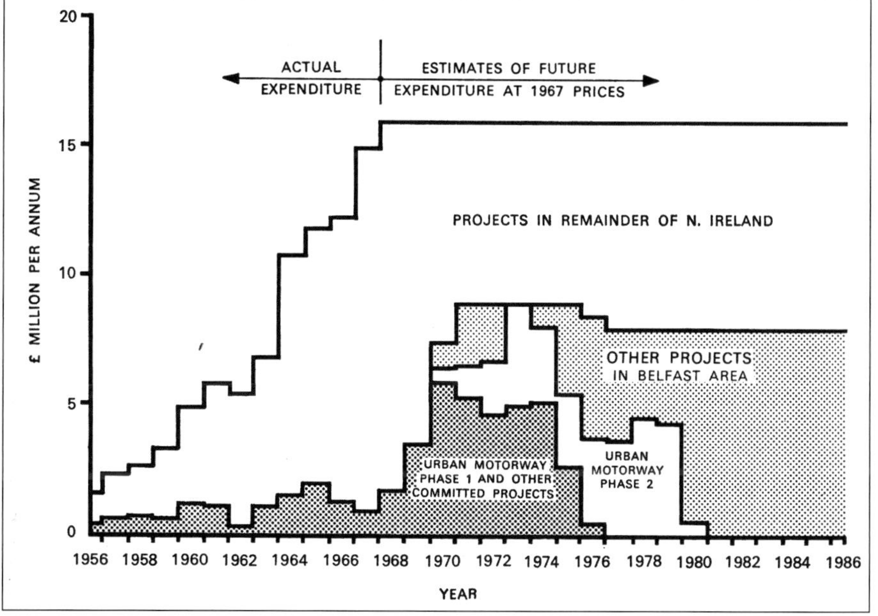

Proposed expenditure profile on Northern Ireland roads up to 1986, as envisaged in 1969. The Belfast area accounts for roughly half the spend. *(Belfast Transportation Plan, Courtesy of DRD Roads Service)*

planners at R Travers Morgan, and the realisation that a phased approach to road building was necessary was prominent in the Belfast Transportation Plan that they released in 1969.

Phase 1 is Approved

On 17 April 1968 the Ministry of Development announced that they had given permission for the construction of Phase 1 of the Belfast Urban Motorway. Their permission was required since they were putting up 92.5% of the money required to build it (the Corporation providing the rest). However they withheld permission for Phases 2 and 3 due to the wider UK government policy of reducing public spending. The Ministry explained:

> *...in view of the need to limit further commitments, it is impossible as yet to agree to any timetable for phases two and three and the Ministry regrets therefore that a decision when to proceed beyond phase one will have to be deferred until the present situation is clearer.*[17]

A press release was issued on the same day indicating that Phase 1 of the Belfast Urban Motorway had been approved by Belfast Corporation and that work would begin in 1970. The cost of all three phases of the scheme was given in this press release as £76.5m,[11] almost the same as given in 1967.[5] The scheme then went to a public inquiry.

The public inquiry, which sat in 1969, lasted two and a half days[6] and was "characterised by a virtual absence of objections".[18] Some of those involved in the scheme later congratulated themselves on this lack of objections as evidence of the skill of their own preparations and the concerted attempts they had made to involve the public over the previous four years. City Engineer JT Noble later commented that:

> *The public acceptance of major urban schemes depends as much on good communication with the public as it does on acceptably fitting the scheme into the fabric of the city. Keeping the public fully and frankly in the picture from the outset requires the agreement of the elected representatives to proper and careful public relations at all stages ... In particular, the policy of putting full time employees into the field to meet the people who are to be displaced to hear their troubles and to help wherever possible, has paid great dividends.*[6]

It is true that the planners sought the views of thousands of people from across the social spectrum in preparing the plans. However, it must be noted that these people were never asked whether or not they supported the plan, and were never asked for their opinion on how the objective of funnelling traffic through the central area should be accomplished. Instead, the planners appear to have felt that 'consultation' meant no more than telling people, frankly, where the road would run and then helping them to find new homes. The planners were not so much gauging public opinion, as simply keeping them informed of their decisions. As a result, the public could see that their opinions were largely irrelevant, and thus had little motivation to engage with the planners.

M Cinalli, writing in 2003, argues instead:

> *...the smooth approval of the plan mirrored the consultants' failure to stimulate public participation during the elaboration of their scheme. While local authority representatives*

had played a positive role in the planning process through the Steering Conference and through direct consultation, the response to requests to the general public for their views on interim proposals, which were publicised through the news media and exhibitions, had been almost insignificant.[18]

Belfast Transportation Plan

R Travers Morgan published the 'Belfast Transportation Plan' on 19 June 1969,[10] with the associated 'Belfast Urban Area Plan'[19] being launched the next day. The authors of the 'Transportation Plan' pointed out that the issue of congestion was so serious that it was costing millions of pounds per year in wasted time and lost business. Transport planner Tim Morton recalls:

> *[I] attended the public launch of the Plan at the City Hall and remember being struck by the forecast that if nothing were done, then the prevailing peak period traffic conditions would eventually occur throughout the day – which was quite a horrendous thought and would have rendered Belfast unworkable as a city.*[20]

Although the plan included both road-based and public transport proposals, the terms of reference meant that it was essentially a set of road proposals. The plan followed the Buchanan principles of separating different types of traffic, such as local and long-distance traffic, onto dedicated roads. They proposed that there should be a hierarchy of roads consisting of:

- Radial motorways feeding traffic from the edge of the city into the central area.
- An inner ring road (ie, the Urban Motorway) to allow traffic on the radial motorways to orbit around the central area and to access other radial motorways.
- A central distributor box, inside the Urban Motorway: a road with traffic lights at every junction, to provide more precise movements within the central area.
- Widespread pedestrianisation of the city centre with only buses permitted on Donegall Place.
- That secondary radial roads, such as the Lisburn Road and Shore Road, should be widened or otherwise improved to become local feeder roads.

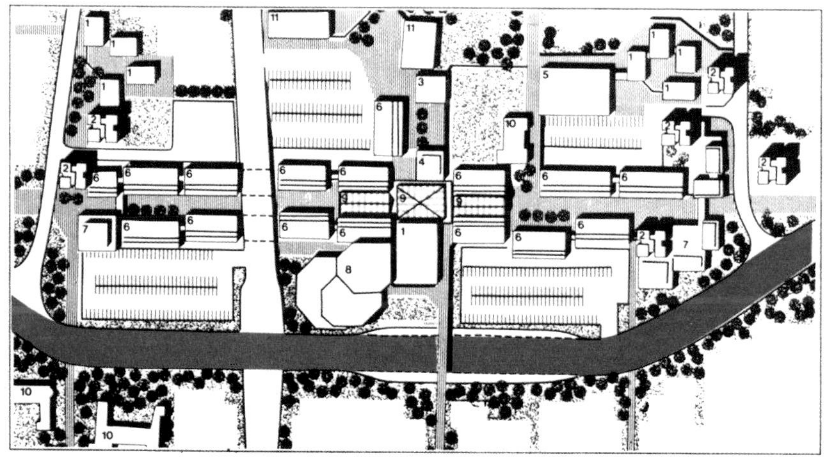

Shankill District Centre
1 Mission halls
2 Multi-storey flats
3 Church hall
4 Banks
5 Health and Welfare
6 Shops with dwellings over
7 Social facilities
8 Leisure Centre
9 Covered shopping
10 Primary schools
11 Churches

Proposals for the Shankill area in the 1969 'Belfast Transportation Plan' show the existing road redeveloped as a pedestrian zone and bypassed by a new road, marked in red. *(Belfast Transportation Plan, Courtesy of DRD Roads Service)*

- An intermediate ring road to provide movements between radials and different parts of the suburbs.
- An outer ring road to provide long-distance connections between different areas of the city.

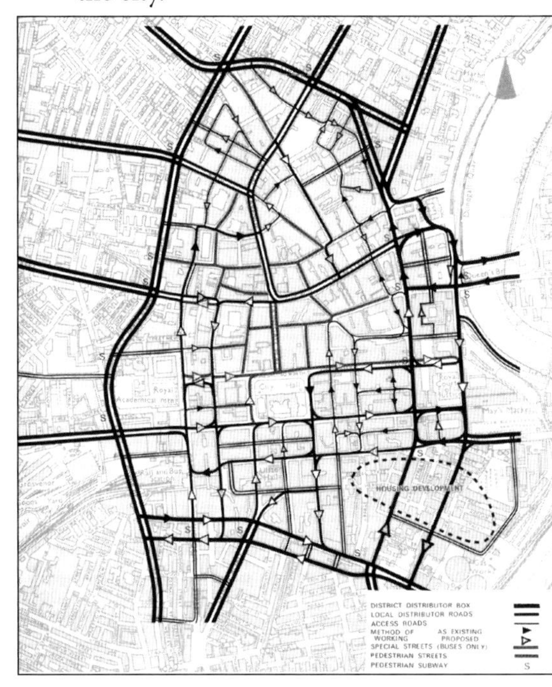

The Central Distributor Box and related one-way systems as envisaged in 1969. *(Belfast Transportation Plan, Courtesy of DRD Roads Service)*

This was the first set of proposals to comprehensively include all-purpose roads as well as motorways, and it is striking that the planners conclude that many of the all-purpose roads were more important than some of the motorway plans. For example, they calculated that the Outer Ring road should have a higher priority than Phase 3 of the Urban Motorway, and also that Phase 1 of the Urban Motorway would perform much better if the Central Distributor Box were built along with it.

The plan also presented much more realistic timescales for construction than had hitherto been the case. It acknowledged that even by 1986 (the year they were planning for) many of the motorways would not be constructed and therefore recommended that a number of schemes

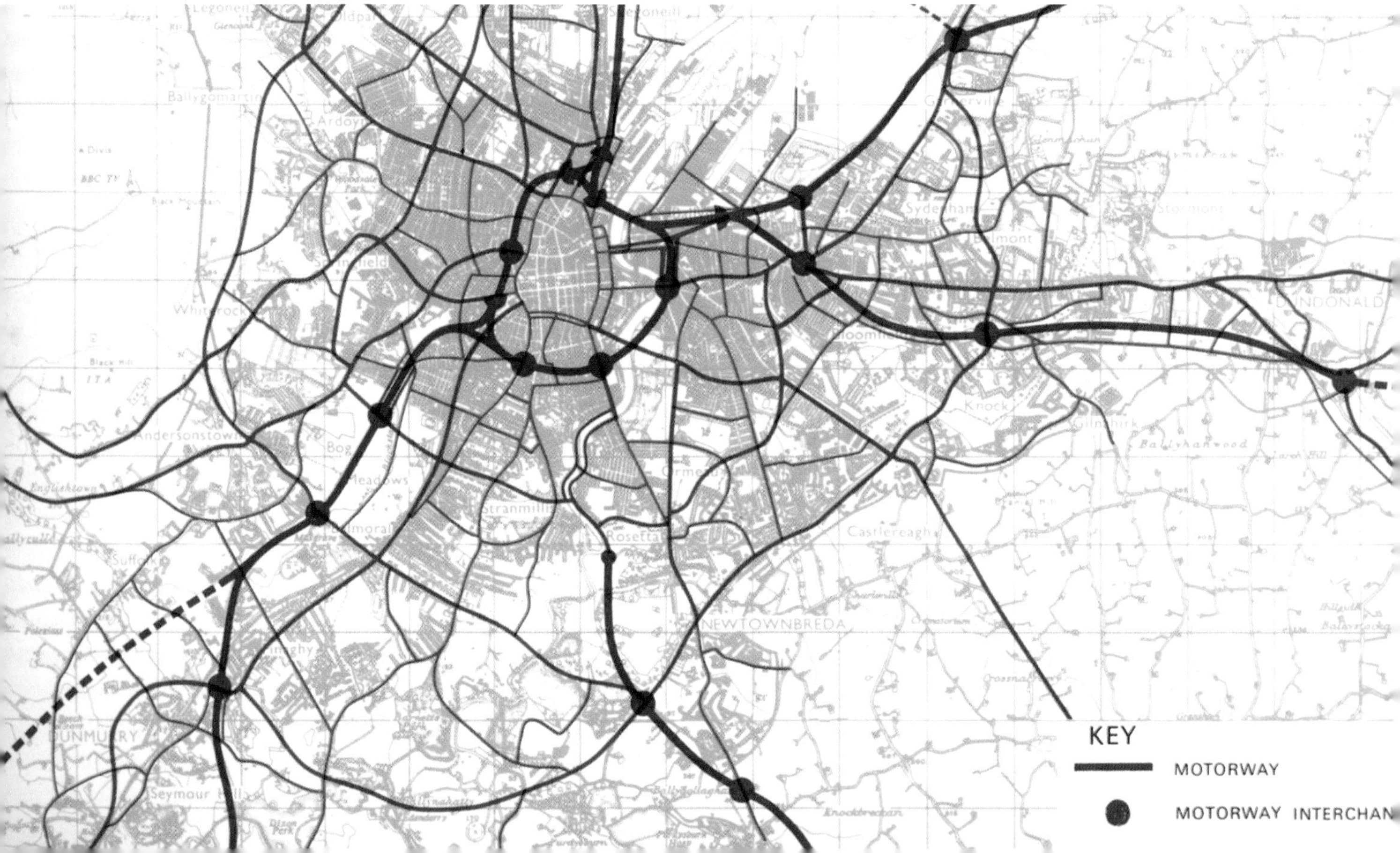

The amended motorway plan in 1969, deleting the innermost section of the M4, along with the M8 and M11 and simplifying the M3/ Urban Motorway interchange. *(Belfast Transportation Plan, Courtesy of DRD Roads Service)*

KEY
MOTORWAY
MOTORWAY INTERCHAN

be deleted, and that the remainder be phased on a strategic basis.

Among the shelved proposals within the Belfast area were the M11 (around northern Lisburn) and the M8 (feeding traffic from the M1 to east Belfast). Interestingly, the planners also recommended that the M4 should not extend to the Urban Motorway, but should instead terminate at Annadale Embankment because the final section had "the greatest cost for the traffic it carries" and because of "its effect on amenity", noting also that "the River Lagan has great potential as an amenity to the City of Belfast and that the impact of the elevated south east approach road would be undesirable". This latter proposal is notable as the first time a motorway scheme in Belfast had been rejected by planners primarily because of its effects on the environment. Although the M8 was cancelled largely due to predicted low usage, a secondary consideration was its impact on the proposed Lagan Valley Park. Finally, they recommended that the freeflow links between the M3 and the eastern leg of the Urban Motorway be omitted in order to simplify the junction and reduce the land take.

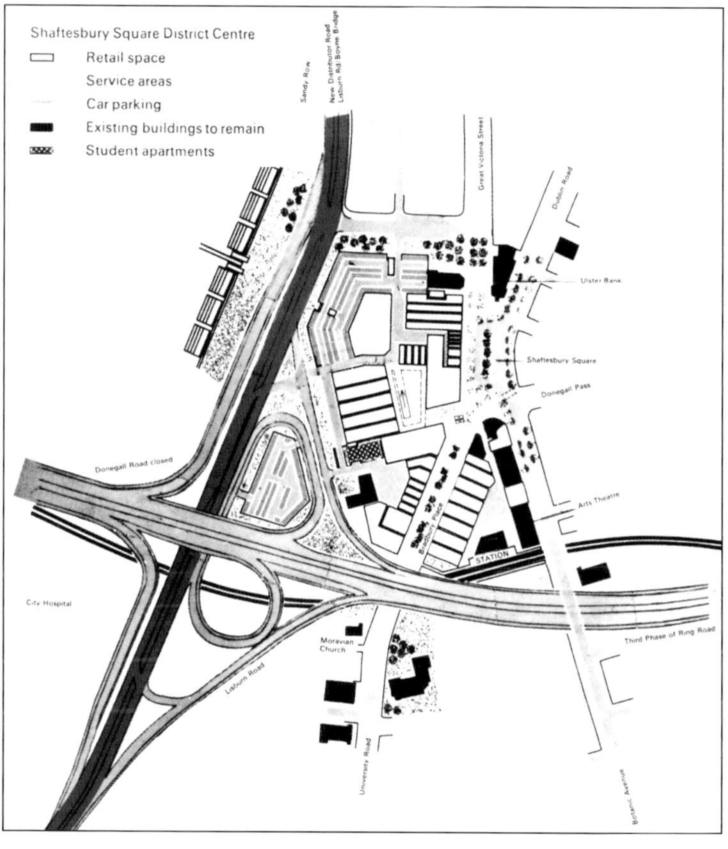

Map showing the proposed Belfast Urban Motorway interchange near Bradbury Place, and the proposed link road passing through Sandy Row, as envisaged in 1969. *(Belfast Transportation Plan, Courtesy of DRD Roads Service)*

These plans resulted in some tweaks to the 1967 design for the Urban Motorway. The removal of the M11 meant that it was now possible to add a junction at Broadway by providing south-facing sliproads here. The deletion of the inner section of the M4 meant that a street level junction could now be provided on the Urban Motorway at Ormeau Road. Several junctions were redesigned, including the pattern of local street access at the M2/Urban Motorway junction. The proposed junction at Bradbury Place was shifted slightly to the west into the southern end of Sandy Row.

The capital investment required for all the road schemes was estimated to be £7.9m per annum at 1967 prices for the period up to 1986, peaking at £11m in 1973. The plan suggested an order of priority and preparation work on the elements relevant to the Urban Motorway scheme were to be constructed as follows. The dates in brackets show the year substantive planning was to begin, and then the year construction would begin:

1. Completion of the M2 foreshore, then under construction
2. Phase 1 of the Urban Motorway (1968/1971)
3. Central Distributor Box (1969/1970)
4. Outer Ring, east Belfast (1969/1971)
5. Phase 2 of the Urban Motorway (1970/1975)

6. Outer Ring, west Belfast (1974/1975)
7. M3 from Urban Motorway to Tillysburn (1977/1977)
8. M7 from M3 to Knock (1977/1977)
9. Phase 3 of the Urban Motorway (1977/1979)
10. M7 from Knock to Dundonald (1978/1979)
11. M3 from Tillysburn to Bangor (1979/1980)
12. M1 widening at Belfast end (1979/1980)
13. M4 from Carryduff to Annadale (1982/1983)

Note that the rather unrealistic ambition to have the entire Urban Motorway completed by 1976 was now abandoned in favour of a much more realistic timeframe, where construction was unlikely to be completed before the mid 1980s.

The planners made fairly detailed recommendations for bus routes and fare structures, but essentially acknowledged that the use of buses in the city was in decline and would likely continue to do so. However, the planners did investigate the role of the Central Railway upon the request of the Corporation. This line connected the terminus of the Dublin line at Great Victoria Street to the terminus of the Bangor line at Queen's Quay and had been disused ever since the construction of the Queen Elizabeth Bridge one-way system had severed it in 1965. It may have come as a surprise at the time that their calculations showed a substantial cost benefit to reopening the line, building a new 'central' railway station at Maysfield on East Bridge Street, a second halt near Shaftesbury Square and closing both Great Victoria Street and Queen's Quay stations. They concluded that "the advantages [of reopening the Central Line] seem far to outweigh its disadvantages." This decision did not result in moving the

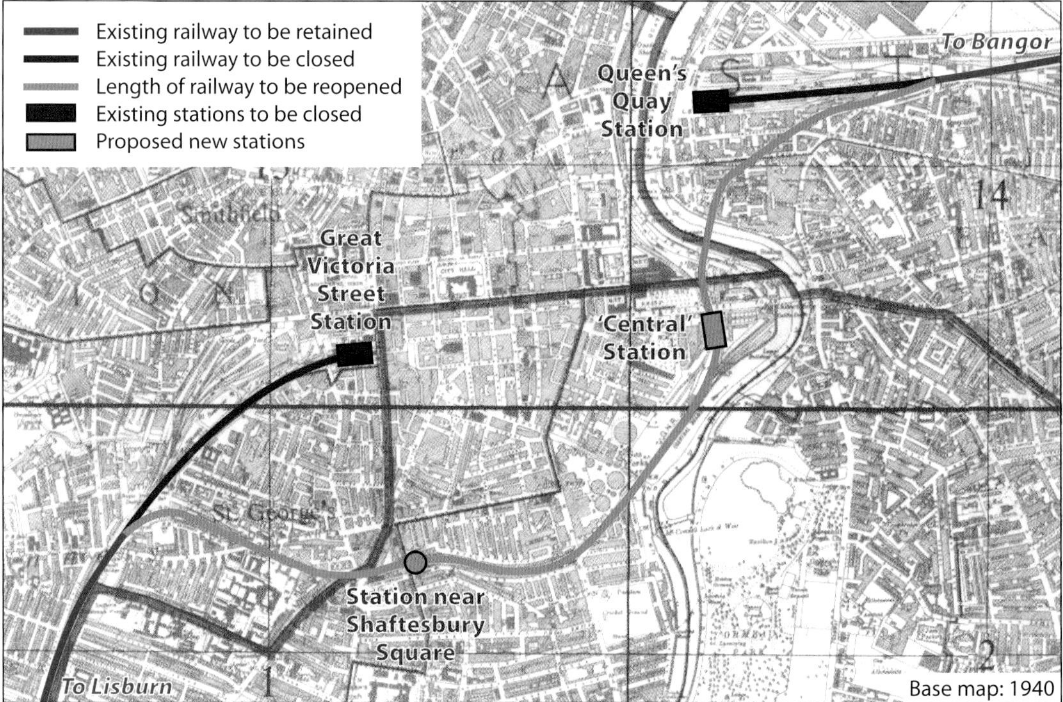

Map of the 1969 proposal to reopen the Central Railway and construct a new 'central' station. *(Base map 1940, Ordnance Survey)*

Urban Motorway – presumably it was to remain in a cutting beneath sections of the road, or else in the central reservation.

The plan was received very positively by the press, with the *Belfast Telegraph* noting that the plan would be pedestrian-friendly, create more homes in the city centre, lead to an increase in office space and make the experience of shopping in Belfast more pleasant.[21] The Lord Mayor of Belfast described the plan as "of paramount importance to our city" while Werner Heubeck, managing director of Ulsterbus, welcomed a plan to construct a new central bus station.[22] Even the *Irish News*, which had poured scorn on the plans for the Urban Motorway, was generally receptive to this plan.[23]

Over the following year members of the general public examined the plans, and some 150 enquiries were received.[24] People tended to object to parts of the plan that impacted on their homes, rather than the plan in principle. Most objections related to Phase 3 of the Urban Motorway, Outer Ring East and specific proposals for Fortwilliam Park, Sandy Row and Stranmillis. The Northern Ireland Hospitals Authority (referring to the planned City Hospital) and Stranmillis College, who would both lose land to roads, also made objections. Requests for meetings with the Town Planning Committee at Belfast Corporation were turned down on the grounds that there would be a public hearing in due course.[24]

Comments were formally invited in Autumn 1970, and 272 objections were received to the Urban Area Plan, 239 of which related to the transport proposals.[25] Of these, all 239 were objections to the road proposals. The bus and railway proposals produced no objections at all.

Other Developments in Public Transport

The railways, which had been in decline since the 1950s, had suffered considerably during the early 1960s from a lack of government support and investment. As already discussed, the Central Railway had been closed in 1965, severing the only link past the city centre. In the same year the UTA ceased all road and rail freight (except for cross-border freight). Although the railways were still very busy with freight, freight no longer made money. According to transport historian Norman Johnston, "between 1965 and 1967 the mood was that the whole [railway] system would be gone by 1970".[29]

This had all changed in 1967 when the Stormont government gave the railways a second chance by permitting competition between buses and trains. In his 1963 report into the future of the railways, Benson had recommended retaining the commuter lines into the city. During 1966 and 1967 railways were detached from buses with the establishment of Northern Ireland Railways (NIR) and Ulsterbus. This brought immediate benefits: "There was a vast improvement in morale. Ulsterbus made the buses pay. NIR introduced conductors on trains and for a while actually made the railways pay as well".[29] The railways phased out steam locomotives and introduced diesel railcars, and (in 1966) even won the four-year contract to supply the infill for the M2 foreshore motorway, then under construction in north Belfast. The recommendation in the 1969 'Belfast Transportation Plan' to reopen the Central Railway and consolidating rail services at a new central station was a further boost.

Nevertheless, buses in Belfast suffered a decline in parallel with the experience of other cities in the UK. Since buses used the same congested streets as cars, there was little point in taking the bus when a car driver could sit in the same traffic jam with more comfort and privacy. Although the mileage operated by buses actually rose through the 1960s, the proportion of people commuting by bus fell from 48% in 1960 to 37% in 1971.[30] In the same period, train commuters fell from 12% to 6%, while car commuters rose from 40% to 57%. This trend would continue into the 1970s. However, it was the start of the 'Troubles' in 1969 that fuelled a steeper decline than similar cities.

Problem of Housing Shortages and Redevelopment Areas

It had been 14 years since the 1956 Housing Act had declared a quarter of all homes in the province 'unfit'. That Act had committed the authorities to replacing all these homes over the relatively long period of 20 years, but in that time little had actually been done. In Belfast during the early 1960s around 26,000 homes (almost a quarter of the city's total of 115,000) were deemed unfit, but new homes were not being built fast enough to meet the 20 year deadline.[26] In 1961, for example, only 350 new homes were built in the city – a quarter of what would be needed annually to achieve the aim.

Wiener[26] argues that there were two reasons for the lack of house building. The first was the lack of building land. The Corporation only had about a quarter of the land within the city limits that it would need to build all these homes.[26] This resulted in the much-derided blocks of flats and lack of recreational space that typified the period. Writing about these years in 1977, Lavery says:

Model of the East Bridge Street/Short Strand area of Belfast in 1969, envisaging significant high rise development. The road at the bottom left is Cromac Street. The Urban Motorway is seen in the background crossing over Middlepath Street/Bridge End. *(Belfast Transportation Plan, Courtesy of DRD Roads Service)*

In the early 1960s there was considerable pressure to rehouse the maximum number of people in the area from which they had been displaced for redevelopment. This required very high gross and nett densities of 130 and 95 persons per acre and the consequent use of multi-storey flats and maisonettes.[27]

Indeed, such was the dislike of these types of homes that they would be largely phased out by the mid 1970s. Lavery continues:

This type of development had been the subject of considerable criticism and the densities of development had [by the 1970s] dropped considerably ranging from 65 to 95 persons per acre. Most [1970s] redevelopments comprised two or three-storey terrace houses with some three-storey flat blocks.[27]

According to Wiener, the second reason for the housing crisis was the "class interests of the running party" and "a lack of due concern for the needs of working class people" combined with the "corruption and ineptitude" of Belfast Corporation.[26] Evidence from the time does seem to suggest that the decision making process in Belfast was either consciously or unconsciously motivated by the interests of the middle and ruling classes.

For these two reasons, the situation in Belfast had reached a critical point by the late 1960s, in what Morrison describes as "an urban crisis" characterised by the issues of "urban renewal, housing, industrial overspill and traffic".[28] Only major redevelopment plans and a centralisation of house building could hope to deal with it.

It was partly to counter criticism of sectarianism and discrimination in the allocation of housing, and partly to better coordinate the construction of thousands of new homes, that the decision was made in 1969 to take the responsibility away from local authorities and place it into the hands of a single, new body. The Housing Executive, as it was known, therefore came into being in October 1971, but did not immediately lead to an improvement in the situation.

Divis Tower, built in 1966, and today the only remnant of the Divis Flats complex. *(Author's collection)*

In any case, the manner of the redevelopment plans created a tension in the city during the late 1960s. Those attempting to solve the city's desperate traffic problems needed the redevelopment land to make their plans a reality. Yet, those in desperate need of better housing needed the same land for new homes. It was obviously not going to be possible to fully meet the needs of both groups. The stage was therefore set for an inevitable showdown.

CHAPTER 7
WORK AND TROUBLES

The Troubles

During the 1960s, Catholic and Nationalist discontent with the Unionist-dominated government of Northern Ireland formulated itself into the civil rights movement, that sought to reform the political and economic status quo of the province, which had been the solid establishment since the state's formation in 1921.

Under the moderate Unionist Prime Minister Terence O'Neill (in office March 1963 to May 1969) reforms were introduced into the governance of Northern Ireland in an attempt to tackle the sectarian divide, and there was a thaw in the relationship with the Republic of Ireland. However, O'Neill's policies were unpopular amongst grass-roots unionists, and he was ultimately unable to sustain his position and was forced to resign.

The tension between the two communities worsened until, in 1969, it erupted into full-scale civil disorder quickly dominated by Republican and Loyalist paramilitaries, and opposed by the British Army which came into the province in the summer of 1969. The disorder, which became known as the 'Troubles', defined the history of Northern Ireland up to the Millennium and resulted in over 3,000 deaths, tens of thousands of injuries and millions of pounds worth of damage to property and the economy.

During the late 1960s the Stormont government had been following a policy of centralising government functions. The decision had already been taken to concentrate responsibility for housing in the Housing Executive (October 1969; see Chapter 6). However, they were keen that the remaining functions (such as planning, education, water, sewerage and road construction) should also be taken away from the dozens of local authorities that existed at the time. In December 1969, the government asked Patrick Macrory to report into the feasibility of such reforms. His report was published in June 1970[1] and recommended shifting the bulk of government functions to central bodies, reducing the number of local councils to no more than 26, and limiting the powers of these new councils to community and environmental matters such as parks and refuse collection. Due to the civil disorder and the increasing instability of the Stormont government, these reforms were not implemented as soon as they might have been, but they were actively taken forward and were finally in effect by late 1973.

The civil disorder got steadily worse from 1970 and reached its peak in 1972 when almost 500 people were killed. Nationalists withdrew from Stormont in July 1971 and it soon became apparent that the Unionist government was unable to control the worsening security situation. After Stormont refused to surrender control of policing to the central UK government, Westminster suspended the Parliament of Northern Ireland on 30 March 1972, replacing it with an ill-fated Assembly that soon collapsed. As a result (with several brief exceptions) 'Direct Rule' Ministers appointed from Westminster governed Northern Ireland for the next 34 years.

Clearing Land

Despite the deteriorating security situation, those in the Improvement Committee and Belfast Corporation who were responsible for the Urban Motorway scheme pressed ahead with Phase 1, which had been approved by the Corporation in 1968. In February 1970 a Vesting Order was made using the new motorway legislation that had been passed in 1963.[2,3] Phase 1 required the acquisition of the following properties:

- 1,200 houses
- 104 shops, 27 pubs and 2 banks
- 84 commercial/industrial premises
- 6 church buildings
- 3 schools
- 2 hospital buildings
- 2 police stations
- sections of 18 further industrial premises. The total cost of these properties was later estimated at £6.5m at 1970 prices (approximately £140m in 2010 prices).[4]

Booklets were published for both householders/tenants and businesses affected by the Vesting Order. In keeping with tradition these leaflets did not leave any space for people to express opposition to the scheme, but simply set out the facts of what was going to happen to their properties and how they could go about claiming compensation.[5] The leaflets also set out the argument for the Urban Motorway by invoking the principle of the 'greater good', ie that the Urban Motorway may be causing upheaval for individuals, but arguing that the economy of the city as a whole would ultimately benefit from it, and hence workers would benefit. It is interesting to note that only 30% of poorer Belfast households owned a car in 1966.[6]

Land cleared at the north end of Phase 1 of the Urban Motorway in the New Lodge area. Note the distinctive 'M' logo. *(Workers Party of Ireland)*

The process of land acquisition and the relocation of homes and business started off well, but soon became bogged down in a quagmire of legal paperwork and practical complexities. It quickly became apparent that acquiring the 1,400 properties would be much more complicated than anticipated. Although the timetable set out in the 1969 Transportation Plan suggested that construction could begin at the end of 1970,[6] in practice property acquisition was still not completed by 1971.

Legal problems included issues such as locating the owners of property and dealing with the enormous number of compensation claims. The Public Record Office contains literally hundreds of pages of solicitor's letters claiming compensation for loss of property and the costs

Older properties (left) at Townsend Street near the Shankill Road in the early 1970s, with high rise flats beyond that were known locally as the 'weetabix blocks'. The graffiti reflects the local sentiments at the time which had turned against the redevelopment project. At the time of writing the site of the nearer building is now waste ground, while the high rise has been replaced by lower density housing. *(©Buzz Logan/ www.rbgbelfast.com)*

of relocation.[7] Even though Phase 1 was the only part of the scheme to have been approved, the issue of 'blight' (being unable to develop or sell a property due to a possible future road scheme) resulted in claims for property that was not even affected by Phase 1, adding to the burden of bureaucracy. For example, the following letter was received from a solicitor representing a fertiliser company based in Short Strand:

> *The line of [Phase 2B of] the proposed new Ring Road runs through [our client's] premises and, as it will be necessary for our client to find other suitable accommodation, they have asked us to enquire if the Corporation would purchase the property now thus enabling them to make suitable arrangements for the future.*[6]

There is no record of whether this particular request was successful.

The issue of blight had been taking its toll for years. The houses at Roden Street had been blighted by the proposed extension to the M1 motorway since the 1950s, so that even by 1958 a local politician was complaining that "There is no inducement for either landlord or tenant to keep the houses in good repair, and the complete uncertainty as to the future is very disturbing".[8] By the early 1970s, blight had been afflicting some properties for well over a decade with the result that buildings were in a very poor state, shops had closed and dereliction was marring the appearance of the communities. The Public Record Office preserves dozens more documents detailing many compensation claims for property affected by blight.[7]

The compensation system at the time was still not well developed, and often did not take account of 'collateral' damage to businesses. For example, it was often the case that property acquisition removed most of the clientele of some businesses, even if the business was physically unaffected by the scheme. This had the effect of devaluing the business. For instance, in late 1968, Liberal MP Sheelagh Murnaghan raised the case of a shop affected by the southern extension of the M2 (part of Phase 1 of the Urban Motorway):

> *The shop in question is not being acquired at present and there is no provision for compensation. It is in an area which is designated for slum clearance at a later stage. The occupant's problem is that by the time slum clearance takes place in three or five years, with luck the value of the business will have depreciated to an extent, and if compensation is measured on the diminished value he will incur a great loss.*[9]

Demolitions at Cullingtree Road associated with both redevelopment and Phase 1 of the Urban Motorway. *(Workers Party of Ireland)*

In this case the root problem was that blight was destroying the market that the shop relied upon. The urban desolation being wrought by blight and demolition, injustices in the compensation system, and the social upheaval caused by the relocations, contributed to growing popular discontent with the entire scheme during the early 1970s. Retired Director of Network Services, Grahame Fraser, comments that "The York Street area was basically decimated, and it lay that way for years".[10]

The documents preserved from the period suggest that the Corporation was unprepared for the huge scale of legal work that would have to be done to prepare Phase 1 for construction, and the solicitors were kept busy into 1971. The slow pace of housing construction in the city (both high rise flats and traditional houses) meant that even when homes had been acquired, it was often not possible to relocate the occupants. By early 1972 a quarter of the families affected had still not been re-housed.[2] The problem was exacerbated by the fact that the Army then requested that some empty, vested properties not be demolished straight away as they provided useful barriers for dealing with the civil disorder that was particularly bad in west Belfast.[11] A further problem was that the unrest had meant that it was impractical to publish a realistic programme with set milestones,[12] giving the impression that the project was not making progress.

Re-housing Families and Industry

As well as fuelling latent anger through demolition, the government also created further public dissatisfaction by the design of the new public housing. Although the decision to build high rise flats was mainly motivated by the need to house large numbers of people in a reduced area of land, in locations near the Urban Motorway it was also motivated by a desire to use the buildings as noise barriers.

It was calculated[13] that the elevated road would produce typical noise levels of 83 dBA at the road edge, well in excess of the 65 dBA which was then regarded as the maximum acceptable background noise. The planners recognised that the elevated nature of the road would enable the noise to travel much further, and would still be around 73 dBA at a horizontal distance of about 150 feet (46 metres) from the road. For residential homes, a daytime maximum of 50 dBA was recommended, dropping to 35 dBA at night.

To resolve this issue, the planners sought to use the land adjacent to the motorway for non-residential uses, but where that was not possible it was proposed to construct flats that would double as noise barriers (despite there already being a public backlash against flats). As has already been discussed, the living/sleeping areas were to be on the side away from the motorway, with kitchens and bathrooms on the near side. The Belfast Urban Study Group (an academic group which opposed the motorway) later calculated that even this would require double-glazing with an 8-inch gap between the panes, sound insulation in the walls and mechanical ventilation.[14]

By contrast, the relocation of industry proceeded more smoothly. In 1968, the government had passed a bill in Stormont that gave local authorities the power to acquire land specifically for the relocation of industry displaced by road developments. The Minister of Development, William Fitzsimmons, said during the debate in November of that year:

> *The various road and development schemes now planned will undoubtedly create a high level of demand for suitable sites when the businesses affected begin to look for new premises. By establishing trading estates local authorities will benefit not only those firms which re-establish themselves on the estates; they will also be easing the pressure on other sites, and so indirectly providing firms which do not want to move into an estate with better opportunities for resettling themselves.*[15]

Stormont intended that many industries would relocate to other 'growth towns', especially Craigavon. However, Belfast Corporation, keen not to lose the tax revenue from industry in the city, had already planned to provide a major new industrial estate by reclaiming the Bog Meadows; part of the flood plain of the River Blackstaff which lay on either side of the M1 motorway between Donegall Road and Stockman's Lane. The land on the eastern side of the M1 was indeed reclaimed by the early 1970s and developed for industry, and is today bisected by the Boucher Road. The planned reclamation on the west side did not occur on the same scale, partly for environmental reasons. Ironically, the removal of the natural flood plain of the Blackstaff here had the effect of worsening the pre-existing flood threat in the areas around.

Many of the industrial buildings in the city centre were old, pre-war edifices that required modernisation but had limited scope for expansion. In many ways, the change forced upon firms by the Urban Motorway was an ideal opportunity to relocate – at government expense – to new, modern facilities further out of the city. A full time Industrial Liaison Officer was appointed by the Corporation to assist firms in the move and by late 1971 'most' of the firms affected by Phase 1 had either already moved or were to do so imminently, and the new industrial estate at Boucher Road was "almost completely booked".[2]

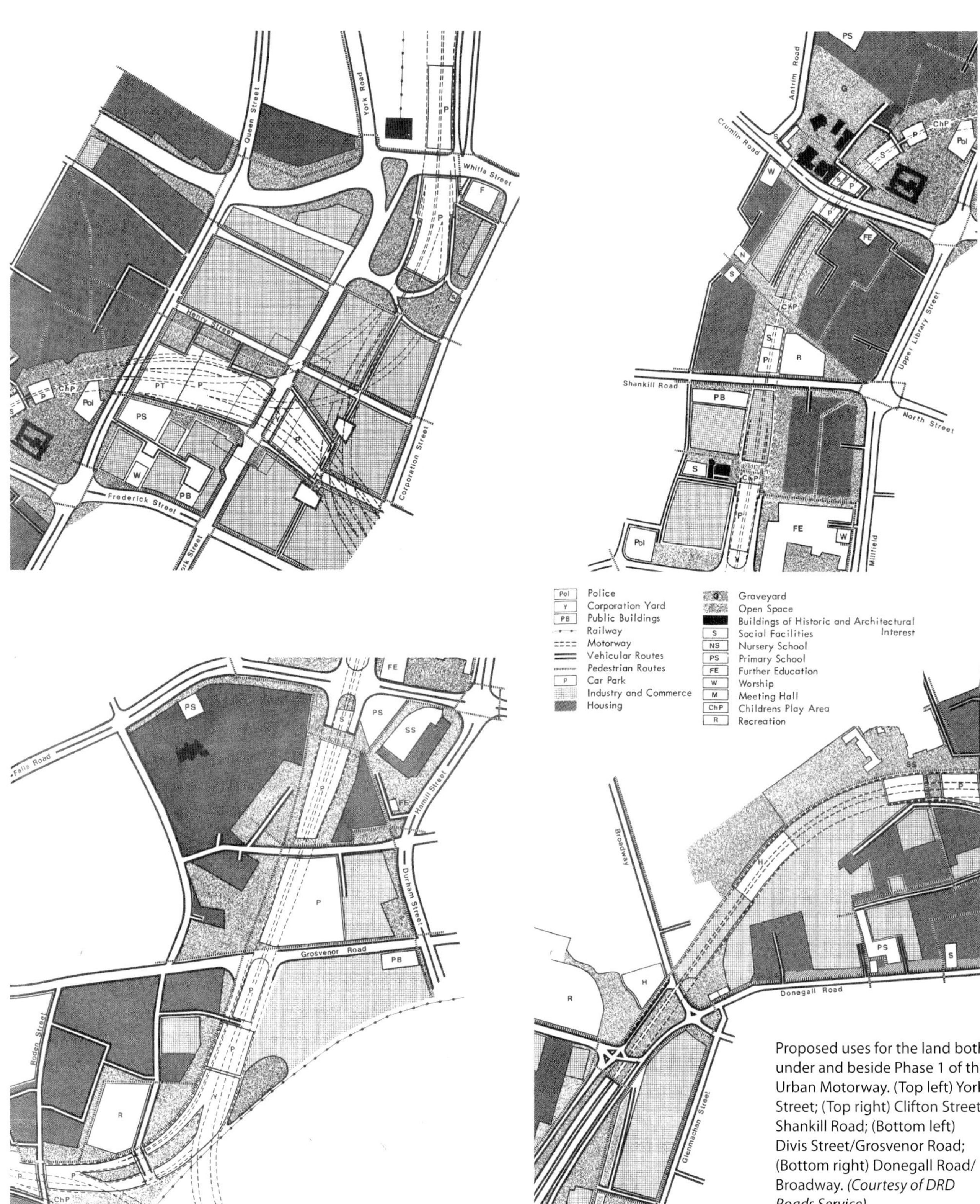

Proposed uses for the land both under and beside Phase 1 of the Urban Motorway. (Top left) York Street; (Top right) Clifton Street/ Shankill Road; (Bottom left) Divis Street/Grosvenor Road; (Bottom right) Donegall Road/ Broadway. *(Courtesy of DRD Roads Service)*

The M2 Motorway

Despite the lack of work on the ground during the land-acquisition phase, work was progressing on a related part of Belfast's motorway system – the M2 'foreshore' section. An isolated section of the M2 motorway from Greencastle to Glengormley (at Sandyknowes) had opened in October 1966, but it was initially poorly utilised because it did not extend into the city and on its own offered only limited benefits to traffic.[16] Work to extend the motorway into Belfast began in November 1966 by infilling the foreshore of Belfast Lough with four million tons of basalt.[17] This work was finally completed in May 1970.

The M2 hill section, seen looking south-east from Bellevue Bridge (Antrim Road) shortly after opening in 1966. The third 'climbing' lane provided up the hill was a late and very worthwhile addition to the scheme. *(Deputy Keeper of the Records, Public Record Office of Northern Ireland PRONI INF/7a/12/9)*

View looking south towards the Fortwilliam interchange on the M2 foreshore under construction around 1971/72. The land for the junction had to be first reclaimed from the sea, then built up high enough to provide a roundabout above the motorway. *(via DRD Roads Service)*

The Greencastle interchange on the M2 motorway seen looking south in May 1973. It connected the existing hill section (to the right) with the more recently completed foreshore section. The stubs for the planned M5 motorway, which was opened in 1980, can be seen at the point the motorway curves to the right. All the land visible to the left of the railway was reclaimed from the sea for the motorway. *(via DRD Roads Service)*

The temporary terminus of the M2 foreshore on Whitla Street is visible at the right of this photograph from 1979. The empty ground in the middle of the picture had been cleared for the planned extension of the M2 to meet the Urban Motorway, as indeed it does today. The roads running parallel to either side of this area of ground are (upper) York Street and (lower) Corporation Street. This whole area was previously occupied by housing. *(Cecil Newman, BELUM.Yn6655.7, © National Museums Northern Ireland, Collection Ulster Museum)*

Because it was planned to fork at Greencastle to feed into the existing M2 and the planned M5, the M2 foreshore section was constructed with dual-five lanes (except for a short section beneath the Fortwilliam interchange), which made it the widest motorway in the British Isles at the time. It opened to traffic on 22 May 1973, after almost seven years of work.[17] Even after all this time the Urban Motorway still did not exist, and so the M2 was forced to terminate in a rather ungainly manner at a set of temporary traffic lights on Whitla Street, close to the docks. Although criticised for its extravagance at the time it opened,[17] the wisdom of the scale of the foreshore section has been confirmed in the decades since. Because of its high capacity, few realise that it is Northern Ireland's busiest road, carrying over 113,000 vehicles per day in 2009 – significantly more than either the M1 or Westlink.[18]

Attempts at Construction

The first proper work on the Urban Motorway scheme began in spring 1970, with a £600,000 contract to relocate some of the many utilities that ran beneath the route of Phase 1.[2,11] Due to the piecemeal nature of the land clearances it was decided in 1970 that the construction works would be broken up into smaller chunks. This was partly to allow construction on the cleared portions of the site to begin straight away, and partly to afford smaller local companies a greater chance of winning contracts to work on the scheme.

A year later, in March 1971, the main construction contracts had still not begun, with the government saying that the plan was to open the tenders at the "end of the year" with work to begin "possibly spring next year [1972]".[19] The work eventually did go out to tender, but the developers then found it almost impossible to find anyone willing to carry out the work. This was almost entirely down to the violent civil disorder, which reached its peak that year. As Wiener explains:

> *...firms were ... reluctant to commit men and materials to these areas especially as the scheme was bitterly opposed by local residents. The Official IRA from the beginning, and later parts of the Ulster Defence Association, made it clear that they were prepared to take more direct action to stop the road going through ... this was clearly not a bluff and it was something well within the capabilities of the organisations to arrange...*[14]

Such was their desperation to find a way to advance the scheme that a prominent industry journal would report in late 1973 that there was then "a somewhat unorthodox contractual idea" consisting of "a £4m 'pay as you go' piling contract" which would be payable to the contractor on the basis of "the cost per foot of pile driven".[20] An attempt was made to carry out piling for the M2 end of the scheme at Whitla Street late in 1973,[10] but was quickly abandoned.[21] It was abundantly clear that until the civil disorder subsided it would not be possible to progress with the scheme.

1972 Public Inquiry

With the changed political landscape in the wake of the introduction of Direct Rule, planning laws in Northern Ireland were brought into line with the rest of the United Kingdom. Coupled with the evident opposition to the Belfast Urban Motorway and other road schemes in the city, the government decided to hold a public inquiry into the 1969 'Belfast Transportation Plan', with the exception of Phase 1 of the Urban Motorway since it was theoretically already under construction. The inquiry heard evidence between 28 February and 31 May 1972 and was chaired by Brian M Rutherford, a solicitor for the Ministry of Development.[14]

R Travers Morgan, the consultants who had developed the various plans, had a surprising amount of input to the inquiry, not only providing dossiers to support the scheme at the inquiry, but going so far as to offer advice on how the inquiry itself should be structured.[3]

In contrast to the uneventful inquiry three years previously, this inquiry saw vocal opposition to all aspects of the Transportation Plan. Cinalli notes two significant features of the 1972 inquiry that distinguishes it from the 1969 one. Firstly, after three years of violence the people of Belfast had become highly politicised and now understood how the system of government worked and how it could be influenced. Secondly, the violence had led to the establishment of numerous community and government groups that gave people a collective voice with which to express themselves. The fact that both of these elements were missing in 1969 helps explain why they proceeded so differently.[22] At the same time, it is also interesting that, in the main, opponents to the scheme chose to act within the legal boundaries of the 1972 public inquiry, choosing to present facts and conduct research as their chief tools of opposition rather than simply refusing to co-operate.

Opposition came from several quarters. The Sandy Row Redevelopment Association (SRRA) presented a comprehensive critique of the plan, later published as a book, in which they argued that Phase 3 of the motorway scheme (and particularly a plan for a trunk road to relieve Lisburn Road that would run north-south through Sandy Row)[6] would herald the wholesale destruction of their community through the demolition of 1,450 of the 2,400 houses in the area. They argued for the principle of the 'superior value of the community', ie that a community had an intrinsic value that surpassed economics:

Adults and children on Sandy Row protesting against the Urban Motorway, carrying a monster seemingly representing the redevelopment programme. 28 February 1972. *(Belfast Telegraph)*

> *If the proposals put forward in the Belfast Urban Area Plan were implemented, the historic and thriving community of 7,000 people living in the Sandy Row area would be annihilated and the resultant environment, in which a quarter of the present population would be expected to live, would be intolerable.*[23]

They believed that cancellation of the entire Urban Motorway scheme was the only option:

> *In light of its evidence and prevailing opinion in the city, the Belfast Urban Area Plan should be reviewed and the whole concept of an Urban Motorway which encircles the city centre, and to which everything else is subservient, should be rejected.*[23]

This is not to say that the residents objected to rebuilding their ageing homes, just that they wanted them rebuilt in the same location, a point that was made repeatedly in many areas of the western world at the time.[38] As resident Janet Magilton said "The sooner they get some of these houses knocked down the better. Many are almost falling down already".[24]

Nationalist representatives of west Belfast similarly argued that the road would run too close to newly constructed housing and lead to unacceptable levels of noise and air pollution. After the public inquiry the SDLP's Tom Donnolly summed up his view of public opinion:

Close study has convinced [the residents] that the motorway would be a monstrosity. Areas like the Cullingtree Road-Divis Flats complex in the Lower Falls and Sandy Row and the Shankill Road would be greatly affected by increased noise and exhaust pollution … the people of the areas are completely opposed to the motorway plan.[25]

Others argued against the road plan from different angles. The Churches Central Committee For Community Work (comprising the Presbyterian, Church of Ireland, Methodist and Roman Catholic churches) and the Northern Ireland Council of Social Services argued that the road scheme would 'box in' residents and physically prevent the reintegration of segregated communities.[22] They gave evidence that the M1 and the land cleared for Phase 1 of the Urban Motorway had already led to increased sectarian polarisation and that the elevated motorway would perpetuate this. They said "it looks as if we are putting into fixed moulds, and in physical moulds, and in physical form, segregated areas in the city … for the next one hundred years at least".[26]

Some argued that the province lacked the economic and physical resources for such an ambitious scheme. Others questioned the predictions of the rate of rising car usage in the city. Still others argued that the various roads wasted huge amounts of land that would be better used for houses and businesses.

In addition, many opposed the plan due to the perceived negative impact that major road schemes had had on other cities. Some argued that public transport was being sidelined, and that it was possible for public transport to eliminate the need for the motorway with less overall investment than was proposed for all the roads in the Belfast Transportation Plan. Nottingham was elevated as an example of a city that had successfully placed public transport at the core of their transportation plans, although some have questioned the validity of the comparison.[27] Students opposed to the Urban Motorway even staged an impromptu 'street theatre' on Royal Avenue on 29 February satirising the whole plan.[28]

The planners argued that, while the road certainly would have many of the negative effects outlined by others, these costs were not as serious as the problems that would be caused by doing nothing. Currently the city's two motorways ended in a very unsatisfactory way on city streets – the M1 at a roundabout on Donegall Road and the M2 at traffic lights on Whitla Street. The city streets were already almost gridlocked, and traffic levels were rising all the time. Without the Urban Motorway to link everything together, they argued, city traffic would soon cease to move at all. The consultants, R Travers Morgan, commented:

…we feel that many objectors do not appreciate the scale of the increased car ownership and usage expected … and do not fully realise the effects the predicted traffic growth

would have on ease of movement about the Urban Area, and on environmental conditions within the Area.[29]

Congestion, they argued, would result in Belfast Port losing vital income for the city, industry relocating to other parts of the UK and business being unable to operate. The city would then descend into a downward economic spiral. For the planners, the consequences of cancelling the scheme were too horrific to contemplate.

Interestingly, the planners did privately concede that if the road plan was not adopted, then the next-best option would be "deliberate traffic restraint methods", although they felt that this would be "inferior to a roads-investment strategy". They also noted that "road pricing may be a suitable way to operate an improved road system beyond the Plan period".[29]

In addressing the issue of community severance, the planners clearly felt that this issue was exaggerated. R Travers Morgan noted that many psychological barriers already exist in cities, such as rivers, railways and roads and that the Urban Motorway and associated road schemes would "in time, become accepted" and predicted that as new development occurred around the structures, "in the course of time [the] road will become largely integrated with its surroundings".[30]

In the end, the Inspector agreed with the planners that the benefits of the current transportation plan outweighed the costs, again appealing to the principle of the 'greater good'. In his report, published in September 1973, he admitted that "it is regrettable but inevitable that some people will have to be adversely affected for the benefit of the community at large" but said that in light of the evidence he had heard he did not see sufficient cause "to recommend the abandonment of motorway construction in Belfast, the use of available land for house and office buildings and the transfer of available funds from motorway construction to the improvement and subsidy of public transport".[26]

Protestors disrupting bus services in protest at the Urban Motorway in October 1973, a month after its approval by the government. *(Workers Party of Ireland)*

He also recommended that the policy of seeking very high densities in the re-housing programme should be discontinued, that further development of high-rise flats should end, and that in future new housing should be provided in two or three storey houses at ground level with no more than 125 persons per acre.[31] This recommendation was accepted, and has informed public housing policy ever since.

The government accepted the bulk of the Inspector's recommendations on 12 September 1973.[31] They accepted that the Urban Motorway should be built ("without it, the relief of the Central Area from congestion … could not be achieved").[31] They also suggested that the Lagan bridge element of Phase 2 (referred to hitherto as Phase 2A) could be built ahead of the rest of Phase 2 to realise its benefits at the earliest date. However they reiterated that a decision on whether to construct Phases 2 and 3 was being deliberately being left to a later date:

It could be that changes in traffic forecast for future traffic or a radical shift in public attitudes on the role of the car could alter the present view that the motorway ring should be completed … it would be possible to go ahead later [with Phases 2 and 3] but equally it would be possible to postpone it.[32]

These words would prove prophetic.

The transportation plan had survived the public inquiry with few material changes. However, as has been discussed previously, no significant construction work was able to take place on Phase 1 of the Urban Motorway during 1972 or 1973 due to civil disturbances in west Belfast. Meanwhile, not happy with the outcome of the public inquiry, many groups in Belfast decided to continue their battle against the Transportation Plan.

Changing Attitudes

The early 1970s saw changes in the attitude of the London government to urban road building. The British government itself admitted in 1972 that there was "increasing public concern" about urban road building and noted that current policy seemed to be leading to "the swamping of city streets by private motor cars and intrusive heavy lorries".[33] A Select Committee of the House of Commons recommended that "national policy should seek to promote public transport and discourage the journey to work by car in city areas" and that "the urban roads programme should be abolished".[33] Even the Northern Ireland government itself admitted in 1972 that "thinking in certain other major cities has turned against urban motorway projects".[31]

A large number of high profile schemes were cancelled or scaled back during these years in the face of overwhelming opposition and deteriorating finances. The hugely expensive 'Ringways' scheme, which would have seen the construction of four concentric motorways in and around London, including one in the city centre, was eventually stopped in 1973 after several years of protest – the M25 being the cobbled-together remnant of the plan. The government appeared to be losing its resolve to press ahead with controversial motorway schemes in urban areas.

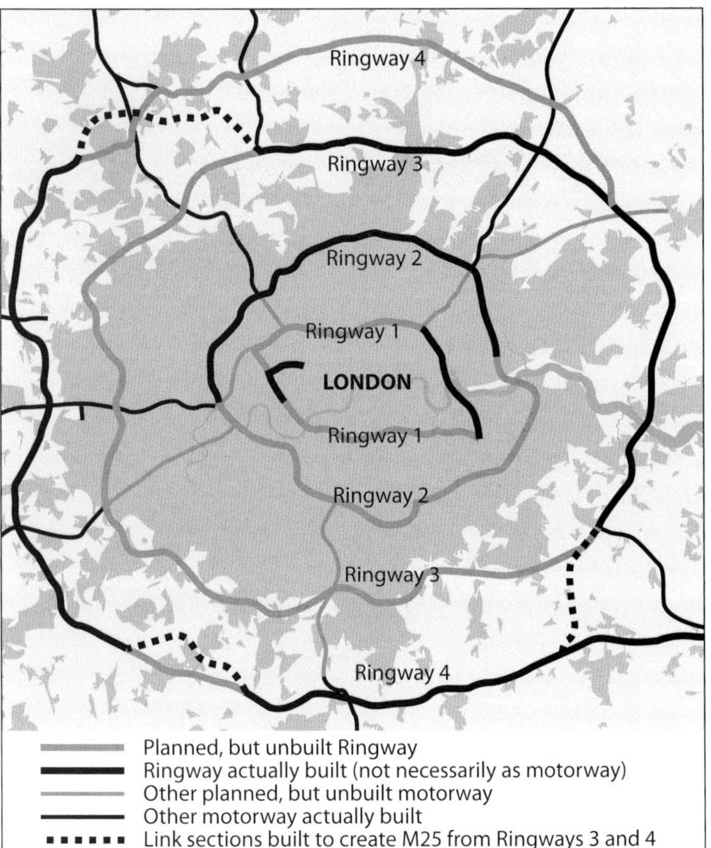

Simplified map of the proposed London Ringways, and the parts which were actually constructed. *(Based on research by Chris Marshall and others, www.cbrd.co.uk)*

The UK government had set up the Urban Roads Committee in 1969 to examine the whole area of urban road policy. They produced two major reports in 1972 which recommended a new approach to the planning of urban roads.[34,35] They emphasised the consideration of indirect costs, and the need to involve the public to a greater degree during the planning stages. They emphasised that urban roads must pay better attention to severance, air pollution, noise, pedestrian access and visual impact. They also suggested changes in the law, which came into effect in Northern Ireland under the *Land Acquisition and Compensation (NI) Order (1973)* and which gave a greater number of people more rights to compensation for the effects of new road schemes, and required the government to install mitigating measures (such as double glazing) free of charge in affected properties.

In 1973, in the wake of the 1972 public inquiry, a diverse group of academics and professionals centred at Queen's formed the Belfast Urban Study Group (BUS).[22] The aim of the group was to inform reasoned debate about the Urban Motorway by conducting and publishing research, and their first report was published later the same year.[36] In the report the group challenged the underlying rationale for the motorway, ie that traffic levels would render the city unusable to industry and trigger an economic collapse. They argued that an alternative outer ring road that avoided the city centre entirely could accommodate traffic to and from the docks. They then offered a detailed rationale of how the aim of preventing commuter gridlock could be achieved at lower economic and social cost by the provision of a subsidised public transport system coupled with measures designed to dissuade people driving cars into the city centre. The BUS urged politicians to "abandon the Travers Morgan road plans; halt all road building in Belfast and to commission one or two teams of consultants to produce alternative plans based on a commitment to public transport".[36] Due to the influence of the members of the BUS, many politicians were attracted to the meetings that it held.

Looking back at this era with the hindsight of the early twenty first century, this view of public transport as a 'magic pill' that would solve traffic problems may appear a little naïve. The experience of the 40 years that have passed since shows that the convenience and security of the private car is so great that motorists are prepared to accept even quite severe congestion before they will consider public transport alternatives. By this logic (unless cars are actually banned) congestion is essentially inevitable, and any notion that it can be eliminated cannot be taken seriously. It seems likely that, even with an entirely free public transport network, many people would have continued to choose to use their cars for many journeys. It thus seems unlikely that the public transport alternative espoused by the BUS could have had the degree of impact on congestion that they predicted at the time. Indeed, if it had had the effect of reducing congestion to such a high degree, it would likely have encouraged more people to drive on the less-congested streets, leading to a return to the original situation.

Weiner characterises the opposition to the motorway as one battle in a wider class war between the working classes and the ruling elite.[14] Seen from this perspective, those most likely to benefit from the motorway (the Protestant middle and ruling classes) were implementing a scheme whose impacts would be primarily borne by those least likely to benefit (the Protestant and Catholic working classes). Weiner therefore sees the scheme in socialist terms as a prime example of the exploitation of the proletariat and identifies a conscious effort on the part of the working classes to form a coherent opposition. This was most successful in Catholic areas, partly because Phase 1 primarily affected Catholic areas, but partly because the Nationalist community was already mobilising itself politically. The various groups came together under the umbrella of the Greater West Belfast Community Association (GWBCA).

The Republican Clubs (Official Sinn Féin) also supported the opposition to the scheme; whilst they regarded armed action against the state and the pursuit of Irish unity to be their primary activities, they also seem to have attached importance to social struggle. In a 1973 document heavily influenced by socialist thinking, Republicans set out their opposition to the road on the grounds that it would cause enormous damage to working class communities, proposing a total ban on private cars from the city centre. However they clearly see it merely as a facet of a bigger ideological issue: "The Belfast Urban Motorway is only one symptom of a common disease, capitalism, which must be got rid of".[37] The document makes a series of accusations of bribery and corruption against prominent retail and industrial companies in the city. Interestingly, the Republican Clubs were not opposed to road building, merely the building of roads in inner cities. The same document advocates the completion of the M2 foreshore, the cross-harbour bridge, the Outer Ring and a motorway from Craigavon to Newry.

With the notable exception of the SRRA, the Protestant working classes found it more difficult to formulate a coherent opposition. On the one hand, they were in a similar position to their Catholic neighbours in having their homes demolished and communities displaced. On the other hand, the fact that Republicans were leading opposition to the motorway rendered it almost impossible for them to join the campaign. Perversely, their loyalty to the unionist cause made them reticent to speak out against the plans formulated by unionist politicians because opposition to the Urban Motorway became entangled and confused with opposition to Stormont.[14] It therefore took much more time for widespread opposition to formulate in these areas.

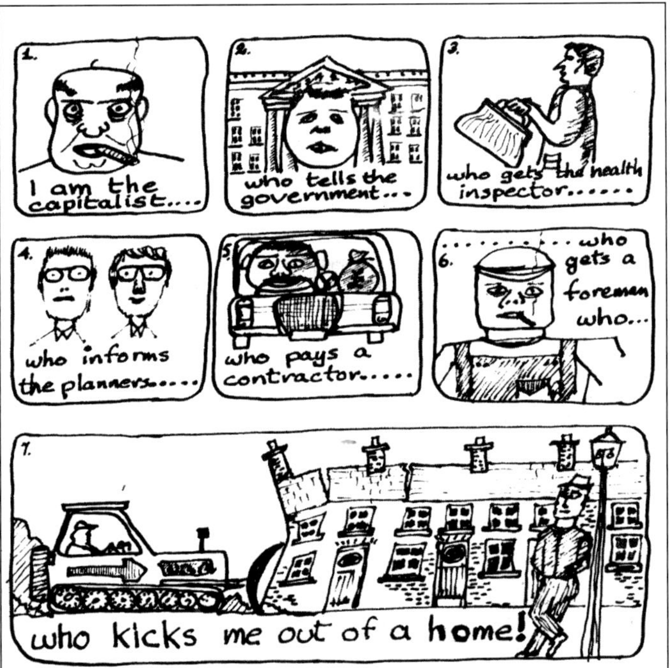

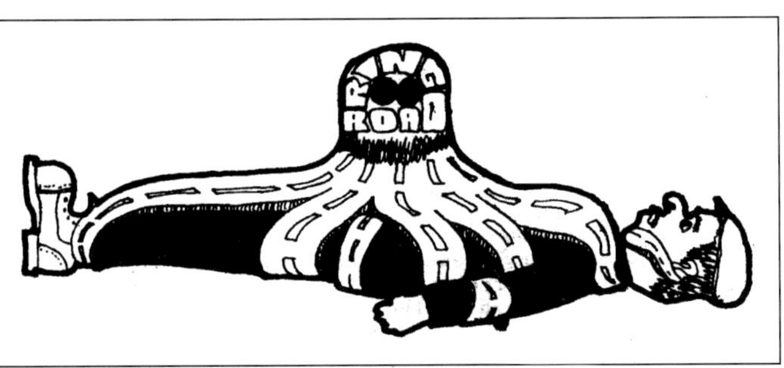

Various cartoons from the early 1970s depicting the Belfast Urban Motorway as various kinds of monster, and as a capitalist conspiracy to exploit working class communities in the pursuit of wealth. *(Workers Party of Ireland)*

Although it is possible to paint the events of the early 1970s as a socialist class struggle, one can paint a different picture of naïve planners being caught off guard by changing times. During the Second World War and the years that followed, the authorities got used to a top-down 'command-and-obey' approach to government that was not seriously questioned until the late 1960s. While it is true that the planner's efforts to involve communities in their decisions were lamentable, it is also true that they were simply following the established practice of the day, a point that had been made already.[38] The political mobilisation of the early 1970s would have come as a genuine surprise to planners who were used to looking at problems with detachment, presenting high-level plans to the public and then proceeding directly to construction. Unsure what to do in the face of such unprecedented opposition, many probably decided to single-mindedly press ahead with the scheme in the hope that once it was actually completed, the dust would settle and dissent would dissolve.

However, the changes that took place in public attitudes in the early 1970s were for good. Never again would it be possible for planners to progress major schemes without serious public consultation. This was not a bad thing. As Tim Morton recollects:

> *It created great work for us transport planners because we had to start thinking much more rigorously and start analysing in greater depth the reasons for new roads and their benefits in order to support schemes at Inquiry stage. The strength of opposition forced us to considerably raise the bar in our modelling and analytical techniques in order to be able to answer the questions from objectors, and justify what we were proposing.*[39]

Belfast City Council

In October 1973 Belfast Corporation officially ceased to exist as the 26 new local councils came into being, along with the new Belfast City Council. The new council had lost all its powers to build roads, and had therefore lost control of the Urban Motorway scheme. On the same date, responsibility for roads was handed to the newly formed Roads Executive (re-named Roads Service in 1974) under the leadership of Noel Prescott.[40] Roads Service itself was under the direction of Westminster via the Direct Rule Ministers.

Since the Urban Motorway was no longer a council project, some local councillors may have at last felt free to air their true feelings about the road. At the first meeting of Belfast City Council, SRRA chairman and Unionist councillor Harry Fletcher, along with an Alliance Party councillor, put forward a motion "calling on the government to reconsider the need for the ring road".[14] The Unionist majority was not united on the issue; some councillors abstained, while others supported the motion, with the result that the council actually passed the motion, by 27 votes to 8. This decision was important for the scheme since it provided an indication to the government that the city of Belfast was now opposed to the very scheme that its earlier leaders had launched.

Nevertheless, support for the scheme was very strong in other quarters. Local road planners were still very much convinced of the need at least for Phase 1 of the Urban Motorway. The traffic growth forecasts remained as terrifying as they had always been and the city's streets continued to clog up with more traffic every year. In addition, almost all planning decisions over the previous three decades had been made on the assumption that there would be an upgraded road system. The two existing motorways were not joined together in anything approaching a satisfactory matter, and Belfast port remained accessible from the south only by travelling along city centre streets. Finally, so much planning, relocation and demolition had already taken place for Phase 1 of the motorway that it seemed foolish to stop work so late in the day. Many politicians outside of west Belfast remained convinced that the road was needed. Even the newly formed Alliance Party, whose own members were actively opposing the scheme, declared in 1974 that "Belfast needs its urban motorway".[41] The argument that the greater good for Northern Ireland would be served by the motorway, despite its local impact, remained a compelling one.

The Urban Motorway debate was now essentially a direct standoff between the people of west Belfast and the London government, with Belfast City Council sitting uneasily in between. With opinion so finely balanced, it would be a combination of relatively small factors that would decide which way the balance would tip.

CHAPTER 8
ROADS OR BUSES?

The Oil Crisis

The Oil Crisis of late 1973 was one of the factors that came out of the blue and had a major impact on Belfast's transportation policy. In response to perceived US support for Israel during the Yom Kippur War, the Organisation of Arab Petroleum Exporting Countries (OAPEC) imposed an oil embargo on key western nations (but not the United Kingdom). This caused almost immediate oil shortages with a resultant surge in fuel prices. From a little over US$3 per barrel in October 1973, the price quadrupled to US$12 per barrel by the beginning of 1974. The crisis continued until March 1974, when a negotiated settlement ended the embargo, but triggered an economic recession that, in the UK, lasted into 1975.

Although the embargo did not apply to the UK, the rapid rise in fuel prices nevertheless led to an energy crisis. This had a major impact on roads, as 25% of petroleum was used for road transport.[1] The government imposed many measures, including a 50 mph speed limit on all roads that had a higher speed limit. As people avoided driving where possible, traffic levels on UK roads fell for the first time since the war. It is estimated that the Oil Crisis resulted in a three-year delay in traffic growth; with 1973 traffic levels not being reached again until 1976.[1]

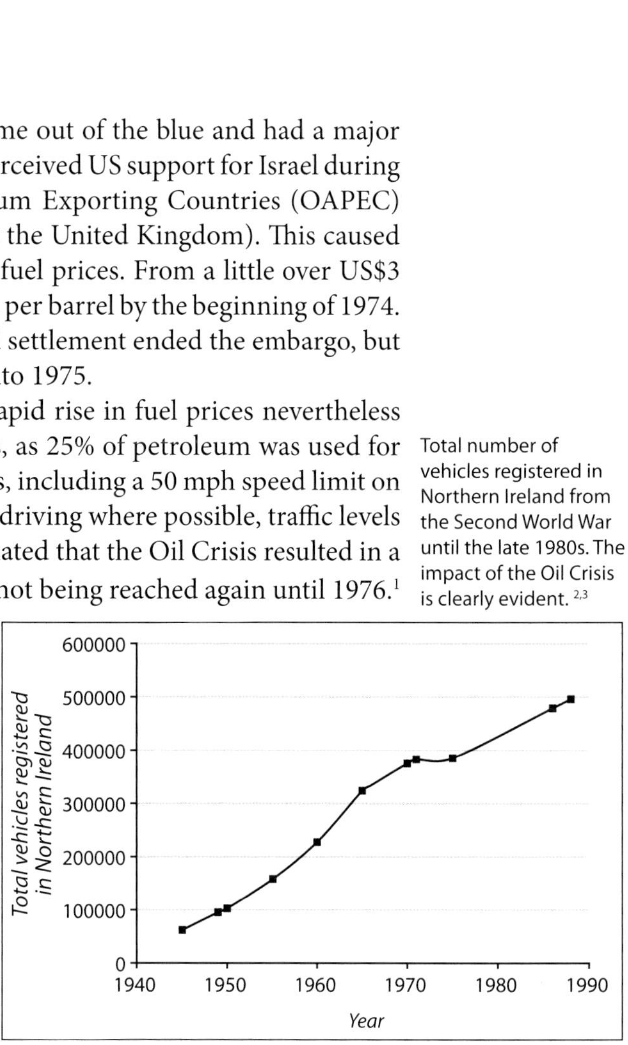

Total number of vehicles registered in Northern Ireland from the Second World War until the late 1980s. The impact of the Oil Crisis is clearly evident.[2,3]

A second trend, which may already have been in motion prior to the Oil Crisis, was that the accelerating growth in car ownership slowed from the early 1970s. This trend showed that the apocalyptic predictions made in the 1960s, which had informed most of the 1969 Transportation Plan, were excessively high. For example, the plan predicted that car ownership in Belfast would increase by 290% between 1966 and 1986. In fact, car ownership in the province rose by a little over 140% in this time period, about half of what was predicted. Traffic levels and car ownership were still going up, of course, but not at the rate predicted.

With hindsight this was predictable, since there are a finite number of people in Northern Ireland who can buy and own cars, and the rapid surge in ownership during the 1950s and 1960s can be accounted for by a high latent demand from a wealthier post-war populace. Without the long-term data that we now have, this trend would not have been quite so obvious in the mid 1970s, and indeed may even have been regarded as a statistical anomaly caused by the Oil Crisis.

To Glasgow and Nottingham

The government was still behind the construction of Phase 1 of the Urban Motorway in some form, regarding it as an essential element of the strategy to attract industry to the province, but the opposition from Belfast City Council was embarrassing. Although the Direct Rule Ministers had the power to proceed with the plan regardless of what local politicians thought, in the current political climate the government felt it would not be prudent to proceed without the council's support. They therefore set about attempting to find a way to persuade the Council to change its mind. (A short-lived Assembly and Executive existed in Northern Ireland from July 1973 until May 1974, in an attempt to restore devolved government. This collapsed and power was once again in the hands of the Direct Rule ministers.)

The government adopted a four-pronged strategy of (a) having discussions with those groups opposed to the plan (b) convincing the councillors that the Urban Motorway would work (c) of offering concessions to the 'dissenting' unionist councillors, since unionists held the majority and were therefore the only ones who could sway the vote and (d) gaining the support of the media for a compromise solution.[4,5]

The first approach involved having discussions with various interested parties. As this coincided with the short-lived Assembly, this involved meetings with the Ulster Unionist Minister of the Environment, Roy Bradford. Wiener describes these meetings as "the least successful" approach by the government since the Minister's view was essentially that the road should go ahead, and the discussions seemed rather pointless to the scheme's opponents. The BUS group argued again for an outer ring road combined with subsidised public transport. Mr Bradford admitted that noise might well be an issue in flats closest to the motorway, but if so the flats would be put to alternative uses. He also argued that the motorway would allow "freedom of choice for car owners".[6]

A key element of the second approach was the organisation of visits for members of the City Council to Glasgow and Nottingham to view successful examples of urban motorways and public transport respectively. Although a much larger city than Belfast, Glasgow had developed an urban motorway plan that was very similar in substance, incorporating a motorway ring around the city centre with radial motorways leading away from it.[7] Glasgow, however, had begun work earlier and by the time of the visit half of the inner ring (the M8) had been constructed as well as a number of the radials. The visit to Glasgow took place during the first part of 1974 and was followed up in June of the same year by a visit to Nottingham to view the widely-acclaimed public transport system that had been developed there in response to the city's traffic problems. The result of the two visits seems to have been to convince some of the sceptics, including the vocal SDLP opponent Tom Donnolly, that the Urban Motorway would be good for Belfast.[5]

Although the M8 in Glasgow is arguably best known today for its daily peak time traffic jams, in 1974 it was brand new. As a masterpiece of functional engineering, it is as impressive and imposing today as it was when first built. The fact that parts of the M8 are depressed below ground level (to reduce the physical, visual and acoustic impact on the city streets) may have been one observation that helped to change the politicians' minds. In addition, although 4,400 homes had been demolished to make way for the central part of the motorway,[1] the city now sported numerous new high-rise flats and the visitors may have become convinced from Glasgow's experience that re-housing all the displaced families really could be achieved in a satisfactory manner.

Interestingly, both cities retain their respective foci today. Glasgow's half-finished plan was cancelled in 1980[7] but was later resurrected, with a modified form of the southern flank (the M74 extension) completed in 2011. Nottingham, meanwhile, was named in 2010 as England's least car-dependent city by the organisation 'Campaign for Better Transport', a group that lobbies for increased public transport investment.[8]

The M8 in Glasgow, here seen from Baird Street bridge above junction 15, forms part of an inner motorway box around the city centre. Both highly ambitious and destructive, Glasgow's urban motorway system was brand new in 1974 and would have appeared very impressive to the visitors from Belfast. *(Author's collection)*

The third approach was to offer concessions to unionist politicians opposed to the scheme in an effort to gain their support.[5] Fred Proctor of the DUP represented the Shankill Road area, which would be bisected by the Urban Motorway, and was strongly opposed to the scheme. Harry Fletcher was the UUP representative for the Sandy Row area who had put forward the motion against the motorway to the City Council. The government apparently acceded to Proctor's demand that the plan to widen the lower Shankill Road from two to four lanes be dropped, and agreed that if the noise levels were too high, then the flats adjacent to the motorway would not be used for residential use. Proctor was apparently also impressed by what he saw in Glasgow. The government made "significant concessions" to Fletcher, in line with the recommendations of the 1972 inquiry, which would drastically reduce the impact of the southern leg of the Urban Motorway and other related road schemes on Sandy Row. The result was that by July 1974 Proctor had been won round to accepting the motorway while Fletcher decided to abstain in a vote on the subject (see later in this chapter).[5]

Finally, the government brought the media round to the view that the motorway should proceed in some form. They did this by promoting a compromise: that Phase 1 of the Urban Motorway should proceed, as should the relatively uncontroversial Phase 2A (Lagan bridge) but that Phase 2B (at Short Strand) and Phase 3 (the southern leg) would be put on ice and reviewed only once Phase 1 was completed and could be observed in action. They also made changes to other proposed new roads at Sandy Row and promised greater environmental impact assessments.[5] This proposal achieved "the open support of the media".[4]

This process of reconsidering took nine months, a period of time in which the Council seemed unable or unwilling to make a decision, asking for additional information from Travers Morgan, and arranging meetings with representatives from the Belfast Urban Study Group (BUS) and the Greater West Belfast Community Association (GWBCA). Some have argued that the lengthy period of indecision was the result of a deliberate delaying tactic by the government.[5] The extent to which this is true is unknown, but there was also an element of genuine uncertainty on the part of public representatives who were faced with two very strong, but opposing, viewpoints on the right way forward. A vote was eventually taken in July 1974 at which Belfast City Council voted 25 to 12 in favour of proceeding with Phase 1 of the motorway.

Cold Realities

If 1973–74 was a time of changing viewpoints within Belfast City Council, then the same was true to an even greater extent within the British government. The Oil Crisis and the subsequent recession had brought cold economic realities to bear on the situation. The fact was that the ambitious 1969 'Belfast Transportation Plan' was now totally unaffordable. Since the plan depended on a very specific ordering of road schemes over a set plan period to meet predicted changes in the city, not being able to carry these out jeopardised the entire plan and its aims. The government was also acutely aware that public attitudes towards urban motorways had changed markedly since the 1960s.

However, even deeper problems were emerging with the 1969 plan, stemming from the fact that so many of its assumptions about the future were proving to be quite wide of the mark. These included:[9]

- Belfast's population was now expected to decline, rather than increase as had been predicted, due largely to population movements triggered by the 'Troubles', smaller household size and rising unemployment.
- The rate of increase of car ownership was not as great as had been anticipated (as discussed earlier in this chapter).
- The number of bus journeys was likely to be much lower than predicted due to general lack of investment. For example, between 1966 and 1971 the proportion of commuters in Belfast using the bus declined from 48% to 43%, while the number using a car increased from 20% to 26% (walking accounted for most of the remainder).[10]

On this basis, and notwithstanding their recent efforts to regain support for Phase 1 of the Urban Motorway, the government decided in late 1974 that a more comprehensive review of the entire transportation strategy was in order. In November 1974, R Travers Morgan (the firm responsible for the 1969 strategy) and Building Design Partnership were appointed to conduct the review. Their terms of reference were to study the feasibility of a new transportation plan that reduced costs by either (a) omitting the Urban Motorway entirely or (b) limiting it to Phase 1 and Phase 2A only. In keeping with the government's current policy they were also instructed to place a greater emphasis on the environment and provision for public transport in their proposals. They were asked to present a range of preliminary options for a revised transportation plan by early 1975 so that the government could decide which they wished to have studied in more detail.[11]

The consultants went to work, speaking once again to the various community groups and other interested bodies. To those who supported the Urban Motorway, especially the engineers who had devoted years of their professional careers to the scheme, this must have been a disappointing and frustrating period. They would have been aware that, had it not been for the 'Troubles', Phase 1 would almost certainly have been completed and in use by then, bringing tangible benefits to traffic in the city centre and on the two motorways. With public opinion moving away from urban motorways, there was a sense that Belfast had 'missed the boat' entirely, in a way that Glasgow (which at had at least completed half its ring) had not. However, with the land for Phase 1 already cleared, they must still have felt confident that at least that part of the plan would proceed in some form.

Central Distributor Box, Intermediate and Outer Ring Roads

Other than the Urban Motorway itself, one of the elements of the 1969 'Belfast Transportation Plan', which the authors of the plan regarded as essential, was the Central Distributor Box (hereafter referred to as the 'Box'). While the Urban Motorway was designed to link the various radial motorways in a freeflow manner, the Box was a ground level ring encircling the city centre within the circle of the motorway. The road was to have two or three lanes in each direction with regular traffic lights at each road it met. The idea was that vehicles arriving into the central area on the Urban Motorway would leave at the nearest exit and then join the Box to guide them more precisely to their destination. The 1969 Plan explicitly stated that the Urban Motorway would not work optimally without early provision of the Box.

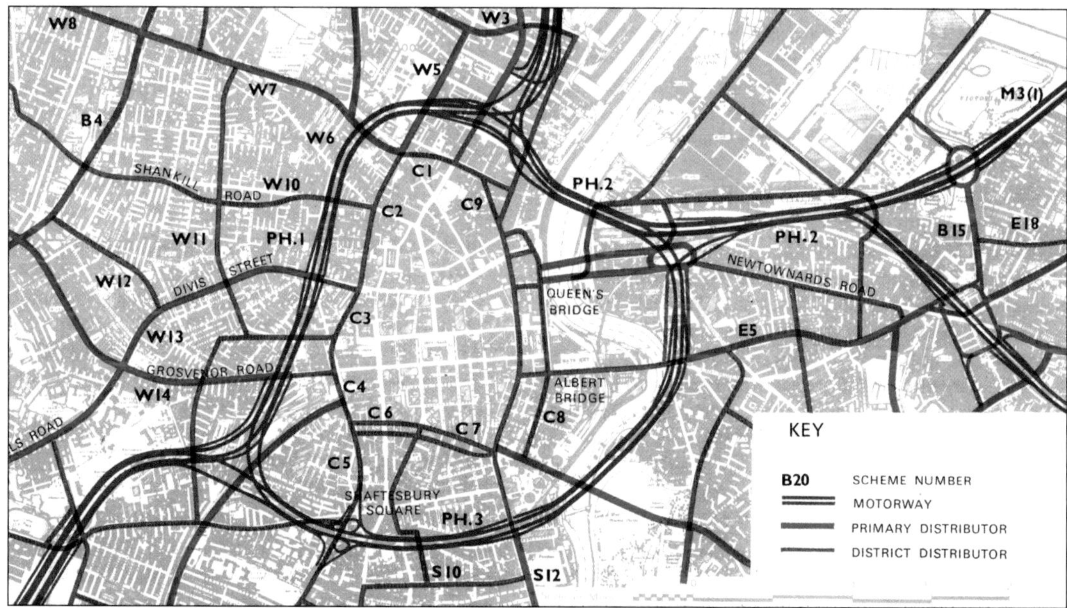

The Central Distributor Box (marked in green and labelled with C-numbers) as it appeared in the 1969 'Belfast Transportation Plan'. Note also the new junction on Ormeau Road and the relocated Shaftesbury Square junction, both facilitated by the deletion of the innermost section of the proposed M4. *(Courtesy of DRD Roads Service)*

The route of the northern half of the Box passed generally through commercial land and was relatively uncontroversial. The route of the southern half, in contrast, passed through four residential areas (Hamill Street, Sandy Row, lower Ormeau and the Markets), all but the first of which were also designated Regeneration Areas. It is not surprising, therefore, that by the mid 1970s the work that had been completed was exclusively on the northern half of the Box.

Although the 1969 Plan had recommended that work on the Box begin in 1970, in fact only limited work had been carried out on the north western part (widening of Carrick Hill and Millfield) and the eastern flank (improvements to Oxford and Victoria Streets). Plans to connect these two parts together via the northern flank (widening of Frederick Street and construction of Dunbar Link) were at an advanced stage (the latter opening in June 1980).[12]

While these sections of the Box functioned well, there was virtually no attempt to incorporate them into the fabric of the urban area. Dunbar Link, to pick an example, was a purely functional dual-carriageway that ploughed a diagonal path through the existing streets and buildings behind St Anne's Cathedral. As a road it was well engineered, but as part of the city centre fabric it was appalling; no serious attempt was made to reconstruct the truncated streetscape around it, almost no frontal development occurred, and pedestrian facilities were sparse. The

Dunbar Link, as seen from Corporation Street junction prior to the construction of the St Anne's Square development. As part of the Central Distributor Box it is a highly functional road but unsuccessful as a city streetscape. *(Author's collection)*

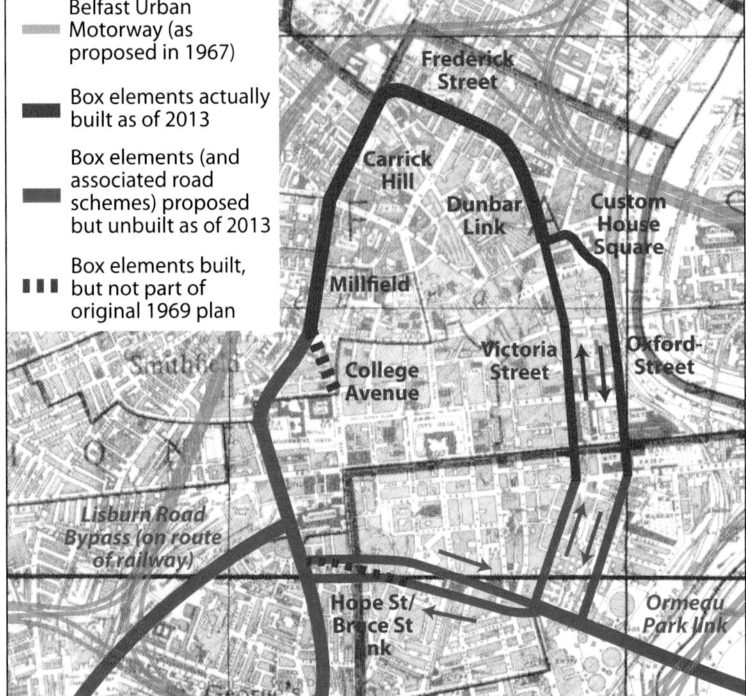

The sections of the Central Distributor Box and associated schemes that were built (green) and which remain unbuilt at the time of publication (red). One-way sections are marked by arrows. *(Base map 1940, Ordnance Survey)*

result was that it remained an urban wasteland devoid of life for the next 30 years. The Box, therefore, helped traffic move about but became a significant barrier to the free movement of people between the city centre and the surrounding residential areas. Important lessons were (eventually) learned from the development of the Box.

The major objections by the residents of places like Sandy Row, which have been previously described, were one reason for the lack of progress on the southern part of the Box, as was the slow progress of construction on replacement homes for those displaced by the redevelopments. Practically no work had taken place on the Outer Ring Road (sections between Knock and Belvoir[13] had been improved in the 1950s and early 1960s but only later would these become part of the coherent Outer Ring). No work at all had taken place on the Intermediate Ring Road which by now "had blighted good housing for some years ... particularly in the Cliftonville area", according to Belfast Divisional Planning Officer Neville Hawker.[11]

Developments in Public Transport

With the abolition of Belfast Corporation in 1973, the bus system in the city was re-formed as Citybus Limited, which came under the ownership of Ulsterbus. Ulsterbus was government owned and had been responsible for buses in the rest of Northern Ireland since 1967. Ulsterbus had been turning a profit, albeit with falling patronage, and they did manage to get Citybus to 'pay its way'.[14] However, they were unable to halt the steeper decline in patronage of Citybus services, which had started during the 1960s and accelerated with the advent of the 'Troubles'. Between 1966 and 1975 patronage of Citybus fell 51%.[10] The problem was exacerbated by the appearance of 'black taxis', which had replaced withdrawn buses in west Belfast and did huge damage to the viability of public transport.

There was some positive news with public transport when the Central Railway was reopened. This had been one of the few non-road recommendations of the 1969 'Belfast Transportation Plan'. The line had connected the Dublin railway line, with its terminus at Great Victoria Street, to the Bangor railway line, with its terminus at Queen's Quay, until its closure in 1963. The plan involved replacing the two termini with a single, central station. As railway historian Norman Johnston explains, "they realised it wasn't just people going into Belfast; there were people who wanted to go from Lisburn to Holywood. People who might leave their cars at home." [15]

The project involved substantial work, including new bridges over Middlepath Street and the River Lagan. In addition, whole sections of track bed had to be reconstructed. "No maintenance had been carried out to the drainage system over the previous ten years, with the result that the track bed was waterlogged and had to be dug out and rebuilt from scratch".[15] Work began on the project in 1973 with a total project cost of £2m. However, selling a large area of railway land near Great Victoria Street station, for the Urban Motorway project, offset £1m of this cost.[16]

The Central Railway reopened fully on 26 April 1976. On the same date, the newly built Central Station on East Bridge Street opened to the public. Great Victoria Street and Queen's Quay were then closed. For the first time in over ten years trains could run straight through from the Bangor line to the Dublin line.

Changes in Planning

In Belfast the lesson that the public did not want high-rise blocks of flats had been learned and further work on such schemes had been terminated. New developments by the Housing Executive concentrated instead on two or three-storey houses and maisonettes. Many of the flats were subsequently demolished (the demolition of Divis Flats was announced in October 1986) and likewise replaced by lower density housing. This had the side effect of creating a further shortage of residential building land.

The 'Matthew Plan' of 1962 was still the framework within which all regional planning decisions were being made. The plan envisaged decentralisation through a combination of a 'stop line' around Belfast (to prevent further expansion) and the planned growth of seven regional towns. This decentralisation was to be facilitated by the network of motorways and trunk roads.

The many changes in government policy that had occurred since the 'Matthew Plan' meant that, in December 1975, the government decided to adopt a new strategy to replace it. The

'Regional Physical Development Strategy 1975–95' (RPDS) confirmed Belfast's role as the major city, but did allow a relaxation of the stop line at Poleglass to tackle the chronic shortage of housing land for Catholic west Belfast. It also scrapped the idea of growing seven regional towns, with growth spread more thinly over 23 'district towns', equitably based around the 26 new district council areas.[17] The plan was adopted in 1977.

Buses or Roads?

The Consultants who were reviewing the 1969 'Belfast Transportation Plan' submitted their interim report to the government in May 1975, although it was not made public at that time.[11] The document set out six possible directions that a revised transport plan could take the city. These were:

A. Substantially improving the road network but making only modest changes to bus services.
B. Modest improvements to the road network, but with substantial improvements to bus services.
C. Modest improvements to the road network, but with substantial improvements to rail services.
D. Modest improvements to the road network, but with substantial improvements to both bus and rail services.
E. A balanced approach with roughly equal improvements to both the road network and buses.
F. Improvements to pedestrian and cycling facilities, plus some improvements to the bus services.

The government then consulted Belfast City Council[18] and the Council in turn canvassed public views.[9] This translated into an invitation for public comment with a six week deadline which did not attract a great deal of public interest.[17] The Council resolved on 2 July 1975 that they supported further study of options A and B only.[11]

The idea that Option B could have won out over Option A in the planning climate of the time is implausible. It seems that the government, too, saw a risk in being seen to offer up a 'straw man' as an alternative to a roads-based strategy. Therefore in August 1975 they announced that three options were to be developed further; the roads-based strategy (A), the bus-oriented strategy (B) and a mixed strategy (E).[19] In keeping with the current government policy of favouring buses over trains, the public transport options were almost entirely based on buses, and no rail-related options were taken forward to stage two. One of the Travers Morgan consultants, Ian Wallis, explained that in their view the rail network in Belfast "was very sparse compared with the bus network and for that reason there was little hope … of attracting passengers from the buses by improving the rail system".[9]

The consultants carried out their work using a computer system that predicted traffic levels on roads by feeding in various data. They included up-to-date figures and predictions of car ownership, population distribution and accurate figures on bus and rail usage. They did not repeat the traffic surveys carried out for the 1969 Plan to the same level of detail because they believed that the 'Troubles' were distorting patterns of travel. Although with hindsight we know that the 'Troubles' were to last over 30 years, this was not known at the time. Lavery, writing in 1977, notes that "the consultants did not assume that the troubles had never happened, but they did assume that the troubles would come to an end".[11] The computer system did, however, receive some new figures from various roadside counts and Roads Service's biannual traffic census. They also made predictions on commercial road usage based on current government policy. The consultants first developed the roads-based strategy (A) and then used a cost/benefit analysis to measure strategies B and E against this, taking into account fuel costs, bus fares, congestion, travel times and pollution.

Summary of the roads that would be built under each of the three options announced in 1975 and analysed at the 1977 Lavery Inquiry.

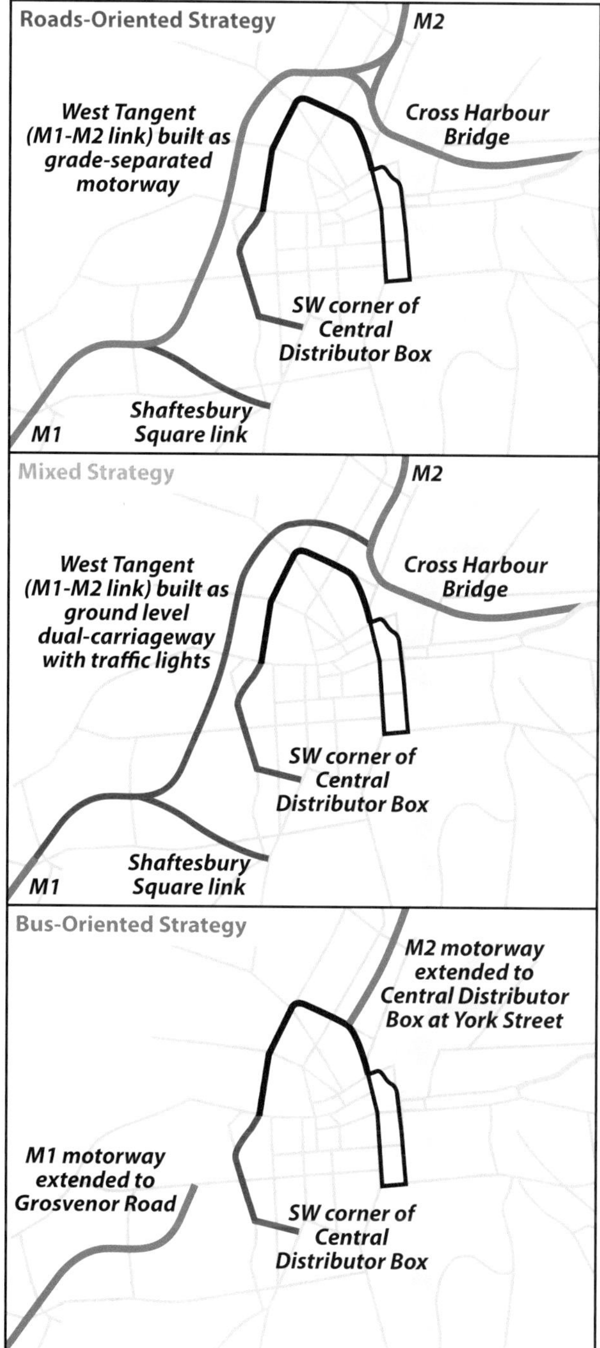

The consultants published their report setting out their calculations of the costs and benefits of each of the three options in September 1976.[20] All three options contained some element of road building, but the allocation of money for the ten years to 1986 was markedly different in each case, as set out below:[9]

STRATEGY	NEW ROADS	IMPROVED ROADS	TOTAL ROADS	BUS SYSTEM
ROADS (A)	£44m	£16m	£60m	£6m
MIXED (E)	£31m	£13m	£44m	£27m
BUSES (B)	£8m	£24m	£32m	£47m

The consultants' conclusions were largely based on economics rather than impacts on the city's streetscape and environment. They stopped short of making a recommendation but their figures show that, based on the cost/benefit analysis, strategy A (the roads-based strategy) was the most cost effective, with strategy B (the bus-based strategy) the least cost effective. Their calculations also showed that the bus-based strategy would only slightly reduce bus journey times (average 27 minute journey compared to 31 minutes in the roads-based strategy).

The plan for the roads-oriented strategy was to construct Phase 1 of the Urban Motorway (referred to in the report as the 'West Tangent'), with grade separated junctions at each of the main radial routes. It also included construction of Phase 2A of the Urban Motorway (the cross-harbour bridge connecting the West Tangent to the Sydenham Bypass); the extension of the M2 to meet the Urban Motorway at York Street; a link road from the West Tangent to Shaftesbury Square; and the south western corner of the Central Distributor Box. Phases 2B and 3

City centre streets to be pedestrianised under proposals in the mid 1970s.

of the Urban Motorway (the eastern and southern legs) were not to be built in this strategy.

The mixed strategy was a scaled back version of the roads-oriented strategy. In this plan, the West Tangent would be built at ground level with traffic lights at each junction. The money saved would be used to provide extra investment in bus services.

In the bus-oriented strategy none of the elements of the Urban Motorway would be built. Instead, the M1 would be extended by about 1 km to terminate at Grosvenor Road, and the M2 would be extended by a short distance to terminate at York Street. The significant amount of money this would save would be used to boost the bus fleet to increase their frequency by 140% at peak times and 250% at other times, as well as funding a subsidy to reduce average fares from 13p to 9p. It also proposed increasing city centre car parking charges for commuters by a massive 450% to act as a disincentive to commuting by car which, it was estimated, could remove 40% of the current number of cars from the city centre.

All three strategies involved the pedestrianisation of city centre shopping streets to improve the environment for shoppers.

The government released a publicity leaflet in September 1976[9] which set out the three options for public consultation, although the document has been criticised for being "essentially shallow with little detail".[17] A number of observations can be made about this document.

Firstly, its summary emphasised numerical measures, such as the number of minutes shaved off bus journeys or the average road speed of a car (facts of limited relevance to members of the public), while providing little information on the factors that the public found profoundly important, such as severance and the impact of major roads on residential communities. For example, the main objection of the groups who supported buses was that road building was destroying the city, not the fact that it took 31 minutes rather than 27 minutes to get into the city centre by bus. At the time this document was perceived as an attempt to steer public opinion towards the roads-oriented strategy, although the somewhat naïvely framed conclusions suggest that the planners at R Travers Morgan had not really grasped the nature of the objections to the plan.

Secondly, the document was essentially a scaling-back of the 1969 'Belfast Transportation Plan', rather than a genuine attempt to go back to first principles. This is not surprising, given that the planners were explicitly reviewing the 1969 Plan and were instructed to make as few changes as possible to land use allocations in that plan. However, an opportunity was probably missed to go back a further step and reappraise transport at a more fundamental level. It has been admitted by Roads Service itself that despite policy changes the government was a rather reluctant convert to environmentally sensitive transport:

> *[The scaling back of road plans] reflected a more realistic view of the likely level of funding. While there was an increasing awareness that new roads could have detrimental effects on the environment, there was little change in the overall policy direction of Transportation in the 70s and 80s.*[21]

While the land for the West Tangent had been cleared for many years, the road had not been constructed and numerous options for use of the land were genuinely still open. Given the major land shortages for housing, in Catholic west Belfast in particular, this was not an insignificant point.

Thirdly, the document did not adequately recognise that the roads-orientated and bus-oriented strategies would have markedly different impacts on two very different socio-economic groups. Middle class people generally owned private cars, although there was increasing penetration into the working classes. The roads-oriented strategy would therefore benefit this socio-economic group while offering few improvements for the working classes. The bus-oriented strategy, by contrast, would primarily benefit the working class communities who lacked private cars, but would disadvantage the middle classes who had hitherto been able to drive into the city centre and pay for cheap all-day parking. In the 1970s owning a

The land cleared for the west tangent of the Urban Motorway was still lying derelict in 1979 (the inset highlighting the area in question). On the extreme left is Roden Street, while Grosvenor Road runs left-right across the centre of the image with the Divis Flats just above. The Clifton Street area is at the very top of the picture. *(Cecil Newman, BELUM.Yn6652.35 © National Museums Northern Ireland, Collection Ulster Museum)*

car was an aspiration of most people, and even with the traffic problems it provided freedom on a huge scale. With hindsight it seems optimistic to suggest that large numbers of middle class people would have switched to buses, even with drastically reduced fares and increased parking charges. Fundamentally the choice was whether transportation in Belfast would be developed to favour the working or the middle classes. The document, therefore, effectively pitted the ambitions of two social groups against each other.

Finally, it is noteworthy that all of the plans involved some road building. The criticism that the option of building no new roads was not even considered was levelled repeatedly at the time, and was held up as proof that the planners were secretly trying to maintain a roads-oriented planning strategy. This, however, is unfair for two reasons. Firstly, the bulk of new road investment in the bus-oriented strategy was actually intended to 'finish off' the temporary termini of the M1 and M2 motorways by extending them to more satisfactory termination points at Grosvenor Road and York Street respectively. The M1, in particular, ended very poorly in the middle of a residential area on Donegall Road. There is no doubt that these two projects would have brought real environmental benefits. Indeed it was noted at the public inquiry in 1977 that even those most viciously opposed to the road plan (for example, the Republican Clubs) nevertheless advocated the construction of other roads (such as the Outer Ring) as alternatives to the West Tangent.[11] Secondly, buses also require roads, and in order for them to work effectively there had to be investment in road space to permit quality bus lanes, bus laybys, etc without compromising the needs of (at the very least) commercial and goods vehicles. The bus-oriented strategy planned to use 75% of the roads budget to improve existing roads, compared to just over 25% in the roads-based strategy.

In relation to the Urban Motorway, the most significant statement in the public information leaflet was that "the Urban Motorway originally proposed will now not be built".[9] Since none of the strategies identified construction of the eastern or southern flanks of the Urban Motorway, September 1976 effectively marked the death of the Belfast Urban Motorway as originally proposed. Indeed, this is the last time that the term 'Belfast Urban Motorway' was used officially, being consigned to history along with its unfortunate acronym.

Coincident with the publication and distribution of the leaflet, a public consultation period began which centred on an exhibition in Clarendon House. This exhibition lasted from 28 September 1976 until 20 May 1977 and although "attractively laid out",[11] it was very poorly attended with only 200 members of the public visiting over the entire eight month period. Planners were left with the distinct impression that, despite vocal opposition in certain areas, the wider Belfast public was uninterested and apathetic towards the entire issue of transportation in the city.

A public inquiry was scheduled, to begin in mid 1977. On 5 January 1977 Belfast City Council voted 17–13 in favour of the mixed strategy,[22] also passing an amendment by Unionist councillor Frank Millar which appealed to the government to consider building a railway link between the new Central Railway and York Road station (terminus of the Larne line) in the north of the city.[11] The Alliance Party and SDLP opposed the main motion, with the latter describing the plan to construct the West Tangent as "motorway madness" which "by its very conception … seeks to bring more and heavier traffic into the city".[22]

Towards the end of the consultation period, in March 1977, the government released a statement indicating that it too favoured the mixed strategy, albeit with some alterations to the proposals for the West Tangent.[23] The government also indicated that it would proceed with work on the elements of the road plan that were common to all three strategies (the short extensions to the M1 and M2), despite the requirement for a public inquiry on the proposals.[11] Just prior to the public inquiry it indicated that it would also consider Frank Millar's rail link proposal.

A month later community groups opposed to road building held a one-day conference at the YMCA where they agreed to set up an umbrella group, known as the Community Groups Action Committee on Transport (CGACT). In an advert released shortly afterwards urging people to support them, the CGACT stated that their primary aim was "to fight for a reliable, cheap public transport system and against wasteful road construction".[24] Since the last inquiry in 1972 community groups had lost much of their faith in inquiries and there was debate within CGACT about whether they should engage with the inquiry or boycott it as a sham. Blackman quotes an academic observer who said: "There was a feeling from the start that the dice were loaded. People didn't expect much out of it. Nobody had much belief in the inquiry, that it would yield benefits for the working class".[17] In the end the group decided to engage in some form. The distrust, however, would manifest itself in the opening days of the inquiry.

CHAPTER 9
THE LAVERY INQUIRY

The Inquiry Opens

The public inquiry into the review of the transportation plan opened on 31 May 1977, heard by CM Lavery, QC. The scope of the inquiry was considerably wider than the Urban Motorway proposals, and as such an in-depth analysis of the many aspects of the inquiry is beyond the remit of this book. The inquiry was, however, a significant event in the history of planning in Belfast and those interested are directed to the detailed discussion in Blackman[1] and Cinalli[2], as well as the inquiry report itself.[3]

On the first day of the inquiry the Community Groups Action Committee on Transport (CGACT) was represented by Francis Keenan, who immediately requested an adjournment to allow the community groups to come up with a 'fourth option', and funding to enable them to do so – a request which was refused. The CGACT had also arranged for John Tyme (an English campaigner who had been given funding by the Rowntree Trust to campaign full-time against road construction[4]) to assist them in formulating their opposition.

When he addressed the inquiry, Mr Tyme made a passionate case around the principle of natural justice, and demanded that the inquiry be adjourned indefinitely[5]. He attacked the very legal basis for the inquiry, the moral authority of central government, the impartiality of R Travers Morgan and alleged the existence of a powerful 'roads lobby' that worked throughout all levels of the political system to ensure that roads construction could continue. He said:

> *[My clients] have no faith in your [Mr Lavery's] office … or its supposed independence of the Department. They have no faith in the Secretary of State … no faith in their Parliamentary or Local Government Representatives who they see as no more than the helpless, manipulated puppets of the Department/Roads Lobby machine that has … achieved no less than the destruction of the representative function of British democracy.*[5]

He went on to suggest that, should his request be turned down, his clients would turn to civil disobedience "in increasing numbers, entirely passively interposing their bodies and their plain courage between you … and the injustice and cruelty that would be perpetrated were you to deny the adjournment that I now seek".[5]

The Inspector, however, did indeed turn it down, noting that such matters were for the national government to decide, and beyond the remit of the Inspector of an individual inquiry. The next day there were noisy protests and a large section of the public gallery attempted to disrupt the inquiry,[6] with some success, as the Inspector eventually retreated to a back room. The CGACT withdrew and mounted a picket outside, while Mr Tyme returned to England.

Protestors outside the Lavery Inquiry. *(credited to Northern Ireland Poverty Lobby)*

On 2 June one of the protestors' demands – that work on the road elements that were common to all three options should stop entirely – was met, and preparatory work for the M1 and M2 extensions was suspended.[7] After several more days of protests the Inspector's resolve hardened, and he accused the protestors of denying the people of Belfast their legitimate right to have their objections heard at the inquiry.[8]

The CGACT continued to press for time to develop a 'fourth option', estimating that this would take "nine months to a year" and objecting strongly to the fact that the Department of the Environment had spent £1m developing their three options, whereas they were being offered no funds at all to prepare alternatives.[9] This issue of funding for objectors was later recognised as legitimate and provided for in subsequent public inquiries but was not available for the CGACT.

The Inspector eventually agreed to an adjournment, despite protests from the DOE, but only for 9 weeks from 21 July to 26 September 1977. Immediately after this victory the CGACT warned their supporters that "seasoned campaigners are not so sure that any new plan put before the inquiry will be decided upon" but celebrated the fact that the adjournment showed that "working class Catholics and Protestants can make the Establishment sit up and listen when they want to".[10] During the adjournment the CGACT carried out a small-scale questionnaire in west Belfast. However, following the adjournment they appeared either unwilling or unable to present much further evidence, and failed to present the promised 'fourth option'. From their statements at the time, it is unclear how serious the CGACT actually were about coming up with a fourth option.[10] With no further evidence to hear, the Inspector therefore closed the inquiry on 7 November 1977.

Although a very acrimonious affair, it is interesting to note that the public inquiry did not attract much interest from the general populace of Belfast. With the exception of a small number of individuals, the majority of objections were made by groups representing a specific locale or community, and in their substance objected more to the impact of specific road proposals on communities than on the overall transport strategy itself.

It is impossible to detail all the objections here, but the following is a summary of the position taken by various interest groups. Page numbers are references to the inquiry report.[3]

The **Department of the Environment, Roads Service,** and their contractors argued for further investment in roads primarily on the grounds of the positive benefits of car ownership. They predicted that 64% of households in the city would be car-owning by 1986, compared to 44% in 1971 (p212), and that cars offered "greater mobility, cheaper travel, more extensive opportunities for travel, flexibility and privacy" (p32) arguing that "people who owned cars were entitled to expect regular use of them and reasonable access to the city centre" (p40). They gauged that car ownership would continue to rise whether roads were built or not, and that failure to build new roads would simply result in more and more traffic congesting existing roads, leading to ever-poorer living conditions (p34). They felt that banning cars from the city centre was not an option, as this would simply drive people to out-of-town shopping centres and kill the city centre (p35). In terms of the West Tangent, the planners argued forcefully that it should be built, in order to take through traffic out of the city centre (p43). They felt that it was vital that it was not built with at-grade roundabouts which would lead to "low speed, start-stop progress, giving longer journey times, a reduction of capacity on the new route and a corresponding severe interference with traffic flows on the five main radial routes" (p38). They recommended that if it was constructed at-grade, then land should at least be reserved for future grade separation. In response to the community severance issue, they pointed out that the land cleared for Phase 1 of the Urban Motorway had lain empty for so long that it was already a community barrier, and that constructing a road there would not make the situation any worse (p34).

The department argued against the bus-oriented strategy. Ian Wallis, a planner with R Travers Morgan, noted that experiments in Stevenage in England showed that while increased bus frequency did lead to significant increases in passenger numbers, it "had little effect on commuter car traffic" which contradicted the common assumption that more people on buses would mean less congestion (p30). They felt that a system discouraging cars from the city centre would impinge severely on civil liberty, offering a detailed critique of the Nottingham 'zone and collar' system which, they said, had not produced very good results:

> *The experiment has shown that extremely severe restraint is needed to achieve a substantial shift from car to bus. We had to ask ourselves how much artificial congestion could reasonably be imposed, and economic considerations are much more important now than when the experiment was conceived* (p134).

They argued that people would not move to buses simply by providing them, and argued that the bus-oriented strategy would merely result in lots of empty buses (p37). They also noted that there was "no evidence that bus priority measures in the UK had a substantial effect in boosting bus patronage or in controlling car commuting" (p115). Finally, they noted that there were hidden costs in a bus-based strategy because investment in buses had to be continuous (new buses had to be purchased regularly) whereas road maintenance was a much smaller ongoing financial commitment (p29).

A number of **residents associations** gave evidence at the inquiry (p82+). The most vocal was the CGACT, which had already expressed its total lack of confidence in the inquiry on day one. In their submission they argued that the planners had always intended to build an urban motorway, that the review was not genuine and was being carried out purely because of paramilitary threats, and that all three strategies would achieve the same roads-based result through different steps. During the adjournment in the inquiry they carried out a survey of 80 residents in the Lower Ormeau, Short Strand, New Lodge, Shankill, Lower Falls, Mountainview and Twinbrook areas of the city. This showed strong support for more buses but, surprisingly, little opposition to road building even from non-car owners.

The Greater West Belfast Community Association (GWBCA) was also critical of the way the inquiry and public consultation had taken place, but was more concerned with the impact of specific proposals on west Belfast (p123+). They supported the bus-oriented strategy, but were very critical of the intention to invest little in rail. They suggested a zone-and-collar system to prevent cars reaching the central area, showing a video presentation of such a system operating in Southampton, and suggested that the West Tangent could be tolled to pay for decking it (ie building it in a covered tunnel) to reduce severance. They indicated that provided it was decked, they would support construction of the West Tangent. They put forward an alternative plan that included provision of the Outer Ring road around west and north Belfast. R Travers Morgan calculated that this strategy would cost £133m, compared to £90m for the three strategies under consideration, and was therefore unaffordable. The DOE felt that tolls would not work, since the disruption that toll booths would cause to traffic flow would negate all the benefits of the road.

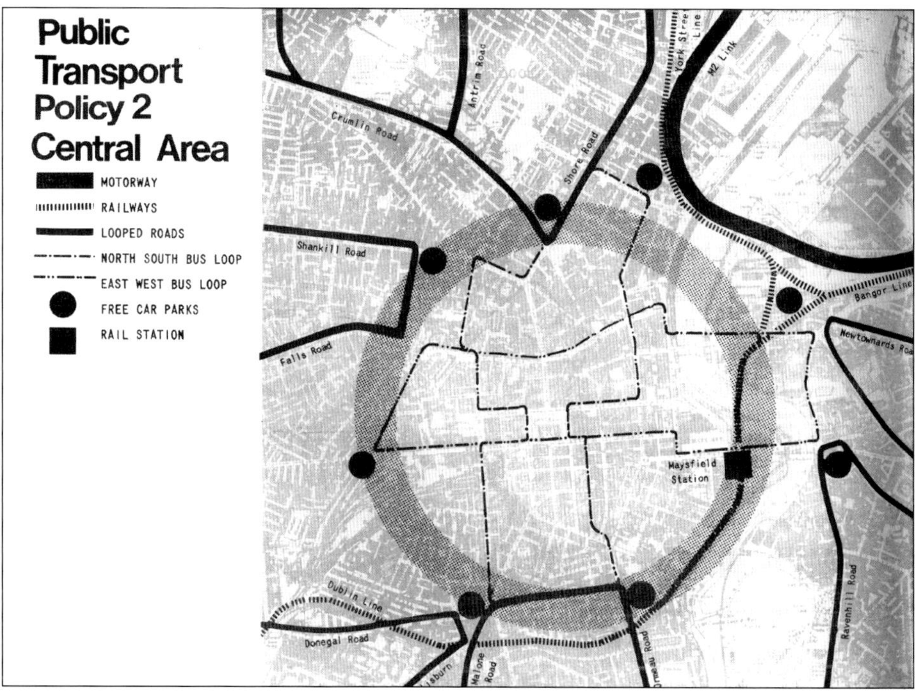

The zone-and-collar system of traffic restraint proposed for the central area by the Republican Clubs at the Lavery Inquiry. *(Workers Party of Ireland)*

The Republican Clubs (Official Sinn Féin) were, like the CGACT, convinced of the existence of a capitalist 'roads lobby' who wanted to build an urban motorway at all costs (p117+) and for their own self-interest. They argued that the West Tangent was unnecessary as traffic could be managed by completing the Central Distrbutor Box and by using innovative traffic management on existing streets. They wanted the cleared land to be turned into a linear park. They ridiculed the proposal to construct the West Tangent depressed below ground level as a "sort of urban moat". Interestingly, they did advocate the construction of further rural motorways, most notably a motorway connecting the M1 and M2 via Nutt's Corner to take more through traffic out of Belfast. They supported the bus-oriented strategy with bus priority measures and a zone-and-collar restraint system.

The Sandy Row Redevelopment Association was critical of the DOE's whole approach to planning, but supported the mixed-strategy because they supported the construction of the West Tangent: the only community group to take this view (p60). They argued that the temporary terminus of the M1 on Donegall Road had caused them to suffer from excessive car and freight traffic, which led to accidents and wanted the West Tangent built to solve this problem.

Various **business and industry groups** gave evidence, all in support of the roads-oriented strategy. The Institute of Highway Engineers argued that transport costs for industry were much higher in Northern Ireland than elsewhere in the UK (up to 50% of total costs in some sectors) and that a lack of new roads would stifle industry and lead to industrial decline (p52). The Confederation of British Industry gave evidence that investors were put off coming to Belfast by its poor road infrastructure (p60). The Northern Ireland Chamber of Commerce attacked the bus-oriented strategy on the grounds that cars were "no longer a luxury", but a "necessity" and despite the fact that car users were essential to the economy of Belfast, "planners seemed to take masochistic delight in hounding the commuter" (p78). Belfast Harbour Commissioners argued strongly for the provision of the West Tangent, noting that the port of Belfast takes 50% of Northern Ireland's seaborne trade and provides almost 10% of Belfast's employment. They felt that the absence of the West Tangent would clog up the roads around the port and jeopardise its viability (p63).

The view taken by **public transport** managers was somewhat surprising. The Northern Ireland Transport Holding Company (which owned Ulsterbus and Citybus) opposed the roads-oriented strategy on the grounds that the private car was a waste of energy and an inefficient way to move people. But they also opposed the bus-oriented strategy, which they felt was too idealistic and relied too much upon restricting civil liberties. They said the strategy was "impracticable and attempted to reverse the historical trend by fiscal means. If people wanted to use cars within a democracy one could not prevent them by very severe financial restraints" (p67). It was their view that even free buses would only increase passenger numbers by a marginal amount (p69). Werner Heubeck, the manager of Ulsterbus, advocated the mixed strategy (p98+), arguing that the huge ongoing costs associated with the bus-oriented strategy would render it impossible to sustain. Noting that "it was no use having 200 extra buses if they could not move" he described that strategy as "totally unnecessary" and "a misuse of public funds". But he also argued against further road building because he felt that innovative traffic management could push sufficient capacity from the existing road network.

Trade unions took a mixed standpoint. The Belfast and District Trade Union Council (TUC) felt that the West Tangent was needed in function, but that in form it should be replaced by completion of the Outer Ring around west and north Belfast to provide an alternative route to the port (p108). The DOE felt that it was very unlikely that commercial traffic would use such a circuitous route to the port (p133). The TUC said that they had seen the effects that roads had had in carving up communities in the USA and said they were "appalled" at the prospect of this occurring in Belfast. The Irish Congress of Trade Unions (ICTU) supported construction of the West Tangent, provided it was depressed below ground level and limited to commercial traffic only. The DOE responded to this with calculations that showed this proposal would represent extremely poor value for money, since even a single-carriageway road limited to commercial traffic would operate well below capacity. Sir Robert Porter, arguing for the DOE, said that "if experience is anything to go by these restraints [limiting roads to commercial vehicles] do not seem to make public transport as attractive to car users as might be hoped. That is the fear." (p113)

The **Northern Ireland Housing Executive**, which had never been particularly enamoured with the Urban Motorway, privately supported the mixed strategy[11] but refused to give public support to any of the options (p46). In fact, they appear to have actively sought to distance themselves from the planners to avoid any suggestion of "some form of collusion with the Roads Service".[11] At this point in time, the issue of housing was a very divisive issue between the two communities, and the Housing Executive were presumably keen to avoid appearing to be "on the Department's benches".[11] Nevertheless, they seem to have been intrigued by the possibilities that would have been available to them if the bus-oriented strategy were adopted. For example, during 1976 they had worked with Building Design Partnership to explore how the land reserved for the West Tangent could be used in this scenario.[12]

Political parties were not well represented at the inquiry, with only the nationalist SDLP and the Northern Ireland Labour Party (NILP) making submissions. No unionist parties made submissions. The NILP described the three options under consideration as "entirely bogus" since the difference in bus versus car patronage in the three strategies was relatively slight (p103) and described the inquiry as a "trap" set by road planners. They argued (correctly, as it turned out) that the estimates of future growth in car ownership were exaggerated, and that since only a minority had access to cars it was socially unfair to spend so much building roads for them. The SDLP argued that the roads-oriented strategy was "grossly inefficient, environmentally disruptive and economically wasteful" (p108). They opposed construction of the West Tangent which, they claimed, was merely a "back door road oriented strategy". A number of private individuals also addressed the inquiry making points that generally reflected the thrust of submissions made by groups.

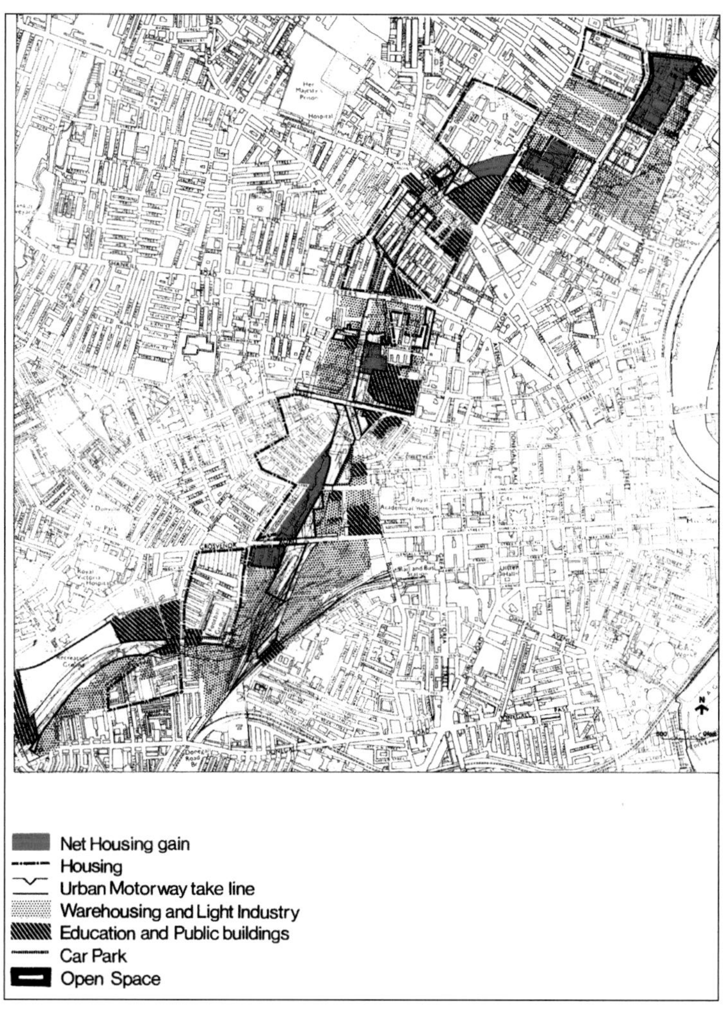

A 1976 map produced by Building Design Partnership identifying alternative uses for the land cleared for the Western Tangent of the Urban Motorway in the event of no road being built at all. *(Base map LPS/Ordnance Survey)*

The 1978 Transportation Strategy

Lavery submitted his report to the DOE in December 1977. His proposals were largely accepted by the DOE, though modified in some of the details, and both the report[3] and the DOE's new transportation strategy[13] were published on 28 April 1978, formally replacing the 1969 'Belfast Transportation Plan'. The result was a form of the mixed strategy, with increased investment in buses and a reduction in capital expenditure on new roads. It assumed a budget for transportation of £90m between 1977 and 1986, ie £10m per year which represented a very substantial reduction in ambition to the 1969 Plan.

The proposals for the central area focused on the completion of the Central Distributor Box, albeit in a modified form, installation of an Urban Traffic Control System to link all traffic signals together via a single computer system and the pedestrianisation of many of the main shopping streets in the city centre.

Construction of the West Tangent would proceed in the form of a dual-carriageway with two lanes in each direction between the M1 (at Donegall Road) and York Street, via Grosvenor Road. The existing junction at Donegall Road would be enlarged, but would remain at ground level to save money, and due to the presence of the Blackstaff and Forth/Clowney Rivers on

Summary of road proposals for the central area of the city in the new 1978 Transportation Strategy (blue for motorways, red for all-purpose roads) which replaced the much more audacious 1969 Plan.

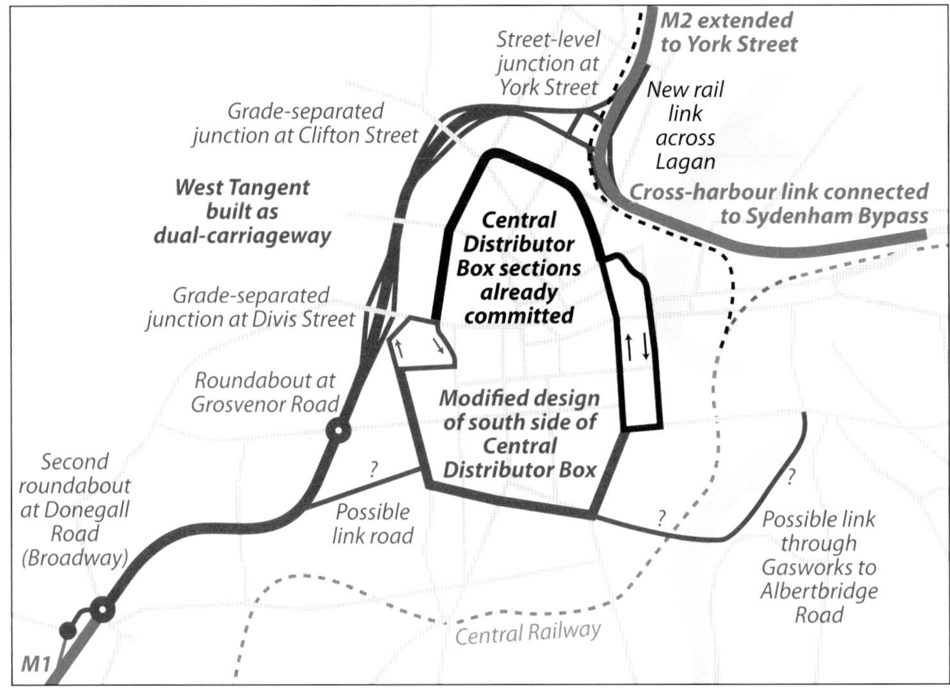

the site. The section between Donegall Road and Grosvenor Road would be constructed at ground level, while the section from Grosvenor Road to York Street would be depressed below ground level and grade separated, in order to reduce the effect of severance, with junctions at Divis Street and Clifton Street. Due to very poor ground conditions it was decided that the road could not be depressed where it met Grosvenor Road, so this junction would instead be built as a ground level roundabout. The design of this roundabout would allow the later addition of a flyover, if finances permitted, and if traffic levels justified it. The inspector proposed a road connecting the West Tangent just south of Grosvenor Road to the Central Distributor Box at Great Victoria Street, but the DOE decided not to progress this proposal as it would conflict with plans for a new central bus station.

The whole road would be built on the land originally cleared for Phase 1 of the Urban Motorway, but would not take up as much land as the elevated motorway would have required. Therefore the road could be shifted as far as possible from adjacent housing and the strips of land left over on either side would be landscaped. (Note that the DOE refer to the northern end of the West Tangent – Clifton Street to York Street – in this document as the 'North Tangent', a term not used in the plans for the Urban Motorway.)

The M2 would be extended from its temporary terminus at Whitla Street to a new junction at York Street, and then extended further onto a bridge across the River Lagan (referred to as the 'Cross Harbour Bridge') connecting it to the Sydenham Bypass on the line originally reserved for Phase 2A of the Urban Motorway. The Cross Harbour Bridge would carry three lanes in each direction (two for the mainline, one for the sliproads) to reduce the danger associated with weaving movements on the bridge. The connection between the West Tangent and the M2/Cross Harbour Bridge would be handled by a street level interchange, as the freeflow junction proposed here was, in the inspector's view, too visually intrusive and unjustified in light of revised traffic forecasts. The design of the junction, therefore, would not take future grade separation into account.

Proposals for the East Tangent (Phase 2B of the Urban Motorway) and the South Tangent (Phase 3) were officially abandoned and the blight on property in affected areas finally lifted.

In terms of public transport, there was to be an increase of 15% in the Citybus fleet, significant increases in bus frequency, and the introduction of flat fares. A new central bus station would be built at Great Victoria Street. Most significantly, the DOE agreed to connect York Road railway station (terminus of the Larne Line) to the new Central Station via a new, elevated, cross-harbour railway line running alongside the Cross Harbour Bridge. This represented a major departure from previous policy, which did not invest significant amounts of money in rail.

In the event, the civil disorder meant that the proposal to pedestrianise parts of the city centre proved the easiest to implement. Looking back from 1998, Roads Service noted that "one positive effect [of the 'Troubles'] was that the pedestrianisation of town and city centres took place virtually overnight, overtaking years of debate and argument about the pros and cons of such measures".[14]

The Nature of Objections

The 1977 inquiry was very different from the 1972 inquiry, primarily in that local people had clearly lost all faith in the value of inquiries. This was partly because previous inquiries had largely rubber-stamped the proposals on offer, despite objections; and partly because inquiries were now seen by nationalists as part of the British establishment, and therefore illegitimate by definition. Unionists, perversely, felt compelled to support inquiries for the same reason. The objectors also felt that they were not given adequate resources to make an articulated objection, a criticism that was certainly valid and has been backed up by research.[1]

Objections to the road proposals came almost exclusively from three very specific quarters: (a) groups claiming to represent the people through which the West Tangent and associated roads passed, (b) trade unions, and (c) nationalist or socialist politicians. It is even more interesting to note that there were little or no objections from (a) the population of Belfast more generally, (b) working class communities unaffected by road proposals, and (c) unionist and 'middle class' politicians. This suggests that the objections to the road proposals were motivated primarily by their direct impact on specific communities rather than a more general objection to the principle of a roads-based transportation policy. The people of Belfast, as a body, remained almost entirely silent on the choices put before them, indicating that they had no strong opinion on the question of roads versus buses. Even the CGACT's own survey in working class communities of west Belfast showed no strong objections to new roads *per se*.[3]

The Inspector himself cast doubt on who exactly the community groups represented, and the extent to which their views really were typical of the people of west Belfast. In his conclusion he wrote:

> *The [CGACT] members who appeared at the Inquiry appeared for the most part to be young, articulate, well-educated persons, some of whom were graduates in social science then engaged in social work. They claimed to represent the working class communities*

> *of Belfast and to be the authentic voice of those communities … I think I can recognise members of the Belfast working class communities when I see them. These young University graduates were by no means typical and I suspect that they were largely self-appointed. In the course of the Inquiry I heard persons who could be said without doubt to speak on behalf of those communities. I had no such conviction when I was listening to these members of the [CGACT].* (p144)

The allegation implicit in the inspector's analysis is that the CGACT were overstating the scale of opposition to new roads. Since no independent surveys of opinion, other than the CGACT's own, were carried out at this time it is impossible to gauge the extent to which this was or was not true. But it is certainly difficult to ignore the apparent ambivalence displayed by the vast majority of the public to the proposals on offer.

If the objections really were centred upon the impact that the roads would have on specific communities, then they are quite understandable. The West Tangent, whether or not it was grade separated, would place a permanent tarmac barrier between the west of the city and the central area. Pedestrians would be forced to cross it at a small number of wind-swept road bridges or junctions. In addition, the road would run very close to existing residential areas in the Roden Street, Divis Street and Shankill Road areas, with the associated problems of noise and pollution. Few people would welcome the construction of such a road close to where they live and, if asked, most would acknowledge that it would be an eyesore, and both a physical and psychological barrier.

So were the objectors simply NIMBYs (Not In My Back Yard)? This would be unfair, as the objections ran much deeper than this. Feelings were almost certainly fuelled by an ongoing sense of injustice – which can be traced back to the establishment of the redevelopment areas – at the way the working class communities of west Belfast were required to pay the price of providing a road that would primarily benefit the middle classes. With no choice in the matter, the communities had been uprooted and homes demolished to make way for a major road to service the rest of the city. Only a relatively small number of homes in middle class areas were being affected by roads proposals, so there was a perception that the wealthy were riding roughshod over the poor to service their own self-interest. The way the public inquiry appeared intransigent and unwilling to offer even the most basic assistance to the community groups only enhanced this perception. As has been noted in previous chapters, there is indeed some merit to this point of view.

It was thus abundantly clear what the community groups objected to, ie what they did *not* want to happen. However, their Achilles heel was the great difficulty they had in formulating a *positive* response to the arguments being put forward for the roads-oriented and mixed strategies, both of which would lead to construction of the West Tangent. Ultimately, the community groups failed to present a coherent argument and were unable to unite around a single, agreed proposal, instead presenting evidence and suggestions that "were often in contradiction with each other".[2] One of the community workers present at the inquiry later noted that they "lacked the positive power to bring forward alternatives and to conceive and draw these alternatives, to get them on paper and argue them".[1]

The result of this was that the strong arguments presented in support of the construction of the West Tangent were not countered in an effective way with arguments that went much beyond "we do not want the road running through our community". In particular, the arguments presented in favour of a largely or exclusively bus-oriented transportation plan were weak and easily dismantled, and weakened further by the fact that even the bus operators themselves expressed the view that they were impractical.

Undoubtedly some saw campaigning for an entirely bus-oriented transportation policy to be an ideal ostensible defence, when their actual objection was the presence of an unwanted road. For others, particularly nationalist/socialist politicians and trade unions, there were strong ideological and social reasons for arguing for a bus-oriented strategy. In either case, the argument made consisted of essentially the same series of axioms:

1. Road building was destroying the fabric of the city and ripping communities apart.
2. Private cars were generally owned by the middle classes; hence investment in new roads was inherently socially unjust.
3. Since the private car was the motivating force behind road building, cars must therefore be severely restrained or banned from the central part of the city.
4. This could best be achieved by placing huge financial disincentives on car drivers, such as high parking charges and tolls, or by a legislated ban from certain localities.
5. Those who could no longer drive into the central area would instead use buses, alongside those who did not own cars.
6. To be practical, buses therefore had to run on many routes, run very frequently and run late into the night.
7. To encourage bus travel, and to reduce social inequality, buses should be cheap or free at the point of use.
8. All of this would sufficiently reduce the number of cars in the central area so that the streets would no longer be congested, and further road building would be unnecessary.

This is a very well formed argument, and if the results envisaged could actually be achieved it would be a strategy worth pursuing. The problem is that it is highly unlikely that such a plan would have worked, and both the transport planners and the bus operators in 1977 knew this.

The argument could be unpicked in 1977 by taking it in reverse. Firstly, points 7 and 6 necessarily imply a huge up-front investment in buses, followed by further annual investment *ad infinitum*. Cheap fares (ie fares priced below operating costs) require a continuous input of money, while buses need drivers and regular repairs, which are a further cost and, since buses are machines, they will need regular replacement. By contrast, road construction is a one-off investment and road maintenance is a very low ongoing cost compared to the operating costs of buses. A bus-oriented transportation strategy, therefore, would eventually work out to be significantly more expensive to the public purse than a roads-oriented strategy. Of course, such an investment may still be judged to be worth the expense during boom times, but was financially unsustainable for much of the 1970s and 1980s. This was the fear expressed by Werner Heubeck, the head of Citybus, in his evidence to the inquiry.

Points 5 and 4, that people would be put off driving cars by major financial disincentives and more frequent buses have been proven to be naïve wishful thinking by the experience of the late twentieth and early twenty-first centuries. The relentless rise in traffic levels in the UK has created ever more congested roads, yet car drivers continue to use their cars for journeys that take longer every year. Why? The advantages that car owners see in their vehicles – privacy, safety, comfort, choice of travel time, limitless destinations, status, easy movement of luggage and small children – are so strong that drivers have proven themselves willing to absorb enormous financial burdens and endure extremely high levels of congestion before they will consider public transport alternatives. With hindsight it seems highly likely that, even if presented with very expensive inner city car parking and free buses, most Belfast car owners would have continued to choose to use their cars. The transport planners in 1977 knew this and said so at the inquiry, and the experience of the subsequent 30 years has proven them correct. The plan to use buses to get people out of their cars, therefore, would have failed. With the roads likely to remain congested, buses would also have got stuck in traffic unless there was further investment to upgrade the road network to provide dedicated routes for buses, and employ the staff to enforce them.

Points 3 and 2 are ideological arguments which highlight the fact that the increased use of private cars is the primary motivation for road building and that, due to the unequal distribution of car ownership, road investment was socially unjust. The problem in a liberal democracy is that an approach that either severely restricts or bans private cars from parts of a city has to be weighed against the principles of freedom that underlie the political system. There is no doubt that private cars offer many advantages to their owners, and in almost all other areas of western life the acquisition of a device that makes life easier is seen as a laudable goal. Yet there is also no doubt that society's accumulation of labour-saving devices comes at an environmental cost. The question, therefore, comes down to the extent to which society is prepared to compromise freedom in order to bring benefits to society as a whole. Since those in the western world appear very *un*willing to compromise in this way, approaches such as restricting the use of cars will necessarily cause severe conflict with the liberal principle of freedom.

The argument in favour of a bus-oriented transportation plan is also flawed in that it does not take account of the needs of industry and commerce. In an area the size of Northern Ireland it is impractical today to use any mechanism other than lorries to transport raw materials and goods to/from factories and ports, and to transport goods from distribution centres to shops. All of these require roads, and with these likely to remain congested with cars under a bus-oriented strategy (see above discussion) commerce and industry would suffer. The bus-oriented transportation strategy, in its realistic rather than idealistic form, made no provision for this.

Point 1, the damage that road building is doing to cities, is the strongest argument in the whole case and the only one that could not be countered at the inquiry. There was no denying the social and physical harm that construction of the West Tangent would do to that part of the city. The problem for the inspector was that with the bulk of the arguments in favour of the bus-oriented strategy having been refuted, the roads-oriented and mixed strategies were clearly the only viable options available for his consideration. His choice, therefore, was between building the West Tangent and damaging the communities through which they passed, or not building the West Tangent and accepting a city centre perpetually choked with traffic. It is therefore not surprising that he attempted compromise and chose the mixed strategy.

All of this is not to say that a choice of either the roads-oriented or mixed strategy was necessarily the *correct* course of action. The criticism that the inquiry did not consider all viable alternatives may well be valid. Firstly, by being based exclusively on buses, the bus-oriented strategy was fundamentally flawed. Buses had the poorest image of all forms of public transport and were the least likely to attract patronage from the middle classes. Trains, bicycles and trams, by contrast, did not have such an image problem and in other parts of Europe have retained the patronage of the middle classes. While a rail-based system could not have done much to help movement within Belfast, a tram-based system would likely have been much more successful. Trams would have required much more investment, both up-front and ongoing, and would have needed much more economic courage to build, but would have stood a much better chance of success than buses. Having had them in the past, Belfast was no stranger to trams.

Secondly, public transport *can* be a viable alternative to cars. The least car dependent city in the USA is New York, which features an extensive bus, train and underground system. New York is, of course, much larger than Belfast but it is quite possible for a city the size of Belfast to have an effective public transport system. In common with all UK cities, Belfast adopted an unapologetically car-based transport system in the 1950s and 1960s, and this decision had resulted in numerous interconnected planning decisions, all of which were based on this assumption. This meant that by 1977 much of the modern city had been designed around cars, and it would have proven extremely difficult to 'wind back the clock'. Unfinished road schemes that ended on residential streets, out of town shopping centres, industrial estates in the middle of the urban area and the accelerating effect of the 'Troubles' had all started Belfast down a slippery slope of car dependency that would have been almost as difficult to reverse in 1977 as it is today.

Thirdly, there is the argument that congestion will have to reach a crisis point sooner or later, and that road building simply postpones the inevitable. At the turn of the twenty-first century, traffic levels in Belfast were rising at a faster rate than the authorities could provide new road capacity – in other words, little of substance had changed since 1977. It is hard to avoid the observation that (unless we adopt a new phase of large-scale urban road building, which seems unlikely) a critical level of congestion, ie gridlock, must eventually occur. In the bus-oriented strategy this point would have been reached by the 1990s. In the strategy actually adopted, the point might be reached at some point in the next 20 years. It can be argued that, since this point will occur, we could have saved a huge amount of money and upheaval by simply letting the critical moment arrive and then adapting to the consequences. Economists will, of course, counter that postponing the inevitable is still a rational course of action as a driver of economic growth, just as human beings still choose to decorate their houses and have regular health checkups, despite the inevitability of death.

The Legacy of 1977

What are we to conclude from the events of 1977? Essentially Belfast's planners seemed unwilling to consider a wider range of viable public transport options; almost certainly lacked the money to implement them even if they had; and were not prepared to sit back and let the city's roads become ever more congested. They therefore effectively chose to continue their historic roads-oriented strategy, adding an element of the bus-oriented strategy in order to placate opposition, so-called "concessions to public opinion",[15] but without really believing that the buses would make much difference. This may explain the subsequent lethargy in implementing the bus proposals; while many of the roads included in the 1978 strategy were implemented, investment in public transport did not take place at the level recommended by Lavery.

Those who derided the inquiry as an attempt to develop a roads-based strategy 'by the back door' have been proved essentially correct in the years since. This represents a major failure on the part of the authorities to embrace, review and adequately implement their own transportation plan, while the lack of mainstream opposition to this represents passive acceptance of a roads-oriented strategy by the people of Belfast.

Roads Service immediately resumed their design work on the West Tangent, which had been suspended due to pressure in the early days of the inquiry. The relatively straightforward Donegall Road to Grosvenor Road link would be built first, followed by the extension to York Street. The proposed road, on the line of the West Tangent, became known as the 'Belfast West Link', changed to 'Westlink' upon opening.

CHAPTER 10
WESTLINK IS BORN

Work began immediately on the three main elements of the West Link plan. The stretch from Donegall Road to Grosvenor Road (termed Phase 1) opened first, followed by the section from Grosvenor Road to York Street (Phase 2). The third element was the extension of the M2 from Whitla Street to York Street.

Protests

The public inquiry had given West Link the go-ahead. However, not all of the opponents of the scheme were prepared to sit back and let construction take place in the wake of what they regarded as a flawed inquiry. A feeling that their concerns had not been addressed motivated most of these people, in particular problems of noise, safety and pollution. With all legal processes exhausted, some opponents took to civil disobedience as their next strategy. Unlike during the attempts to construct the Urban Motorway ten years earlier, paramilitaries did not directly interfere with construction, perhaps due to the fact that by 1979 the violence was at a lower level than in 1971.[1]

In mid November 1979, for example, residents of North Queen Street began a blockade of machinery at a site to be used for the construction of Phase 2.[2] Alderman Seamus Lynch, a member of the Republican Clubs who had argued against the project at the inquiry, explained that the residents were carrying out the protest because (a) "the [road] is due to pass within 25 yards of Churchill House high-rise blocks and two sets of pensioners dwellings", (b) "the effects of vibration on these buildings", (c) that "traffic noise alone will cause serious nuisance" (d) the recent concerns about lead pollution on children, (e) that "the proposed road is stealing [recreational] ground badly needed by the community",[2] and (f) that the attention of school children would be affected by the noise.[3] Around the same time he became chairman of a new protest group calling itself the North Queen Street Action Committee.[4] The group called for a suspension of the contract and talks with the government, but by-and-large relied upon physical disruption as a strategy. This was ultimately aimed to "force the DOE into a revaluation of transportation strategy".[5]

Their meetings with various government bodies did not lead to any change in the plans. The view of the DOE and Roads Service was that all of these issues had been addressed in the public inquiry, and there was therefore neither a legal nor a moral reason to reopen the discussion. They likely regarded the protestors simply as people who were unwilling to accept the outcome of a legitimate inquiry.

The protest continued for six months until late May 1980, at which point the government finally lost its patience and removed the protestors from the site.[6] By that point, the focus of the opposition was on the noise and disruption being created by the work itself, in particular the alleged lack of fencing around the deep excavations when workers went home and the long hours that the work went on for.[7]

At the other end of the scheme, residents of Donegall Road appear to have been less united. Some organised a similarly disruptive protest against contractors at Glenmachan Street,[6] but others supported the scheme because it would reduce traffic on Donegall Road. One resident branded Alderman Lynch "selfish" for opposing the scheme, pointing out that at present vehicles from the M1 "pass not 25 yards … but five feet from bedroom windows",[8] a view that promoted Mr Lynch to publish a defence of the protestors, arguing that they were not against all road proposals, merely this one, and that the Central Distributor Box should go ahead.[5]

On the day before Phase 2 of the new road opened (probably deliberately timed for maximum impact) Alliance Assembly member Will Glendinning launched a blistering attack on the DOE for having no legislation in place to deal with noise pollution, ie that there were "no proper guidelines for measuring noise levels".[9] Because this meant that residents in privately owned homes would have no choice but to pay for their own noise insulation, he poured scorn on the idea that "the department will protect the residents from the effects of this road". This was a valid point. Although a 1973 law did allow homeowners to claim compensation for loss of property value from noise, residents were not given the legal right to funding to install noise mitigation measures until 1995.[9]

In the end the protests failed due to the sheer physical size of the work site, the apparently resolved political will to proceed, the inability of opponents to secure any policy change after various meetings, and the failure of the scheme's opponents to form a united front. This last fact was largely due to the violence and upheaval of the 'Troubles', which had created such distrust and polarisation in working class communities that they could not unite even over issues of common interest.[6] Eventually the protests were abandoned and the road was completed.

Construction of Phase 1

A comprehensive discussion of the design and engineering aspects of the entire scheme can be found in Fogarty.[10] The discussion below is therefore a summary highlighting the key points. A list of the contractors follows the discussion. The total cost of the scheme was £23m[11] (£80m in 2007 prices[12]).

Although detailed ground investigation works had already taken place along the route of the West Tangent, these had been oriented towards assessing the difficulty of piling and the distance to bedrock, ie with the assumption that the motorway would be elevated. These results proved inadequate for the revised plan for a part ground level/part depressed road and new investigations were needed. Due to the strong desire to begin construction at the earliest opportunity, there was not enough time to award a site investigation contract for Phase 1, so Roads Service employees instead carried this out in September and October 1978.[10] By working quickly, the detailed design documents for Phase 1 were ready by October 1978 and the contract was advertised, with construction scheduled to begin in April 1979.[10]

This stretch of the road followed the route of the River Blackstaff, which presented unique challenges to the engineers. The greatest challenge was in the vicinity of the connection to the M1 at Donegall Road, where the relatively tame Blackstaff River was joined by the Forth/ Clowney, a 'spate' river draining a large area of the Belfast Hills around Divis mountain, which had the tendency to flood during heavy rainstorms.[13] The geometry of the road was such that the existing roundabout (which terminated the M1 at Donegall Road) would have to be augmented by a much larger roundabout to the north east, and the meeting point of the two rivers would lie directly beneath this proposed roundabout. This ruled out the construction of a depressed road in this location, while the high cost associated with building a flyover meant that the junction was built as an at-grade roundabout. The junction became known as *Broadway Roundabout*, due to the fact that the new roundabout severed an existing local road known as 'Broadway' that ran from the Falls Road to Donegall Avenue.

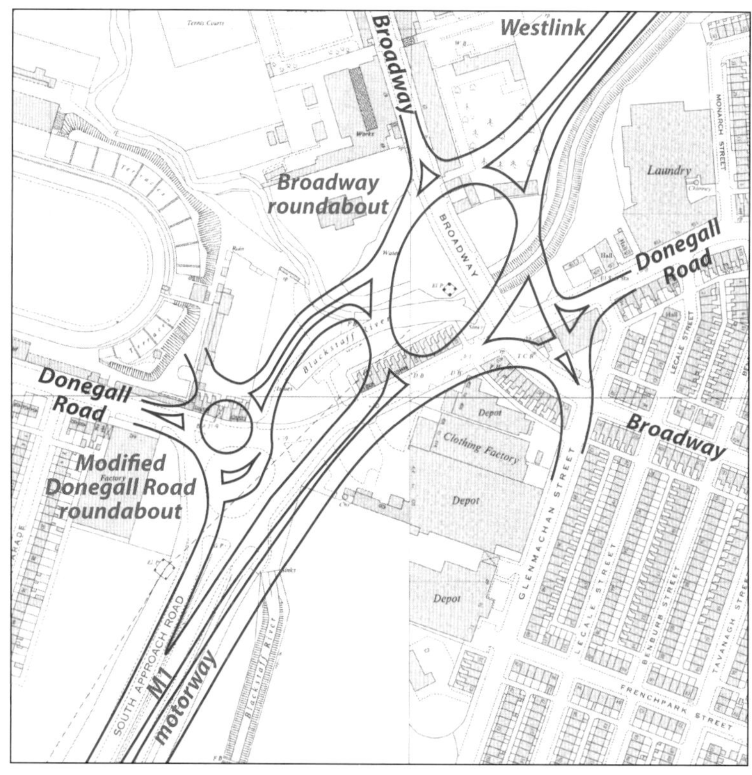

(Above) The new 'Broadway' roundabout superimposed on a map of the area from 1965/71. *(Base: LPS/ Ordnance Survey)*

To build the road the Blackstaff River had to be culverted for 850 metres (half a mile), a sorry fate for a river that had helped to shape the early history of Belfast. The fact that such a long stretch of a waterway was being culverted did not seem to attract much opposition, even from environmentalists, other than the odd letter to the paper.[14] The project also required the diversion of numerous water and sewer pipes, as well as the replacement of 900 metres of a Victorian sewer called the 'Asylum Wall Sewer', a most unpleasant job which required an unfortunate diver to swim down to a depth of 3 metres in raw sewage in order to install and remove stoppers as the pipes were severed and reconnected.[10]

The road itself was then built at ground level with a 300 mm continuously reinforced concrete slab on a 200 mm stone sub-base with a 95 mm asphalt surface. The road terminated at a new at-grade roundabout on Grosvenor Road. However, in order to future-proof the junction for a possible flyover during better economic times, the two carriageways were splayed to leave a 20 metre (70 foot) gap on the approach to Grosvenor Road. The roundabout initially operated as a conventional priority roundabout.[15]

At the point where the new road severed Roden Street, a traffic-light controlled junction was provided giving access to Roden Street to the south and to the Royal Victoria Hospital, via Mulhouse Road, to the north.

(Below) The completed footbridge at Roden Street.

(Above) Grosvenor Road roundabout, looking north, circa 1982 before the extension to York Street had opened. At this time it was operating as a conventional roundabout.

A pedestrian footbridge was provided here to reduce severance, although the bridge quickly became a focal point for sectarian tensions, and it had to be completely enclosed in wire mesh to prevent objects being dropped onto the traffic below.

Section 1 of the West Link was built on what was originally to have been the final section of the M1 motorway, while the Grosvenor Road junction was to have been on the Belfast Urban Motorway. This means that the 90° turn between Roden Street and Grosvenor Road was originally to have been occupied by motorway sliproads, not the mainline of a dual-carriageway. For this reason the curve on the West Link here was much tighter than would normally be provided on such a road, with an inner radius of about 150 metres (490 feet).[12] In a similar contrast to the original plans, the presence of a set of traffic lights at Roden Street – a location once intended to be part of the M1 motorway – served to highlight how far the mighty Urban Motorway plans had fallen.

Unlike the remainder of the West Link, Phase 1 was designated 'all purpose', meaning that pedestrians and cyclists could use it. Indeed, a footpath was provided along the entire length of Phase 1 between Broadway and Grosvenor Road.

The road opened to traffic without ceremony during the evening of 4 February 1981 after almost two years' work and at a cost of £3.837m[10] (£13.3m in 2007 prices[12]). The *Belfast Telegraph* declared the next day that "traffic flows smoothly on the section", commenting that it should help "some drivers to avoid the rush hour bottleneck at Shaftesbury Square".[16] Compared to the large-scale, enthusiastic coverage of earlier road plans in the city, there was

(Below left) The smaller Donegall Road roundabout occupies the site of the original terminus of the M1. (Right) The 'Broadway' roundabout shortly after opening in 1983.

very little media interest in the opening, perhaps due to the general air of pessimism under which the city lived after more than a decade of civil disorder. Because the road only went as far as Grosvenor Road when Phase 1 opened, the West Link was initially of limited use to through traffic.

(Above) Fairly light traffic following the opening day of Phase 1 of West Link in February 1981. Traffic levels soon soared. *(Belfast Telegraph)*

Construction of Phase 2

Phase 2, connecting Grosvenor Road to York Street, via Divis Street and Clifton Street, was challenging for

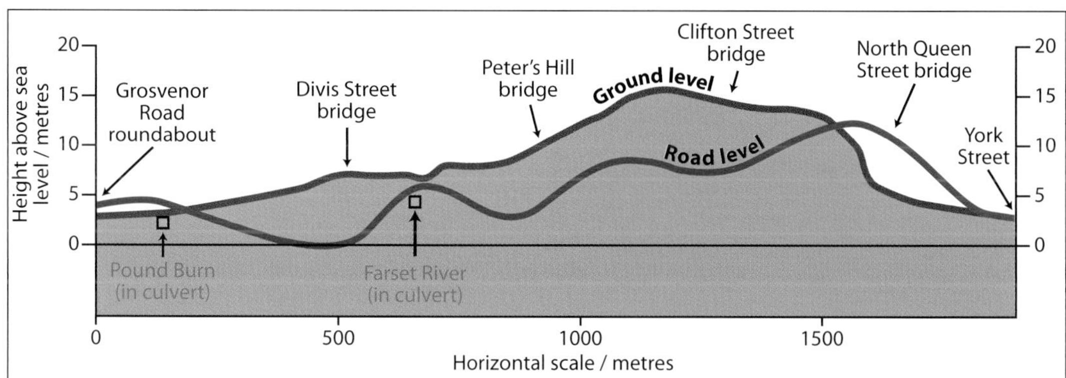

(Left) Longitudinal section of Phase 2 of West Link showing its depth in relation to ground level and two rivers. Note that it briefly approaches sea level at Divis Street. *(Based on Fogarty, 1983)*

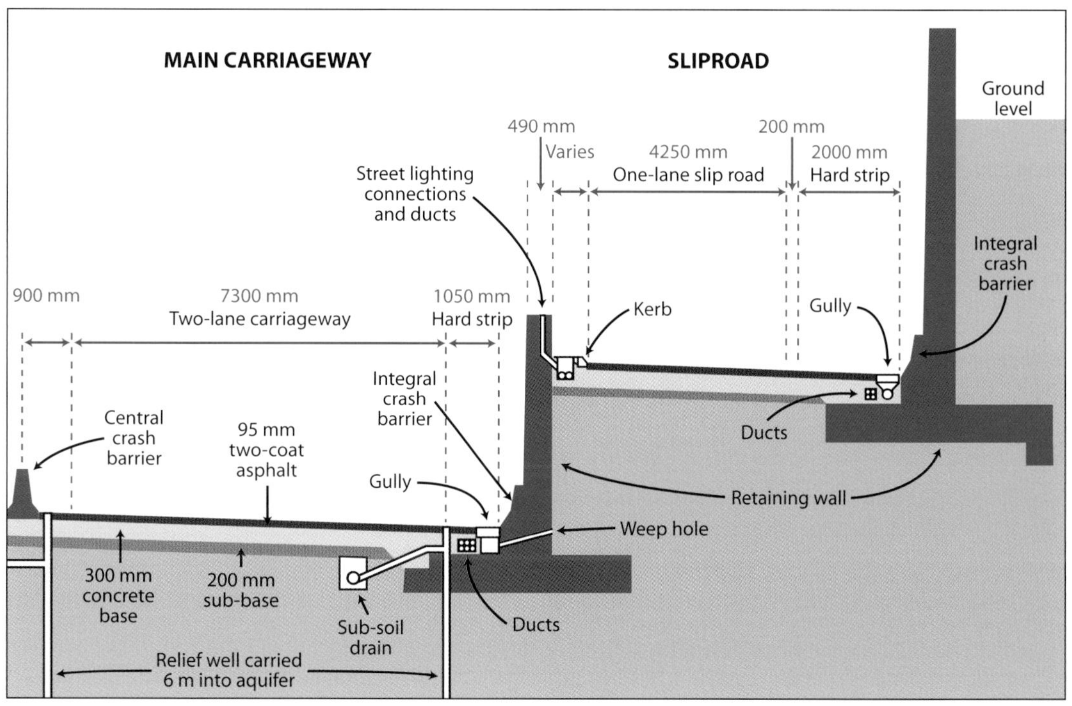

(Left) Indicative cross-section of part of West Link Phase 2, showing half of the main carriageway and a sliproad. The design of the actual road varies depending on its location and curvature. *(Based on Fogarty, 1983)*

different reasons. Firstly, much of the road was to be constructed in a cutting with vertical walls, which required extensive engineering work. Secondly, this section ran through land that had been heavily developed and was hence riddled with services, as well as the River Farset, which crossed the route of the road just north of Divis Street, and a smaller stream to the south known as the Pound Burn.

Between January and August 1979 further site investigations were carried out along the length of Phase 2. This part of the route was at a higher altitude than Phase 1, so that instead of Belfast sleech the ground consisted of sandstone bedrock overlaid by a thick layer of glacial gravel and subsoil. The investigations revealed that the gravel carried a suppressed water table under pressure. The fear was that, once the channel for the road had been excavated, the reduction in weight of the overlying material would result in this water forcing the material at the base of the excavation upwards. The problem was sufficiently serious at the Divis Street and Peter's Hill underpasses that a complex system of over 100 relief wells had to be installed to reduce the pressure. Nevertheless, the excavation at Peter's Hill did suffer from a pressure failure before the relief wells were fully operational.[10]

(Top) Early earthworks underway at Divis Street, here seen looking north, circa 1981.

(Bottom) View south towards Divis Street circa 1982. Note the culvert for the River Farset on the right. *(Both photos courtesy of DRD Roads Service)*

A separate contract was carried out between May 1979 and December 1980 to divert the sewers; the rivers were diverted as part of the main contract. The River Farset and an adjacent sewer were diverted north from their original course to a point parallel to Melbourne Street, where the new road would be high enough to let them pass beneath in culverts. To the south of Divis Street, the Pound Burn was diverted south to a point near Albert Street and brought under the new road in a culvert. In total 800 metres (870 yards) of culverts were built. The total cost of these diversions alone was £1.15m[10] (£4m in 2007 prices[12]).

Work on the main contract was underway by April 1980 and involved the construction of a 'canyon' that varied in depth from 1.5 metres to 10 metres (5 to 33 feet). This required the installation of 4 km (2.5 miles) of reinforced concrete cantilevered retaining walls. These were constructed in lengths of 12 metres (39 feet). At Divis Street and Clifton Street there were two such walls on either side, to facilitate the sliproads onto and off the depressed road. For aesthetic reasons, the exposed surface of the walls was textured with a 'rock like' finish, the design being based on a scheme that had previously been carried out in Craigavon.[10] The lowest 900 mm (35 inches) of each wall was reinforced to act as an integral crash barrier, negating the need for separate metal crash barriers. In total the retaining walls contained 23,000 cubic metres of concrete and 2,500 tons of steel.

(Left) Work on the Divis Street junction well underway in 1982, here seen looking south with the Divis Flats beyond. The retaining walls for the sliproads are in place. *(Photo courtesy of DRD Roads Service)*

(Below) Divis Street underpass fully excavated and the bridge being built above it, seen here looking north in 1982. *(Photo courtesy of DRD Roads Service)*

Three road bridges were required on the canyon section, carrying Divis Street, Peter's Hill and Clifton Street. All three bridges were of the same prestressed concrete beam design with a 160 mm (6.3 inch) reinforced concrete slab and a span of 21 metres (69 feet). The bridge abutments were finished identically to the retaining walls, giving drivers the impression of a continuous structure. Divis Street bridge is by far the widest at 43 metres (141 feet; over twice its span) in order to accommodate a single-point urban interchange (SPUI) road layout (where right-turning traffic passes to the right of opposing traffic) and remains unique at the time of writing as the only road junction in the entire United Kingdom with this layout. Peter's Hill is the narrowest bridge at 21 metres (69 feet), while Clifton Street is 26 metres (85 feet). These latter two are at slight skews of 5° and 4° respectively.

At the northern end of Phase 2 the ground slopes rapidly downwards (actually a post-glacial raised beach) so that the road emerges from its canyon close to Clifton Street and must then immediately cross over North Queen Street. To facilitate this, North Queen Street was excavated and lowered by one metre. The bridge has a span of 22 metres (72 feet), a width of 25 metres (82 feet), clearance of 5.2 metres (17.1 feet) and is skewed at 23°. The abutments were finished with a different variation of the rock-like finished used on the West Link itself. Unfortunately, corrugated iron security barriers had to be attached to the guard rails of the bridge shortly after opening.

Divis Street junction close to completion, looking north circa late 1982. Work is focused on preparing the road structure itself through the completed underpass. *(Photo courtesy of DRD Roads Service)*

(Above left) The view east from Clifton Street bridge circa 1982, showing the sliproads taking shape. *(Photo courtesy of DRD Roads Service)*

(Right) Completed Divis Street junction in 1983. *(Author's collection)*

(Below) Mural of McGurk's Bar and a memorial on the abutment of the bridge that carries Westlink over North Queen Street. *(Author's collection)*

This bridge is located on the site of the former McGurk's Bar, which had been the scene of a terrorist bombing on 4 December 1971. Fifteen people were killed and many others injured. Today, a mural depicting the bar's original appearance has been painted on the bridge abutment, along with a memorial.

The road itself was constructed to dual two-lane standard with no hard shoulder. The extremely short merge distances provided for the southbound onslip at Clifton Street and the northbound onslip at Divis Street (less than 100 metres; 330 feet) have continued to cause problems since construction, as a vehicle travelling at the maximum 50 mph speed limit can cover this distance in just four seconds. With the benefit of hindsight, connecting the sliproads of these two junctions together as a continuous lane would have gone a long way to reducing these problems. Unfortunately, due to the enormous challenges involved in building the Peter's Hill underpass it would likely be too expensive and disruptive to retro-fit such an arrangement today.

Due to the depressed nature of the road and the Northern Ireland climate, it was necessary to provide a pumping station at each of the three underpasses along Phase 2. Three pumps were provided at each location: one would be used for everyday weather, two for a once-in-five-year storm event, and all three only if an alarm was triggered by water levels reaching a dangerous level. Each pump had a maximum discharge of 890 gallons per minute (56 litres per second), an arrangement that has since proven sufficient.

Two dedicated pedestrian routes were provided. The first was a subway beneath the West Link adjacent to the north side of Grosvenor Road roundabout. The route consisted of ramps at either side and then

The completed Westlink seen (left) looking east from Clifton Street and (right) looking north towards Divis Street from the footbridge near Cullingtree Road shortly after opening. *(Author's collection)*

two underpasses, one under each carriageway, with an exposed section in the central reservation to improve lighting and reduce the claustrophobic sense of being in a long tunnel. Other measures were taken to reduce the attractiveness of the tunnel to 'loiterers'[10] but nevertheless the tunnel was not popular and was eventually removed as part of the 2006 upgrade.

To the north, a pedestrian footbridge was built over the 'canyon' section just south of Divis Street to connect the Divis Flats complex at Cullingtree Road to Durham Street. This bridge was built as a continuous vertical curve from T-shaped reinforced concrete beams. The total length of the bridge was 78 metres (256 feet) consisting of a 36 metre (115 foot) central span and two 21 metre (69 foot) approach spans. The approach spans were initially provided with a normal steel parapet, while the central span was covered with an anti-vandal cage.[10] This cage was later extended to enclose the whole structure.

Phase 2 of the West Link was opened to traffic at noon on 29 March 1983. There was no official ceremony, although Roads Service's Deputy Divisional Roads Manager John Fogarty was on site to oversee the opening.[17] Although referred to by most drivers as 'the Westlink', Roads Service continue to use the name without the definite article, ie simply as 'Westlink'.

The *M1-M2 Link (Belfast) Order (Northern Ireland) 1983* was passed before Phase 2 opened, which designated the stretch from Grosvenor Road to York Street as a 'Special Road', prohibiting pedestrians. Although motorways are also legally created using Special Road legislation, the content of the 1983 Order was deliberately insufficient to turn Westlink into a motorway. Hence it was given an 'A' classification as A12. Until 2003 (when the A101 opened at Sprucefield) Westlink was the only A-class road in Northern Ireland that was a dual-carriageway for its entire length.

Construction of the M2 Extension

The third element of the Westlink plan was the extension of the M2 motorway. In order for Westlink to lead directly to the M2 it was necessary to extend the M2 southwards by 800 metres (0.5 miles) to York Street, on the same route as the originally planned extension to meet the Urban Motorway. Since 1973, the M2 had terminated abruptly at a set of traffic lights on Whitla Street.

Because the extended M2 would cross the existing road network at Dock Street, it was necessary to raise the road 8 metres (26 feet) onto an embankment. This proved extremely challenging since the sub-surface at this location consisted of 14 metres (46 feet) of sleech. It was estimated that following construction of the embankments, the land would subside by 1.2 metres (4 feet) over the course of 12 years. As this was both an excessive amount of subsidence and much too long a timescale, work was carried out to reduce the settlement time.

Between March and June 1979, 6,500 sand drains were installed along the route of this section of embankment, complete with monitoring equipment, down to the depth of the underlying glacial till. The embankments were then built up to their final height. The entire structure was then left for a year and monitored until, by June 1980, the degree of settlement had reached its final value of 1.2 metres. The remaining sections of embankment were not quite so challenging, but required the installation of a further 1,700 sand drains between November 1979 and February 1980, with the last of the embankments completed by September 1980.

Two views of the Dock Street bridge being constructed around 1981. (Left) The view east from York Street, and (right) the view north from the future M2, with Nelson Street visible on the right. *(Author's collection)*

Dock Street bridge was built to a width of 37 metres (121 feet) and with a headroom of 5.6 metres (18.4 feet). It consists of four spans of prestressed M-beams with lengths of 12.6 metres, 16.5 metres, 16.5 metres and 10.4 metres (41 feet, 54 feet, 54 feet, 34 feet). All 24 concrete supporting columns have a similar textured finish to that used in the Westlink 'canyon' section. The bridge was subsequently widened by approximately 5 metres (16 feet) in 1991.[18]

To the north, a pedestrian underpass was provided through the embankment at Whitla Street. It has a total length of 50 metres (164 feet) and doubles as a conduit for gas, water and electrical services.

Work on the road surface itself did not begin until late 1981.[10] As it was the intention to build the Cross Harbour Bridge, the embankments were built wide enough to accommodate four lanes in each direction, and a 'ski jump' was provided at the south end so that two lanes each way could eventually continue onto the Cross Harbour Bridge. Initially, however, the M2 extension was marked out with three lanes northbound and two lanes southbound. The Whitla Street terminus was reduced to a southbound-only exit taking three of the M2's five lanes, while two continued to York Street.

At York Street, where both the M2 and Westlink terminated, an at-grade junction was created with a one-way gyratory system controlled by traffic signals. The Lavery Inquiry had rejected the notion of a three-way freeflow junction here on the grounds of its appearance and traffic predictions. Instead, freeflow movements were to be limited to the connection between the extended M2 and the planned Cross Harbour Bridge.

Upon its completion, Roads Service's Deputy Divisional Roads Manager John Fogarty declared that this was "not just another road, it is a main artery through the heart of a city". He went on to affirm that "Westlink is here for hundreds of years to come and historians will record that despite the bombings and destruction the people in Belfast are still capable of building a better future".[10]

Contractors

The following contractors worked on the West Link and M2 scheme:[10]
Advance works: Cementation Ltd, Ulster Foundations Ltd, Glover Site Investigations, GKN (NI) Ltd.
Main contract: JMJ Contracts Ltd, Charles Brand and Son Ltd, Farrans Ltd, Maralin Quarries Ltd, Terratch Ltd, John F Owens and Sons Ltd, RJ Maxwell (Ballymena) Ltd, CW Contracts Ltd.
Suppliers: Macrete Ltd, Wavin Pipes (NI) Ltd.

Urban Traffic Control System

The Lavery Inquiry had recommended the installation of a traffic control system for the city centre streets, and this was implemented and came into operation in 1981.[9] The system, one of the first of its kind in the UK, used phone lines to send information from various parts of the city centre road network to a central computer that then adjusted the microprocessors in the traffic signals to optimise traffic flow. The system was augmented by 12 CCTV cameras, and was very successful in squeezing extra capacity out of the road network and responding quickly to sudden incidents.

The 1984 Junction Upgrade

Upon completion of Westlink it was immediately obvious that the at-grade roundabouts at Broadway and Grosvenor Road were not working because "the main flows were prevented from gaining access to the roundabout by relatively small volumes of circulating traffic", resulting in delays of 5–10 minutes at each roundabout.[19] Although this design was basically a rural design – which is not always appropriate in urban situations – this was not naïvety on the part of the designers: it was quite obvious even before the road opened that the design was likely to be inadequate. The situation was created by the requirement on the engineers to stay within the remit set for them by the Lavery Inquiry. Retired Director of Network Services Grahame Fraser explains:

> *The public inquiry had determined what would be built. To start trying to change the design at this stage would have caused, at best, serious delays, and in the political climate of the time, perhaps the loss of the project.*[21]

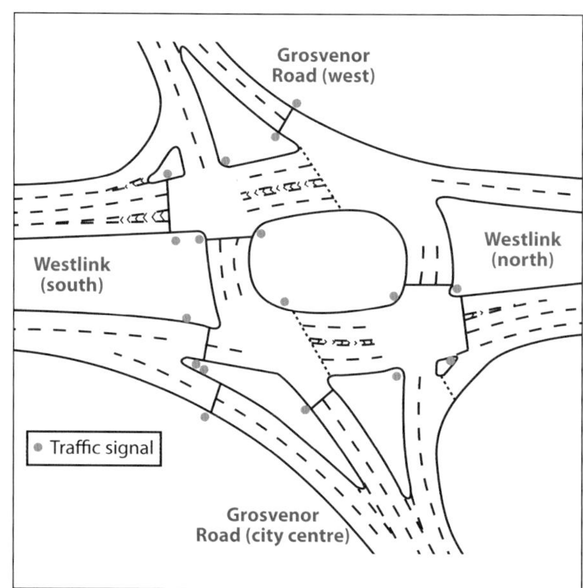

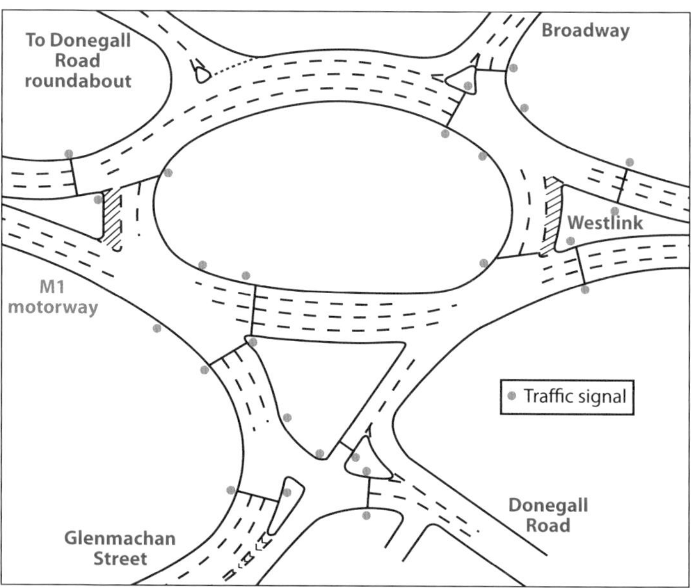

(Above) Lane layout at (left) Grosvenor Road and (right) Broadway following the 1984 signalisation schemes.

(Below) Grosvenor Road roundabout, looking south, after the 1984 signalisation scheme. (*Author's collection*)

Once the road was opened, however, the problem came under the remit of 'maintenance' and could be tackled. In 1984 the decision was therefore taken to modify both roundabouts. Cost restrictions meant that the money available for engineering works was minimal, so the engineers' only option was to add traffic signals to the existing roundabouts, albeit with some minor adjustments to the central island and deflections. At Broadway, additional capacity was obtained by allowing three lanes to pass through the junction between the M1 and Westlink.

This was achieved by widening the approaches from two to three lanes just before they reached the roundabout, and dropping the third lane just after. On the M1 this meant removing the hard shoulder for a short distance.

The two schemes were completed in 1984, around six months apart.[20] The solution "worked very well", "like honey flowing from a pot" according to one journalist who was shown round the scheme by Roads Service.[20] Throughput increased by almost 25% and the problem of through traffic being unduly held up by turning traffic was eliminated. Its success hinged on the use of the newly installed urban traffic control system. Denis O'Hagan, the Principal Engineer in charge of Traffic Management in Belfast at the time, stated that "we couldn't have done it without the computers".[20]

Effect on Road Users

Motorists embraced the new road enthusiastically, with approximately 23,000 vehicles per day choosing to use the road in 1983.[22] In fact, just six years later it was admitted that "traffic generated by the opening of this road was far in excess of any forecast".[23] By the following year (1990) traffic levels had almost doubled to 42,830 vehicles per day (measured at Roden Street)[24] and the road was experiencing regular congestion at the signalised junctions at Broadway and Grosvenor Road.

Since roads are designed as methods of transporting people and goods from one location to another, the 'success' of a road is directly related to the amount of traffic it attracts. This traffic is made up of both (a) traffic that was already making the journey but which could now do so more conveniently and (b) traffic that did not previously make the journey, but was empowered to do so by the provision of the new road. By this definition, Westlink was an extraordinarily successful project, attracting much more traffic than even its designers had anticipated. Of course, this created its own problems, since it was almost immediately apparent that the chosen design (with two at-grade roundabouts and two signalised junctions) was insufficient to cope with the traffic it attracted. But in the words of Denis O'Hagan "it was a very popular traffic jam – people still wanted to use it despite the congestion".[20]

What can account for the unexpectedly high levels of traffic? Or, to put it another way, why were the high levels of traffic apparently unexpected?

In the 1960s the planners of the Belfast Urban Motorway had recognised that there were a lot of people that wished to make journeys from one side of Belfast to the other, especially between the north and south and between the north east and south. The city centre streets were catering for all of these journeys. The Urban Motorway had been designed to carry this traffic, and the M1 and M2 motorways were therefore designed assuming the future provision of the Urban Motorway. However the 16 year hiatus between 1967 and 1983 had allowed the build-up of an unprecedented degree of pressure on the streets of the central area of Belfast, akin to water building up behind a dam, as demand for cross-city journeys continued to rise despite the lack of road space.

Although theory would suggest that this would result in people switching to public transport, this does not seem to have occurred in Belfast. Between 1971 and 1981 the number of work journeys made via buses by Belfast residents fell from just over 58,000 per day to just under 33,000,[25] a drop of 43%, despite the increasing traffic congestion. This decline was mirrored in Great Britain, although not at such a steep rate (a drop of 30%[26]). One reason was the lack of bus priority measures in the city, which meant that a bus offered few advantages over a car in heavy traffic. Belfast, of course, had its own unique problems at this time, such as the effect of the 'Troubles' and a general lack of funding for public transport, but the fact remains that increasing traffic congestion does not seem to have turned the residents of Belfast into public transport users.

When the dam finally burst with the opening of Westlink, not only did the north-south cross-city traffic immediately transfer onto the new road from the city centre, but huge numbers of people discovered that it was now viable to make journeys that were previously too time consuming to be worthwhile. This is a perfect illustration of how new roads not only cater for existing road users, but generate new road users (the 'induced traffic' effect). This is often perceived as a bad thing, and in the sense that new roads in urban areas tend to become congested again, it is. But it also means that more people are able to make journeys that were previously not possible to make. Despite the fact that the streets of the city quite quickly returned to a level of congestion following the opening of Westlink, in absolute terms more journeys were happening than were previously possible. In that sense, Westlink provided liberation for many people and businesses, despite its obvious design flaws. The 'success' of Westlink, therefore, should be measured not by how freely traffic moved, but rather by the number of additional journeys that it permitted. Westlink was, therefore, exceptionally successful as an engine for increased movement, economic growth and more widespread social activity.

Aerial views of Westlink in early 1985 showing (top) the Roden Street and Grosvenor Road stretch, and (bottom) Broadway roundabout. *(Photos courtesy of DRD Roads Service)*

The Lavery Inquiry seems to have taken the view that a more conservative road design could be used to save money and address the concerns of objectors. The assumption seems

Aerial views of Westlink in early 1985. (Top) The terminus of it and the M2 at York Street. Note the 'ski jump' ready for the planned Lagan bridge. (Bottom) The Clifton Street area. (*Photos courtesy of DRD Roads Service*)

to have been that a lower capacity road would attract less traffic, and therefore at-grade junctions would be sufficient.[27] This was not borne out, since it seems that the same amount of traffic would have attempted to use Westlink upon opening, regardless of its design. Therefore the provision of a lower specification design simply resulted in immediate congestion, rather than lower demand.

Lack of money prevented the construction of the Cross Harbour Bridge at the same time as Westlink. Therefore, traffic wishing to travel between the south (the M1) and the north east (the Sydenham Bypass) had to continue using the central area of the city and the Queen's Bridge. Even at this stage, therefore, it would have been clear to Roads Service that Westlink was not carrying the total amount of traffic that could be expected to use it once the Cross Harbour Link was provided. The planners, therefore, were aware that it was only a matter of time before the design of Westlink would have to be revisited. For instance, early steps were taken to secure additional land at Grosvenor Road and Broadway to permit the future addition of flyovers.[23]

Effect on West and North Belfast

The provision of Westlink had a profound and permanent effect on the areas through which it passed. Part of Phase 1 passed along the route of the River Blackstaff and hence did not create much more severance than already existed. However the rest of the road had the effect of restricting access to the central area of the city to just five streets (Grosvenor Road, Divis Street, Peter's Hill, Clifton Street and North Queen Street) and one footbridge (serving Divis Flats).

It has been alleged that this was a deliberate policy to 'control' the people of west Belfast.[28] While it is certainly true that Westlink must have assisted the security forces in monitoring traffic entering and leaving the central area of the city, it is wrong to conclude that this was the reasoning behind the road's design. The junction strategy had been decided almost 20 years previously, before the 'Troubles' had begun, while the justification for depressing the road below ground level is clear and sufficient, without appealing to such sinister motives.

Restricting access to the city centre to just six routes had the effect of severing the organic links that had previously existed across the route of Westlink. The road significantly reduced the connectivity between the city and west and north Belfast, a fact that is very evident 30 years on. As The Forum for Alternative Belfast noted in 2011 "the route [from north Belfast] to the city centre is frustrated by road barriers and poor quality frontage environments".[29]

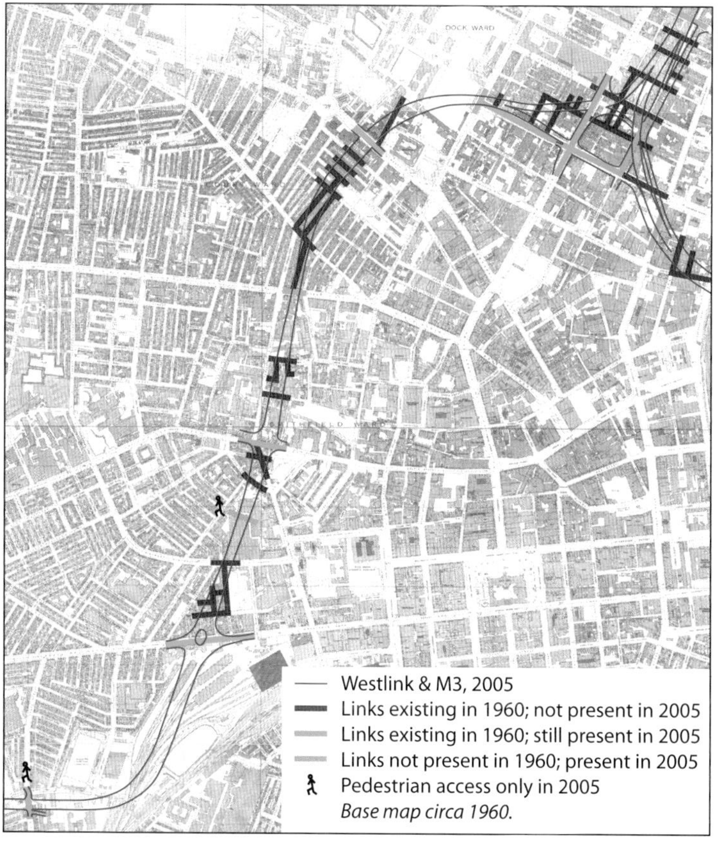

Map showing the links between the city centre and west/ north Belfast that were severed by Westlink, reducing the number of crossing points significantly. *(Base map 1958/60, LPS/Ordnance Survey)*

Of the five roads, the worst impact was on Divis Street and Grosvenor Road, both of which were severed by vast areas of tarmac devoted almost wholly to motor vehicles, with no frontal development to mitigate this impression of negative space. Such areas are extremely unappealing to pedestrians, and combined a significant psychological barrier with the more obvious physical barrier. Clifton Street experienced moderate severance in that, despite the presence of four sliproads, it managed to maintain frontal development in close proximity, which mitigates it to some extent. Peter's Hill and North Queen Street suffered less severance, as the lack of sliproads created no physical barriers for pedestrians, although there was still the psychological barrier of crossing the empty space above or below Westlink. Because the inter-community boundaries in this locale ran at right angles to Westlink, not along it, this part of the road did not create major new sectarian boundaries between communities in the way that it did between them and the city centre.

To the south of the central area of the city, the impact on communities was subtly different. The severance at Roden Street was almost total, with the footbridge (which now provided the only link across Westlink) becoming a focal point for sectarian tension and a cultural no-mans-land, with Westlink marking the barrier between the Nationalist northern end, and the Loyalist southern end.[6] At Broadway, the enormous new Broadway roundabout effectively split Donegall Road in half, and similarly became a border zone between the two communities. This southern section of Westlink became the permanent boundary between the

(Top) The southern side of Clifton Street still bears the scars of demolitions that took place 40 years earlier to make way for the Urban Motorway and then Westlink. *(Author's collection)*

(Bottom) Townsend Street, which lost all buildings on its eastern side, is still largely derelict today. *(Author's collection)*

loyalist 'Village' and Catholic Falls Road areas. This division already existed in 1983 but, while Westlink did not create these divisions between communities, it did freeze them in concrete and therefore may have helped to perpetuate them.

Because Westlink occupied less space than the planned Belfast Urban Motorway, there was an opportunity to use some of the land on either side of the 'canyon' section for other uses. This included a linear park between Peter's Hill and Clifton Street, and similar landscaping and tree-planting along the north side of Westlink between Broadway and Grosvenor Road. In other areas, the spare space remained undeveloped, such as at Townsend Street where the land remains undeveloped and unattractive at the time of writing. More recent low-density housing developments, mainly built in the 1980s, were constructed within a few feet of the finished Westlink: notably at Henry Street, Stanhope Drive, Barrack Street and Cullingtree Road (successors to the Divis Flats) reducing the number of strips of unoccupied land along the road and demonstrating that more modern construction methods could provide a habitable environment even in close proximity to Westlink.

Public Transport Developments

The Lavery Inquiry had recommended a series of measures to enhance public transport, especially buses. It is notable that while work on Westlink began within weeks of the DOE accepting the bulk of Lavery's proposals, the public transport initiatives were not taken forward with the same urgency. Among proposals accepted but not implemented were: a rail link between York Road and Central Station, a central bus station, the elimination of black taxis, a study into bus priority measures and the nationalisation of car parks.[30] Indeed, the only significant proposal that was implemented was the introduction of concessionary fares.

Expenditure on public transport in the period until Westlink opened was even lower than had been anticipated by Lavery.[30] What can account for this? One reason is the coming to power of Conservative Prime Minister Margaret Thatcher in 1979. Although it is unlikely that she really did say that "a man who, beyond the age of 26, finds himself on a bus can count himself as a failure", this apocryphal quote does summarise the view of public transport under Thatcherism. By 1981, 71% of commuter trips in Belfast were being made by car, compared to 27% by bus and train.[25] This compares to 57% and 43% in 1971. The main reason for the soaring use of cars was a continued aspiration to car ownership, a trait common to the whole UK, but reinforced in Belfast by declining investment in buses and the upheaval of the 'Troubles'. In Belfast, the gap between the most mobile (ie car owners) and the least mobile (ie bus users) grew during the early 1980s.[30]

All of these trends fuelled the feeling that buses were a transportation method of 'last resort', and that in an ideal world everyone really ought to have a car. This influenced planners by giving the impression that, in such frugal times, spending on roads made much more sense than spending on buses, which were only going to decline anyway. This led to a climate where progress on public transport was lethargic, while road schemes were pursued with vigour. Regardless of the merits of the road schemes, this skewing of focus was **not** what the Lavery Inquiry had recommended and was **not** the strategy that the DOE had agreed to follow. In the end the lack of any kind of oversight, or meaningful review of the transportation strategy, meant that Lavery's 'mixed' strategy on 1977 morphed into a de-facto roads-oriented strategy, essentially because there was no political will to question how the money was being spent in practice. Westlink's opponents always suspected that the DOE would try to pursue a roads-oriented strategy if left to their own devices[27] and, when they actually were left to their own devices, this is indeed what occurred. This represents a fundamental weakness in the planning process.

Public Housing

By the start of the 1980s there was still a housing crisis in Belfast, despite the efforts of the previous 20 years and the disastrous experiment with high-rise flats. In 1981 the government identified housing as its number one priority in Belfast.[31] During the following decade the Northern Ireland Housing Executive built 10,000 new homes in the city, consisting almost entirely of two storey terraced houses and maisonettes. The housing areas redeveloped at this time included virtually the whole length of Westlink from Roden Street to Clifton Street, including the notorious Divis Flats. Consensus is that these developments finally struck the right balance between density and quality of environment and have been praised for their quality and architectural merit.[32]

Although the debate about expenditure on social housing continues to this day, the disappearance of the worst standard housing during the 1980s took some of the vitriol out of the debate on roads versus houses, and marked a belated recognition by the authorities that local communities did have a right to a say in how their areas were modernised, in marked contrast to the experience of the previous decade.[28] Groups such as the Save The Shankill Campaign were ultimately successful in forcing the government to listen to the wishes of residents when engaging in redevelopment. The battle fought over housing between the representatives of these communities and the planners is a striking one, but beyond the scope of this book.[33]

CHAPTER 11

CROSS HARBOUR BRIDGES

A New Plan

By the early 1980s urban planners had moved away from the idea of large scale government plans, such as allocating huge sums to enormous 'regeneration areas'. They now supported a greater role for the private sector in advancing schemes, with the majority of individual projects merely guided by statutory plans rather than implemented because of them.[1] This shift was in keeping with Thatcherite politics, although it was accused of being about "policy following purchasing power" and for ignoring those at the bottom end of the economic ladder.[2]

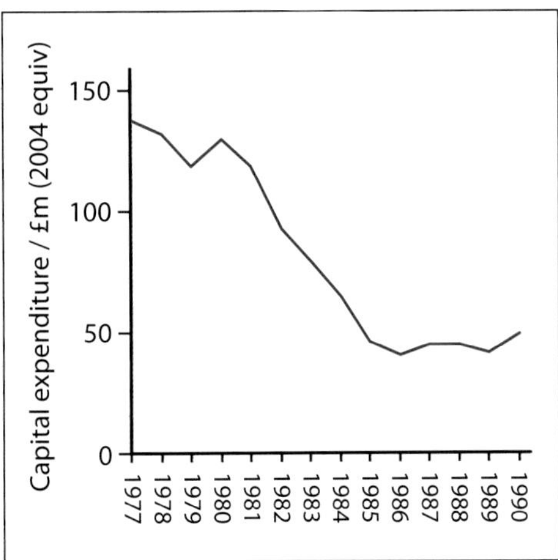

Roads Service capital expenditure on roads in Northern Ireland more than halved in the period from 1977 to 1990.

In addition, there had been two further developments in road transport. Firstly, in 1974 the UK Minister of Transport had issued new standards for roads.[3] These were introduced because it was observed that many roads were now carrying more traffic than their 'design capacity' without apparent difficulty.[4] In other words, it was accepted that a given road could carry more traffic than had been estimated in the 1960s. The government thus increased the traffic flow threshold used to justify the provision of dual-carriageways. This meant that many planned dual-carriageways were no longer seen as justified. Secondly, Roads Service's capital budget was cut drastically from over £100m per year in 1980 to around £35m per year in 1985 (prices are 2004 equivalents), a level that was maintained until around 2000.[5] This severely limited Roads Service's ability to carry out capital schemes, so they tended to focus on short stretches of bypasses and dualling schemes rather than major new roads.

In June 1985, two years after Westlink opened, the government announced that it would begin work on a new plan, guided by the above principles, which would shape all aspects of planning policy for Belfast until the Millennium.[2] It would be known as the 'Belfast Urban Area Plan 2001' (BUAP). The last time such a plan had been prepared was 1969[6] but the DOE stated that the transportation proposals in BUAP would be based upon the scaled-down transportation plan of 1978, not the ambitious plan of 1969.[7] The government gave three key reasons for the review:[7]

1. The need for a revision of the stopline and greenbelt to provide more housing land.
2. The need to rejuvenate the city centre and especially the waterfront area.
3. The need to review both public and private transport policy.

By this stage, the major transportation schemes accepted by Lavery had only been partially implemented, with the Cross Harbour Bridge being the most obvious road scheme still not constructed, along with the Outer Ring West and several stretches of the Central Distributor Box; the lack of progress on the Box being due to major problems with land acquisition.[8] In terms of public transport, concessionary fares had been introduced, but there was still no cross harbour rail link and no central bus station.

The BUAP would consider all aspects of the development of Belfast, and it gave rise to protracted debates about both the conduct of the planning process and the proposals that resulted. As such, the bulk of the debate is beyond the scope of this book which shall limit its treatment of the BUAP to matters directly related to transport. A wider discussion of the development of the BUAP can be found in Blackman.[2]

Work got underway during late 1985, and included a separate 'Belfast Transportation Strategy Review', which involved the creation of a traffic modelling system.[5] Preliminary proposals were published in May 1987[9] and envisaged between £200m and £280m being available for transport in Belfast during the plan period, ie up to 2001.[7] In this document all road proposals were subjected to reappraisal. The planners first listed the existing road proposals that remained unbuilt, which included the Cross Harbour Bridge amongst numerous others. They then added in new proposals not previously considered. The principal one of these (prompted by the high level of traffic that had come to use Westlink since its opening) was a proposal to widen the M1 to three lanes each way, and to upgrade Westlink

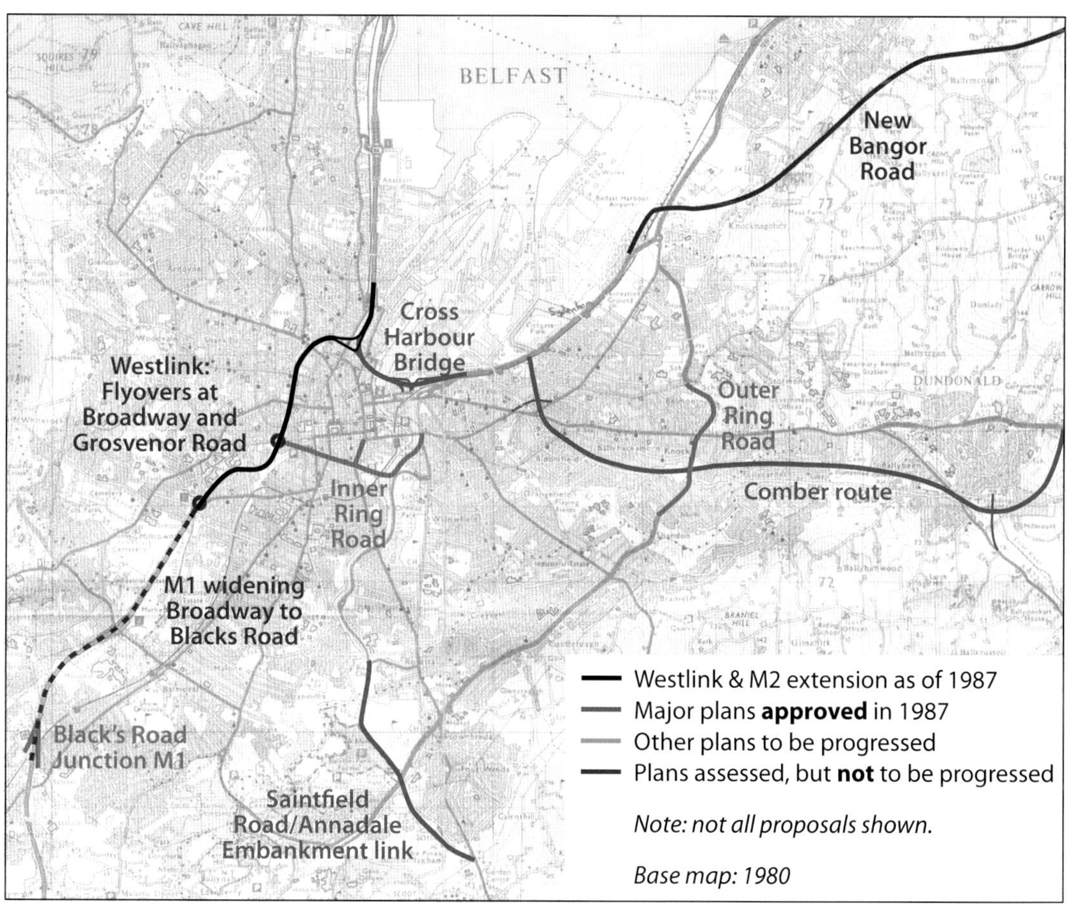

Map showing all road proposals that were considered in the 1987 review. Those that were taken forward are shown in blue, while those rejected are marked in red. It is interesting that only one of the blue schemes actually occurred, while two of the red schemes eventually took place. *(Base map 1980: LPS/ Ordnance Survey)*

by adding the missing flyovers at Broadway and Grosvenor Road. Also added were scaled-down, all-purpose versions of the ambitious M3, M4 and M7 plans: a new cross-country road to Bangor; a road link between the Saintfield Road and Annadale Embankment, adjacent to Belvoir Park Forest; and a new road from Holywood Arches to the Outer Ring at Knock, along the route of the disused railway line. This last proposal was known as the 'Comber route'. Various other proposals were made.

After appraising the economic case for each of these, and considering the budget limitations, it was decided that only three of the schemes should go ahead:

1. The Cross Harbour Bridge
2. The Saintfield Road/Annadale Embankment link
3. The Comber route

It was further recommended that the Cross Harbour Bridge be prioritised ahead of the others, with a suggestion that completion be planned for 1993/94.[9] Notably, the proposal to upgrade Westlink was not taken forward for the period up to 2001 but relegated to a list of proposals to be reviewed at a later date.

These preliminary proposals were sufficient to allow the Direct Rule Minister for the Economy, Richard Needham, to approve construction of both the cross harbour road bridge and the cross harbour rail bridge in May 1987.[10] Although the BUAP had not yet published its draft proposals, let alone been the subject of a public inquiry, the minister felt able to proceed because both these proposals were part of the existing (ie 1978) transportation strategy. When challenged on this point, the DOE responded: "The cross harbour bridges have been processed through public inquiry on a previous occasion. They are now confirmed schemes..."[7] This did not look good: some activists claimed that the DOE had given the impression that all elements of the 1978 strategy were 'on the table'.[2] While the DOE were, technically, perfectly entitled to go ahead with these schemes, there is no doubt that the decision to press ahead with the bridges ahead of the outcome of the public inquiry compromised the credibility of the process as a genuine review and gave ammunition to those who suspected that the plan masked a continued, hidden 'roads agenda'.[2]

The draft BUAP was published on 17 November 1987. The transportation proposals were almost identical to the preliminary proposals, except that the draft BUAP used less certain language about the Saintfield Road/Annadale Embankment link because it had attracted vocal criticism for running so close to Belvoir Park Forest. A public inquiry was scheduled for May 1988. The BUAP "provoked much less interest and passion than its predecessor [the 1969 Plan]",[11] mainly because the BUAP involved "nowhere near the scale of reconstruction that was planned in 1969 to meet the needs of a new manufacturing industry, and instead [emphasised] the needs of the 'post industrial' sectors of retailing, offices, leisure and tourism".[2]

Around this time (in December 1988) a scheme to add a new junction on the M1 at Black's Road, with east-facing sliproads only, was completed at a cost of £2.3m.[12] The new junction was given the number 3, using one of the three missing numbers between Belfast and Lisburn.

The 1988 Inquiry

The public inquiry into the BUAP began on 4 May 1988 in Central Hall, Belfast, under the direction of the Planning Appeals Commission. Having learned from the experience of the Lavery Inquiry ten years earlier, groups such as Community Technical Aid (which backed those who wanted a greater emphasis on public transport) attempted to engage professional help from the earliest stages of the process, and were successful in obtaining a grant of £50,000 towards this end from the DOE in November 1987, a grant which was described by CTA as "disappointing" in size, but "enough to commission" Reid McHugh, a professional planner, and three graduate planners.[2] They also held a series of meetings beforehand to settle disagreements within the opposition camp. The result was that by the time of the inquiry, opponents to the BUAP proposals were largely able to present a united front and, crucially, make well-argued technical points, both of which were factors that had been absent in 1977.

The case of the Department first of all focused on their breakdown of planned expenditure, which for the proposed strategy was £128m for roads and £96m for public transport. The roads figure included £45m for the Cross Harbour Bridge, while the public transport figure included £14m for the cross harbour rail bridge and £40m to sustain the concessionary fares, which were recommended by Lavery in 1977 as a cornerstone of a viable public transport system. Thus 57% of the transport budget was allocated to roads, which the department felt was "not unduly biased towards private transport bearing in mind that 80% of daily trips … are made by private transport".[7] It was also very close to the ratio of 55% roads/45% public transport recommended by Lavery in 1977. In addition, it was pointed out that the rail link and proposed central bus station were both major investments, so it was not true to say that there would be no improvements to public transport.

The Department then argued that it had carried out a detailed financial appraisal of the costs of implementing alternative forms of public transport, by investigating a light rail system. They found that such a proposal would be too limited in terms of the areas it could serve, and too expensive when compared to the patronage it would attract to justify its construction. It rejected major investment in park-and-ride sites on the grounds that there was no demand for them, since existing and planned car parks (especially the proposed multi-storey at the planned Castle Court shopping centre) would "ensure that forecast demand is satisfied".[7] They argued against restraining the private car because, in the fragile climate of the 'Troubles', doing so "would have adverse effects on city centre growth".[13]

Finally, the case was made that the Cross Harbour Bridge was the single most important piece of transport infrastructure needed in Belfast. They said that it was "of fundamental importance in coping with traffic flows in and around the central area" and were recommending its construction "as soon as resources permit".[14] The bridge would take the majority of traffic travelling between the M1/M2 and Sydenham Bypass off the city centre streets that they were currently forced to use.

The case of the Objectors was, as it always had been, the argument that local communities were being asked to pay too high a price to serve the perceived needs of car owners and that not enough was being spent on public transport. They argued that bus services were cramped and dirty, and that the Department was making no effort to improve services or make them more attractive to car users, preferring to simply sustain what already existed. The strategy of merely maintaining public transport was contrasted with the road proposals which were designed to cater for the predicted expansion of 40% in traffic levels by 2001.[2]

While the Department's figure that 80% of journeys were made by car was accepted, they pointed out that 50% of households in the city did not own a car and were forced to rely on what they regarded as a sub-standard public transport system in a way that clearly impacted social equality.[2] The Consumer Council presented a report at the inquiry which argued that only 15% of transport expenditure since 1978 had gone directly to public transport, just a third of the 45% figure recommended by Lavery.[2]

They also argued that the approach being taken to roads was far too *laissez-faire*: there was going to be no effort to actually restrain the use of the private car; car parks were going to be provided in the city centre to continue to meet demand; and there would in fact be further road building and widening throughout the city, albeit on a reduced scale due to financial constraints. They argued that cars should be restrained by a combination of (a) halting new roads and (b) catering for the rise in demand for journeys through priority bus lanes or light rail, especially in east Belfast where the road along the 'Comber route' was proposed.

The Outcome

The inquiry closed on 24 June 1988. Unlike the events of 1977, the 1988 inquiry had not been disrupted by protests, but was characterised by genuine engagement on the part of the objectors. Although still heavily criticised,[2] the experience of 1988 was the most positive of the three key inquiries relating to the Belfast motorway system. In the first, in 1972, opponents engaged with the process but felt their objections had been ignored. By the second, in 1977, many objectors had lost all faith in inquiries and adopted a strategy of disruption and civil disobedience, but in the end were unsuccessful and still felt that their objections had been ignored. In the third, in 1988, objectors once again engaged with the process and this time were able to do so on a much more equitable footing and ultimately achieved genuine modifications to the plan.

For the first time in Northern Ireland, an inquiry resulted in significant changes to a transport plan. The Planning Appeals Commissioners were convinced by the objectors of the merit of the public transport arguments, and recommended that more attention be given to the needs of non-car owners, and that more consideration should be given to restraining city centre car parking and ways of making public transport more attractive. The Department, with the exception of restraining car parking, accepted all of the recommendations.

They then dealt with the road proposals. All three key proposals survived the inquiry intact. The Cross Harbour Bridge, then already approved by the Department, would go ahead as planned. The Commission recognised that the construction of the 'Comber route' would result in loss of amenity on the former railway line, part of which had now been converted into a nature walk, but that the needs of city transport outweighed this loss. The Saintfield Road to Annadale link would also go ahead, but with an option to review it. In many other cases, however, the Commissioners sided with the objectors. Thus, schemes such as a planned flyover on the Outer Ring at the Castlereagh Road, the widening of the Upper Newtownards Road past Stormont and through Dundonald, and further widening of Albertbridge Road were all thrown out.

Looking back at this era of private-sector-focused Thatcherite politics, it is probably a fair criticism that there was not enough effort to improve or enhance the image of public transport. It was clearly regarded as the backup transport method 'for those without cars', rather than a method people might actually choose to use. At the same time, given the attractiveness of private cars and the apparent willingness of people to sit in quite serious congestion before considering alternatives, it is probably optimistic to think that the growth in demand for road space could have been largely or entirely managed by the provision of light rail, improved bus services and priority bus lanes. The Department's concerns about damaging the city centre by restraining car parking were likely correct, since this was an era when increasing numbers of shops and businesses were choosing to set up in the periphery of the city in order to reduce costs and improve access. Increasing parking charges or reducing parking provision would inevitably have accelerated this retreat to the suburbs. If severe forms of planning restraint had been imposed to prevent this, the result could have been the departure of some businesses from the city entirely.

While the inquiry could hardly be called a victory for the objectors, it was nevertheless remarkable as the first time that objections appeared to have been considered important enough to result in material changes to a plan. As was the case at both the 1972 and 1977 inquiries, the debate was once again between two equally unattainable dreams (unrestrained car use versus a perfect public transport system) which resulted in a compromise that did not satisfy anybody entirely, but which did represent the approximation of a workable, pragmatic strategy. The adopted strategy was one of maintaining and slightly improving public transport while providing some, but not all, of the infrastructure needed to cater for private transport.

Planning the Cross Harbour Bridges

The new road bridge would provide a direct link between the M2 motorway in north Belfast and the Sydenham Bypass in east Belfast by following a tightly curving route along the line reserved for Phase 2A of the Belfast Urban Motorway. The link would be built with dual two-lane carriageways, and was designed for a 50 mph speed limit. This reduced speed limit was justified because of the tight curve that the road would follow and the close proximity of junctions. Although the road would have motorway restrictions, it would have hard strips on the bridge itself, rather than full size hard shoulders (hard shoulders are not actually a requirement on motorways).

The Lavery Inquiry of 1977 had recommended proceeding with the Cross Harbour Bridges, but had suggested that the road bridge should be two lanes each way with a third lane each way for the sliproads.[14] However, when the bridges were being designed, traffic engineers became convinced that this design would lead to significant congestion on the bridge due to (a) weaving between the sliproads and the mainline and (b) the high percentage of traffic predicted to use the bridge to 'hop' across the river by going up the onslip and immediately down the offslip. The outcome of this analysis was that the bridge was redesigned to accommodate four lanes each way: two for the mainline and two for the sliproads. This change made only a moderate difference to the cost but made a significant difference to traffic flow.

Indeed, all the sliproads would be two lanes wide, with the offslips widening to four lanes when they reached the local road network. The space between junction 1 (Middlepath Street) and junction 1A (York Street) would set the record as the shortest distance between any two motorway junctions in Northern Ireland, with a total weaving length of 340 metres (1115 feet) eastbound and just 310 metres (1017 feet) westbound. This weaving stretch coincided with the river bridge itself, which would therefore be four lanes wide in each direction. The section of road that connected the river bridge to the M2 would carry two lanes each way and be

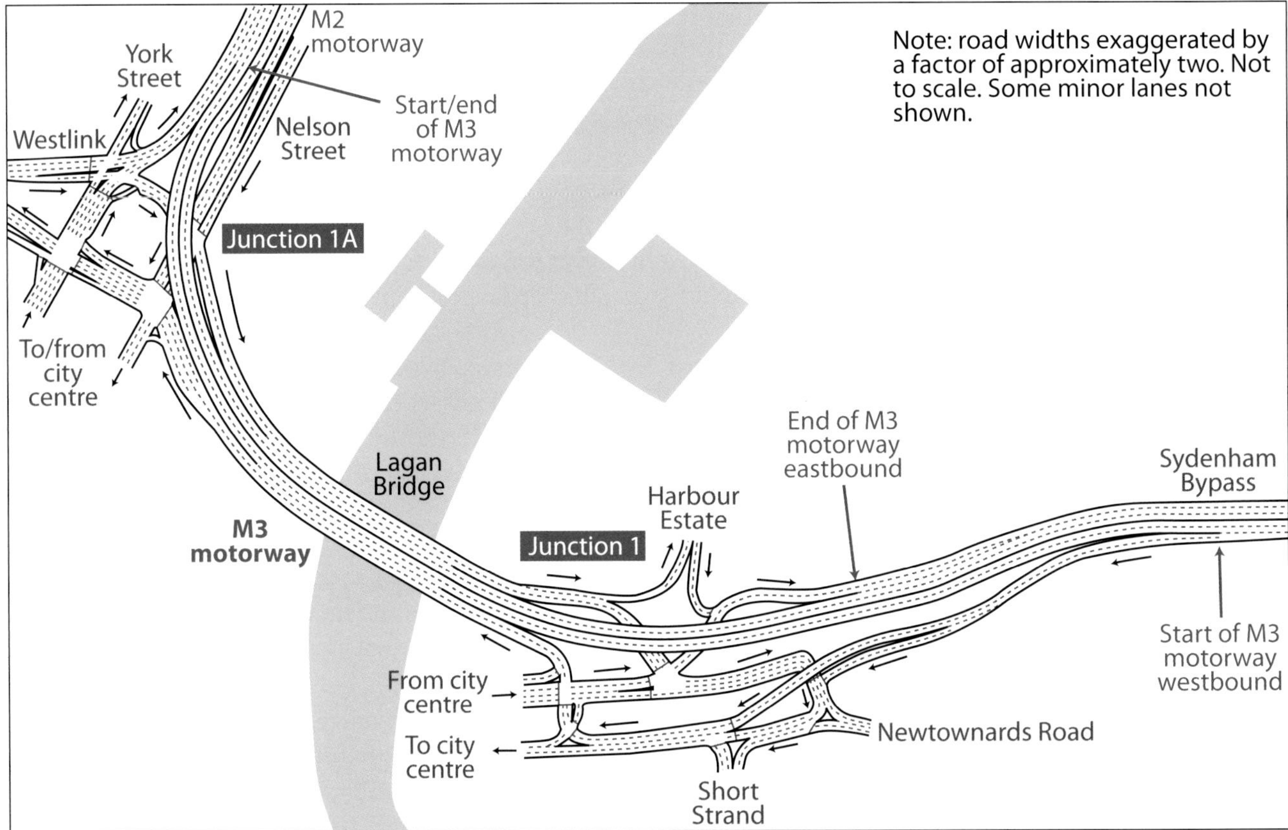

Stylised map showing the layout of lanes on the completed M3 motorway and the adjacent local road network. Note that the M3 is considerably longer westbound than eastbound due to the positioning of the last opportunity for non-motorway traffic to exit the road.

elevated on a viaduct over the local road network. The section of road that connected the river bridge to the Sydenham Bypass would also be two lanes each way, but would be elevated on an embankment rather than a viaduct as it was not necessary to avoid so many local roads in this locality. Thus, the engineering challenges on the west and east banks were markedly different.

At the extreme eastern end, the road would tie in to the existing Sydenham Bypass, although the next junction along (at Dee Street) would remain a signalised T-junction, despite being just a few hundred metres from the end of a motorway.

Because the decision had been made in 1977 that Westlink would only have a street-level interchange with the M2 and Cross Harbour Bridge, the 1988 design did not incorporate any provision for freeflow links either then or at a future date. As a result of this, it was decided that the cross harbour railway viaduct could be constructed adjacent to, and at the same elevation as, the south/west side of the road link. This decision made sense at the time, but would lead to difficulties when the design of the junction was re-examined 20 years later.

Despite the fact that the existing rail network in Belfast was entirely double track, it was decided that the railway viaduct would have only a single track between Dock Street and Middlepath Street, albeit with a short passing loop half way along. Those campaigning for the rail link saw this decision in a poor light, as it would create a bottleneck on the railway network requiring commuter trains to take turns crossing the bridge. In addition, the decision had been made to relocate the railway maintenance yard to north Belfast, which would generate more rail traffic across the bridge. However, the government had only agreed to press ahead with the rail link under public pressure, and it was made clear that the choice was between a single-track bridge and no bridge at all.[15] The railway managers therefore accepted the single-track bridge as the 'best deal in town'.

The project was by necessity split into two phases. The connection between the new road bridge and the Sydenham Bypass required the demolition of Northern Ireland Railways' maintenance depot at Queen's Quay. However, this could not be carried out until a replacement depot was opened at York Road. This replacement could not be built until York Road railway station was demolished, which itself could not be carried out until a replacement station at Yorkgate was built. Since the opening of Yorkgate station required the construction of part of the approach embankment on the west bank, it is obvious that there was much to co-ordinate. The solution was to build the railway and road bridges in Phase 1, along with the sliproads connecting the road bridge to Middlepath Street. Then, once Queen's Quay maintenance yard had been demolished, the bridge would be connected to the Sydenham Bypass in Phase 2.

Construction of Phase 1

The tender process commenced in November 1988,[10] and six consortia were carried through to the second stage of the process, with each submitting designs in October 1989. These were then assessed by the Royal Fine Art Commission which suggested changes, mainly that the structure should have smooth, continuous lines and that the bridge piers should be moulded to make them easier on the eye.[10] These changes were incorporated into the design. Three consortia were then invited to tender, with the winner – Graham-Farrans Joint Venture – being awarded the design and construct tender by the DOE in July 1991.[16]

Work began the following month, although some work on the road embankments for the road at Station Street (on the east bank) had been carried out in 1990 and early 1991 in order to allow enough time for settlement of the soft ground. In 1991 preliminary work was also required to widen the M2 to five lanes northbound, which meant widening Dock Street bridge, which had only opened 11 years earlier. It had originally been planned that there would be two lanes northbound from York Street and two from the Cross Harbour Bridge, but since its construction it had been determined that three lanes would be required northbound from York Street to accommodate anticipated traffic flows. The widening scheme was completed in May 1992. Finally, work was carried out in 1991 and 1992 to realign the railway line at York Street, and Yorkgate station was opened in October 1992, albeit as a temporary terminus awaiting the construction of the railway viaduct beyond.

The embankment for the future M3 in place near Station Street in October 1991, where it was left for some months to settle. *(Aubrey Dale)*

As the road did not pass through any residential areas, there were no issues associated with public protest during construction. Nevertheless, the construction of an elevated motorway less than 1 km from City Hall was highly visible and attracted much public interest from the commuters who crawled past the site each day on the Queen's Bridge.

(Above) View south from York Street railway station at Dock Street in October 1992 showing work underway on the railway viaduct. The 'ski jump' on the M2 is also visible. *(Author's collection)*

As an exhaustive treatment of the engineering aspects of the design and construction of the bridges is available elsewhere[16] the discussion below is a summary.

The road bridge consists of a viaduct of 950 metres (3116 feet) in length with a river crossing of 165 metres (541 feet). The adjacent railway bridge is longer at 1500 metres (4921 feet). The bridge foundations were constructed in very poor ground conditions along most of the scheme, as this part of Belfast is situated on deposits of maritime sleech and glacial deposits up to 40 metres deep.[17] With the exception of the abutments at the east end of the bridges, all the piers were built on piled foundations. Ten piers (five on the west, five on the east; eight for the road, two for the railway) were constructed in the River Lagan itself, facilitated by a temporary cofferdam. The ten piers rest on 112 tubular steel piles, each 610 mm in diameter, and contain 2500 cubic metres of concrete. Each pier was designed to withstand an impact from a 5500 tonne vessel travelling at two knots. The piers for the approach spans on land were founded on 1269 precast concrete piles, the bulk of which were on the west bank of the river for the elevated section over the existing city streets around Corporation Street.

(Below) View west along Great George's Street from Corporation Street in January 1993. The street was removed to make way for the M3. *(Aubrey Dale)*

The bridge decks were constructed from precast segments which, in their simplest form, were boxes 5.0 metres (16.4 feet) wide and 2.2 metres (7.2 feet) deep ranging in length from 2.0 to 4.0 metres (6.6 to 13.1 feet). To facilitate the arch required for the river section (which is a circular arc) the segments there are deeper, reaching a maximum

(Top left and above) Building and using cofferdams to construct the piers for the Lagan bridges. *(Photos courtesy DRD Roads Service)*

(Left) Pillars taking shape at Corporation Street in January 1993. *(Aubrey Dale)*

(Below) Work on the decks of the M3 and railway viaducts circa mid 1993. The westbound offslip is visible in the foreground. *(Photo courtesy DRD Roads Service)*

(Top) One of the three specially made moulds used for casting the bridge segments.

(Bottom) One of the completed bridge segments awaiting transportation to the site.

(Photos courtesy DRD Roads Service)

depth of 5.0 metres (16.4 feet). The segments used on the road bridge were augmented by cantilevers on each side, which vary in size but have a maximum width of 3.05 metres (10.01 feet) on each side. The main span of the road bridge actually consists of four adjacent bridge sections, each carrying two lanes. In total, 1058 box segments were required, sufficient to justify the construction of a temporary factory in the Harbour Estate which, using three moulds, constructed the segments at a maximum rate of 15 per week between April 1992 and early 1994. The segments weighed between 50 and 90 tonnes and 828 of them were transported to the site via a multi-axle low-loader during the night. The remaining 230 were floated to the river section by barge.

Work on erecting the deck segments began in October 1992 using the balanced cantilever technique. This required the use of a 230 tonne cantilever crawling crane for the land sections, and a crane mounted on a barge for the river bridges. The river sections required the largest number of balanced sections on either side of a pier (11), while some of those on land had only three. The deck structures were completed by May 1994 (rail) and August 1994 (road).

The trackwork for the rail link was in place by October 1994, and the railway bridge came into use on 28 November 1994. It was named Dargan Bridge in honour of the Victorian engineer William Dargan, who was responsible not only for the first railway in Ireland (Dublin to Kingstown) but also the Ulster Railway (Belfast to Portadown and Ballymena), the Ulster Canal, and the development of Victoria Channel in Belfast harbour.

The road bridge was completed in August 1994, and the sliproads connecting it to Middlepath Street in January 1995 (the embankments that would carry these sliproads having been left to settle since January 1992). The road bridge was opened to pedestrians for one day on 26 November 1994, to raise money for charity and to allow people to view the completed railway bridge, and many people took the chance to walk across.[12] The road bridge was opened to traffic on 22 January 1995 and was named Lagan Bridge. Both bridges were officially opened by Queen Elizabeth II on 9 March 1995.[16] Until Phase 2 was built, all traffic on the road bridge was directed down the offslips to Middlepath Street. This was accomplished by dropping the leftmost lane eastbound and directing the three remaining lanes down the offslip, an arrangement that was in place until 1998.

Perhaps it was the experience of being prevented from realising the dream of a network of motorways in the Belfast urban area that prompted Roads Service to give the road across

The deck of the Lagan Bridge takes shape circa early 1993. Note the barge-mounted crane. The land in the distance is now home to the Odyssey complex. *(Photo courtesy DRD Roads Service)*

the new bridge the number 'M3', the number originally reserved for the Belfast to Bangor motorway. This was a slight misnomer, as the Urban Motorway itself never had a number, while the planned M3 was only to have begun near Bridge End. The Lagan Bridge, therefore, inherited a number that it would not have had if it had been built as part of the Urban Motorway scheme.

The total cost of the scheme was £89m, of which the road represented £56m and the rail link £33m. The European Regional Development Fund provided £22m towards the costs of the rail link.

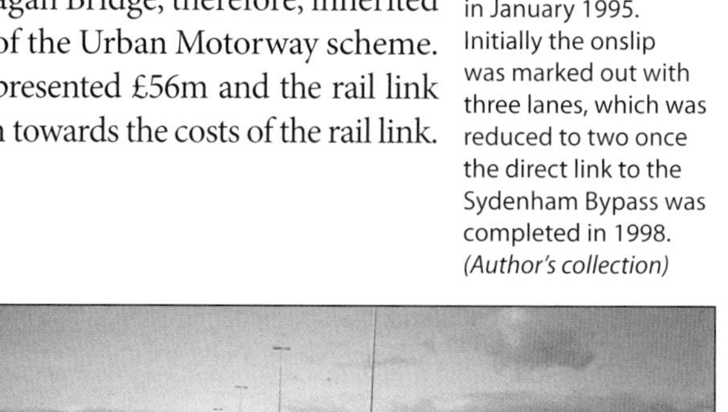

The view west across the M3 Lagan Bridge shortly before opening in January 1995. Initially the onslip was marked out with three lanes, which was reduced to two once the direct link to the Sydenham Bypass was completed in 1998. *(Author's collection)*

Impact of the Cross Harbour Bridge

The opening of the M3 Lagan Bridge on 22 January 1995 brought half a century of road planning in Belfast full circle, as it was designed to tackle the cross-river traffic problem: the issue that had first triggered the process that led to the conception of the Belfast Urban Motorway. It is also unique in being the only part of the Urban Motorway that was constructed essentially as planned, as an elevated, four-lane highway cruising above the city streets while its impoverished sibling, Westlink, had been reduced to two lanes with at-grade roundabouts. The M3, therefore, provides the most accurate illustration of how the rest of the Urban Motorway would have looked had it been completed.

The completed Dargan Bridge and, beyond it, the M3 Lagan Bridge in 1995. *(Author's collection)*

Aerial view of the M3 Lagan Bridge in 1995 before the direct link to the Sydenham Bypass was completed. *(Photo courtesy DRD Roads Service)*

The new road was received very positively by the citizens of Belfast. As the hour of opening approached there was severe congestion as 'M3 mania'[18] hit the city with "hundreds of cars lined up as far back as the Queen Elizabeth Bridge … which remained motionless for an hour".[18] When the road was opened, two police cars led off, followed by the first member of the public, biker Steven Constanzo, with his wife Alison riding pillion. He explained that "this will save me at least 30 minutes on my way from the Ballysillan Road to Comber. It skips the city centre traffic".[18]

Mr Constanzo's comment was typical of thousands of motorists who wanted to travel across the periphery of the city and who had, since the earliest days of the motor car, been forced to drive through the city centre to do so. The M3 allowed all this traffic to get out of the city streets and onto the network of urban dual-carriageways and motorways. Like Westlink 12 years before, the M3 unleashed a tidal wave of frustrated demand that had been building up behind the Queen's Bridge dam for decades. It almost immediately became the second busiest road in Northern Ireland (after the M2), and was carrying almost 91,000 vehicles per day by 2004,[19] more even than Westlink. Its importance to transport in the Belfast region is demonstrably immense, and there can be little doubt that it has contributed to greater economic relations between the two sides of the river, and opened up new opportunities for people to seek a wider variety of employment opportunities. When measured against the yardstick of how many journeys it facilitates, the M3 has been a staggering success.

The road immediately took an enormous amount of traffic out of the city centre, most specifically the routes leading to the Queen's/Queen Elizabeth Bridges, as well as the Bridge End one-way system on the east bank. A number of pieces of infrastructure once required to meet the high demand were left looking somewhat over-engineered with the reduced traffic levels. For example, the Station Street flyover at Queen's Quay, and the Queen Elizabeth Bridge itself, which features excessively wide footpaths in addition to four traffic lanes. With the city centre now having a diminished role for cross-city traffic, planners were able, over the next decade, to introduce a range of measures to improve the streetscape in the city centre, for example, routing traffic out of Custom House Square, which was redesigned as an attractive pedestrian space. Further measures of this kind, such as reducing the width of the Inner Ring Road, are at the proposal stage. None of these measures would have been practical without the M3 Lagan Bridge.

At the time of writing, over 15 years on, the M3 continues to cope fairly well with the high traffic levels it attracts. It is true that the weaving section on the bridge itself is unpopular with motorists and can lead to slow-moving traffic. However the fact that there are traffic signals at the bottom of both on-slips means that the bridge has an effective 'ramp metering' system which cuts off the supply of vehicles just as stop-start conditions begin to develop and allows the congestion to dissipate. Despite carrying more traffic than Westlink, the M3 suffers less severe congestion at peak times, due to its higher specification, freeflow design.

Completing the Link

Of course, all was not yet finished: there was still the matter of tying the M3 directly into the Sydenham Bypass. This was possible only once the Queen's Quay railway maintenance depot was vacated by NIR, and once that had happened the work was carried out by Farrans at a total cost of £6.2 million and came into use in May 1998.

Until this road link was completed, the Sydenham Bypass crossed over the railway line on a bridge, the Ballymacarrett Flyover, which had been constructed in 1959. This bridge was not compatible with the design of the new road link, which ran parallel to the north side of the railway line, and was thus demolished. This enabled the Sydenham Bypass to flow directly onto the M3 without crossing the railway. Traffic wishing to join the Sydenham Bypass eastbound was instead directed along a new onslip which departed from Middlepath Street, passed under the M3, and merged as a sliproad shortly before Dee Street. A second sliproad facilitated traffic wishing to exit Sydenham Bypass westbound. This new road required the construction of a new bridge over the railway line slightly to the east of the original Flyover. Many readers will remember the temporary 'wiggle' that diverted traffic off the alignment of the new M3 onto this offslip before the main section of M3 was opened. At its western end the sliproad connects to the Bridge End Flyover, which dates from the construction of the Bridge End one-way system of 1966 and which survived the completion of the M3.

Because the westbound offslip is situated much further east than the corresponding eastbound onslip, the M3 is 520 metres (1700 feet) longer westbound than eastbound. The motorway restrictions must begin and end at these points for legal reasons. The total length of the M3, therefore, is 1.45 km (0.90 miles) eastbound but 1.97 km (1.22 miles) westbound.

The Dee Street junction on the Sydenham Bypass, with the M3 beyond, here seen in December 2006. Visible in the distance is the westbound offslip to Middlepath Street, which is on the original line of the 1959 Sydenham Bypass. *(Author's collection)*

The opening of the rest of the M3 in 1998 marked the completion of the Urban Motorway in the reduced form envisaged by Lavery in 1977. Phases 1 and 2A were now built, albeit in very different forms from what was planned in 1967. It is almost impossible to conceive of Phases 2B or 3 of the Urban Motorway ever being built.

Other Developments in the 1990s

Contemporaneous with the opening of the M3, Roads Service commissioned a brand new £5.5m traffic control system[10,5] to build upon the one installed in 1980.[20] The system connects virtually all the traffic signals in Belfast, as well as numerous traffic cameras and variable message signs, to a central control centre. The system allows computers or human operators to constantly tweak traffic signals and, on the motorways, introduce advisory speed limits to keep traffic moving optimally and has been greatly expanded in the years since its installation.

In 1991 Lavery's dream of a central bus station for Belfast was finally realised with the opening of the Europa Bus Centre on Great Victoria Street. The Bus Centre is located less than 500 metres from City Hall and consolidates the majority of long-distance buses connecting Belfast to the rest of Northern Ireland into a single site (Citybus/Metro services generally departing from City Hall). The building is large and spacious, and accommodates a multi-story car park above, allowing people to park their cars and continue their journey on the bus, as well as providing additional city centre car parking. Nevertheless, prevailing government policy in the 1990s placed limits on how much subsidy was available, insisting that bus services had to largely pay for themselves.[21]

On 30 September 1995, the re-opening of Great Victoria Street Railway Station, adjacent to the Bus Centre, further developed the public transport hub at the site. For the first time, this allowed the direct integration of province-wide bus and rail services. Coupled with the new bridge that allowed trains to run directly between north, east and south Belfast, it is little wonder that transport chiefs hailed "the dawning of a new era for railways in Northern Ireland".[22] Sure enough, between 1991 and 2001, the number of people commuting by train in Northern Ireland rose by 40%,[21] reversing a decline that had begun in the early 1970s. The events leading up to the reopening of Great Victoria Street railway station are fascinating, but beyond the scope of this history.

Variable message sign and advisory speed limit signs on the M2 foreshore, which are part of the DRD's sophisticated traffic control system. The signs can be changed from a central control room. *(Photo courtesy DRD Roads Service)*

The Europa Bus Centre and adjacent Great Victoria Street railway station, seen here in 2001. *(Author's collection)*

CHAPTER 12
A NEW ERA

Environmentalism

During the early 1990s it was increasingly clear that attitudes to roads and cars were changing as environmental concerns grew. Issues such as lead poisoning, acid rain, the hole in the ozone layer, deforestation, excess carbon emissions and global warming followed in quick succession, contributing to the growth of a large constituency who felt that mankind (or at least the West) was now exerting an unacceptably high impact on the Earth and its resources. It was argued that the human race must change its behaviour to avoid major environmental degradation. One aspect of this was the idea that humans should take no more resources from the Earth than it replaced: the doctrine of 'sustainability'. Campaign groups took on various forms and issues, but most pointed the finger at industrialisation, consumerism and increasing energy use as the ultimate culprits.

Since cars conflicted with the doctrine of sustainability on many fronts, cars and roads found themselves particularly susceptible to attack from what had become known as the 'environmental lobby'. Cars, after all, used fossil fuels and were not only polluting the atmosphere, but were mostly doing so in densely populated areas. Additionally, since every car had its own engine, they were using a finite resource (oil) very inefficiently and their emissions were contributing a sizeable proportion of global anthropogenic carbon emissions. And their numbers just kept rising. Cars, it was argued, were unsustainable and the environmental lobby therefore concluded that continuing to provide new road space to accommodate the growth in traffic was not only futile from a practical point of view, but was actually taking society further from the goal of sustainability. (The point that traffic kept growing was not new, but the rationale of sustainability as a reason to reverse the trend was.)

The arguments that could be presented against this conclusion were few in number – perhaps the strongest being that of freedom and liberty, manifested in the enormous resistance that would be encountered from the car-owning masses. Nevertheless, by the 1990s, the environmental lobby had embarked on an unapologetic crusade against the unhindered use of cars. This is not to suggest that environmentalism was a new phenomenon in the 1990s – environmentalists had been opposing road construction for decades – but in the 1980s and before, environmental objections tended to focus on the physical impact of cars in cities and the countryside, and the social impacts of road construction on existing communities, rather than the impact on global climate. The 1990s saw much more elucidated environmental arguments, on a much wider range of environmental issues and in much more detail than hitherto.

Public transport, long regarded in government circles simply as the default transport system for those without cars, found itself fiercely championed as the solution to the whole issue of sustainability and environmental concern. While, hitherto, advocates of increased expenditure on public transport had argued the case on the grounds of social equality and the need to reduce traffic in cities, proponents now presented new arguments, such as reduced pollution (especially in terms of anthropogenic carbon emissions) and a more efficient use of energy resources, as reasons to embrace it.

These arguments finally found some sympathy within the UK government during the early 1990s. The most recent predictions of traffic growth, made in 1989, suggested that traffic levels in the UK would grow by between 83% and 142% over the following 35 years and that this increase could not be accommodated by road building without enormous cost.[1] In 1993, the EC published a White Paper that advocated a change in transport policy to reduce congestion caused by cars and to promote public transport. In 1994 the UK government issued new planning policy guidelines that aimed to reduce the need to travel by discouraging developments that would lead to a significant growth in the number of new car journeys made.[1] This was directly at odds with much previous policy, for example the decentralisation of population and growth of commuting advocated by the 1962 'Matthew Plan'.[2]

These changes finally filtered down to Northern Ireland early in 1995, when Conservative Direct Rule minister Malcolm Moss issued a statement signalling how Northern Ireland would respond to this shift in UK policy.[3] There were seven key points:

- The need to minimise, where possible, the effects of transport on the environment.
- A recognition that it is no longer acceptable to seek to meet the full demands of future traffic growth simply by building roads, particularly in urban areas.
- An improved public transport system which will include better co-ordination of bus and rail services.
- Fuller integration of land use and transport planning.
- A more integrated approach to transport planning and funding.
- The maintenance of good strategic transport connections both within Northern Ireland and between Northern Ireland and the rest of Europe.
- A realistic assessment of what is achievable, in both the short and medium-term, having regard to the availability of future financial resources and changing public attitudes.

This was a bold statement of intent, and highly principled when taken at face value, but was unspecific and did not set out what it would actually mean in concrete terms. While it explicitly mentioned improving public transport, it stopped short of saying that new roads should not be built. However, the minister did go on to make a statement that was probably intended to silence those who would accuse him of offering mere words:

> *There has been considerable public disquiet about one of the options under consideration – the proposal to run a new road through Belvoir Forest Park [the Saintfield Road/ Annadale Embankment link]. I have now ruled out this option in the light of our new policy direction: not only would it have an unacceptable environmental impact on a unique urban forest, but it would also run counter to the principle of not seeking to meet the demands of commuter traffic through new road building. The options for a solution*

to the problem need to be determined in the light of the principles which I have set out today... [4]

Of course, public opposition would quite likely have thwarted this particular scheme even without the change in policy, but announcing the decision on this date certainly helped the Minister make his point. It was a clear contradiction of the existing Belfast Urban Area Plan that had been adopted in 1987 and was supposedly still in force until 2001. That plan had included three major road schemes for Belfast: the cross-harbour bridge (then nearing completion), the aforementioned road link adjacent to Belvoir Park, and the Comber route. The latter two were essentially commuter roads, and the 1995 announcement showed that London's Direct Rule Ministers no longer regarded such schemes as acceptable in Northern Ireland. This left Roads Service's plans for the period following the completion of the M3 somewhat in limbo.

On the same date, the Minister also announced that the three main public transport organisations (Ulsterbus, Citybus and Northern Ireland Railways) would be combined as a single body called Translink, the hope being that this would allow much closer integration between the three brands.

The End of Predict-and-Provide

The Department of the Environment spent most of the year digesting the government's shift, finally releasing a document in October 1995 setting out their new policy towards roads.[5] Most importantly, it signalled an end to the era of building new roads to meet future demand, the so-called 'predict-and-provide' policy. The department explained that:

...road building in the coming years will be targeted at removing bottlenecks and completing missing links on the existing road network... [specifically]
- *the improvement and upgrading of the key strategic routes*
- *the completion of bypasses of a number of towns presently on those key routes*
- *the construction of schemes in Belfast to relieve serious traffic congestion, eg Forster Green [where the A24 Saintfield Road meets the A55 Outer Ring], Westlink."*[5]

This meant that a 'strategic network' (made up of a small number of existing key road links) would be identified, and investment would be channelled primarily into efforts to remove bottlenecks on this network, and complete missing links between the various elements. In other words, Roads Service would give up attempting to provide enough capacity to accommodate all those who wanted to use the road network and concentrate instead on dealing more modestly with problem sections of the existing road network. In light of Roads Service's very limited budget, this was largely a *de jure* recognition of what was already true *de facto*.

The first two bullet points implied that new roads would still be built, but only to enhance the existing strategic road network and provide bypasses of towns that were presenting bottlenecks (for example, Toome). In greater Belfast, the strategic road network consisted of: the motorways; Westlink; the Sydenham Bypass; the Outer Ring in south and east Belfast;

Comber Road; and the sections of the Saintfield Road and Newtownards Road that lay outside the Outer Ring. The new policy, therefore, essentially ruled out all new road building within Belfast, other than providing enhancements to these specific roads. Beyond the strategic road network, the new policy left little scope for road building schemes of all but the most minor nature. It seemed that traffic levels would continue to increase on city roads, but that only tactics that did not involve new roads would be adopted to manage the problem. In essence, this marked a final acceptance at the highest levels that road building could not keep pace with increasing traffic levels.

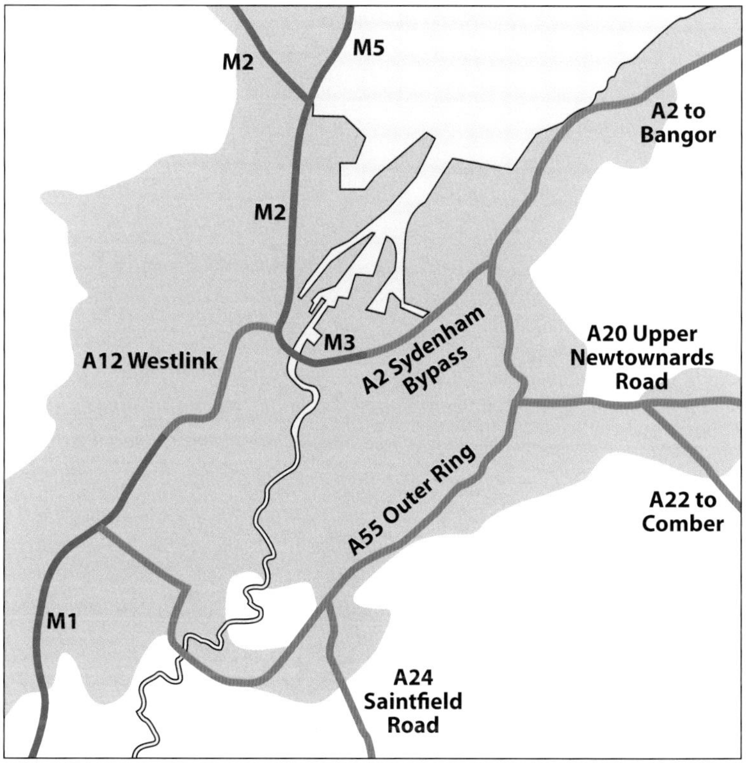

Both the Comber route and the Saintfield Road/Annadale Embankment link road proposals were abandoned, and the M3 became the last major new strategic road to be built in Belfast at the time of writing. As such, the M3 is the last, and arguably the greatest, monument to the era of major road building in Belfast that began in the 1960s and ended, it now seems, in 1998.

The 'strategic road network' in the Belfast area consists of those key routes deemed most essential for longer distance travel and links between key economic nodes.

With the Comber route and Saintfield Road/Annadale Embankment link road abandoned, attention turned to the proposal to upgrade Westlink. This had been included as a future option in the 1987 Plan, but had not been prioritised. In the new post-1995 landscape, this scheme was one of the few remaining schemes that could still be carried out in Belfast, as it involved upgrading a 'strategic' road. Without any other competing schemes on the agenda, Malcolm Moss announced in March 1996 that work would begin immediately to assess the scope for upgrading the section of the M1 from Black's Road to Broadway, and Westlink, to improve capacity.[20] Although used by many commuters, Westlink was not purely a commuter route as it also connected the surrounding regions and ports.

The Peace Dividend

Just as things were settling down, transport planning was thrown into chaos again in 1997 when the Labour Party won the UK general election with a manifesto that made explicit pledges to safeguard the environment and develop an integrated transport policy for the UK. This resulted in all transportation policies going back to the drawing board to be reviewed. In November 1998, Lord Dubs (now the Direct Rule Environment Minister) published a statement that committed the DOE to producing a Regional Transportation Strategy (RTS) covering the period from 2001 onwards.[7]

1998 also saw the signing of the historic Good Friday Agreement, which signalled an end, at least in major part, to the violent sectarian 'Troubles' that had raged since 1969. The

Agreement finally ended Direct Rule by setting up the devolved power-sharing Northern Ireland Assembly, which received its powers on 2 December 1999 and ran in a faltering manner for three years before being suspended on a long term basis in October 2002. During the period 1999–2002, therefore, historians find a curious mixture of decisions made by local ministers and Direct Rule politicians.

The next few years saw an incredible number of master plans and documents that in quantity exceeded the total produced for Belfast in the previous 40 years. The 'Regional Development Strategy 2025' was published in September 2001, and was followed in July 2002 by the 'Regional Transportation Strategy 2002–2012 (RTS)'.[8] This latter document was published by Peter Robinson, the DUP Minister for Regional Development: the department which assumed oversight of transport after the Good Friday Agreement.

The signing of the Good Friday Agreement, and the financial 'peace dividend' that followed it, came at a critical juncture in the efforts of the local environmental lobby. As the public emerged from the 'bunker' mentality that had characterised the previous 30 years, they looked across to Great Britain and realised just how far behind the rest of the UK the local transport system was. While motorways linked most cities in Great Britain, drivers travelling between the two main cities of Belfast and Londonderry were still negotiating twisty single-carriageway roads and trundling down the main streets of towns such as Toome and Dungiven. With the conflict now much diminished, money was suddenly available to do something about it and both the government and much of the general public were not willing to let the opportunity pass them by.

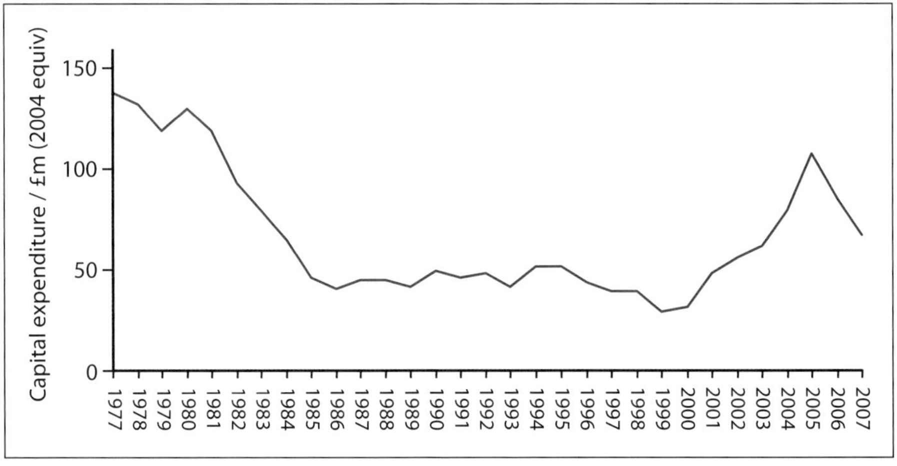

After remaining at a low level for almost 20 years, capital investment by DRD Roads Service climbed again following the 1998 Good Friday Agreement.

The vision of the RTS was strongly influenced by this mindset when it committed to providing Northern Ireland with "a modern, sustainable, safe transportation system which benefits society, the economy and the environment and which actively contributes to social inclusion and everyone's quality of life."[8] On its opening page, the RTS laments the "decades of underinvestment in roads and public transport", and states that "there is now an acceptance that investment in roads and transport is a high priority for public expenditure". The RTS committed the new Executive to substantial investment in the rail network, the provision of commuter bus corridors in Belfast, the provision of a rapid transit system in Belfast and a huge investment in the strategic road network.

It envisaged an expenditure of £3.5 billion on transport over the following decade to 2012, with 35% going to public transport, 63% to roads and 2% to walking and cycling. The document is perhaps more remarkable for the amount of expenditure it envisaged than for the percentages allocated to each form of transport, percentages that were in keeping with the policy of the previous 20 years. Although the rail and bus network would benefit from an unprecedented level of new investment, the road network would benefit from a level of investment unheard of since the motorway building era of the 1960s and early 1970s. That said, public transport policies for the Belfast area were genuinely new and bold by the standards of the previous 20 years, envisaging a major reallocation of road space to buses at peak hours, along with a high profile rapid transit system. Nevertheless, environmentalists were not impressed, with Friends of the Earth noting that:

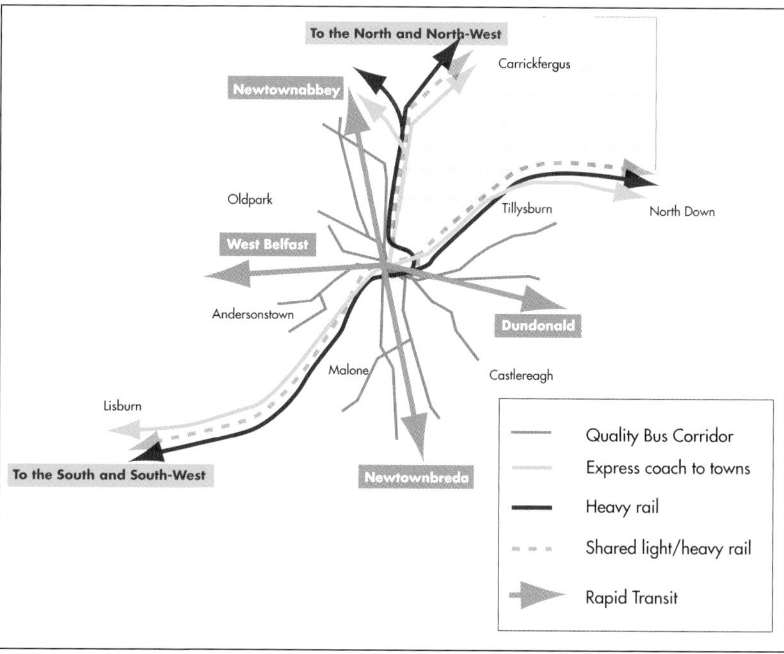

The 2002 'Regional Transportation Strategy' envisaged the development of a much more integrated public transport system in the Belfast area over the following 25 years. *(Image courtesy DRD Roads Service)*

> *The Department has been canny enough to make sure, that in the event of a funding shortfall, it is the public transport investment which will suffer. This is evidence, if more were needed, that the old-fashioned 'roads first' approach lives on in the Department.*[9]

The RTS committed the government to developing three further transport plans: one for Belfast; one for the strategic road network; and one for the rest of the road network. However, these were still in the future and in the meantime there had been further developments on Westlink.

Managing Traffic

The population of the Belfast Metropolitan Area (as defined in 2011) had risen only slightly from 631,000 in 1981 to 647,000 in 2001, but the population of the core Belfast City Council area had fallen by 12% from 316,000 to 277,000 over the same period.[10] This represented both the voluntary and forced flight of people out of the inner city to the suburbs and nearby towns.

In the first half of the twentieth century Belfast was an industrial city, with around 50% of the population employed in manufacturing. After the Second World War, this began to decline, reaching about 25% in 1981 and around 10% in 2001.[11] By the same token, employment in the service sector increased to around 90% by 2001. Despite the loss of industry, the city centre remained a key employment location: in 2001, despite having only 16% of Northern Ireland's population, Belfast City Council area provided almost 29% of the province's jobs, and hence dominated the local economy. It also meant that at least 13% of Northern Ireland's population was commuting into inner Belfast each day.[11] The issue of catering for large-scale commuting, therefore, was as strong as ever.

In Belfast, traffic was still growing, but there were signs that the rate was slowing. Between 1990 and 1994 daily traffic levels on Westlink (measured at Roden Street) grew from 42,830 vehicles to 52,890 vehicles – a rise of 5.4% per year, and higher than the rate for other key roads in Belfast.[6] In the period 1993 to 1998 the rate of growth had fallen to 2% per year,[12] and in 1999 it was predicted that traffic increases would fall to an annual rate of 1.7% by 2005,[12] However, it was also noted that this reduced rate of growth on Westlink would be primarily due to the fact that it was approaching (or had indeed surpassed) its capacity and that traffic speeds would slow each year over this period until sections of Westlink became congested throughout the working day. In other words, the lack of capacity on the road was once again acting as a collar, restricting the number of new journeys that travellers could contemplate.

Between 1996 and 1998, Roads Service explored the possibility of using private sector investment to pay for a Westlink upgrade (known as the Public Finance Initiative), but this was dismissed as being too costly at that time.[1] On 13 May 1998 Westlink briefly became a political tool in the attempts to achieve peace in Northern Ireland. The Chancellor of the new Labour government, Gordon Brown, came to Belfast and announced that they would provide £87m funding for upgrading the strategic road network, including Westlink. This would be part of a larger financial package to be paid only if the province voted 'Yes' in the referendum on the Good Friday Agreement, which was due to be held (not coincidentally) nine days later. With funding in place in the form of a thinly-veiled bribe, Roads Service were able to produce concrete plans for exactly how the M1 and Westlink could be upgraded. Sure enough, the province did indeed vote 'Yes' on 23 May 1998.

By 1997, Roads Service had already produced a shopping list of specific improvements that could be made to the M1 and Westlink if money were no object.[13] These were:

1. West-facing sliproads at Black's Road (M1 junction 3).
2. A bus priority system between Stockman's Lane and Roden Street.
3. Ramp metering on on-slips between Black's Road and York Street (ie using traffic signals to limit the rate at which vehicles could join the M1 and Westlink).
4. Improve the capacity of three nearby routes, namely Falls Road, Lisburn Road and Malone Road.
5. Grade separate Grosvenor Road and Broadway roundabouts, widen the section of Westlink between them to three lanes in each direction, and close the Roden Street junction.
6. Widen the M1 to dual three-lanes from Black's Road to Broadway.
7. Grade separate the York Street (M2/M3/Westlink) junction.
8. Widen the canyon section of Westlink, ie between Grosvenor Road and York Street, to dual three-lanes.

On the basis of the available cash, Roads Service decided that only items 1, 2, 5 and 6 should be taken forward. Grade separating the York Street junction was very desirable, but it was deemed too expensive at that time. This was unfortunate, as it was known even then that there would be increased congestion at York Street after the upgrade until such times as this final junction was improved. In 2005 Roads Service's Roy Spiers, who spearheaded the eventual upgrade, said:

> *The reality is that I am where I am. I have to start somewhere and I have to stop somewhere. I would like to be a position where I could say 'Yes we'll go the whole way through' [ie, include York Street]. What I am doing is removing two of the main bottlenecks on the route.*[14]

Widening the canyon section to three lanes was also rejected, as the presence of the 1980s retaining walls would have meant essentially reconstructing the entire section of road from scratch.

First off the mark were the bus priority measures, and a citybound hard-shoulder bus lane was introduced on the M1 between Stockman's Lane and Broadway just two years later in 1999, delivering significant time savings for buses at peak times as they could bypass the congestion approaching Broadway.[1]

The M1 hard shoulder bus lane (seen on the left in this photograph) begins part way between Lisburn and Belfast and continues to Broadway. It operates at peak times to give buses priority for commuters. *(Aubrey Dale)*

Detailed planning then commenced for upgrading the rest of the road. Most importantly, it was proposed to add flyovers above Broadway and Grosvenor Road roundabouts. Flyovers were by far the cheapest option, as it required no major excavations in the soft ground. Broadway, in particular, presented significant challenges for excavations given that the Forth/ Clowney and Blackstaff Rivers actually met beneath the roundabout.

Roads Service realised that, due to the proximity of the Grosvenor Road and Divis Street junctions, it would not be possible to provide both north-facing sliproads at the former and south-facing sliproads at the latter. Numerous permutations were tested, but eventually it

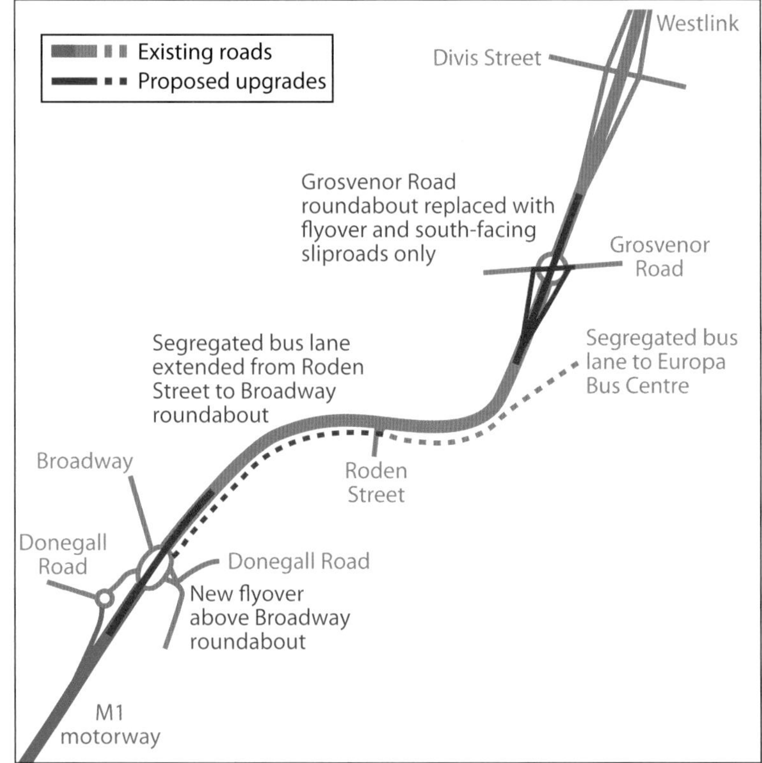

DRD Roads Service's original proposals for upgrading Westlink, as examined at the 2000 public inquiry. Both Broadway and Grosvenor Road would have received flyovers in this plan.

was decided to only provide south-facing sliproads at Grosvenor Road, and retain Divis Street in its unmodified form. This decision would have major implications for traffic in the city centre, as traffic coming from the M2 would no longer be able to enter the city at Grosvenor Road, and would instead transfer to Divis Street. Additionally, a segregated road exclusively for buses would be constructed parallel to Westlink, connecting Broadway roundabout directly to the Europa Bus Centre.

Objections

Unlike the previous rounds in the many years of development of the Belfast Urban Motorway/Westlink, this time the main objections were based on environmentalism rather than on the impact on communities. Although a number of organisations campaigned against the proposals, the most vociferous was Friends of the Earth (FoE) who objected to the scheme on principle, as it did nothing to move Belfast towards sustainable transportation and perpetuated (and even encouraged) continued growth in the use of the private car, and hence congestion, pollution, severance and transport poverty for those without cars. Their campaign was well-informed, intelligent and appealed to firm figures and academic studies rather than general sentiments, and it has been praised as providing "a crucial point of reference to protesters, thanks to its nationwide organization and its ability to frame and fight environmental campaigns".[15]

FoE challenged not only the proposals, but the legal framework within which they were carried out.[16] This had unwelcome hallmarks of the 1977 Lavery Inquiry, where there was a conviction that the whole inquiry process was a sham that would merely rubber stamp the proposals. This was clearly not an issue in the 1988 inquiry, suggesting that by 2000 there had been another deterioration of confidence in the inquiry process, at least amongst environmentalists, due to the suspicion that the government's newfound fondness for environmental issues was mere whitewash to camouflage an unrepentant roads agenda. In this light, Green Action (a group within QUB Students Union) felt able to dismiss Roads Service as "bankrupt intellectually, environmentally and morally in its planning policies".[13] The BBC, by contrast, took the line that Roads Service should have built Westlink with flyovers from the beginning (something that Roads Service would certainly agree with), lampooning their short-sightedness for building the road with roundabouts. But they also expressed cynicism that the upgrade would work in the long term. These two comments were likely typical of the views of the general public.[17]

FoE were joined in the protest by four other organisations: the West Belfast Partnership

Board (WBPB), the Roden Street Community Development Group (RSCDG), the Roden Street Action Group (RSAG) and the Dunmurry Residents' Association. The last of these objected specifically to the sliproads at Black's Road, which is beyond the scope of this book. The RSCDG and RSAG represented the residents of the north (Nationalist) and south (Loyalist) ends of Roden Street respectively, which Westlink severed, and who feared worsening living standards in their communities. The RDCDG's Isobelle Black said: "We are going to try to highlight what we lost when we got the Westlink, the number of streets, the population of people moving. I think you need to highlight the things you are losing for motorways."[18] The WBPB represented a variety of organisations in West Belfast and worked closely with FoE. WBPB Chief Executive Roisin Donough summarised their view of the proposals thus:

> *Road building on this scale destroys communities. The Westlink cut a swathe through the city 20 years ago and now it is jammed with polluting traffic. Further widening and the construction of flyovers provide no solution. The whole of west Belfast will be cut off from the rest of the city and the city centre by a wall of concrete.*[18]

Various publicity events were carried out. On 23 February 2000, members of these groups placed dozens of crosses onto Grosvenor Road roundabout, each bearing the name of a street that was supposedly destroyed during the construction of Westlink – although many had, in fact, been demolished years before Westlink was built, as part of the wider regeneration works of which the Urban Motorway was a key, but by no means the sole, element.

Cinalli credits the campaign with success by creating the threat of "a progressive spreading of the mobilization",[15] and Roads Service did indeed undertake to review other options in the face of the criticism.[19] Nevertheless, Cinalli perhaps over-states the impact of the campaign. While a number of prominent members of political and university circles did indeed get involved, and while the campaign did receive publicity in the media on several occasions, it appears to have stirred up little public interest outside the membership of the groups themselves. Politically, the only major party to take an official stance was Sinn Féin, who argued that the scheme should not proceed (hence it is particularly ironic that in 2006 it was a Sinn Féin Regional Development Minister who would cut the first sod on the scheme). From the general public, only 76 objections were received,[20] and 71 of these were pre-printed 'Friends of the Earth' postcards and letters. 76 objections from a city of half a million residents is certainly not indicative of widespread public opposition to the scheme. Therefore, despite their efforts, the opponents of the scheme ultimately failed to persuade the wider public that the scheme was a bad idea.

The objection had been raised (not incorrectly) that Roads Service had not seriously considered any public transport alternatives to the scheme. In response to this criticism, Roads Service conducted an appraisal of the Westlink upgrade against 24 alternatives, including some that were exclusively public transport.[13] This appraisal was based on detailed traffic modelling and found that the two best solutions were (a) the scheme as proposed and (b) a scheme to provide significant new park-and-ride facilities, more frequent buses and trains, more bus lanes and a daily 'congestion' charge of £6 for private cars entering the city centre. As a result of this appraisal, Roads Service took the view that the scheme as proposed still offered the best solution. This was, of course, a case of 'our word against theirs', and it was challenged.

The 2000 Public Inquiry

Between 20 November and 7 December 2000, Belfast witnessed the fourth public inquiry into the now long-running Belfast Urban Motorway/Westlink project. Chaired by Francis G Guckian, it was technically an examination of the Environmental Statement, but was, in practice, an inquiry into the proposals more generally.

The case of Roads Service[13] was centred on the problems being created by congestion on the route. The key objective was "to reduce congestion on M1/Westlink and encourage the transfer to it of traffic from parallel routes". The road was now running at capacity, and it was predicted that traffic speeds would fall by 28% by 2005 in the absence of any action. The Port of Belfast was under increasing competition from Dublin, especially due to the plan to open the Dublin Port Tunnel giving lorries fast access from the M50 to Dublin Port. If Westlink continued to be congested, hauliers would switch to Dublin. The congestion on Westlink was mostly caused by the presence of at-grade junctions but also, to a lesser extent, the number of lanes. Since Westlink was a general-purpose road, all types of vehicles could use it, not just commuters and freight, but also long-distance traffic that was just passing through. It was not possible, therefore, to provide benefits for one specific group. Roads Service accepted that the proposed scheme could not provide for unrestrained demand (which they estimated would require at least four lanes each way) and did not suggest that it would.

Secondly, current congestion was causing large numbers of drivers to switch to parallel routes, specifically Falls Road, Lisburn Road and Malone Road. Roads Service argued that improving flows on Westlink would take traffic back off these roads, leading to a reduction in noise and pollution in these areas. While admittedly increasing the visual impact, flyovers would reduce severance by making it much easier to walk or cycle across Westlink.

Roads Service admitted that they had initially not considered public transport alternatives, but argued that it was doubtful that providing even significantly enhanced public transport would really encourage many people to leave their cars at home. In other words, even providing much improved public transport could not compensate for people's strong preference for driving their own car, despite bad congestion. They said that there was "no evidence before the Inquiry [that such alternatives] would achieve the objectives in terms of relieving congestion and facilitating strategic traffic". Therefore, they argued, the scheme as proposed was the only realistic option.

The Port of Belfast "wholeheartedly supported the objectives of the scheme".[13] They noted that 50% of port traffic used Westlink, which represented 30% of Northern Ireland's total seaborne trade, and that the number of ships arriving had increased by 55% since 1995.[12] However, they argued that a 'freight-only' lane should be provided, instead of allocating all the road space to general use.[13]

The case of Friends of the Earth and the WBPB has already been set out. They presented evidence prepared by Professor Austin Smyth of the Transport Research Institute at Napier University[13]. Prof Smyth's study indicated that a bus-based alternative would produce only a negligible shift to public transport, and that the scheme as proposed would probably become congested again quite quickly due to the effect of releasing suppressed demand. A rail-based park-and-ride, combined with improvements to buses, would offer the biggest shift to public transport, but even this would be "very modest overall". Prof Smyth suggested increasing multiple-occupancy. Noting that currently 25% of cars at peak times had more than one person, he claimed that there was potential to reduce vehicle miles by 10%.

The Green Party made a submission[13] arguing that the solution lay in eliminating the need for freight to use Westlink by closing Belfast Port entirely, and shifting operations to Larne, and basing future transport in the city centre on bicycles and trains.

Despite there being no major objections to the proposed flyover at Broadway, two submissions (by SDLP Councillor Margaret Walsh, and Forest of Belfast) were made that suggested replacing this with an underpass, and this was subsequently supported by several others, including Friends of the Earth and WBPB. A local residents group, the Greater Village Regeneration Trust, were concerned about the potential of an underpass to flood due to the historic flooding in the area.[21] Roads Service objected that an underpass would add almost £10m to the project bill, and would involve significant work to divert the rivers and equipment to continuously pump out rainwater.

The Inspector submitted his report in February 2001,[20] and it was released to the public in September – a delay that did not go unchallenged.[22] He concluded that the scheme should proceed, and that the objectors had not offered any alternatives that could credibly compete with the benefits. However, he did find the case for a 'freight-only' lane, or high-occupancy vehicle (HOV) lane compelling and recommended that these be considered. Given that the scheme as proposed would likely become congested again in the medium term, he recommended that consideration be given soon to what options would be considered next, and implied that public transport should have the main role here. The only other major recommendation was a preference for the underpass at Broadway, rather than the proposed flyover.

Roads Service accepted the recommendation for an underpass at Broadway. Since this change would leave Grosvenor Road as the only flyover on Westlink, they decided to alter Grosvenor Road to a partial underpass for consistency, despite this not being flagged up by the Inspector. In terms of a dedicated lane for freight or HOVs, Roads Service merely said that they would "consider" this option in the future, but made no commitment to it.

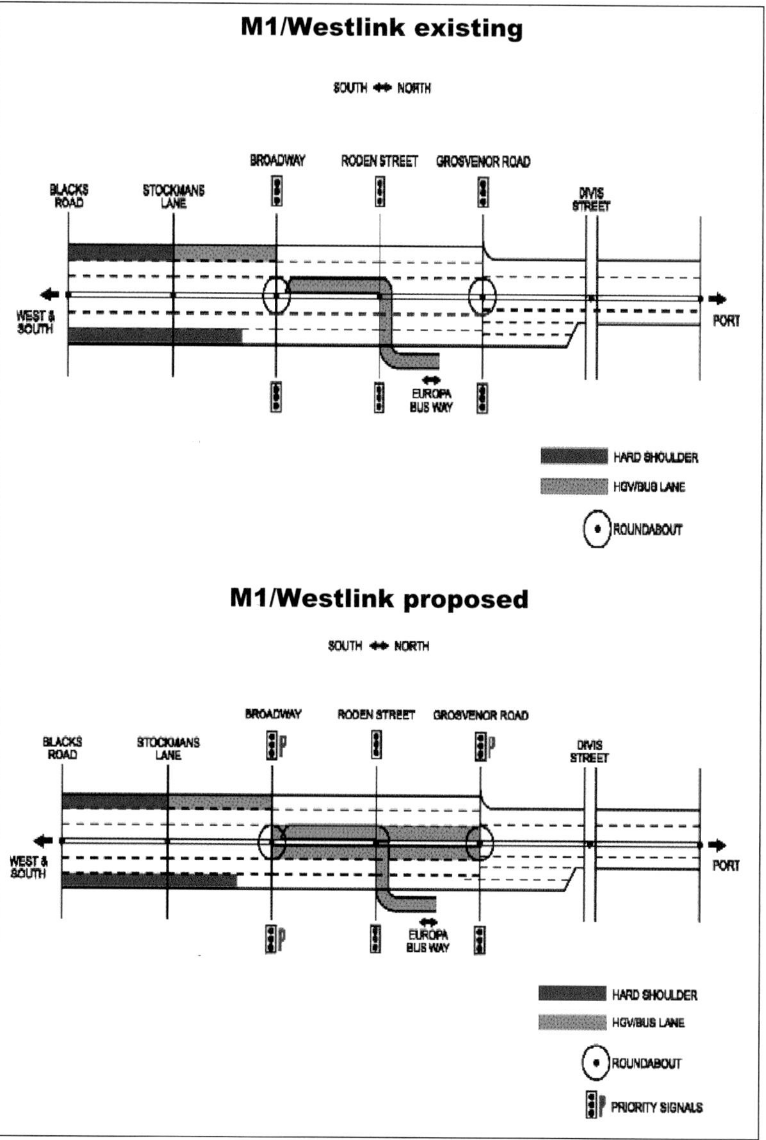

In the HGV/bus only lane proposal developed by Friends of the Earth, the road would not have been widened or had flyovers added. Instead, one lane would have been allocated to these vehicles in order to give them priority over other vehicles. *(Friends of the Earth)*

The Scheme Proceeds

Over the following year, Friends of the Earth (FoE) developed the 'freight-only' lane proposal,[23] even producing a report showing how it could be accommodated on the hard shoulder of the M1 and on lane 3 of Westlink between Broadway and Grosvenor Road. The case for freight priority measures is compelling, and the concept itself has been somewhat vindicated by the opening of the Dublin Port Tunnel in 2006. On Westlink it would be an ideal way to ensure that increasing general traffic levels do not impinge on the freight traffic upon which the province's economy depends.

However, to give Roads Service its due, it is difficult to see how such an arrangement could be safely accommodated on Westlink. Firstly, HGVs would be travelling in the third lane, adjacent to the central reservation, potentially at a slower speed than vehicles to their left, so it would be hazardous for HGVs to manoeuvre into and out of this lane. Secondly, to be of real benefit, such a lane would have to traverse the entire length of Westlink, rather than stopping at Grosvenor Road as FoE proposed. However, between Divis Street and York Street Westlink would remain two lanes wide. Merges from sliproads into a single lane are not safe, and thus merges at intermediate junctions would become much more dangerous. This is a demonstration of how Westlink will always suffer from being originally built as an all-purpose road.

The 'widened' Westlink near Roden Street after the 2002 upgrade, where the removal of the hard strips adjacent to the edges of the road, and a slight narrowing of the lanes, allowed two lanes to morph into three, including the bus lane shown. *(Author's collection)*

Meanwhile, in the light of continued congestion, a limited upgrade was carried out on Westlink in 2002. This involved re-painting the carriageway between Grosvenor Road and Broadway to provide three lanes in each direction. Southbound all three lanes were allocated to general traffic. Northbound, the third lane was limited to buses between Broadway and Roden Street, where buses could turn right onto a bus-only road link directly into Europa Bus Centre. This was a cheap-and-cheerful stopgap measure, but provided short-term benefits while the main upgrade was planned.

Roads Service decided to press ahead with construction. A second public inquiry, into the Designation Order, was carried out in November and December 2002. The objectors continued their opposition: although they appeared to have accepted that the scheme was going to happen, they argued forcefully that the additional space should be allocated specifically to freight, not general traffic.[24] Lisa Fagan of FoE said:

> *Roads Service ought to abandon their extravagant pipedream in favour of a realistic and affordable solution, one which can satisfy the business and environmental lobbies: freight priority measures and decent public transport alternatives ... Port of Belfast and the*

Inquiry Inspector have already indicated their support for a freight lane. Roads Service should return from Cloud Cuckoo Land and weigh in behind it too.[24]

These arguments carried considerable weight, not least because the Inspector at the 2000 inquiry had backed the idea.

The 2002 inquiry was also chaired by Francis G Guckian, and FoE objected to this on the grounds of his "age [75], frailty and scant note-taking" and also claimed he had a conflict of interest as a Director of Londonderry Chamber of Commerce.[25] Nevertheless, the inquiry reported and the (once again, Direct Rule) Minister Angela Smith announced on 14 March 2003 that the scheme would be proceeding unmodified, at a total estimated cost of £70m to £80m, and that it would go out to tender in April 2003.[26] She also announced that the M1 between Black's Road and Stockman's Lane would be widened first, followed by Westlink, around 2006. A Vesting Order was published in September 2004.

Belfast Metropolitan Transport Plan

The 'Regional Transportation Strategy' of 2002 had required the production of three further transport plans. Of these three (which also included the 'Regional Strategic Transport Network Plan' and the 'Sub-Regional Transportation Plan') it is the 'Belfast Metropolitan Transport Plan' (BMTP) that is relevant to this study. It included transport proposals for the council areas of Lisburn, Belfast, Castlereagh, North Down, Newtownabbey and Carrickfergus (strangely omitting the Newtownards urban area) and was part of the wider 'Belfast Metropolitan Area Plan' (BMAP) that covered the period up to 2015, and replaced the 'Belfast Urban Area Plan 2001'.

Work on BMTP had involved three years of consultation with stakeholders, and the draft document was published in November 2004.[27] It envisaged £1.9bn being spent on transport in the city by 2015, broken down at 48% for roads, 46% for public transport and 6% for walking/cycling measures. Of the public transport proposals, the key measures were the commencement of a bus-based rapid transit system (nothing had happened on this since it had been first proposed), new park-and-ride facilities and a growing network of quality bus corridors (mainly, bus lanes).

Of the road proposals, the plan noted that due to "the real constraints on major new road construction", which presumably meant public opposition more than money, any proposals would be "based mainly on the network of roads that currently exists".[27] In reality, this limited road proposals to the strategic network first envisaged in 1995. There were a number of significant road proposals in the 2004 BMTP, but the ones relevant to Belfast's urban motorway network were:

- The M1/Westlink upgrade that had already been approved.
- Widening the Sydenham Bypass from two to three lanes (reminiscent of the 1969 plan to upgrade the Sydenham Bypass to motorway standard).
- Widening the M2 hill section from two to three lanes citybound, ie between Sandyknowes and Greencastle.

In terms of roads these were expensive, but hardly ambitious, proposals. Their aim was essentially to add capacity to the existing road network, despite the fact that the funeral of 'predict-and-provide' had already taken place. Notably missing from the proposals was any plan to grade separate the York Street junction, which was now the focus of Belfast's road system where the M1/Westlink met the M2 and M3/Sydenham Bypass at Northern Ireland's busiest road junction. Although capacity improvements were proposed on all three routes, the plan still appeared to be that all this traffic would be squeezed through a series of traffic lights at York Street. Nevertheless, Roads Service did commission a study in 2004 which proposed short term solutions to the congestion at York Street,[28] and suggested that more radical solutions were practical, albeit expensive.[29]

Public Transport

Provision of bus lanes in Belfast had been slow during the 1990s with just one in place in 1990, growing to 15 in 1999. The early bus lanes were tentative, in many cases ending before major bottlenecks in order to avoid creating excessive congestion for private vehicles, and therefore limiting the benefit to buses.

After the Millennium, work took place much more rapidly with 65 lanes (totalling 30 km) in place by 2005, a total of 30 km.[1] Just six years later, in 2011, the length of bus lanes has jumped by over 50% to 47 km.[30] 2011 also saw the publication of 'Belfast on the Move', an initiative to reallocate road space in the city centre to public transport and cyclists. Announced in August 2011,[31] key elements of the plan had been implemented by the end of the year. The accelerating pace of implementation of these initiatives suggest that a 'tipping point' in terms of governmental attitudes to public transport in Belfast may finally have been reached.

This dedicated bus lane was introduced on Oxford Street in July 2012, part of a package of similar measures built under the 'Belfast on the Move' project that began in 2011. *(Author's collection)*

The decline in public transport usage in Belfast, continuous since the late 1950s, was finally reversed during the first decade of the twenty-first century. In 2003–2004, 19.5 million journeys were made by Citybus in Belfast,[32] which contrasts with 25.7 million journeys by Metro (the successor to Citybus) in 2010–2011,[33] an annual increase of 4%. Similarly, the level of rail patronage in Northern Ireland in 2010–2011 stood at 10.4 million journeys,[34] the highest level since 1967.

At the time of writing, it seems that public transport is likely to play a more significant role in commuting into central Belfast in the years to come. For those travelling into the city from outside the Metro zones, a number of park-and-ride sites have been provided on the periphery of the city, notably at Cairnshill on the Saintfield Road, Sprucefield on the M1 and Black's Road near the Lisburn Road. Although there are plans for others, for example at Sandyknowes on the M2, some of these have been hampered by opposition from local residents.

The rise in the percentage of Belfast residents commuting by car, continuous since the 1950s, finally peaked at 67% around 2004, and then began to decline, standing at 59% in 2008.[35] Curiously, the biggest winner from this reduction was not public transport, but walking. The number of people commuting on foot rose from 12% in 2001 to 22% in 2008, suggesting that either people were willing to walk further, or were working closer to their place of residence. This is despite the fact that, over the same time period, the number of homes without a car in the city fell from 46% to 40%.

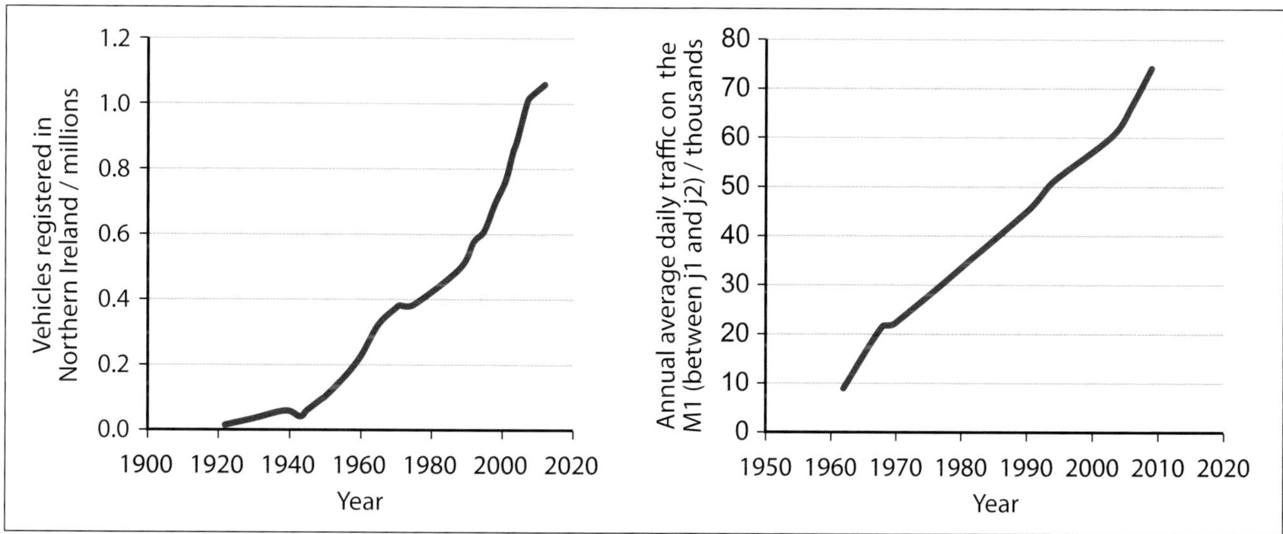

(Left) The number of vehicles registered in Northern Ireland has risen at an increasing rate since the 1920s.

(Right) Traffic levels (as measured here on the M1) have also risen steadily.

Numerous cycle lanes have also been created, some of which (such as the Comber Greenway and Lagan Towpath) are totally segregated and very popular. Others, particularly those implemented early on, are of low quality and are seen in a poor light by cyclists. However, experience has been gained, and there are plans for more significant and proactive cycling provision in the inner city area.[31] As of 2008, 3% of Belfast residents were commuting by bicycle, a not insubstantial percentage.[35]

The BMTP envisaged work commencing on a Rapid Transit System for Belfast by 2015, and at the time of writing the planning for the system does seem to be progressing towards construction. It has been watered down from what many had hoped, becoming essentially a high-frequency bus service (albeit with special vehicles and off-vehicle ticketing) running down an almost continuous bus lane. The three routes currently planned are on the Falls Road, Newtownards Road and Titanic Quarter, all converging in the city centre.

CHAPTER 13
RENAISSANCE

Most 1960s-era road schemes in the UK tend to follow a familiar pattern. Firstly, a hugely audacious plan is announced. Next, a series of complications and public opposition lead to the plan getting watered down and key elements dropped. Finally, a much more modest scheme with lots of untidy, unfinished elements gets built.

The Belfast Urban Motorway followed this pattern from its zenith in 1967 until its eventual 'completion' as Westlink in 1983. However, in Belfast's case, this was not the end of the story. The early twenty-first century has seen something of a renaissance of the original plans, with the upgrades that were carried out representing a return to many of the basic concepts of the 1967 Plan, namely three lanes each way with fully grade separated junctions. The only other city in the United Kingdom that has seen a similar reversal is Glasgow, which finally completed its inner motorway box, albeit in a slightly modified form, in 2011.[1]

The M1 and Westlink Upgrade

In August 2003, in the middle of the period of intensive plan-writing, work on Phase 1 of the M1 upgrade had got underway with the widening of the M1 from two to three lanes from Black's Road to Stockman's Lane. This was the more straightforward and cheapest part of the whole scheme, but was still a significant project in its own right. It was completed almost exactly a year later on 10 August 2004[2] at a total cost of £5.8m. The contractor was FP McCann. The third lane initially ran only between junctions 2 and 3.

In 2004, Roads Service looked again at the option of using private finance to pay for schemes, and this time it resulted in a series of schemes being grouped together under two public-private partnership (PPP) agreements which included Design, Build, Finance and Operate (DBFO) elements. The first, DBFO1, was eventually awarded to Highway Management Construction (HMC), a joint venture of engineering firms – John Graham (Dromore) Ltd, Farrans Ltd (later Northstone) and Bilfinger Berger Ltd – on 17 February 2006,[3] with Arup as designers. It included the M1/Westlink upgrade (£104m) as well as the proposed upgrade to the M2 hill section. The second, DBFO2, involved upgrades to the A1, A4 and A5 beyond the Belfast area.

The project was going to take over three years to complete and there was a sense of dread among road users about what impact the works were going to have on traffic. Everyone could see that there was congestion even without the works. Prior to work commencing, Roads Service made significant efforts to minimise disruption, including:

- Producing leaflets for road users, and specifically for hauliers, outlining what exactly was proposed.
- Upgrading parts of the B23 Hillhall Road, which was an obvious alternative route.

- Undertaking to keep two lanes open for general traffic at peak times, and to keep the M1 and Westlink bus lane open.
- A marketing campaign promoting car share and park-and-ride.
- Initiating travel time information on VMS displays on the M1.

In addition, Roads Service printed and gave away over 200,000 copies[4] of a one-off 32 page magazine[5] detailing the history of the scheme, what was proposed, and a range of ideas on how people could minimise disruption.

Preparatory work began in November 2005, and Sinn Féin Regional Development Minister Conor Murphy cut the 'first sod' at Broadway roundabout on 17 January 2006. Work slowly spread across all sections of the route over the following six months. The works disrupted traffic (especially when Grosvenor Road roundabout was closed and the recently-widened stretch of Westlink reduced back to two lanes each way) although not as badly as had been feared. This partly manifested itself as a reduction of 16% in traffic levels on the southern part of Westlink between 2005 and 2006,[6] likely due to people avoiding the area. In March 2006, the *Belfast Telegraph* proclaimed that the works "passed their first major test today as thousands of commuters enjoyed a problem-free journey to work … while motorists coming into the city faced traditional Monday morning rush-hour delays, fears of chaos on the Westlink were unfounded".[7] Early in the work a serious road accident at the start of a contraflow at Stockman's Lane[8] resulted in the police vigorously enforcing the 30 mph speed limit.[9]

As before, the following discussion is not intended to be an exhaustive engineering description, but a more general overview of the works involved. A fuller engineering description has been published elsewhere.[10]

Stockmans Lane

The original 1962 bridges on the M1 at Stockman's Lane were replaced by new structures. The main reason was that they were too narrow to accommodate the proposed three-lane road with hard shoulders. However, the bridges were also at the end of their natural lifespan and would have been due for replacement even without the upgrade. The original plan was for two pairs of bridges, with an earth embankment in the centre of the roundabout.[5] This was changed at a late stage to a pair of parallel viaducts traversing the entire roundabout.

In June 2006 all four lanes were diverted onto the southbound bridge – quite an accomplishment – and the northbound bridge was demolished. This bridge had actually failed a strength test, so Roads Service could not be certain that it could cope with this much traffic for nine months, so the structure was continuously monitored for deterioration. Had the stresses become too great, the bridge would have been closed and all M1 traffic accommodated on the roundabout. Fortunately, although there was some movement, a closure did not become necessary.

The new northbound bridge came into use on 26 May 2007, at which point all traffic was switched to it and the southbound bridge was demolished, after nine months of glory carrying the entire M1. The new southbound bridge opened in mid December 2007. Initially only two lanes were opened over both bridges, since the rest of the upgrade closer to Belfast was still underway. The official opening took place on 27 May 2008 when the new traffic signals on the roundabout were activated.[11]

(Above left) The original bridges at Stockman's Lane and (right) during the demolition of the citybound bridge in June 2006. *(Author's collection)*

The effect of 50 years of engineering advancement is laid plain by observing that each of the old bridges was carried on 40 concrete piers, compared to just six piers for each of the new, larger bridges, which also feature individual spans almost three times the length. The new structure has 72 precast prestressed beams cast integral with the internal pier supports and placed on bearings above the abutments. The beams vary between 21.5 and 23.4 metres (70.5 and 76.8 feet) in length and are 1.1 metres (43 inches) deep.[12]

The M1 itself was widened from two to three lanes between Stockman's Lane and Broadway. This was accomplished by asymmetrically widening it on the eastern side, as it was not possible to encroach on the Bog Meadows nature reserve to the west. The existing road structure was found to be in good condition, and was re-used within the wider road.[3] A vertical concrete step barrier, in line with current practice, replaced the existing steel central barrier. The third lane was tied in to the previously upgraded section of motorway from Stockman's Lane to Black's Road.

(Below) Construction of the new citybound bridge at Stockman's Lane (on the left) took place while four lanes of traffic used the original countrybound bridge (on the right). *(Author's collection)*

View beneath the completed bridges at Stockman's Lane in May 2008. Note how few pillars are necessary today compared to 1962. *(Author's collection)*

Broadway

The works to provide the underpass at Broadway roundabout were the most complex and time-consuming element of the whole plan, mainly because two rivers – the Forth/Clowney (a spate river, prone to flash floods) and the Blackstaff – met underneath the existing roundabout. An existing underground overflow structure directed some of the flow north along the remainder of the Blackstaff River channel, while diverting excess water east along the artificial Blackstaff Relief Culvert, which flows underground to the south east, below Broadway, to the Lagan.[13] This entire system had to be relocated so that it did not conflict with the underpass before any road construction work could be carried out.

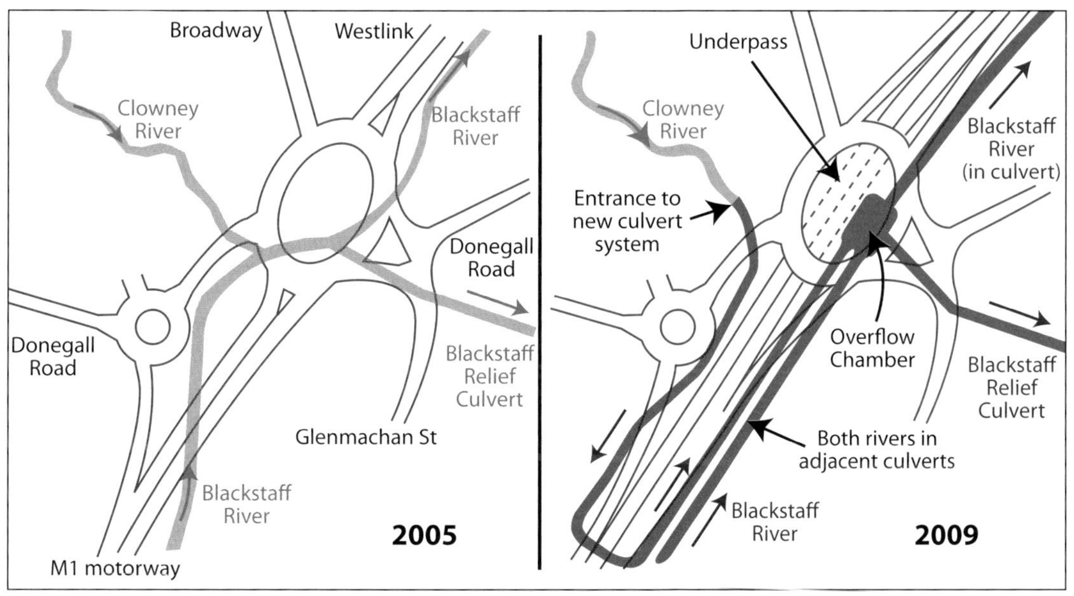

Sketch maps showing the courses of the Clowney and Blackstaff Rivers through the Broadway junction before the upgrade, and how they were re-routed through a series of culverts and a new overflow chamber to accommodate the underpass.

The Blackstaff River in its channel through Broadway roundabout in late 2006, before being diverted underground. The new Clowney culvert can be seen taking shape on the left. *(Author's collection)*

The original plan had been to divert the Clowney through a channel built into the roof of the underpass to connect with the Blackstaff on the east side.[3] However, at the detailed design stage this was changed: the Clowney was instead diverted 200 metres south west along the M1, crossed under the M1, and then 200 metres back north again, adjacent to the Blackstaff culvert. The two rivers would then merge in a new overflow structure under the east side of the roundabout.

A length of high-voltage (33 kV) electrical cabling which crossed the junction on pylons had to be relocated underground. In addition, multiple sewers, water mains, telephone cables, electrical cables and fibre optic cables had to be relocated, while simultaneously keeping two lanes open and maintaining the existing roundabout. It is not surprising, therefore, that the river and service relocation works lasted throughout 2006 and well into 2007.

Due to the nature of Belfast 'sleech', the alluvial clay that underlies much of the city, bedrock lies up to 25 metres below ground level. In addition, the water table is only 1–2 metres below ground level. Therefore, it was decided to construct the continuous sides of the underpass from the top down, using secant bored piles, 1.2 metres in diameter. Broadway consists of a 140 metre (459 foot) tunnel with 500 metres (1640 feet) of approach cuttings,[3] and this required 834 piles with an average drilling length of 19.6 metres (64 feet) and incorporating 1650 tonnes of reinforcement steel.[14] These walls had the key advantage of being waterproof. A pumping station with three pumps was constructed to drain surface and rain water from the underpass, capable of pumping 570 litres (over half a tonne) of water per second.[15]

The reinforced roof slab in place in the centre of Broadway roundabout in November 2007. *(Author's collection)*

With the walls of the underpass in place, and before any excavation works had taken place, work was carried out on the reinforced roof slab of the underpass between July and November 2007. The slab has a clear span of 27.2 metres (89 feet) and is 1.3 metres (51 inches) deep.[12] On 10 December, the River Clowney burst its banks and flooded the western part of the site to a depth of two feet,[16] an event that would be repeated a year later with more severe consequences. Once the slab was completed, the underpass was excavated during December and January, with the breakthrough occurring on 28 January 2008.[17]

Works in early 2008 involved lining the sides of the underpass, and providing the reinforced concrete slab below the road base. Attractive curved portal entrances were provided at either end of the underpass for aesthetic appeal. The road itself was fairly quick to construct through the completed underpass, and was opened to the public on 4 July 2008, some six months ahead of the original programme. Roads Service announced that the opening had gone "according to plan, with drivers experiencing an instant improvement",[18] a statement that seemed to be consistent with the experience of motorists. The *Irish News* hailed "a new era for motorists".

The final phase of work at Broadway involved reconstructing the roundabout on top of the permanent slab, albeit slightly modified from the original layout. These works continued until early 2009. On the western side of the roundabout, an attractive textured red brick wall was constructed both as a sound/privacy barrier and a high-quality visual feature for this prominent location. Thanks to the fully depressed underpass, the completed roundabout looked very similar to how it did before the works began, except for the huge reduction in traffic and more attractive finish.

Work taking place on the iconic curved portal entrance at the north end of the Broadway underpass in March 2008. *(Author's collection)*

Broadway to Grosvenor Road

On this stretch, the existing road base was utilised for the widened road, which consisted of three full lanes in each direction close to ground level. Due to the extremely tight corner south of Grosvenor Road, the superelevation (angle of the road surface) of the existing road was increased significantly. All access to Roden Street (south) was closed off permanently as part of the upgrade, while Mulhouse Road (on the north side) was reconstructed as a

The view north east along Westlink from the same point on Broadway roundabout in (top) August 2005 (middle) September 2007 and (bottom) December 2008, showing progress on excavating and opening the underpass. *(Author's collection)*

left-in/left-out junction with two sliproads. The provision of the junction at Mulhouse Road was not desirable from a design point of view, but was necessary in order to maintain access to private property, and to provide sufficient access to the Royal Victoria Hospital. The road on this stretch was largely completed by early 2008.

The existing footbridge at Roden Street was both unsightly and too short to span the widened road, and was replaced by a more modern Vierendeel truss structure.[3] The 'landmark' status of this conspicuous structure was seen as very important at the design stage, and the resultant design consisted of a single, gently curving 37 metre (121 foot) span with an elliptical cross section. Ramps at either end comply with current disability legislation, while a discreet but effective wire mesh discourages vandals from targeting vehicles with missiles – a persistent problem at the location. The footbridge came into use on 1 April 2008. The existing footpath along the east side of Westlink here was closed, and replaced by a segregated footpath on the west side. Along the west side, adjacent to the hospital, a wire fence with a low brick footing was provided to open up views into the surrounding area for aesthetic reasons.

(Top) Cars dwarfed by the scale of the works between Roden Street and Grosvenor Road in July 2007.

(Bottom) The completed Mulhouse Road junction.

(Author's collection)

The bus lane that ran from Westlink at Roden Street to the Europa Bus Centre was retained, but the lane on Westlink itself was replaced by a fully segregated inbound busway on the east side of Westlink. Starting at Broadway roundabout, it came into use in early June 2008. Outbound buses were facilitated by a south-facing onslip directly onto Westlink. Although a bus-only onslip is not unusual in itself, the inclusion of a bus stop less then ten metres from the merge point certainly raises eyebrows.

(Above) The iconic Roden Street footbridge, which was finished to a very high standard due to its prominence.

(Inset) The view along the segregated busway to/from the Europa Bus Centre from the footbridge. Note the bus stop located less than 10 metres from the merge onto Westlink. *(Author's collection)*

Grosvenor Road

Grosvenor Road junction was rebuilt as a partial underpass. The confines of the site and the nature of the upgrade meant that it was not possible to keep the junction open during the works. Right turns were banned from 13 March 2006, with the junction closing completely on 9 October the same year. The same date saw the opening of a 137 metre (449 foot) bailey bridge just to the south of the roundabout that carried Grosvenor Road over the Westlink for 19 months.[3]

Without the need to keep the junction open, works here were more straightforward with all traffic passing on either side of the underpass site. This permitted the engineers to install the sides of the underpass via secant bored piles 1.2 metres in diameter, the same as at Broadway. The underpass has 312 metres (1024 feet) of approach cuttings,[3] and this required 602 piles with an average drilling length of 9.6 metres and incorporating 1000 tonnes of reinforcement steel.[14] As at Broadway, the bored wall was waterproof. A pumping station was constructed to drain surface and rain water from the underpass.

These works were complete by December 2006, and excavation work on the two approach cuttings was carried out up to February 2007. The central section was not excavated until after the bridge beams had been placed above them in mid March. Each of the 12 precast prestressed beams forming the deck is 33 metres (108 feet) long and 1.6 metres (63 inches) deep, cast integral with the walls of the underpass, and is positioned at an skew of 26.05°.[12] The completed bridge is approximately 28 metres (92 feet) across: almost as wide as it is long. The

The bailey bridge which carried Grosvenor Road over Westlink from October 2006 until October 2007. It had the additional benefit of affording interested members of the public a grandstand view of the works below. *(Author's collection)*

footpaths on the bridge are so wide that it could comfortably accommodate six traffic lanes if required, almost certainly a deliberate exercise in future-proofing. This has already been proved wise at the time of writing, as the bridge was briefly earmarked to carry the western route of the planned Belfast Rapid Transit system, although this proposal was later dropped.[19] The remainder of the earth was excavated and the reinforced concrete base slab was in place by mid June 2007.

Traffic on Westlink was re-routed through the underpass on 2 September 2007, while the bridge came into use on 22 October, at which point the bailey bridge was removed. The two sliproads were then constructed, and the whole junction came into use at 7 am on 4 March 2008 (usefully, two days before the opening of the landmark Victoria Square Shopping Centre).[20]

The iconic railings on the Grosvenor Road bridge were designed by Helen Miner. *(Author's collection)*

The view north from the Grosvenor Road bailey bridge towards the former roundabout in (top) October 2006 (middle) March 2007 and (bottom) October 2007. *(Author's collection)*

Due to its prominent location, much thought went into designing the parapet railings for the Grosvenor Road bridge. The eventual design was produced by Helen Miner, and represents four phases of Belfast's industrial development: linen (a silver ribbon), shipbuilding (twisted rope along the top edge), engineering (blue cogs) and information technology (the holes in the cogs).[10] The railings were to have been illuminated from below, but unfortunately the spotlights suffered repeated vandalism soon after construction.

The three lanes of the upgraded Westlink were carried through to the Divis Street junction where the outermost lane was dropped at the sliproads. This entailed widening a short 150 metre (490 foot) section of the original 1983 canyon section by demolishing the original retaining wall and reconstructing it further back. The seam between old and new occurs parallel to Albert Street.

Completion

All three lanes of the M1 and Westlink were opened on 29 November 2008, although ancillary works continued well into 2009. The construction phase required over 2.1 million man hours (equivalent to 25 people working for 40 years),[12] involved the excavation of 375,000 tonnes of sleech, the pouring of 60,000 cubic metres of concrete[12] and the laying of 100,000 tonnes of road surfacing material.[3] It also required 156 miles of ducting, 31 miles of piping, 18 miles of piles and 10 miles of kerbstones.[12]

The scheme was officially opened by Regional Development Minister Conor Murphy on 4 March 2009.[21] Speaking at the event, the Minister highlighted the main benefits of the scheme as ensuring "shorter and more reliable journey times, which will benefit all road users, including public transport, the haulage industry, as well as private car users".[21] The total cost was £104 m.

Runners competing in the 'Between the Bridges' fun run on 6 March 2009 were allowed to run on the M1 and Westlink. *(Author's collection)*

Two days later, on 6 March, the entire road was closed to allow a charity fun run ('Between the Bridges', for the Northern Ireland Hospice) along the route from Stockman's Lane to Divis Street. Despite the sleet, almost 5000 people took advantage of a rare opportunity to run or walk through the underpasses. The winner of the 10 k race was David Morwood of Annadale Striders who completed the run in 32 minutes 21 seconds.[22]

The impact on traffic was not as instantaneous as the opening of Westlink in 1983 or the M3 in 1995, because the upgraded road was opened in stages. Nevertheless, the road has been significantly less congested since it opened. As predicted, it has led to increased queuing at York Street, although this effect has not been as severe as feared. Even before the third lane opened, the media was reporting that "drivers [are] seeing an instant improvement after [passing] the Broadway underpass".[23] Nevertheless, there were a few anomalous events, including a spontaneous ten-mile tailback along the M1 from Westlink on 11 November 2008 that defied explanation, but attracted negative publicity.[24]

The upgrade has almost certainly allowed more people to use the road (the induced traffic effect). In particular, motorists who may have used the Hillhall Road/Outer Ring corridor to travel between the M1 and A2 Bangor Road were now able to use the Westlink/M3 corridor instead, something which is highly desirable from the point of view of keeping strategic traffic on strategic roads. Traffic levels at Roden Street were just over 63,000 vehicles per day in 2005, the last full year before the upgrade. In 2009, following the upgrade, this had jumped by 29% to almost 81,000 vehicles,[6] again illustrating the amount of latent demand that exists on this route. The upgraded road is clearly facilitating many more journeys than were previously possible, although the capacity of the road is still finite, as may be demonstrated within a couple of decades if traffic levels continue to grow.

With access to Grosvenor Road no longer possible from the north, traffic on the local road network at Divis Street has increased, and in particular the problem of vehicles 'rat running' along Barrack Street. The latter effect contributed to the decision to introduce a one-way system on Barrack Street in 2012, and then sealing off its southern end completely.

At the time of writing, it is too early to assess the longer term impact of the M1/Westlink upgrade, but to date the works seem to have facilitated more travel and quicker journeys, and have been very well received by the travelling public and the haulage industry.

The Broadway Flood

Saturday 16 August 2008 saw a prolonged spell of heavy rain over Belfast during which 67.3 mm of rain fell on the city.[15] The rain caused flooding across Northern Ireland, but particularly on the Forth/Clowney River which drains a sizeable proportion of the Belfast Hills. At this time, the new culverts for the Clowney and Blackstaff Rivers at Broadway were completed and in use, while the underpass itself had been open to traffic for just six weeks.

At 4 pm the Clowney finally burst its banks at the entrance to the new Broadway culvert and began flowing onto the roundabout.[15] At 4.30 pm this water found its way to the northbound onslip and began flowing along it, before turning 180° and flowing down into the underpass itself. Drivers coming from Westlink could see the water, but traffic approaching on the M1 initially had no prior warning of what was occurring ahead. The flow of water involved (25,000 litres per second) was immense, and videos later posted on YouTube[25] show frightened motorists on the citybound M1 suddenly finding themselves driving into a rapidly filling lake against

Water from the Clowney River pouring down into the Broadway underpass shortly after 4.30 pm on 16 August 2008, as seen from the southbound offslip. Just over half an hour later the underpass was completely full of water. *(Paul Smith)*

Workers beginning the task of cleaning tonnes of mud off the M1/Westlink on the morning after the flood, while pumps positioned above the underpass (inset) removed the water. The road was reopened after just three days. *(Author's collection)*

what was effectively a river. Around this time the police closed the underpass, but one vehicle was submerged in the water: its occupant, taxi driver Kevin Curran[26] having to be rescued. Quick-thinking police officers used an angle-grinder to remove a portion of the steel central barrier to allow the remaining motorists to perform a u-turn and escape the rising water.

Mr Curran later said:

> *There did not seem to be that much water at all then all of a sudden it started flooding. At that stage I was on the roof, the water was up here to my waist. It was frightening. The emergency services were absolutely fantastic. This one guy Mark, who was one of the firemen, he was as brave as brave can be. It's thanks to him that I am standing here today.*[26]

By 5.15 pm the underpass had been completely filled with water, an estimated 75 million litres (or 75,000 tonnes). Water continued to pour out of the Clowney and flow across the site until 6.40 pm when the flood peak passed and the level began to subside. At the time of the flood, the permanent drainage pumps had not been installed, and the underpass was instead being kept dry by two temporary pumps capable of pumping up to 240 litres per second. Neither these, nor the permanent pumps, would have had any chance against the actual inflow of over 25,000 litres per second. Portable pumps were installed that evening and the next morning, but the underpass was not re-opened (and Mr Curran's car retrieved) until the early hours of Tuesday.

Martin O'Neill, HMC's construction manager, later commented: "The drainage system we have in there is more than capable of taking whatever rainfall we have. If the Clowney hadn't been there there wouldn't have been a problem."[27] This illustrates the distinction between pumping rainwater and pumping the flow from a river, and again highlights the very particular nature of the site of the Broadway underpass. It is notable that if Roads Service's original plan for a flyover had made it through the public inquiry, the impact of the flood would have been much less severe.

A subsequent investigation was unable to conclusively explain why the flood had occurred, as the flow of the Clowney had not exceeded the design capacity of the culvert. The flood was between a 1 in 50 and 1 in 70 year event, while the culvert was designed to cope with a 1 in 100 year event. However, it did note that the sluice at the entrance to the Blackstaff Relief Culvert was only half open at the time the flood began. The report recommended remedial measures, including more regular inspection of the trash screen at the entrance to the culvert, raising the flood wall on the unculverted section immediately upstream, modifications to the policy for diverting water down the Blackstaff Relief Culvert and an upstream alarm system.

A £70,000[28] scale model of the culvert system was also built to allow further investigation of the fluid dynamics within the system. It indicated that a partially blocked screen at the entrance to the Clowney culvert had been the primary reason for the flood.[29] Subsequent work was carried out to provide further trash screens upstream, and to modify the layout of the repaired screen at Broadway.

Occurring so soon after the opening of the underpass, the flood attracted ridicule on social media, and received far more media attention than any of the scheme's opening events. The subsequent investigation suggests that this genuinely was an exceptional rainfall event, and the fact that it occurred so soon after opening seems to have been a very unfortunate coincidence. The last time there was a comparable flood event was August 1952, when the same area was submerged under 1.5 metres of water.[13] Ironically, it was this flood that prompted Belfast Corporation to drain large areas of the Bog Meadows, paving the way for the construction of the M1 through the middle of the site in 1962, eventually leading to the choice of this location for the underpass. The Forth/Clowney has always been a violent river and it remains to be seen whether the recent mitigation measures will prevent the flood recurring in an era when climatologists predict more frequent extreme weather events in the years to come.

Subsequent Developments

During 2009 and 2010 a £10m traffic control system was installed on the M1 and Westlink between Black's Road and Clifton Street. The system featured mandatory (as opposed to advisory) variable speed limits, the first time such a system had been used in Northern Ireland and the first time such a system had been used on an A-class road in the British Isles.[30] The system operates using 60 detection loops buried in the road surface, which then automatically select the most appropriate speed limit to minimise congestion. On the M1 this can be the National Speed Limit (70 mph for most cars), 60 mph, 50 mph or 40 mph. On Westlink it can be 50 mph, 40 mph or 30 mph. (The M1 between Stockman's Lane and Broadway had been limited to 50 mph before the M1 and Westlink upgrade, but this was raised to the National Speed Limit once the scheme was completed since the lower limit was no longer seen as appropriate.)

The system came into operation on 16 September 2010, 18 months after the completion of the Westlink upgrade. A public information exercise was carried out to ensure that motorists understood that the variable limits were enforceable (as indicated by the a red circle around the number).[30] The absence of media attention since then suggests that the system is working efficiently at minimising delays on the route. It is the latest in a number of technological developments in Belfast that mean that the M1, M2, M3 and Westlink are now amongst the most closely monitored and carefully managed trunk roads in the UK.

Broadway Rise Sculpture

From the inception of the project it had been the intention of Belfast City Council to place a prominent piece of public art at Broadway roundabout to act as a striking landmark for those arriving at the city from elsewhere in Ireland. In October 2005 a competition resulted in the selection of 'Trillian', a £400,000 45 metre sculpture reminiscent of a flower, by Californian artist Ed Carpenter who described his sculpture in these terms:

> *It represents growth, transformation, evolution, and these are all subjects which are universal and which we can identify with and particularly in a city which has had some negative press around the world, this can be a very positive symbol both internally and externally …. It will provide a kind of very optimistic and memorable large scale monument which will be visible from a great distance night and day and which can be identified with by the people of Belfast.*[31]

Wolfgang Buttress' 'Rise' sculpture that graces the centre of the Broadway roundabout. *(Aubrey Dale)*

Trillian was not to be however: the soaring cost of steel pushed the price up and up, and when the cost of the sculpture passed £600,000 in July 2008, the Council pulled the plug on the project and began a new competition.[32] In November of the same year, an alternative sculpture was chosen. Called 'Rise', it was designed by English sculptor Wolfgang Buttress[33] and consists of two spherical frameworks, one inside the other, representing the rising sun with a total height of 37.5 metres (123 feet). The sculpture was cast in white steel by M Hasson and Sons Ltd of Rasharkin.

The sculpture was erected during 2011 and unveiled on 16 September.[34] Despite public apathy during the planning phases[35] and criticism that it was a waste of money at £486,000, it is a bold, striking addition to the skyline and acts as a gateway to the city. Perhaps inevitably, it was soon nicknamed 'The Balls on the Falls'.

York Street Junction

Even before work began on the Westlink upgrade in 2006, the question of the York Street junction was looming ever larger on the radar. Indeed, in 2006 a Roads Service spokesperson stated publicly that such a scheme would be required within "five, ten to fifteen years" of the completion of the Westlink upgrade.[36]

The 1977 Lavery Inquiry[37] had recommended that the Lagan bridge be connected directly to the M2, but that Westlink should be linked to these via a street level interchange. Writing in his 1977 report, Lavery stated that "taking into account the slower rate of increase in car ownership … cross harbour traffic could then be accommodated on a ground level junction".[37] This policy informed the design of the northern terminus of the 1983 Westlink as well as the 1995 Lagan Bridge and adjacent railway viaduct. With hindsight, it is obvious that Lavery's prediction was wrong, and even with a much reduced rate of increase in car ownership, current traffic levels cannot for much longer be accommodated on a ground level junction.

By 2004 around 111,000 vehicles negotiated the junction per day: higher than the traffic levels on the M2, M3 or Westlink individually.[38] Taken together, the M2, M3 and Westlink are respectively the first, second, and third busiest roads in Northern Ireland. York Street, therefore, is the focus of Northern Ireland's road network and, as such, it is an ongoing embarrassment that it remains a signalised junction when numerous junctions with less traffic have benefitted from grade separation. The M3 to Westlink connection was operating above its capacity in 2004 (less than a decade after it was built), while it was predicted that the three remaining strategic links would exceed capacity by 2015.[38]

In planning the Westlink upgrade, Roads Service made it clear that grade separating

York Street interchange was highly desirable.[39] It was obvious to the engineers that the upgraded Westlink, when combined with the upgraded M2 motorway, would feed vehicles much more efficiently to the one remaining signalised junction at York Street. This would actually exacerbate congestion at this location until this final bottleneck was removed.

Only the lack of money at the time of the 2006 upgrade prevented them from carrying out the work. Indeed the complexity of grade separating the junction was such that doing so would have doubled the cost of the scheme, rendering it unaffordable.[40]

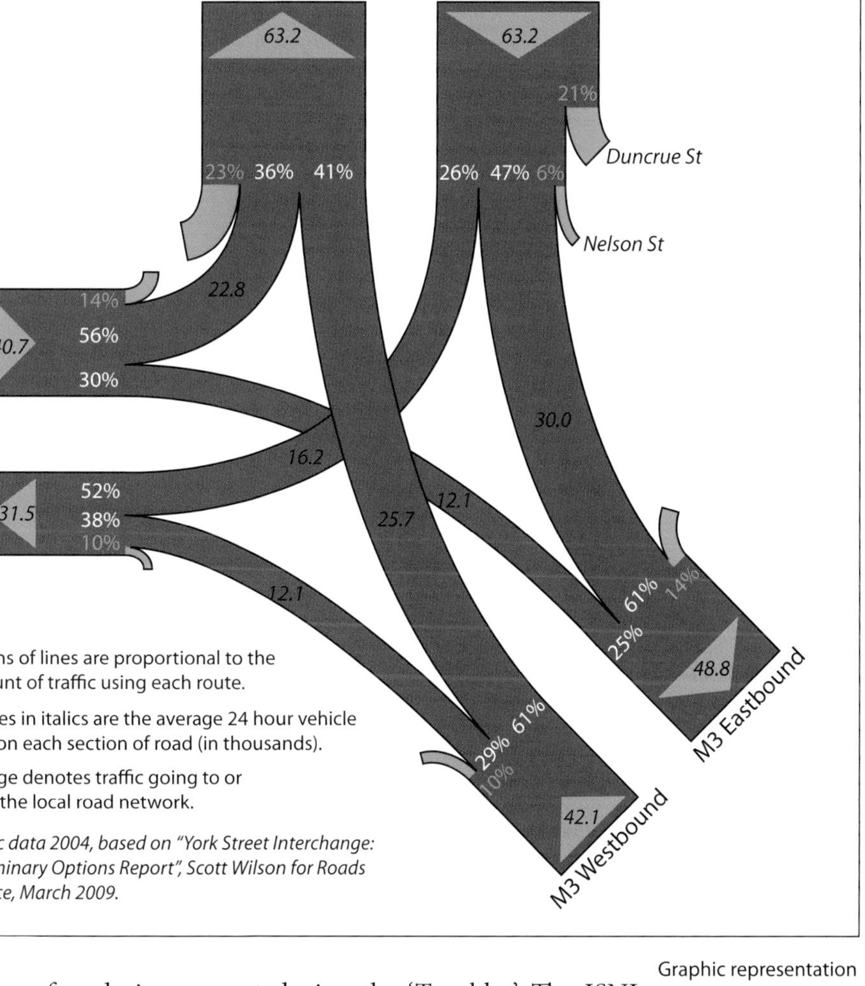

Graphic representation of traffic flows through the York Street junction as they were recorded during survey work in 2004. Contrary to popular belief, Westlink is the least busy of the three routes, while the M2-M3 link is the busiest connection between them. As the meeting place of the three busiest roads in the province, York Street junction can be thought of as the focal point of the Northern Ireland road network.

December 2005 saw the publication of the Investment Strategy for Northern Ireland (ISNI), which was the devolved administration's first real attempt to redress the years of underinvestment during the 'Troubles'. The ISNI envisaged £1.4 bn of investment in road schemes for the period to 2015. However, Roads Service's plans had assumed that only £1.0 bn would be available. In light of this unexpected windfall, work began to identify additional projects that should now be considered.

Roads Service's response in July 2006 included a proposal to grade-separate the York Street interchange at an estimated cost of £50 m.[41] Roads Service then appointed Scott Wilson to do a more detailed investigation of feasibility. Their report, published in March 2009, concluded that it was feasible to make three of the movements free flowing while the fourth (M3 to Westlink) could be accommodated with a degree of difficulty.

Roads Service presented four options to the public in June 2011.[42] In two of the options the M2 to Westlink connection was to be made by building a flyover over the railway viaduct, while the remaining two saw the link follow a more curvaceous route below ground level. All four options were practical, legal and safe, although all featured considerable departures from ideal engineering standards and ranged in cost from £73 m to £100 m. The scheme, it was predicted, could reduce journey times through the junction by between 37% and 67%,

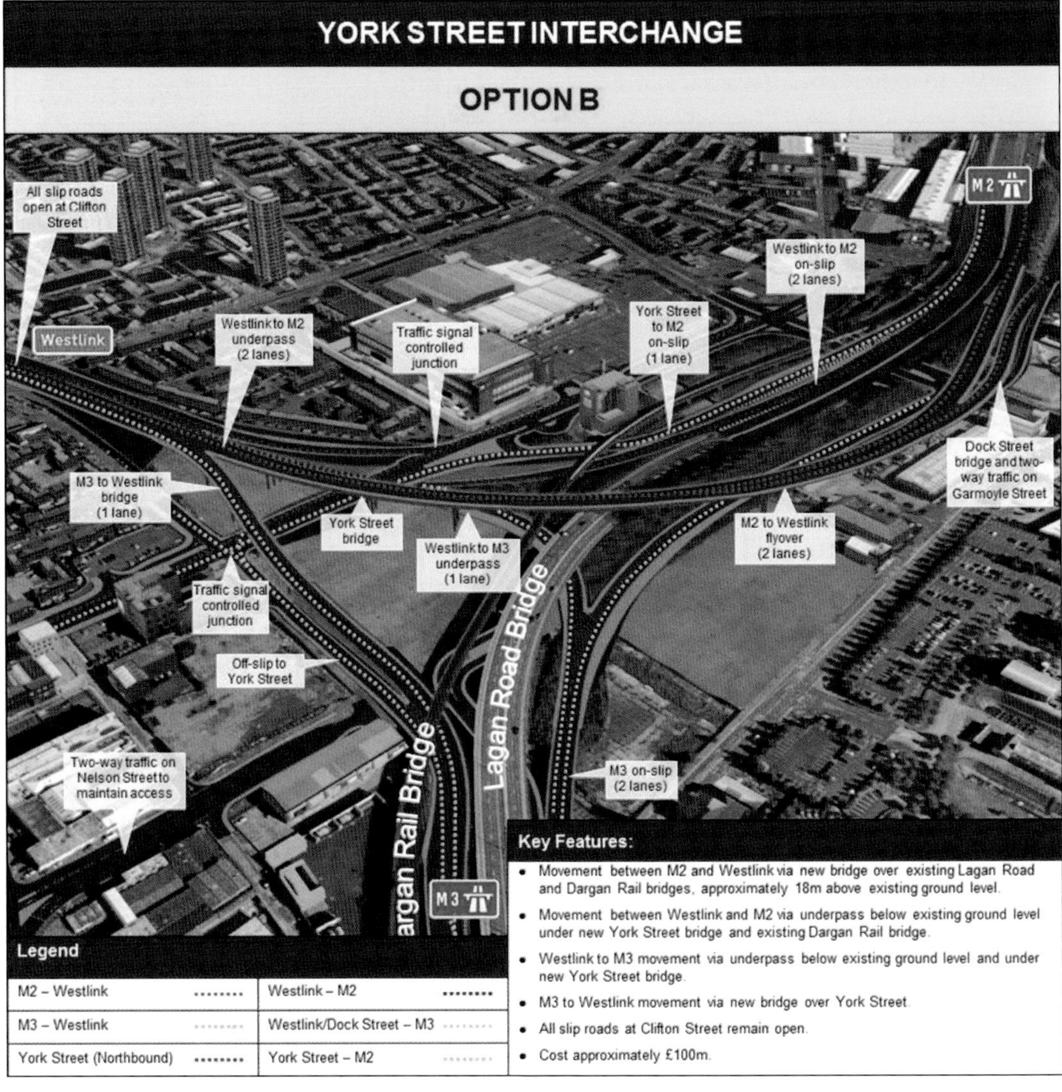

Graphic representation of the 'Option B' design for York Street interchange, published in 2011. This option allowed the fastest design speeds, but required a controversial bridge over the existing M3 which would have reached 18 metres above ground level *(Image courtesy of DRD Roads Service)*

depending on the route and design option.[38] At the same time, it was also noted that some of the links on the upgraded junction could be operating at or above capacity once again by 2029 if traffic levels continued to rise.

All bore more than a passing resemblance to the 1967 Belfast Urban Motorway proposals for this location, and were striking in their boldness. Option B featured a flyover soaring 18 metres (59 feet) above street level,[38] higher than any proposed here in 1967. Following the public consultation in June 2011 it was this aspect of the plan that attracted the most negative comment. Opponents argued that not only would such a structure have a very negative visual effect, but it would permanently jeopardise any attempts to revitalise a very degraded part of the cityscape and reduce the severance between north Belfast and the city centre. One campaign group even hired a crane to lift a lorry 18 metres into the air to illustrate the effect.

There was a concerted, and uniquely constructive, campaign in support of Option C, which would see all four links provided either at or below ground level. The campaigners were

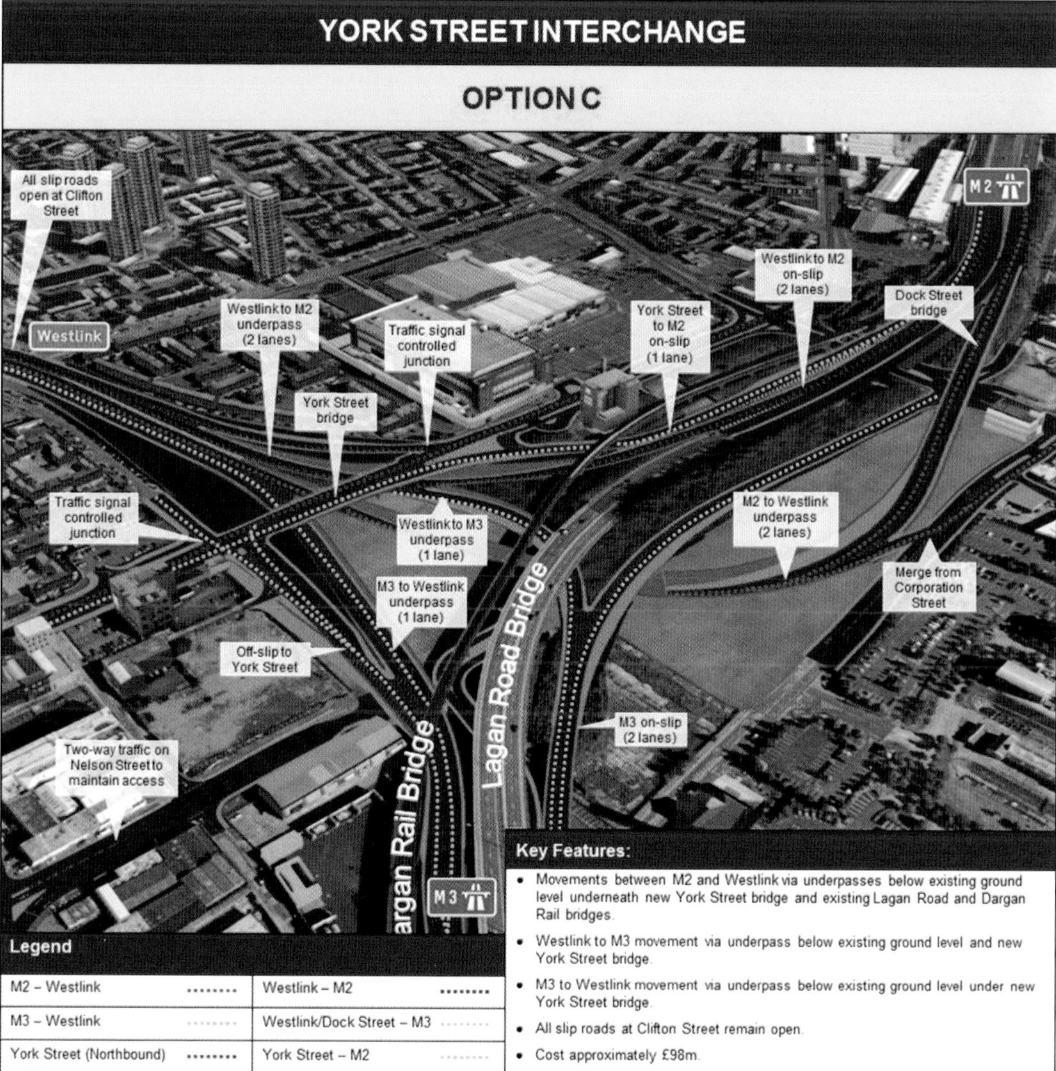

Graphic representation of the 'Option C' design for York Street interchange, published in 2011. Although this option was not quite so optimal for consistent traffic speeds, the fact that all the links were at or below ground level ultimately counted in its favour. *(Image courtesy of DRD Roads Service)*

delighted when, on 5 December 2012, Roads Service announced that they would, indeed, be proceeding with Option C and that no 18 metre flyovers would be built.[42] The revised cost estimate was between £100 m and £135 m.[43]

It is not unfair to say that major road schemes since the 1960s have decimated the urban fabric of York Street. Severance is severe, and the presence of so many vehicles has diminished its desirability for residential, recreational or commercial land uses. Removing the road is not a credible option – in a city the size of Belfast, with a large port and large-scale commercial activity, strategic roads like this are essential. However, a unique win-win opportunity presents itself to simultaneously upgrade the junction and enhance the local area. Fully grade-separating the junction would remove large amounts of traffic from street level roads, allowing a more pedestrian-friendly environment and an enhanced role for public transport. Meanwhile, releasing carefully selected areas of land for development would diminish the sense of an urban wasteland that currently characterises the location, and replace it with more human-scale frontal development and land uses.

A 'lorry' lifted 18 metres into the air by the Forum for Alternative Belfast on 5 December 2012 as a graphic protest against the 'Option B' proposal for York Street junction. *(Mark Hackett, Forum for Alternative Belfast)*

The Forum for Alternative Belfast has come up with imaginative proposals[44] for the junction, which would require only minor adjustments to the design. Since Roads Service currently does not have much remit beyond building the road elements of the scheme, these imaginative proposals would require inter-departmental cooperation directed from the Stormont Executive. This will be no small feat in Northern Ireland where the unusual structure of the Executive ensures that competing political parties often run different departments. However, in his speech at the announcement of the preferred option in December 2012, DRD Minister Danny Kennedy explicitly said that:

> *...while the financial and legislative remit of my Department does not permit the promotion of redevelopment projects, I can assure you as stakeholders that I will continue to work with the DSD [Department for Social Development] Minister to ensure the aims and objectives of both Departments are as closely aligned as possible.*[43]

We may be witnessing a long-overdue maturing of the relationship between the road planners and those with an interest in the social aspects of transport. For perhaps the first time in the history of the Urban Motorway, campaign groups have worked constructively with the planners' designs, making serious efforts to incorporate them into the cityscape, rather than simply opposing them *carte blanche*.[45] Similarly, we are witnessing an apparent, if tentative, will at Ministerial level to see York Street as more than just a road project. Only time will tell if this really is the case.

2014

As of 2014, two things are obvious. Firstly, barring a radical change in government policy or a shift to a trend of much reduced road traffic, the need for a substantial upgrade to the York Street interchange is inevitable in the long term. Indeed, the full benefits of the Westlink and M2 upgrades cannot be realised until such a scheme is carried out, and the proposed widening of the Sydenham Bypass would make the case even stronger. In other words, there is a strong engineering and traffic flow motivation to proceed with the plan.

Secondly, the Global Recession and economic austerity that has gripped the world since 2008 has made the viability of such a scheme far from certain, regardless of its desirability. At the time of writing, the scheme is still firmly on the drawing board, with no funding currently identified. Even if funds are identified, there are still several years of planning and a three-year construction period before it could be brought into use.

The past 50 years have witnessed Belfast's urban motorway system slowly but inexorably develop into something that now resembles the original proposals, at least in terms of the West Tangent and Cross Harbour Bridge. Grade separation of the York Street junction is the last piece in the jigsaw that would see this process finally completed. It is unlikely that any more proposals will be made to upgrade the urban motorway system in the foreseeable future, but the roads themselves are vital pieces of infrastructure that will play a major role in the city for many years to come. The story of the Belfast Urban Motorway is far from over.

A model constructed through the Forum for Alternative Belfast illustrating the high quality urban environment that could be achieved at York Street whilst simultaneously upgrading the junction under 'Option C'. Only slight modifications to the design, such as roofing over some of the links that lie below ground level, would be required. *(Mark Hackett, Forum for Alternative Belfast)*

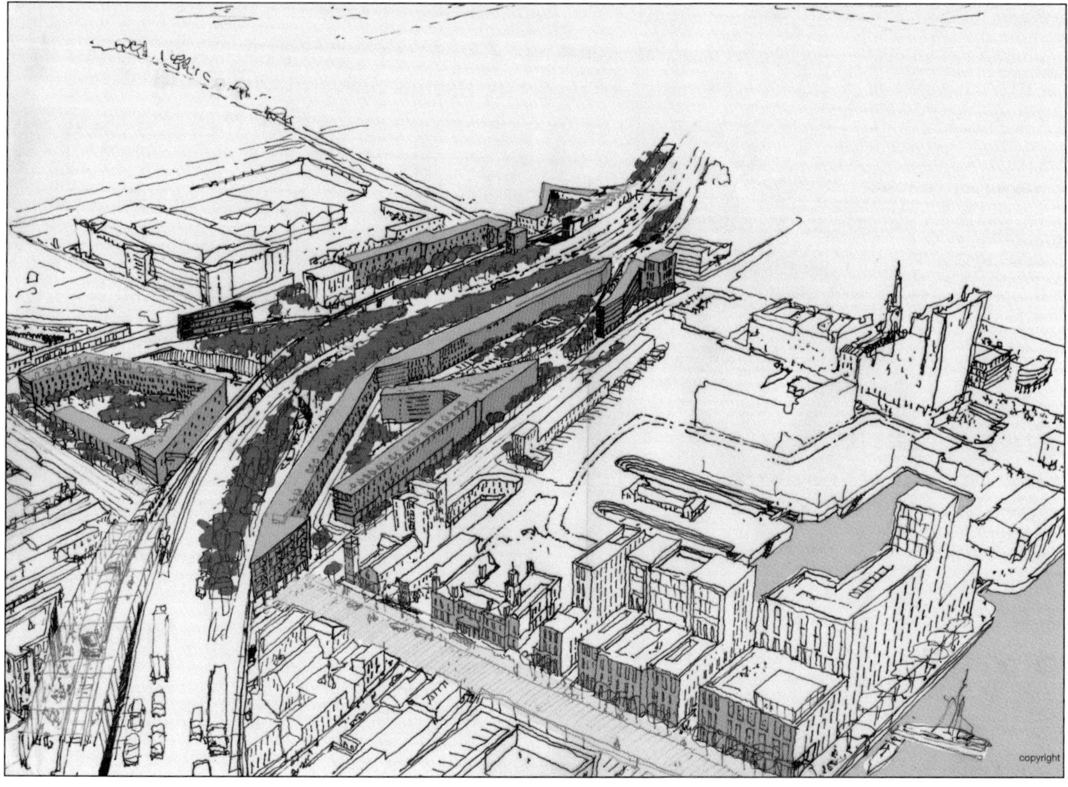

An artist's impression of how the York Street junction could look after being upgraded under 'Option C' and then developing the land around and amongst the elements of the junction to create a people-friendly urban environment. *(Mark Hackett, Forum for Alternative Belfast)*

CONCLUSION

The story of the Belfast Urban Motorway is about much more than engineering. It is woven into the more general story of the development of Belfast during the second half of the twentieth century, and encompasses so many different issues that attempts to draw out conclusions are fraught with difficulties. On the one hand, it would be facetious to characterise it simply as a road plan, making faltering progress through the legal and planning system, as if it existed in isolation from the organic city. On the other hand, providing an exhaustive analysis of every associated issue risks turning it into yet another general assessment of Belfast's urban environment, ignoring the specific story we have been following. I have, therefore, tried to keep the focus on the Urban Motorway and the issues that immediately impacted on it, and to avoid reducing it to a generalised discussion on urban planning in Belfast. I leave that to others.

At the outset, it must be stressed that it is vital to judge past decisions by the knowledge, trends and culture of the time they were taken. With the benefit of hindsight it is tempting to be overly critical of decisions made by our forebears. But although the consequences of their decisions are laid plain before us, they did not have the benefit of such hindsight. In addition, we cannot judge past decision makers through the prism of issues that are of critical importance to us today (such as Global Warming) but which were largely unknown in the mid twentieth century. We must therefore be careful not to read the prominence of a modern issue into the past. For example, it would be tempting to use modern lenses to try to portray the Belfast Urban Motorway as a simple tale of private cars versus public transport. This would be grossly misleading.

Why an Urban Motorway?

Despite being such a major issue in late 1960s Belfast, many people alive today have never heard of the Belfast Urban Motorway. Whenever such people discover what was planned, the initial response is usually some variant of the following:

1. That's amazing!
2. What were they thinking?
3. Why wasn't it built?
4. Thank goodness it was never built.

The first issue that needs to be tackled, therefore, is why the road was conceived at all. The modern observer feels such incredulity at the sheer scale and audacity of the proposals, that it is taken as a given that it should not have been built. Most people today automatically hold this view. Yet, such a consensus did not exist in the late 1960s and there was fierce debate about the pros and cons of the proposals. Many are genuinely surprised not only by the issues that were seen as important to the question at the time, but also by the issues that were not.

Belfast in the late 1940s and 1950s was still predominantly an industrial city, but a city that had been devastated by wartime bombing and austerity. The experience of the Second World War had made people keen to leave pre-war European society – with its perceived stuffiness, imperialism, pomp and ceremony – behind. The new era would be dominated by modernity and practical technology. Industry would be put to peaceful purposes. People would have the freedom to go and do as they pleased. In the light of this worldview, many people began to implicitly judge certain aspects of the city as 'bad' or 'good', where bad was often equated with 'old' and good with 'new'.

Into the 'bad' category fell the old, crusty Victorian buildings with their ostentatious ornamentation. So too did the traditional brick terraces of the working classes with their outside toilets. Many having been bombed to rubble, there was a desire to get rid of this old, over-crowded 'slum' housing and replace it with sleek, futuristic tower blocks where people could truly 'live in the sky'. Huge pressure built up on the government to reconstruct poor-quality working class housing to better, post-war standards.

For many, the railways also fell into the 'bad' category. The 1950s saw the profitability of the railways fall away as wages rose. Still dominated by steam, they were seen by many as dirty and antiquated. By contrast, cars were 'good', being seen as futuristic symbols of freedom and modernity. The public bought cars in their droves. It was assumed that before long everybody would own a car and buses and trains would be relegated to the history books. Few people questioned that this was anything other than a good thing, and few imagined that the public would continue to buy and use cars to the extent that they eventually did. The idea that the government might one day attempt to discourage people from using cars would have seemed bizarrely authoritarian in the 1950s.

As one of the only major powers to have emerged from the Second World War without significant damage to its homeland, the United States became the model to be aspired to. People saw pictures from the USA with its sweeping freeways and elevated motorways filled with prosperous Americans enjoying life, and naturally came to see motorways and factories as two of the essential ingredients of a prosperous post-war society.

As post-war austerity eased in the 1950s, people bought cars in increasing numbers and traffic levels on the roads began to rise. At that time all roads were shared spaces devoted to all kinds of traffic from pedestrians and cyclists to cars and lorries. The resultant conflicts resulted in rapidly rising congestion. The government was keen to grow Northern Ireland's industrial base, and as more and more freight moved to the roads it became increasingly concerning that congestion was stopping people moving about and could eventually cripple the economy.

This was coupled with predictions that Northern Ireland's population would rapidly rise, with the risk that Belfast would mushroom out into the countryside and become unmanageable. The influential 'Matthew Plan' of 1962 is of key significance. Matthew halted the growth of Belfast and encouraged the decentralisation of population away from Belfast to other towns and the new city of Craigavon. All of these people were going to have to commute into Belfast and, as per the thinking of the time, this would naturally be achieved by car. He hence proposed a series of motorways connecting these towns to Belfast. Given that Matthew was on record as attaching more importance to public transport in other cities, it seems likely that planners in Northern Ireland were particularly keen on the use of private cars, perhaps more so than other areas of the UK. It is not entirely clear why this might have been the case.

Realising that all this traffic would be dumped into the already congested streets of central Belfast, it was assumed that some way would be needed to allow all this traffic to quickly find its destination. Hence an inner ring road was conceived: what eventually became the Urban Motorway. Traffic would enter the city on the motorways, circulate around the Urban Motorway and then enter the central area or the port at the most convenient point. In theory it was an excellent plan, but it was built on the assumption that this alone would be enough to absorb all the traffic coming into the city. The planners at the time lacked the practical experience to understand that the central area had a relatively low and finite capacity that could not be increased simply by allowing traffic to circulate around it. However, this dose of realism was for the future.

It was now that the sort of opportunity that comes along only once in a century presented itself. Large areas of inner Belfast were in dire need of reconstruction, the city needed a modern road system and the industrial economy needed to be boosted. Many birds could be killed with the one stone, ie the wholesale demolition of huge tracts of the inner city and their replacement with an entirely new urban fabric of modern roads, factories and tower blocks parachuted in, as it were, into the void. Large tracts of land, most of which were in the west and north of the city, were designated as regeneration areas.

It would be wrong to think that the regeneration areas were conceived primarily to allow the Urban Motorway to pass through. At the same time, it would be wrong to see the Urban Motorway as an entirely unrelated plan that was able to pass through these areas merely by happy coincidence. In reality, the planners wanted to reconstruct all aspects of the city at once, and the Urban Motorway was as much an integral part of the plan as the regeneration schemes.

Early Weaknesses

So far we have seen that it was the mindset of the 1950s that conceived the Urban Motorway and the pattern of commuting. The road was conceived as a means of preventing congestion in the city centre and as a means of allowing commuters to reach their destinations quickly. But how did thinking change as time went on? Trends and policies ebb and flow with the decades, and it was no different with the Belfast Urban Motorway. As the 1960s dawned, there were already signs that opinions of urban roads were changing. Belfast's planners were, on the whole, slow to recognise these changes, slower to accept them and even slower to respond to them.

Among these changes was the realisation that it was unlikely that everyone would own a car in the near future. Public transport, therefore, would continue to have a role – at the very least to provide transport for those unable to afford a car. The 1963 Buchanan Report in the UK noted, for the first time, that urban roads had the ability to severely harm the fabric of British cities and could not, by themselves, solve congestion. The warnings of Buchanan seem not to have been heeded in Northern Ireland at the time. There was also growing opposition to urban roads in the USA, where road building and district-wide reconstruction projects were more advanced than in the UK. When a delegation of Belfast engineers visited the USA in 1963 they came back full of inspiration and enthusiasm by what they had seen. Even though at this time there was a considerable backlash in the USA from the communities through which elevated motorways had been built, it seems that the Belfast planners failed to notice this.

In a sense, who can blame them? Trained road engineers will always be drawn to their passion, the road system. The lessons of the USA were not learned in 1963, but they easily could have been. Perhaps if more politicians and community representatives had gone on the trip the team would have returned with a more balanced perspective on the effect of roads on urban areas. As it happened, the engineers returned home to design the ultimate Urban Motorway, a three-lane elevated structure encircling the city, which was unveiled in 1967. They severely under-estimated the opposition they would receive and seem to have been genuinely surprised by the criticism. The engineers of the early 1960s can rightly be accused of a remarkable level of naivety, but it would be unfair to attribute more sinister motives.

Traffic levels grew at an incredible rate during the 1960s, and by 1967 the Stormont government's concerns about the issue had almost reached hysterical proportions. Planning documents warned that traffic levels would double within ten years, and that the city was going to collapse if more roads were not urgently provided. Provision of the Urban Motorway was elevated to such an extent that it seems to have become the over-arching issue in the entire city. Contemporary accusations that all other issues in the city had become subservient to the Urban Motorway are probably not far off the mark. The language grew increasingly apocalyptic as time went on, and the public were shocked by predictions that if nothing was done the city would eventually become gridlocked throughout the working day. There must have been a degree of positive feedback as each planner made predictions that shocked other planners into devising more drastic solutions.

Around 1967 the plans for the Urban Motorway made a subtle shift away from naivety and towards inertia. By the late 1960s a number of key problems with the plans had become evident, and by 1967 it is difficult to accept that the authorities could have been unaware of them. The fact that the plans continued in the same form after 1967 suggests that the Urban Motorway was no longer motivated purely as a solution to traffic problems, but had been given a life of its own that continued to sustain the plan, as an end in itself, for another decade.

The key problems were:

1. That the general public had never actually been asked if they wanted an Urban Motorway.
2. That the cost, estimated at £1.09bn in 2010 prices, was barely affordable for a small province such as Northern Ireland.
3. That if traffic forecasts were correct, the road would not have enough capacity to function properly after just ten years.
4. That the plan would require the demolition of over 4000 houses, over and above those that had been destroyed in the war or which needed reconstruction due to age.
5. That the plans clearly asked the working class communities to pay the bulk of the costs of a scheme that would primarily benefit the car-owning middle classes.
6. That there was growing opposition to high-rise flats. The plan to use former residential land for the motorway relied on the assumption that housing densities could be increased on the remaining land.

In other words, it could be seen that not only was the Urban Motorway incapable of achieving its own stated aims, but it came at an economic and social cost that the province could arguably ill afford. The Urban Motorway came to be seen in working class Belfast as a beast, controlled by the middle classes, that was eating housing land. The response of the government was to press ahead regardless, and this left them open to accusations of being contemptuous of the working classes, and purely serving the interests of the middle classes.

It must be stressed, therefore, that the growing opposition to the Belfast Urban Motorway at the end of the 1960s did *not* derive from accusations that it promoted cars at the expense of public transport (as would be the case today) but rather from the impact that its construction would have on the communities through which it passed. The primary issues were land use and a dislike for the proposed structure of the road. At this point in time, the issue of explosively increasing traffic volumes was a very real one, and in general the detractors of the scheme did not argue against the need for new roads, just their location: a survey conducted ten years later (1977) in these communities suggested that there was little opposition to new roads in principle, even amongst non-car owners.

Why Was It Never Built?

Despite public opposition in the late 1960s, the Northern Ireland government decided to press ahead with the Urban Motorway as planned. Yet just ten years later the plan was effectively dead. Why did this occur? A number of reasons can be identified.

A. Timing

The Belfast Urban Motorway came at a critical time in the evolution of thinking on urban roads in the UK. The Oil Crisis in 1973, and a growing realisation that the scale of some urban road schemes was causing unacceptable damage to British cities, led to a shift in policy away from widespread construction of such roads from 1973 onwards. Major new roads were still built, but they were mostly outside city centres. This was important for Northern Ireland because its devolved Parliament had been suspended in 1972; henceforth UK road policy was also local road policy. This meant that, generally speaking, any urban road schemes not already underway by 1973 would find it tougher to proceed after that date.

The Belfast Urban Motorway plan was launched in 1967 (the more general transport plan for the city being launched in 1969), giving what we can now recognise as a narrow window of just six years within which it had an excellent chance of proceeding. Had planners known that a stopwatch was running they would probably have proceeded more earnestly than they did. It took until April 1968 for Phase 1 to be approved. A public inquiry in 1969 attracted virtually no public interest, and it was not until 1970 that land acquisition began, coinciding with the worst years of the 'Troubles' that had begun in 1969. The complexity of this aspect of the project was totally underestimated, with the result that land clearance was still not completed by 1972.

Growing anger at the inadequate compensation, poor quality replacement homes, social upheaval and blight combined to the point that the paramilitaries threatened any contractors who came near the site in 1971 and 1972. Eventually the scale of the social disorder in west Belfast was so great that all attempts to begin construction had to be abandoned. The whole transport plan was sent back to a public inquiry in 1972.

Thus the Belfast Urban Motorway was critically delayed, for three key reasons: (a) the length of time it took to acquire and clear the land (b) the negative experiences of those being re-housed, which motivated (c) armed opposition from paramilitaries. It is fair to say that, had these three factors not conspired, Phase 1 of the Urban Motorway would certainly have been built and would likely exist today.

B. Public Opposition

Public opposition to the scheme was at its strongest in the 1970s, and the debate raged ever more vocally as time went on. Two groups emerged. Opponents were generally the working class residents of the areas through which the Urban Motorway would pass, and nationalist or socialist politicians. Supporters were generally transport planners, business owners and (increasingly due to nationalist opposition) the unionist bloc. Interestingly, few Belfast residents outside the affected areas expressed any opinion on the plan. Since almost all the public resistance was from residents of the affected areas, this suggests that the opposition was essentially local in nature, and supports the view that the wider populace was in fact indifferent to the Urban Motorway.

Nevertheless, the two groups that emerged for the showdown were divided not only by their opinion of the Urban Motorway but by social class and (at least to a degree) political opinion. It was, therefore, an ideological confrontation rather than a simple clash of opinions on transport policy.

A further complication was that the two opposing groups were actually arguing different points, and often failed to engage with the points being made by the 'other side'. To the opponents, the issue was primarily a *social* one: the impact that the physical fabric of the road would have on the area through which it passed, the loss of amenity and fears of pollution. Some also saw it as a front in a wider class war. To supporters, the issue was primarily a *transport* one. Every year traffic was getting worse, with hundreds of lorries forced to trundle through residential areas such as the Donegall Road on their way to Belfast Port, while all traffic seeking to cross the city was forced to drive through the city centre, choking the streets. For the planners, it was difficult to see how the city's transportation system could continue to function without a high-capacity road capable of distributing all this traffic.

Of course, the opponents made strong transport arguments. They argued forcefully that massively improved public transport was a viable alternative to the Urban Motorway, and their proposals in this area became increasingly well argued as time went on. These proposals are critical to understanding the development of the Urban Motorway, and will be evaluated more fully later. Nevertheless, these arguments were offered more as a means to achieving their underlying social objectives of opposition to the Urban Motorway, rather than being presented as solutions to the transport issue as an end in itself. This muddied the waters, and tended to make hopes of compromise appear more plausible than was actually the case.

The Inspectors at the 1972 and 1977 public inquiries were hence being asked to weigh transport arguments against social arguments: something that is difficult to evaluate in any meaningful or objective way. Compromise was impossible – even a scaled down road would be unacceptable to opponents, and anything less than that would not satisfy the transport planners.

At the 1972 inquiry, opponents engaged with the inquiry, but the inspector, Brian Rutherford, decided that on balance the economic prospects of the city had to take precedence, ie that the need for the Urban Motorway was stronger than the negative social impact it would have. He made a classic appeal to the greater good. To transport planners, this was an entirely logical position to take – after all, the land for Phase 1 had already been cleared, so would it really cause much additional harm to just go ahead and build it? But to opponents, it was an outrageous decision. To them, the 'greater good' was really just the good of the middle classes. They lost all faith in the inquiry process as a result of the 1972 inquiry. The whole event simply served to demonstrate the subjectivity of the issue.

By 1973 the issue of the Urban Motorway had become hopelessly interwoven with the issue of the 'Troubles'. In that year even Belfast City Council voted against it. Republicans, although genuinely motivated by its social impact, soon saw the whole debate as an opportunity to undermine the unionist ascendancy. At the same time, the fact that nationalist politicians were against the Urban Motorway encouraged otherwise ambivalent unionists to support it, and this served to discourage working class Protestants in affected areas from speaking out against the scheme. In the dark days of early 1970s Belfast, there was little hope of amicably resolving an issue that had become tied so closely to the conflict.

C. Inertia

It has already been noted that the Urban Motorway was characterised by increasing inertia from 1967. The idea of an inner ring road in Belfast dated back to 1944. By 1967 the plan had been gestating for almost a quarter of a century, and during all of this time the basic assumption that there had to be an inner ring road was never questioned. It was reaffirmed by Belfast Corporation in 1964, where it was described as 'inescapable'. When R Travers Morgan were appointed to design the Urban Motorway in 1965, their terms of reference permitted them only to assess the Corporation's ring road plan, not come up with an independent plan. It is hardly surprising therefore that they came up with a design that differed only in detail from the Corporation's plan.

R Travers Morgan received enormous criticism during the late 1960s and 1970s, yet much of this is unfair. As a consultancy firm they had no choice but to do their work within the remit of their employer, Belfast Corporation. The company had considerable experience, and it is quite likely that they would have come up with different proposals (albeit still roads-based) had they been given less constricted terms of reference in 1965. For an investment of the magnitude anticipated for the Urban Motorway, it is not unfair to suggest that the Corporation ought to have considered a wider range of options for managing road traffic when R Travers Morgan were appointed. Their failure to do so supports the assertion that by the late 1960s the plan had a degree of inertia.

This was demonstrated again in 1968 when more detailed traffic forecasts became available. These demonstrated that the south and east legs of the Urban Motorway would be very under-used, and suggested that the system could probably run as effectively with just the West Tangent and river crossing. Given the huge saving this would be in both money and upheaval, it is very surprising that the only change that it led to was a decision to bring the south and east legs down to ground level between junctions. An objective analysis should have recommended scrapping these two sections, yet it does not seem to have been considered in any serious way and the plan continued to be seen as a 'ring'. It was not until 1973 that the government conceded that a reduced (ie non-ring) Urban Motorway might be an acceptable option.

This inertia indicated that the plans for the Urban Motorway became more and more divorced from reality during the late 1960s and early 1970s, and hence became more and more susceptible to rational counter-arguments based on traffic figures. Perhaps the scale and range of opposition was so great that the planners did not know how to cope with it, and hence decided to press ahead with 'Plan A'.

D. Money

The Belfast Urban Motorway was conceived in a time of relative peace and stability, and represented a colossal investment that would have been just about feasible for a growing, prosperous economy. At the same time, even in 1967 the cost was enormous and there are doubts that Stormont could have afforded the whole scheme even were it not for the economic freefall of the 1970s. It is questionable whether the province could have mustered up the quantity of manpower, concrete and steel that would have been required to complete it by the original target of 1976. It would also have required a doubling of the pace of housing construction. The scheme, therefore, began life at the very limits of feasibility.

The general world economy and the particular difficulties in Northern Ireland in the early 1970s made huge investments in infrastructure much more problematic. In addition, the dire traffic predictions of 1967 had not come to pass, Belfast's population was declining rather than growing and bus patronage was going through the floor thanks to underinvestment and the 'Troubles'. By 1974 the government realised that the Urban Motorway was no longer affordable and began looking at smaller-scale alternatives.

The one complicating factor was the 'Troubles'. Without the 'Troubles', the West Tangent would likely have been constructed as planned, even if the later elements were delayed or cancelled. The fact that construction was delayed is largely due to the civil disorder and social upheaval of the period from 1969 to 1973. This led to the scheme passing the crucial policy milestone of 1973 and the crucial cost analysis of 1974. It was, therefore, the conflict between paramilitaries and the state that was responsible for pushing the unwilling Urban Motorway to this point of infeasibility.

In the final analysis, it was the 'Troubles' and the high cost – not public opposition – that really killed the Urban Motorway in the form envisaged in 1967. The government stoically pressed ahead with the scheme, resisting public opposition, right up until it was blatantly obvious that it could no longer be afforded. With no disrespect to the conviction and passion of the opponents, their efforts ultimately failed to have a significant impact on the overall scheme: even after 1974, the government was determined to press ahead with the most controversial (and most needed) West Tangent.

Significance of the Death of the Urban Motorway

As we have seen, rumours of the Belfast Urban Motorway's demise in 1974 were very much exaggerated. The Direct Rule government remained convinced of the need for the road, at least in **function**. While they no longer regarded the Urban Motorway as being an appropriate means of feeding commuter traffic into the city centre, as had been the idea in the 1960s, they still saw it as vital to connect the M1 and M2 motorways, and Belfast Port. In this regard, they were correct. The lack of such a road did not prevent vehicles trying to make the journey, and the result was chronic congestion in the city centre as everything from port-bound HGVs to private cars jostled their way into the city centre and residential areas such as Donegall Road, in the absence of any alternative.

As the streets continued to choke, transport planners concluded that (a) the road was still necessary and (b) that public transport could not address the difficulty sufficiently to solve the problem since public transport was best suited to people travelling into/out of central Belfast, rather than through it, and could not accommodate freight.

Even among those who were opposed to the Urban Motorway in form, there was nevertheless acceptance that a link between the motorways was needed in **function**. The Republican Clubs, for example, proposed that the Outer Ring Road (West) could be used by freight to negate the need for the West Tangent of the Urban Motorway, while the Greater West Belfast Community Association indicated that they would be willing to accept the West Tangent provided it was hidden underground. Once again, this demonstrates that much of the opposition had its roots in the **form** of the road proposed, not the principle of having such a road.

The government's position, therefore, did not change at all. The demise of the Urban Motorway in 1974 was merely an acknowledgement that its current design was no longer affordable, not that it was, or had been, a bad idea – despite the fact that the newly formed Belfast City Council itself turned against the road in 1973. Their policy over the next three years was to try to bring about support for a scaled-down Urban Motorway, for example by expending great effort in getting Belfast City Council back on side, and offering some concessions to the affected communities. Some of these efforts were more successful than others, but the overall effect was to achieve sufficient support to press ahead.

In 1976 they prudently decided to kill off the name 'Belfast Urban Motorway' in a way that led some to believe that the plan itself was now dead. In practice, the Urban Motorway lived on, merely stripped of its emotive name and unfortunate acronym. Given the lack of money, it was no longer plausible that the South and East Tangents of the Motorway would ever be built. Efforts therefore concentrated on the West Tangent and Cross Harbour Bridge.

As a result of mounting pressure from the newly mobilised communities of west Belfast, and the increasingly sophisticated counter-arguments being made against a roads-oriented transportation strategy, for example by the Belfast Urban Study Group, the government conceded that they would have to consider public transport alternatives.

The Nature of the Public Transport Debate

Between 1974 and 1976 the government engaged in a consultation that on the face of it offered a choice of a bus-oriented transport system, a roads-oriented system or a mixture of the two. Any consultation of this nature must set out clearly the terms on which the comparison is being made. Factors that would seem to have been relevant include:

- initial construction cost
- ongoing maintenance cost
- impact on journey times
- impact on the built environment
- impact on communities
- impact on the environment

In practice, not all of these factors seem to have been given the same, or indeed any, weight. The government's 1976 consultation document set out the benefits of a bus-oriented transport system primarily in terms of running costs, journey times and average fares, while completely ignoring the fact that the primary benefit of public transport (according to its advocates) was that the fabric of the city would not be torn apart by road building. By overlooking this point, the benefits of even major public transport investment appeared to be relatively insignificant. It is thus not surprising that the consultation document concluded that a roads-oriented transportation strategy was the most 'cost effective' way forward.

A divisive factor in the debate was that it was not merely a choice between two forms of transport, but actually a choice between the desires of two conflicting socio-economic groups. Car users were predominantly middle class, while public transport users were generally working class. Regardless of the objective reality, the choice was perceived as a 'working class transport policy' versus a 'middle class transport policy'. This was not conducive to a rational transport debate.

The fact that the government subsequently went on to support the *mixed* strategy, despite the roads strategy emerging as the most cost effective option, was almost certainly a concession to public opposition. Despite probably believing the roads-oriented strategy to be the most rational option, adopting it would have been politically difficult to defend. The mixed strategy was the furthest they could dare to go.

Some may argue that what was labelled the 'mixed strategy' was actually the government's preferred strategy all along, and that they presented the 'roads-oriented strategy' merely as a lightning rod to deflect criticism and garner support for the preferred strategy. However, the passion with which the Department of the Environment argued the case for the roads-oriented strategy at the 1977 inquiry indicates that they genuinely believed it to be the best way forward. That the scaled-down mixed strategy Westlink immediately suffered from all the problems the transport planners had predicted at the inquiry lends credence to the arguments they made in 1977.

At the 1977 inquiry, the advocates of public transport were unable to present either a united front or a clear alternative strategy, and their critics demolished their arguments with ease. Two reasons can be offered. The first, favoured by almost all literature written since, is that the groups lacked the skill and money to research and present their case in a more robust manner. The assumption is that if they had more resources they could have presented irrefutable arguments against Westlink and the road would not have been built. The second possibility is that their arguments may actually have been weak, and that no amount of additional time and money could have produced the desired result. Despite repeated talk of a 'fourth alternative', no fourth alternative ever materialised. The Inspector was forced to conclude that only the mixed or roads-oriented strategies were practical. With hindsight, his decision to go with the mixed strategy was inevitable.

Was the Alternative Realistic?

This all leads to the question of why the government was apparently so opposed to the public transport alternatives. Two possible reasons can be put forward:

1. That the government was serving the interests of the middle classes, and that meant more roads.

2. That the government genuinely did not believe that the public transport alternative was viable.

At the time of the 1977 Lavery Inquiry, a Labour government ruled Northern Ireland, but after 1979 Margaret Thatcher's Conservative government took its place. It was certainly the Thatcherite view that cars were a symbol of free enterprise and personal success, and that public transport existed merely for those who had 'failed', ie could not afford a car. It is not difficult to see how the public transport alternative would have been undesirable to a government with this worldview, and this was undeniably a factor in the lack of enthusiasm shown for the public transport alternatives.

However, it must also be said that there are serious doubts about the viability of the public transport alternatives that were proposed in 1977. Opponents of Westlink did not put forward a single alternative, but the most developed option was a zone-and-collar system whereby access for private vehicles would be increasingly restricted the closer they came to the city centre, accompanied by regular, cheap (or free) buses and very high parking charges. Other roads could be restricted to HGVs only, to cater for freight and port traffic. The idea was that this would make buses both cheaper and more convenient than cars for commuters, and that a modal switch would occur. By taking hundreds of commuters out of cars, traffic levels could be sufficiently reduced to render construction of the West Tangent, and indeed many other road proposals, unnecessary.

In practice, this is unlikely to have been the outcome. Experience in the 35 years since (seen particularly in relation to fuel prices) has shown that commuters are prepared to pay very high costs and tolerate severe levels of congestion before they are prepared to consider public transport alternatives. Just as the government's 1976 document naïvely assumed that the case for public transport investment could be analysed purely in terms of fares and journey times, it was equally naïve to think that car drivers could be persuaded to switch to buses by appealing only to the same factors. Car drivers apparently place a great value on the privacy, convenience and comfort of their vehicles, and it seems likely that many drivers would have continued to drive into the city centre even with significantly higher parking charges and free buses.

What is most striking is that even public transport bodies opposed the bus-oriented strategy in 1977. The Northern Ireland Transport Holding Company felt that such a huge expansion in the number of buses would create an unsustainable burden of ongoing maintenance costs, and relied too much on restricting civil liberties, while Citybus manager Werner Heubeck took the view that such a huge increase in the fleet and journey frequency would merely result in hundreds of relatively empty buses running through the city. The fact that the head of public transport in Belfast could describe the bus-oriented strategy as 'a misuse of public funds' supports the view that its rejection was not simply a result of closet support for road building, but because it would not have worked.

The zone-and-collar system as proposed also makes the mistake of assuming that the commercial activity of the city would remain static in the aftermath of such severe restrictions on the use of private cars. In practice, such measures would almost certainly – at least in the 1970s and 80s – have encouraged many businesses to relocate out of the central area and into parts of the city that were more conveniently accessible by car. The huge success of out-of-town shopping centres and retail parks powerfully demonstrates this to be true. In other words, the zone-and-collar system would have encouraged the development of new commercial districts on the periphery of the city, areas that are, in turn, difficult to serve by public transport. The only way to have prevented such a trend would have been to impose very severe planning laws that would have had the effect of very closely legislating where people could run their businesses and spend their money, and such measures would clearly be unacceptable in a western democracy where it would significantly impact on civil liberties and free enterprise.

However, it must be acknowledged that the 1977 Inquiry was not particularly imaginative in the alternatives it considered. Certainly other (albeit more costly) public transport alternatives were ignored, for example recreating Belfast's historic tram system. At the same time, proposals that could have achieved benefits for freight without encouraging further car-based commuting were dismissed on the usual cost grounds. A key example is the proposal to limit the West Tangent to HGVs only. This was dismissed as the cost/benefit ratio was obviously very poor, but with hindsight, cost alone was probably not a sufficient reason to dismiss this option.

Lavery's choice, fundamentally, was between (a) building Westlink and damaging the communities through which it passed and (b) not building Westlink and accepting that the city centre would be perpetually choked with traffic. The question of whether or not it was the correct decision will certainly not be settled in this book, and the debate will rage for many years to come.

A Closet Roads Strategy?

Some at the Lavery Inquiry argued that the 'mixed strategy' was actually a stealth 'roads-oriented strategy', albeit less ambitious than the proper 'roads-oriented strategy' that Lavery rejected. These people were proved largely correct by subsequent events. Lavery recommended a mixture of road and bus schemes, but in practice the money almost always went first to the road schemes, with the bus measures lagging badly behind, or not being implemented at all. While work on Westlink began within weeks of the publication of the inquiry report, Belfast would have to wait 14 years for the completion of the central bus station (the Europa) recommended in the same report.

This fundamental problem, which persisted through the 1980s, was a result of two factors. Firstly, Lavery did not set out a concrete order of priority for each measure to be implemented, except in relation to other similar schemes. So while the list of road schemes was in some sort of order of priority, this list was largely independent of the list of public transport schemes. This left the DOE to decide how to prioritise the two lists, which usually meant road schemes getting priority. Secondly, there was a lethargic approach to oversight of the Lavery recommendations, born out of an apparent lack of conviction that public transport investment really made sense. Since nobody at the top seems to have been particularly concerned with how the investment plan was proceeding, there was little incentive to compare this to the original Lavery recommendations.

At the later 1988 inquiry, objectors successfully exposed this state of affairs, suggesting that the figure spent on public transport over the previous decade had been closer to 15% of funds, rather than the 45% recommended by Lavery. The DOE counter-argued that their plan for the future period up to 2001 showed an investment of only 43% on roads, very similar to what

Lavery had recommended. Given the experience of the past ten years, it is no surprise that this was not a particularly convincing argument to the objectors.

The 1988 inquiry resulted in a genuine refocusing on public transport. A number of road proposals (although not the key Lagan Bridge scheme) were thrown out, and the DOE was forced to adopt a more proactive approach to public transport. This was reinforced after 1994, when the British government adopted a much more critical stance on new roads that would facilitate increased car commuting. The M3 Lagan Bridge was one of the last major road schemes to get the go-ahead prior to this sea-change in policy, and is likely to be the last major new strategic road in Belfast for many years.

Impact on the Urban Fabric

As a component of inner Belfast's urban landscape, it is difficult to find much positive to say about Westlink and the M3 other than the fact that they took a considerable amount of through traffic out of the city centre. Of course, on all the schemes, and especially after 1990, considerable time has been spent on the design of the new road structures with the result that the Lagan Bridge is not an unattractive structure, and the upgraded Westlink has some nice design attributes, such as the Rise sculpture at Broadway.

Nevertheless, Westlink and M3 are fundamentally transport conduits and have a dominating effect on the areas through which they pass. The 'canyon' section of Westlink from Grosvenor Road to York Street has had arguably the greatest impact. Although building the road in a canyon reduces its *visual* impact, if anything it increases the *physical* impact by forcing everybody to cross the road at just a handful of bridges, all but two of which also form major road intersections that are dominated by vehicles. The barrier effect of Westlink here is very great, essentially cutting the central area of the city off from the west and north, an effect that can easily be seen by comparing a map of the area before Westlink with a map today. It is a well-attested fact that cutting off streets in this way destroys city vitality by cutting off the natural linkages between homes, shops, leisure facilities and workplaces. Although the city centre is only a short walk from Divis Street interchange, for example, it is notable how few pedestrians are present there.

The effect is worsened by the presence of the Central Distributor Box just inside Westlink, a street level dual-carriageway road designed to cater for local traffic within the city centre. Any pedestrian who crosses Divis Street junction must then negotiate a second crossing of the Box. This further cuts off the city from its natural hinterland and starves the vicinity of diversity.

There is some limited scope for improving the situation. The DRD currently has long-term proposals to reduce the dominating effect of the Box by reducing its width and turning it into a more pedestrian-friendly boulevard. The crossings over Westlink are more troublesome. The Forum for Alternative Belfast has put forward proposals for how severance at Divis Street, Clifton Street, North Queen Street and York Street might be reduced. The least severance is probably at Peter's Hill (the lower Shankill) where it might be possible to construct a roof structure above Westlink on either side of the bridge. A lightweight (ie removable) building could be placed on top, to provide a continuous façade along Peter's Hill.

The severance effect between Grosvenor Road and Broadway was not as severe, since Westlink took the place of the Blackstaff River, and the boundary wall of the Royal Victoria Hospital, both of which created an almost continuous barrier long before the road was built.

The key exceptions are at Roden Street, which was permanently severed by Westlink, and Donegall Road, which is traversable only by negotiating the huge Broadway roundabout. Both locations are today known as sectarian flashpoints. Westlink did not create these sectarian divisions (both were flashpoints before the road was built) but Westlink did render them permanent by setting them in concrete. It is difficult to know today whether reducing the severance effect here would have a positive or a negative effect. This is a question that only local community groups can answer, and indeed the answer will probably change over time.

Westlink is often accused of having been built to act as a barrier between the two communities. This is not true, as its conception long pre-dates the recent 'Troubles', and indeed in most locations the community boundaries run at right-angles to the road, not along it. It is certainly true that having limited crossing points greatly assisted the security forces in monitoring the movements of people, but this was a side effect of the road's design, not its motivation.

It is impossible to definitively answer the question of whether Westlink ought to have been built, since the answer ultimately depends on what factors each person rates to be of greatest importance. The problem of how to accommodate traffic wishing to go between north, south and east Belfast was a real one that required an actual solution. It could not be wished away. In its absence, vehicles were clogging the city centre. The reality of Belfast's poor finances always ruled out the most elaborate solutions, and simple geography meant that any solution was always going to primarily impact the west of the city.

Problems are much more apparent with things that exist in the real world than with things that exist only in people's imaginations. The status quo, in other words, will always appear worse than the 'might have been'. When considering how the city might appear today without Westlink, it is easy to pinpoint the things that would be better – less severance, more diversity on the western edge of the city centre, more residential land use, etc. Harder to visualise are the things that would be worse, such as a vastly greater number of lorries crawling along congested streets. Had Westlink never been built, the debate today might be about an even more acute traffic problem than we actually have.

The M3 Lagan Bridge is a rather different beast. It is a dominating, but nevertheless rather elegant, structure. It benefitted from the fact that its construction displaced mostly unattractive industrial land uses such as factories, coal and junk yards and a large area of railway sidings, rather than busy residential streets. Its severance effect was largely neutral at the time, although the bridge renders the effect permanent. It generated few objections at the time of its construction, and the reduction in local traffic around the Queen's Bridge has been immense, facilitating the reclamation of spaces such as Custom House Square for other uses. On the whole, its benefits to the fabric of the city seem to outweigh its costs. Today the Lagan Bridge is the second busiest road in Northern Ireland, second only to the M2 and busier even than its older sibling, Westlink. Despite this, it flows fairly well at most times of the day, only becoming badly congested before and after major concerts at the Odyssey Arena.

Westlink as a Road

When Westlink was completed in 1983, it was to a design that Roads Service engineers knew would not function, not so much because of its reduced width of dual two lanes, but because the road featured four at-grade junctions (Broadway, Roden Street, Grosvenor Road,

York Street). This was done primarily to save money, and was hence forced upon Westlink's designers. There seems to have been an assumption at the Lavery Inquiry that building the road with a lower capacity than the original Urban Motorway would attract correspondingly less traffic. This was explicitly stated for the York Street junction. This was a false assumption, and the junctions were so overwhelmed by traffic upon opening that the roundabouts failed to function and had to be signalised almost immediately. The upgrade that took place 25 years later was essentially a correction of this mistake.

The frequent junctions on Westlink also represent a design failing, although one that came about due to its long gestation as the Urban Motorway. The Urban Motorway was intended primarily to feed traffic efficiently into the central area of the city, a strategy that is now accepted to be unworkable. It was hence equipped with the maximum feasible number of junctions to allow drivers to leave at various sites around the periphery of the city centre. Numerous junctions are today rightly regarded as incompatible with the needs of long-distance, strategic traffic.

By the time it was built the primary justification for Westlink was to link the M1 to the M2 and planned Lagan Bridge, not facilitate access to the city centre. Had work on the scheme begun from scratch at this time, ie without the historical baggage of the Urban Motorway, it would have made sense to build it with no intermediate junctions at all between south Belfast and the port at York Street. The presence of intermediate junctions has made Westlink a magnet for commuter traffic. It is possible today that the majority of vehicles on Westlink do not even traverse the full length of the road. The junctions have contributed greatly to traffic congestion, since traffic merging from the numerous sliproads interrupts smooth flows and causes traffic to slow down, often to a standstill. This is particularly the case between Divis Street and Clifton Street where short merge lengths force traffic to brake.

A high proportion of vehicles on Westlink today enter or leave at the intermediate junctions. For example, almost a quarter of traffic reaching Divis Street junction exits there. The most extreme example of local use is the large number of vehicles that join Westlink at Clifton Street and exit immediately at Divis Street, or vice versa, essentially using the strategic route to avoid congestion on the Central Distributor Box, the route that was intended to cater for such localised traffic movements. This contributes to congestion on Westlink, yet it is impossible to prevent this phenomenon without reducing the number of junctions. Attempts to resolve a similar problem on the M8 in Glasgow by preventing people joining the main M8 at certain junctions have met with limited success.

What would be the impact of reducing the number of junctions? The obvious question would be how traffic with a destination within the city would get there if it could not use Westlink. Without these junctions, all local traffic aiming for west and north Belfast, not to mention goods vehicles aiming for the city centre, would be forced to traverse the city streets from the last exits to the south and north of the city centre to reach their destination, likely resulting in severe congestion on these streets. On the other hand, the very fact that these streets would become so much more inconvenient to access by car might well encourage more use of alternative forms of transport in these areas – the attrition effect.

On the other hand, the lack of intermediate junctions would give Westlink a much greater capacity, and had it been built in this way in the early 1980s it would probably have rendered the 2006–2009 upgrade unnecessary. At the same time, it would have required the construction of free flowing sliproads at York Street (at least onto the M2), which would have added considerably to the cost.

With so much of the city's infrastructure and business activity built around the road system as it currently exists, it would be very difficult for any government to justify closing the intermediate junctions at this point in time, despite the advantages it might have for flows on the road itself or the surrounding city. The outcry from the users of these junctions would probably eclipse the cries from supporters of the proposal.

Nevertheless, it must also be said that a key social advantage of having no intermediate junctions would be that it would open up the possibility of partially or totally burying Westlink underground. This would be extremely expensive, but remains an option for future generations to consider. Given the huge severance impact that Westlink has had on west and north Belfast, such a scheme would have considerable merit that could well justify its costs in the years to come. Poor ground conditions, and particularly the presence of the Blackstaff, Farset and Pound Burn rivers, present significant engineering challenges, but they are surely not beyond the talent we have in Northern Ireland today.

One of the primary motivators for the 2006–2009 Westlink upgrade was the fact that traffic congestion was preventing goods vehicles reaching Belfast port, hence shifting business to Dublin. This is a very important point, alleviated by the upgrade. But by allocating all the new road space to general traffic use, the benefits will not last. The surge in traffic levels on Westlink immediately after the completion of the upgrade suggests that the latent demand for this route is very high and will not be accommodated even by the new road. Unless there is some effort to differentiate between traffic types, the problem will simply recur at a later date.

The City of Dublin solved the problem by constructing the Port Tunnel which, although technically open to all vehicles, has a toll structure that is heavily biased towards HGVs. Such a solution may be too expensive for Belfast, as a much smaller city, but remains an option for future generations. The difficulty of safely implementing an HGV lane on the existing Westlink has been highlighted, but the need for some kind of priority system for HGVs is fairly obvious. Imposing a barrier-free toll on Westlink (so as not to interrupt the flow of vehicles) is now technically feasible, but carries with it the danger that it would displace large numbers of vehicles onto the adjacent streets. A very long term solution might be to do the reverse and implement some kind of blanket congestion charge on all inner city streets with the *exception* of Westlink, in order to encourage strategic traffic to stay on the strategic road.

Ultimately Westlink was a compromise that satisfied nobody and carries with it inherent flaws. In essence, Westlink's fundamental problem is its schizophrenic double life as both a long-distance strategic route and a convenient route for local traffic. Regardless of what we would wish for, it exists and we are stuck with it. The problem can be explained more readily than it can be remedied, and it seems that there will be no easy solutions in the decades to come.

Postscript

It is often said that the Belfast Urban Motorway was never built. This is not true. It exists today, incognito, as Westlink and the M3 Lagan Bridge.

That it exists at all is a testament to the persistence and skill of the engineers who built it. That it exists in such a piecemeal form is a testament to the 'Troubles' and changing times that plagued its long gestation. That it has such obvious negative impacts on the surrounding area justifies the fiercely vocal opposition it attracted both then and now.

These negative impacts should not lead us to conclude that the road should not exist. Much can still be done to lessen the impact of the road on the city, and much deserves to be done. But the road itself exists and serves a critical role in the city today.

Few of its users today would claim that they love the road, but few would be willing to do without it. Few have any interest in the extraordinary story of how it came about. This is often the fate of infrastructure, and lack of appreciation is the burden that must be borne by the engineers who provide it.

Cities are never static – their needs change and evolve all the time. None of us can predict what economic, environmental, social or technological changes are coming our way. Westlink and the M3 were built to solve problems of their day, and as long as they continue to serve as solutions they will remain. But it will be future generations, not us, who will decide how the function and form of these roads must adapt to meet new challenges and different needs in the decades ahead.

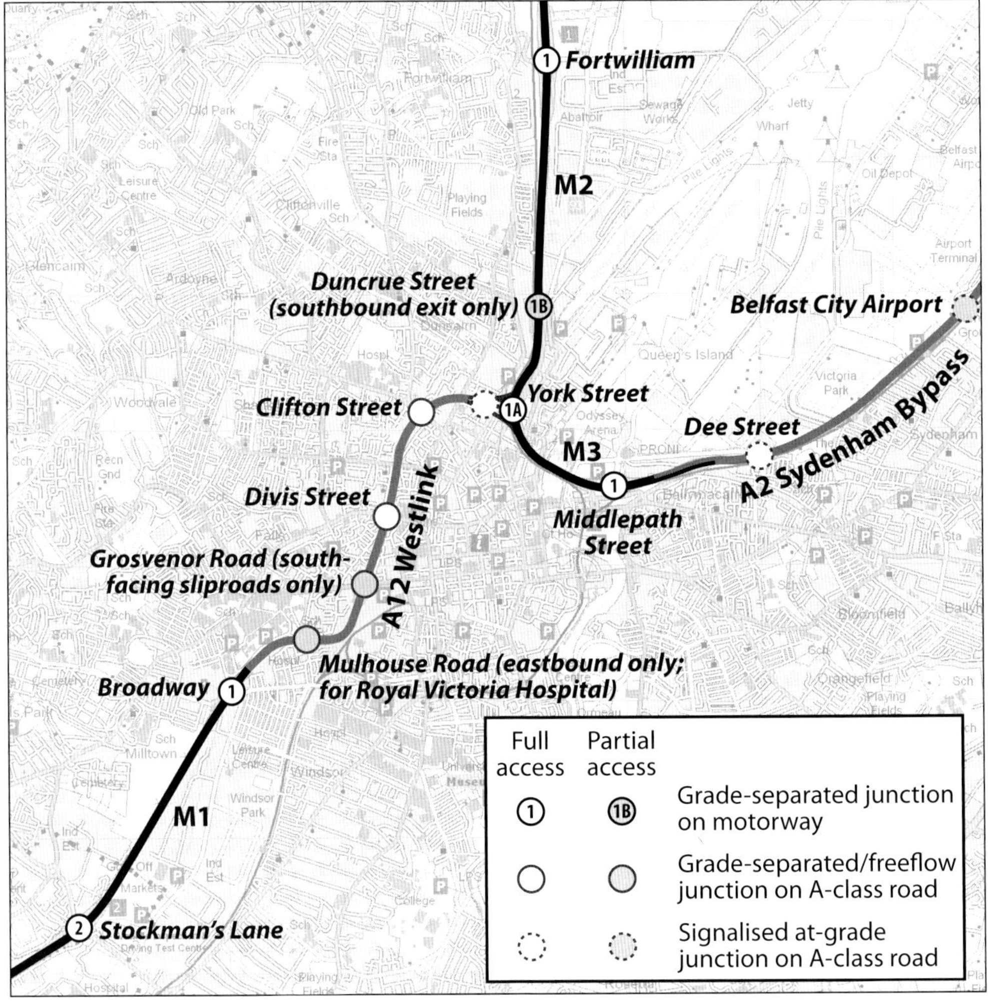

The Belfast urban 'motorway' system as it exists at the time of writing. Approximately 50% of the core Belfast Urban Motorway of 1967 exists today in some form. Elements with motorway restrictions are shown in black, while the rest are marked in grey. *(Base map 2013, LPS/ Ordnance Survey)*

REFERENCES

Chapter 1

1. Eds Frederick W Boal and Stephen A Royle, *Enduring City: Belfast in the Twentieth Century*, Blackstaff Press, 2006, ISBN 978-0-85640-790-1
2. Philip Macdonald, Chapter 3 'The Medieval Settlement', in Ed SJ Connolly, *Belfast 400: People, Place and History, 2012*, Liverpool University Press, ISBN 978-1-84631-635-7
3. *Central Belfast: An Historical Gazetteer*, Ulster Architectural Heritage Society, 1993, ISBN 0-900457-45-7
4. Stephen A Royle, *Irish Historic Town Atlas No 17: Belfast Part 2 – 1840–1900*, 2007, Royal Irish Academy, ISBN 978-1-904890-26-3
5. *Map of Belfast*, Marcus Ward and Company Limited, 1884, Public Record Office of Northern Ireland
6. JT Noble, 'Belfast Urban Motorway', *Journal of the Institution of Highway Engineers*, June 1972, Volume XIX, Number 6, pp 45–54
7. Stormont Papers, 24 March 1938, Volume 21, p 452
8. BC Boyle, *Northern Ireland Road Transport Board 1935–48: Buses in Ulster Volume 1*, Colourpoint Books, 1999, ISBN 978-1-898392-47-7
9. Stormont Papers, 29 April 1936, Volume 18, p 1158
10. ibid, 2 May 1934, Volume 16, p 1336

Chapter 2

1. *The Northern Ireland Motorway Achievement*, The Motorway Archive Trust and Roads Service of Northern Ireland, 2002, ISBN 0-9543056-6-3
2. Stormont Papers, 29 April 1936, Volume 18, p 1181
3. ibid,10 March 1937, Volume 19, p 360
4. ibid, 24 March 1938, Volume 21, pp 432–434
5. ibid, 15 June 1937, Volume 19, p 1636
6. Ministry of Development and Belfast Corporation and R Travers Morgan, 'Report on Belfast Urban Motorway', February 1967
7. George Charlesworth, *A History of British Motorways*, Thomas Telford Limited, 1984, ISBN 978-0-72770-159-6
8. *The System of Motor Roads in Germany*, RGH Clements, German Roads Delegation, 1937
9. Interview with T Jackson McCormick, former head of Roads Service, 20 January 2009

Chapter 3

1. George Charlesworth, *A History of British Motorways*, Thomas Telford Limited, 1984, ISBN 978-0-72770-159-6
2. 'The Northern Ireland Motorway Achievement', The Motorway Archive Trust and Roads Service of Northern Ireland, 2002, ISBN 0-9543056-6-3
3. Public Record Office of Northern Ireland, ref D2669/9
4. Interview with T Jackson McCormick, 20 January 2009
5. Stormont Papers, 13 November 1946, Volume 30, p 2582
6. Ministry of Development and Belfast Corporation and R Travers Morgan, 'Report on Belfast Urban Motorway', February 1967
7. HE Aldington, 'City of Belfast Report on General Traffic Conditions', June 1951
8. Stormont Papers, 26 October 1954, Volume 38, p 2942ff
9. ibid, 15 December 1953, Volume 38, p 394
10. Roads Service Traffic Census data, Site 338, 2000. Note that in 2000 this bridge carried westbound traffic only. The associated eastbound figure for Queen Elizabeth Bridge is 13,800 vehicles, census site 331, 1998
11. Stormont Papers, 16 November 1954, Volume 38, p 3283
12. Interview with bus/railway expert Norman Johnston, 1 January 2009.
13. Interview with ex-railway workers Joyce and Norman Topley, 7 January 2009
14. Michael Collins, *Rail Versus Road in Ireland 1900–2000*, 2000, Colourpoint Books, ISBN 978-1-898392-37-8

15. Eds Frederick W Boal and Stephen A Royle, *Enduring City: Belfast in the Twentieth Century*, 2006, Blackstaff Press, ISBN 978-0-85640-790-1
16. Stormont Papers, 6 June 1956, Volume 40, p 1842
17. ibid, 25 June 1957, Volume 41, p 1690
18. ibid, 23 February 1954, Volume 38, p 939
19. 'Traffic jams mark opening of the by-pass', *Belfast Telegraph*, 23 November 1959
20. Stormont Papers, 24 November 1959, Volume 45, p 948

Chapter 4

1. Eds Frederick W Boal and Stephen A Royle, *Enduring City: Belfast in the Twentieth Century*, Blackstaff Press, 2006, ISBN 978-0-85640-790-1
2. Stormont Papers, 26 April 1960, Volume 46, p 1090
3. The Motorway Archive Trust and Roads Service of Northern Ireland, *The Northern Ireland Motorway Achievement*, 2002, ISBN 0-9543056-6-3
4. Interview with retired Director of Network Services Grahame Fraser, 23 August 2011
5. Documents and correspondence in Public Record Office of Northern Ireland, ref D2669/9
6. R Travers Morgan and Partners, 'Belfast Urban Motorway', 6 February 1967
7. JT Noble, 'Belfast Urban Motorway', *Journal of the Institution of Highway Engineers*, June 1972, Volume XIX, Number 6, pp 45–54
8. R Matthew, 'The Belfast Regional Survey and Plan 1962', 1964
9. Personal correspondence with transport planner Tim Morton, March 2006
10. 'Motorways alone are not the answer', *Belfast Telegraph*, 10 July 1962
11. Documents and correspondence in Public Record Office of Northern Ireland, ref CAB/9/B/74/9
12. H Benson, 'Northern Ireland Railways: Report', HMSO, 1963
13. Stormont Papers, 13 February 1964, Volume 56, p 613
14. Interview with transport historian Norman Johnston, 1 January 2009
15. Jane Jacobs, *The Death and Life of Great American Cities*, 1961
16. 'Queens Quay Belfast: Draft Masterplan', Department for Social Development, 13 December 2011
17. 'Between the Bridges', article from the BBC Northern Ireland website under 'Your Place and Mine', http://www.bbc.co.uk/northernireland/yourplaceandmine/coast/part5.shtml, accessed 31 December 2008
18. Stormont Papers, 5 November 1963, Volume 55, p 478
19. Interview with T Jackson McCormick, former head of Roads Service, 20 January 2009
20. Professor Sir Colin Buchanan, 'Traffic in Towns: a study of the long term problems of traffic in urban areas', 1963, HMSO

Chapter 5

1. R Travers Morgan and Partners, 'Belfast Urban Motorway', 6 February 1967
2. 'Belfast Urban Motorway: Rehousing', Information leaflet, January 1968, Public Record Office of Northern Ireland, ref LA/7/3E/14/27
3. Documents and correspondence in Public Record Office of Northern Ireland, ref D2669/9
4. Using the 'GDP Deflator' measure at measuringworth.com, accessed December 2011
5. GWH Allen, 'Motorways in Northern Ireland', *Journal of the Institution of Highway Engineers,* Volume XIX, No 6, June 1972
6. JT Noble, 'Belfast Urban Motorway', *Journal of the Institution of Highway Engineers*, June 1972, Volume XIX, Number 6, pp 45–54
7. JM Fogarty, 'Belfast Westlink', *Journal of the Institution of Highway Engineers*, April 1983, pp 10–25
8. 'Planning Aspects of the Belfast Urban Motorway', Building Design Partnership in association with R Travers Morgan, August 1968.
9. 'Belfast Urban Motorway – Planning Aspects and its Integration into the Landscape', City Planning Department, Belfast Corporation, 9 November 1972
10. Ministry of Home Affairs press release, 17 April 1968, Public Records Office of Northern Ireland, ref CAB 9B/74/9
11. Based on traffic on the M1 motorway approaching Broadway. Source: Roads Service Traffic Census 1990 and 2009. Data from 2007–2009 is not useful due to Westlink upgrade works

Chapter 6

1. Letter from St Anne's Unionist Association, January 1965, Public Record Office of Northern Ireland, ref D2669/9
2. '£77m road plan shapes the Belfast of 1976', *Belfast Telegraph*, 6 February 1967
3. 'The Road Ahead (Editorial)', *Belfast Telegraph*, 6 February 1967

4. 'A question of priorities (Editorial)', *Irish News*, 7 February 1967
5. R Travers Morgan and Partners, 'Belfast Urban Motorway' main report, 6 February 1967
6. JT Noble, 'Belfast Urban Motorway', *Journal of the Institution of Highway Engineers*, June 1972, Volume XIX, Number 6, pp 45–54
7. Letter from Deputy Town Clerk of Belfast Corporation to the Ministry of Development, dated 17 April 1967 Quoted in Stormont Papers, 2 May 1967, Volume 66, p 810
8. Letter from the Ministry of Development to Belfast Corporation, dated 21 April 1967. Cited in Stormont Papers, 2 May 1967, Volume 66, p 811
9. *The Northern Ireland Motorway Achievement*, The Motorway Archive Trust and Roads Service of Northern Ireland, 2002, ISBN 0-9543056-6-3
10. R Travers Morgan, 'Belfast Transportation Plan', 19 June 1969
11. Northern Ireland Government Press Release, 17 April 1968, Public Record Office of Northern Ireland, CAB 9B/74/9
12. R Travers Morgan, 'Travel in Belfast', 22 May 1968
13. Stormont Papers, 15 December 1966, Volume 65, p 200
14. GWH Allen, 'Motorways in Ireland', National Conference of the Institution of Highway Engineers, July 1971.
15. Stormont Papers, 31 October 1968, Volume 70, p 1422
16. Using the 'GDP Deflator' measure at measuringworth.com, accessed December 2011
17. 'Ring road gets go ahead', *Belfast Telegraph*, 17 April 1968
18. M Cinalli, 'Socio-politically polarized contexts, urban mobilization and the environmental movement: a comparative study of two campaigns of protest in Northern Ireland', *International Journal of Urban and Regional Research*, March 2003, Volume 27, Issue 1, p 158–177
19. R Travers Morgan, 'Belfast Urban Area Plan', 20 June 1969
20. Personal correspondence with transport planner Tim Morton, March 2006
21. 'Blueprint for a city geared to the nineties', *Belfast Telegraph*, 19 June 1969
22. 'What the people think', *Belfast Telegraph*, 19 June 1969
23. 'New Belfast envisaged as city of life by day and night', *Irish News*, 20 June 1969
24. 'Report on the Transportation Plan and Objections to It', Report to the Town Planning Committee of Belfast Corporation, by the City Planning Officer, 21 May 1970
25. R Travers Morgan, 'Belfast Transportation Plan Public Hearing: Notes for Counsel', January 1972
26. R Wiener, *The Rape and Plunder of the Shankill*, Farset Co-operative Press, 1978, ISBN 0-9504292-0-1
27. CM Lavery, 'Belfast Urban Area Plan, Review of Transportation Strategy: Public Inquiry', April 1978, HMSO
28. B Morrison, 'Planning the City; Planning the Region' in Eds Frederick W Boal and Stephen A Royle, *Enduring City: Belfast in the Twentieth Century*, 2006, Blackstaff Press, ISBN 978-0-85640-790-1
29. Interview with railway historian, Norman Johnston, 1 January 2009
30. A Smyth, 'Belfast: Return from Motown?' in Eds Frederick W Boal and Stephen A Royle, *Enduring City: Belfast in the Twentieth Century*, 2006, Blackstaff Press, ISBN 978-0-85640-790-1

Chapter 7

1. Patrick A Macrory, 'Review Body on Local Government in Northern Ireland 1970: Report', June 1970, ISBN 0-337-10546-4
2. JT Noble, 'Belfast Urban Motorway', *Journal of the Institution of Highway Engineers*, June 1972, Volume XIX, Number 6, pp 45–54
3. R Travers Morgan, 'Belfast Transportation Plan Public Hearing: Notes for Counsel', January 1972
4. Written Answers to question submitted by Peter Robinson, MP, to the Secretary of State for Northern Ireland, House of Commons, 14 March 1983, Hansard Volume 39, c66W
5. 'Belfast Urban Motorway – Rehousing', information leaflet, January 1968, in Public Record Office of Northern Ireland, ref LA/7/3E/14/27
6. R Travers Morgan, 'Belfast Transportation Plan', 19 June 1969
7. Documents stored in Public Record Office of Northern Ireland, ref LA/7/3E/14/27
8. Letter from Edmond Warnock to the Northern Ireland Prime Minister, February 1958, in Public Record Office of Northern Ireland, ref CAB 9B/74/9
9. Stormont Papers, 18 December 1968, Volume 71, p 74f
10. Interview with retired Director of Network Services, Grahame Fraser, 23 August 2011
11. Documents stored in Public Record Office of Northern Ireland, ref LA/7/3E/14/41
12. Interview with retired Principal Engineer in charge of Traffic Management in Belfast, Denis O'Hagan, 23 August 2011

13. Building Design Partnership, 'Planning Aspects of the Belfast Urban Motorway', August 1968
14. R Wiener, *The Rape and Plunder of the Shankill*, Farset Co-operative Press, 1978, ISBN 0-9504292-0-1
15. Stormont Papers, 13 November 1968, Volume 70, p 1734
16. ibid, 23 April 1968, Volume 69, p 629
17. *The Northern Ireland Motorway Achievement*, The Motorway Archive Trust and Roads Service of Northern Ireland, 2002, ISBN 0-9543056-6-3
18. Scott Wilson for DRD Roads Service, 'York Street Interchange: Preliminary Options Report', March 2009, document ref S105296/G/01/POR1
19. Documents stored in Public Record Office of Northern Ireland, ref /7/3E/14/39
20. 'Why Guns and Bombs May Halt Belfast's Urban Motorway', *New Civil Engineer*, December 1973
21. JM Fogarty, 'Belfast Westlink', *Journal of the Institution of Highway Engineers*, April 1983, pp 10–25
22. M Cinalli, 'Socio-politically polarised contexts, urban mobilisation and the environmental movement: a comparative study of two campaigns of protest in Northern Ireland', *International Journal of Urban and Regional Research*, March 2003, Volume 27, Issue 1, pp 158–177
23. 'Sandy Row at the Public Inquiry', Sandy Row Redevelopment Association, July 1972. Public Record Office of Northern Ireland ref LA/7/3E/14/42
24. 'Sandy Row: what the people think of a new look', *Belfast Telegraph*, 24 February 1972
25. *Irish News*, 7 November 1973
26. RM Rutherford, 'Belfast Urban Area Plan Public Inquiry', September 1973, HMSO
27. CM Lavery, 'Belfast Urban Area Plan, Review of Transportation Strategy: Public Inquiry', April 1978, HMSO, p 30
28. 'Take 1 – it's the new road show', *Belfast Telegraph*, 1 March 1972
29. R Travers Morgan, 'Belfast Transportation Plan Public Inquiry General Dossier No 5: Implications of Doing Nothing', February 1972
30. ibid, 'Dossier No 10: Severance of Community', February 1972
31. 'Belfast Urban Area Plan: Statement by the Ministry of Development', HMSO, dated 12 September 1973, published 17 September 1973
32. 'Part of ring road plan to be dropped?', *Belfast Telegraph*, 17 September 1973
33. George Charlesworth, *A History of British Motorways*, 1984, Thomas Telford Limited, ISBN 978-0-72770-159-6
34. 'New Roads in Towns – Report of the Urban Motorway Committee', UK Department of the Environment, July 1972
35. 'Development and Compensation – Putting People First', UK Department of the Environment, October 1972
36. 'The BUS Report on the Belfast Urban Motorway', Belfast Urban Study Group/Holy Smoke Press, 1973
37. 'Belfast Ring Road', Pamphlet published by the Republican Clubs (Official Sinn Féin, now the Worker's Party), circa late 1973
38. Jane Jacobs, *The Death and Life of Great American Cities*, 1961
39. Personal correspondence with transport planner Tim Morton, October 2010
40. *A History of Roads Service 1973–2005*, Roads Service, 2006
41. *Belfast Telegraph*, 30 April 1974

Chapter 8

1. George Charlesworth, *A History of British Motorways*, Thomas Telford Limited, 1984, ISBN 978-0-72770-159-6
2. TAN Prescott, 'Maintenance and Reconstruction of Northern Ireland's Main Road Network', June 1972, *Journal of the Institution of Highway Engineers*, Volume XIX, No 6, p 7–20
3. T Jackson McCormick, *The History of Ulster's Roads*, joint publication by The Institution of Civil Engineers Northern Ireland Branch and The Institution of Highways and Transportation Northern Ireland Branch, March 1991
4. M Cinalli, 'Socio-politically polarized contexts, urban mobilization and the environmental movement: a comparative study of two campaigns of protest in Northern Ireland', *International Journal of Urban and Regional Research*, March 2003, Volume 27, Issue 1, pp 158–177
5. R Wiener, *The Rape and Plunder of the Shankill*, Farset Co-operative Press, 1978, ISBN 0-9504292-0-1
6. *Irish News*, 6 April 1974
7. Chris's British Road Directory, www.cbrd.co.uk, Chris Marshall, accessed 31 December 2010
8. 'Nottingham named as England's least car-dependent city', *The Guardian*, 14 September 2010

9. 'Transport for Belfast – What are your views?', leaflet, Department of the Environment, September 1976
10. A Smyth, 'Belfast: Return from Motown?', in Eds Frederick W Boal and Stephen A Royle, *Enduring City: Belfast in the Twentieth Century*, 2006, Blackstaff Press, ISBN 978-0-85640-790-1
11. CM Lavery, 'Belfast Urban Area Plan, Review of Transportation Strategy: Public Inquiry', HMSO, April 1978
12. Halcrow Fox and Associates, 'Review of Transportation Strategy for Belfast 1986–2001', DOE, April 1987
13. Aidan Campbell, *Knock: An Illustrated and Spoken History of Knock, East Belfast*, 2nd Edition, October 2009
14. Werner Heubeck at the 1977 Public Inquiry, see p 99 of Lavery Report[11]
15. Interview with bus/railway expert Norman Johnston, 1 January 2009
16. JM Allen, *Thirty Five Years of NIR: 1967 to 2002*, Colourpoint Books, 2003, ISBN 978-1-904242-00-0
17. T Blackman, *Planning Belfast*, Avebury Academic Publishing Group, 1991, ISBN 1-85628-182-5
18. Department of the Environment, 'Belfast Urban Area Plan Review of Transportation Strategy: Consultation with City Council on Interim Findings by Consultants', May 1975
19. Department of the Environment, 'Government Statement on The Belfast Urban Area Plan Review of Transportation Strategy', August 1975
20. Building Design Partnership & R Travers Morgan and Partners, 'Belfast Urban Area Plan: Review of Transportation Strategy. Main Report', September 1976
21. *A History of Roads Service 1973–2006*, Roads Service, 2006
22. 'Belfast council is split over transport plan, *Belfast Telegraph*, 6 January 1977
23. 'Belfast Urban Area Plan: Review of Transportation Strategy. Statement by the Department of the Environment for Northern Ireland', March 1977
24. 'Spotlight on Transport', undated leaflet probably published around April 1977 by the CGACT

Chapter 9

1. T Blackman, *Planning Belfast*, Avebury Academic Publishing Group, 1991, ISBN 1-85628-182-5
2. M Cinalli, 'Socio-politically polarized contexts, urban mobilization and the environmental movement: a comparative study of two campaigns of protest in Northern Ireland', *International Journal of Urban and Regional Research*, March 2003, Volume 27, Issue 1, pp 158–177
3. CM Lavery, 'Belfast Urban Area Plan, Review of Transportation Strategy: Public Inquiry', April 1978, HMSO
4. 'John Tyme: Obituary', *The Times*, 19 May 2008
5. Transcript of a submission to the Public Inquiry into a Revised Transportation Strategy for Belfast, by John Tyme, 31 May 1977
6. 'Noisy protest delays city transport probe', *Belfast Telegraph*, 1 June 1977
7. 'Transport Inquiry to Continue', *Irish News*, 3 June 1977
8. 'Inquiry won't be bullied – Inspector', *Belfast Telegraph*, 9 June 1977
9. 'Community body slams transport Inspector', *Belfast Telegraph*, 11 June 1977
10. 'Transport in Belfast', undated CGACT leaflet probably published in July or August 1977
11. 'Belfast Transportation Strategy Review', Northern Ireland Housing Executive, internal paper prepared for a meeting on 11 May 1977
12. Map enclosed with letter from Building Design Partnership to Northern Ireland Housing Executive, 18 March 1976
13. 'Belfast Urban Area Plan: Review of Transportation Strategy. Statement by the Department of the Environment for Northern Ireland', HMSO, April 1978
14. 'Roads Service 1973–1998 Jubilee Reflections: 25 Years Caring For Your Roads', Roads Service, 1998
15. 'New Transport Blueprint Bows to Public Opinion', *Belfast Telegraph*, 28 April 1978

Chapter 10

1. D McKittrick et al, *Lost Lives*, Mainstream Publishing, 1999, ISBN 978-1-84018-504-1
2. 'City motorway link protestors deny DOE stance', *Irish News*, 20 November 1979
3. 'Motorway link dangerous – claim', *Belfast Telegraph*, 22 November 1979
4. 'Suspend link road contract – call', *Belfast Telegraph*, 21 November 1979
5. Letters to the Editor, Seamus Lynch, *Belfast Telegraph*, 13 December 1979
6. M Cinalli, 'Socio-politically polarized contexts, urban mobilization and the environmental movement: a comparative study of two campaigns of protest in Northern Ireland', International Journal of Urban and

Regional Research, March 2003, Volume 27, Issue 1, pp 158–177
7. 'Protests and link road go on mid noise and dust', *Irish News*, 29 May 1980
8. JF McCormick, 'Protest 'selfish' ', Letters, *Belfast Telegraph*, 27 November 1979
9. *A History of Roads Service*, 1973–2006, Roads Service, 2006
10. JM Fogarty, 'Belfast Westlink', *Journal of the Institution of Highway Engineers*, April 1983, pp 10–25
11. *The Northern Ireland Motorway Achievement*, The Motorway Archive Trust and Roads Service of Northern Ireland, 2002, ISBN 0-9543056-6-3
12. Scott Wilson for DRD Roads Service, 'York Street Interchange: Preliminary Options Report', March 2009, document ref S105296/G/01/POR1
13. Des O'Reilly, *Rivers of Belfast: A History*, Colourpoint Books, 2010, ISBN 978-1-906578-75-6
14. William Stewart, 'Marshland spot being killed', Letters, *Belfast Telegraph*, 9 October 1980.
15. Based on a series of photographs owned by Roads Service Eastern Division, Hydebank, viewed February 2011
16. 'M-way link road opened', *Belfast Telegraph*, 5 February 1981
17. 'M1 link road opens at last', *Belfast Telegraph*, 29 March 1983
18. 'Building the Bridges', Department of the Environment Northern Ireland, 1995, ISBN 0-9525321-0-7
19. Denis O'Hagan, 'The Optimisation of Traffic Management', *Journal of the Institution of Highways and Transportation*, August/September 1987
20. Interview with retired Principal Engineer in charge of Traffic Management Denis O'Hagan, 23 August 2011
21. Interview with retired Director of Network Services Grahame Fraser, 23 August 2011
22. FG Guckian, 'Report of an Inquiry held into the Environmental Statement Relating to the M1/Westlink (A12) Improvements and into Opinions Expressed in Relation to it', February 2001
23. TA Warnock 'Urban Roads' in '1964–1989: 25 Years On', The Institution of Highways and Transportation Northern Ireland Branch Silver Jubilee booklet, 1989, pp 35–37.
24. 'Road Traffic Census', Roads Service, 1990
25. A Smyth, 'Belfast: Return from Motown?', in Eds Frederick W Boal and Stephen A Royle, *Enduring City: Belfast in the Twentieth Century*, 2006, Blackstaff Press, ISBN 978-0-85640-790-1
26. 'Passenger journeys on public transport vehicles', 1950–2010, Department for Transport, November 2010
27. CM Lavery, 'Belfast Urban Area Plan, Review of Transportation Strategy: Public Inquiry', April 1978, HMSO
28. R Wiener, *The Rape and Plunder of the Shankill*, Farset Co-operative Press, 1978, ISBN 0-9504292-0-1
29. 'Shared Space', Forum for Alternative Belfast, 2011, www.forumbelfast.org
30. T Blackman, *Planning Belfast*, Avebury Academic Publishing Group, 1991, ISBN 1-85628-182-5
31. B Morrison, 'Planning the City; Planning the Region' in Eds Frederick W Boal and Stephen A Royle, *Enduring City: Belfast in the Twentieth Century*, 2006, Blackstaff Press, ISBN 978-0-85640-790-1
32. Paul Larmour, 'Bricks, Stone, Concrete and Steel', in Eds Frederick W Boal and Stephen A Royle, *Enduring City: Belfast in the Twentieth Century*, 2006, Blackstaff Press, ISBN 978-0-85640-790-1
33. *The Rape And Plunder of the Shankill Revisited* (short film), Northern Visions, 2009, http://vimeo.com/channels/64772#6515247, accessed December 2011

Chapter 11

1. B Morrison, 'Planning the City; Planning the Region' in Eds Frederick W Boal and Stephen A Royle, *Enduring City: Belfast in the Twentieth Century*, 2006, Blackstaff Press, ISBN 978-0-85640-790-1
2. T Blackman, *Planning Belfast*, Avebury Academic Publishing Group, 1991, ISBN 1-85628-182-5
3. 'Design flows for motorways and all-purpose roads', DOE (London), Technical Memorandum H6/74, 1974
4. George Charlesworth, *A History of British Motorways*, Thomas Telford Limited, 1984, ISBN 978-0-72770-159-6
5. *A History of Roads Service 1973–2005*, Roads Service, 2006
6. R Travers Morgan, 'Belfast Urban Area Plan', 20 June 1969
7. Response by DOE to objection by Community Technical Aid into Belfast Urban Area Plan, 1988, quoted in Blackman[2]
8. TA Warnock, 'Urban Roads' in '1964–1989: 25 Years On', The Institution of Highways and Transportation Northern Ireland Branch Silver Jubilee booklet, 1989, pp 35–37
9. Halcrow Fox and Associates, 'Review of Transportation Strategy for Belfast 1986–2001', DOE, April 1987

10. 'Building the Bridges', Department of the Environment Northern Ireland, 1995 ISBN 0-9525321-0-7
11. S Mooney and F Gaffikin, 'Belfast Urban Area Plan 1987: Reshaping Space and Society', 1987, Belfast Centre for the Unemployed, cited in Blackman[2]
12. *The Northern Ireland Motorway Achievement*, The Motorway Archive Trust and Roads Service of Northern Ireland, 2002, ISBN 0-9543056-6-3
13. Planning Appeals Commission, 1989, p 391, 1989, cited in Blackman[2]
14. 'Belfast Urban Area Plan 2001', Adopted Plan, June 1990, DOE/HMSO, ISBN 0-337-08252-9
15. Correspondence with railway historian Norman Johnston, 2011
16. PT Donald, RGW Knight, SD Bourne, 'The design and construction of the cross-harbour road and rail links, Belfast', Proceedings of the Institution of Highway Engineers, Volume 117, Issue 1, February 1996, pp 28–39
17. Des O'Reilly, *Rivers of Belfast: A History*, Colourpoint Books, 2010, ISBN 978-1-906578-75-6
18. 'M3 a smash hit with the Irish News', *Irish News*, 23 January 1995
19. Scott Wilson for DRD Roads Service, 'York Street Interchange: Preliminary Options Report', March 2009, document ref S105296/G/01/POR1
20. Denis O'Hagan, 'The Optimisation of Traffic Management', *Journal of the Institution of Highways and Transportation*, August/September 1987
21. A Smyth, 'Belfast: Return from Motown?' in Eds Frederick W Boal and Stephen A Royle, *Enduring City: Belfast in the Twentieth Century*, 2006, Blackstaff Press, ISBN 978-0-85640-790-1
22. 'Building Bridges', supplement in *Belfast Telegraph*, 16 November 1994

Chapter 12

1. *A History of Roads Service 1973–2005*, Roads Service, 2006
2. R Matthew, 'The Belfast Regional Survey and Plan 1962', 1964
3. Statement of Transportation Principles, Minister for the Environment in Northern Ireland, Malcolm Moss, 17 January 1995, Cited in 1.
4. Department of the Environment, 'Lagan Valley Regional Park Local Plan 2005', Adoption Statement 1995
5. Department of the Environment, 'Transportation in Northern Ireland: The Way Forward', 3 October 1995
6. Roads Service, 'Road Traffic Census', 1990 and 1994
7. Department of the Environment Northern Ireland, 'Northern Ireland Transport policy statement: Moving Forward', November 1998
8. Department for Regional Development, 'Regional Transportation Strategy for Northern Ireland 2002–2012', July 2002
9. Friends of the Earth Northern Ireland, 'Transport Strategy: Robinson fails to grasp the nettle', Press Release, 3 July 2002
10. Based on Northern Ireland Statistics and Research Agency 1981 and 2001 Census Data
11. Mark Hart, 'From Smokestacks to Service Economy', in Eds Frederick W Boal and Stephen A Royle, *Enduring City: Belfast in the Twentieth Century*, 2006, Blackstaff Press, ISBN 978-0-85640-790-1
12. FG Guckian, 'Report on an Inquiry Held Into the Environmental Statement Relating to the M1/Westlink Project Stage 1 (M1 Improvements) and into Opinions Expressed in Relation to it', 30 January 2001
13. FG Guckian, 'Report on an Inquiry Held Into the Environmental Statement Relating to the M1/Westlink Project Stage 2 (Westlink A12 Improvements) and into Opinions Expressed in Relation to it', 30 January 2001
14. *Belfast Newsletter*, 28 December 2005
15. M Cinalli, 'Socio-politically polarized contexts, urban mobilization and the environmental movement: a comparative study of two campaigns of protest in Northern Ireland', in *International Journal of Urban and Regional Research*, March 2003, Volume 27, Issue 1, pp 158–177
16. Friends of the Earth Northern Ireland, 'Minister Dumps Human Rights', Press Release, 6 November 2000
17. 'Analysis: Unlocking the Westlink', BBC News Online, 26 November 2002
18. 'Campaign Against Road Expansion Plan', BBC News Online, 23 February 2000
19. *Irish News*, 8 March 2000
20. Department for Regional Development, 'M1/Westlink Project Stage 2: Westlink A12 Improvements', Departmental Statement, undated (circa September 2001)
21. 'Community Group Warned of Flooding', *Community Telegraph*, 20 August 2008
22. Friends of the Earth Northern Ireland, 'Westlink Inquiry Row Escalates', Press Release, 25 June 2001

23. Friends of the Earth Northern Ireland, 'M1/Westlink 'Freight First' Proposal', August 2003
24. Friends of the Earth Northern Ireland, 'Roads Service told: Wise Up On Westlink', Press Release, 26 November 2002
25. Friends of the Earth Northern Ireland, 'M1/Westlink inquiry Inspector: unfit and compromised', Press Release, 14 March 2003
26. Roads Service, 'Team Brief', internal Roads Service newsletter, April 2003
27. Department for Regional Development, 'Belfast Metropolitan Transport Plan", November 2004
28. Scott Wilson for DRD Roads Service, 'M1 Westlink/ M2/M3, York Street Improvements, Traffic Management Options Report', 2004
29. Scott Wilson for DRD Roads Service, 'York Street Interchange: Preliminary Options Report", March 2009, document ref S105296/G/01/POR1
30. Department for Regional Development, 'New Bus Lane for Belfast's Shankill Road', Press Release, 21 November 2011
31. Department for Regional Development, 'One Step Closer to Keeping Belfast 'On The Move', Press Release, 16 August 2011
32. A Smyth, 'Belfast: Return from Motown?', in Eds Frederick W Boal and Stephen A Royle, *Enduring City: Belfast in the Twentieth Century*, Blackstaff Press, 2006, ISBN 978-0-85640-790-1
33. Northern Ireland Statistics and Research Agency, 'Northern Ireland Road and Rail Transport Statistics April to June 2011', October 2011
34. Questions for Written Answer to the Minister for Regional Development, Northern Ireland Assembly, 18 November 2011
35. Figures from the annual Department for Regional Development and Northern Ireland Statistics and Research Agency, 'Travel Survey For Northern Ireland' 1999–2001 to 2007–2009

Chapter 13

1. 'Glasgow's new £692 m M74 Extension Opens', BBC News Online, 28 June 2011
2. 'Motorway scheme gives glimpse of future', *Belfast Telegraph*, 10 August 2004
3. D Ainger et al, 'Westlink/M1 Northern Ireland', in *The Arup Journal*, February 2009, pp 20–31
4. Letter from Chief Executive of Roads Service, Malcolm McKibbin, to Andrew MacKinlay, MP, 7 June 2006. Hansard, reference HC Deb, 690W
5. 'The Link: Investing in the Road Network', Roads Service information booklet, 30 May 2006
6. 'Traffic and Travel Information 2009 Annual Traffic Census', Roads Service, 2009
7. 'All quiet on the Westlink front', *Belfast Telegraph*, 13 March 2006
8. 'Motorway clear after day of delay', BBC News Online, 12 October 2006
9. 'M1 speed cameras plan as drivers flout limit', *Belfast Telegraph*, 9 November 2006
10. R Spiers, K O'Hara, S McCaffrey, J Border, 'Major Improvements to the M1/Westlink, Northern Ireland, Proceedings of the Institution of Civil Engineers, to be published in a future issue as of December 2012, DOI: 10.1680/tran.11.00030
11. 'Stockman's Lane junction completed', Department for Regional Development press release, 27 May 2008
12. Correspondence with Roy Spiers, Roads Service Project Manager of M1/Westlink upgrade, November 2011
13. Des O'Reilly, *Rivers of Belfast: A History*, Colourpoint Books, 2010, ISBN 978-1-906578-75-6
14. Bilfinger Construction, source: http://www.civil.bilfinger.com/C1257130005050D5/vwContentByKey/W277EFX8951MARSEN/$FILE/M1%20Westlink%20Belfast%20engl.pdf, accessed 27 November 2011
15. Amey, 'Broadway Underpass – Westlink, Belfast: Independent Report into the Flooding Incident on 16 August 2008', October 2008
16. 'Rain plays havoc with Ulster roads', *Belfast Newsletter*, 9 December 2007
17. 'Broadway Underpass Breakthrough', Department for Regional Development press release, 28 January 2008
18. 'Westlink upgrade a new era for motoring', *Irish News*, 5 July 2008
19. Department for Regional Development, Transport Projects Division, 'Belfast Rapid Transit Outline Business Case', September 2012
20. Department for Regional Development, 'New Grosvenor Road junction opens in Belfast: Murphy', press release, 4 March 2008
21. Department for Regional Development, 'Minister officially opens £104 million M1/Westlink Scheme', press release, 9 March 2009
22. www.betweenthebridges.org.uk, accessed 9 March 2009

23. 'M1 lane to open next month', *Irish News*, 16 October 2008
24. 'Road rage over 10-mile tailbacks', BBC News Online, 11 November 2008
25. For example, http://www.youtube.com/watch?v=4axkBNH2FN8, accessed 5 December 2011
26. 'Taxi driver tells of terror ordeal trapped in floods', *Belfast Telegraph*, 19 August 2008
27. BBC Northern Ireland News, BBC1, 17 August 2008
28. 'Road builder 'must pay' for flood', BBC News Online, 3 November 2009
29. 'Road anti-flooding moves in place', BBC News Online, 24 November 2009
30. 'Managed Routes M1/A12 Westlink: Variable Mandatory Speed Limits', DRD Roads Service leaflet, 16 September 2010
31. 'Belfast to bloom with new artwork', BBC News Online, 11 October 2006
32. 'Broadway sculpture scrapped amid escalating steel costs', *Belfast Telegraph*, 23 July 2008
33. 'New landmark rises from rubble', BBC News Online, 13 November 2008
34. 'Rise sculpture unveiled in Belfast', UTV News, 16 September 2011
35. 'No show for meeting on Belfast roundabout sculpture', BBC News Online, 20 January 2011
36. The Politics Show, BBC Northern Ireland, 5 Feb 2006
37. CM Lavery, 'Belfast Urban Area Plan, Review of Transportation Strategy: Public Inquiry', April 1978, HMSO
38. Scott Wilson for DRD Roads Service, 'York Street Interchange: Preliminary Options Report', March 2009, document ref S105296/G/01/POR1
39. FG Guckian, 'Report on an Inquiry Held Into the Environmental Statement Relating to the M1/Westlink Project Stage 2 (Westlink A12 Improvements) and into Opinions Expressed in Relation to it', 30 January 2001
40. DRD Roads Service, 'York Street Interchange: Information Leaflet', 1 June 2011
41. DRD Roads Service, 'Expanding the Strategic Road Improvement Programme 2015', July 2006
42. URS, 'York Street Interchange Preferred Options Report', 22 October 2012, released to the public 6 December 2012
43. Department for Regional Development press release, 'Minister Kennedy announces Preferred Option for York Street Interchange', 6 December 2012
44. 'INTER-CHANGE', Forum for Alternative Belfast, http://www.forumbelfast.org/projects/inter-change.php, accessed 3 January 2012
45. Based on a conversation with members of the Forum for Alternative Belfast, 12 December 2012

INDEX

General Index

Index of People

COPYRIGHT NOTES